When Ladies
Go A-Thieving

When Ladies Go A-Thieving

Middle-Class Shoplifters in the Victorian Department Store

ELAINE S. ABELSON

OXFORD UNIVERSITY PRESS
New York   *Oxford*

Oxford University Press

Oxford   New York   Toronto
Delhi   Bombay   Calcutta   Madras   Karachi
Kuala Lumpur   Singapore   Hong Kong   Tokyo
Nairobi   Dar es Salaam   Cape Town
Melbourne   Auckland

and associated companies in
Berlin   Ibadan

Copyright © 1989 by Elaine S. Abelson

First published by Oxford University Press, Inc.,
200 Madison Avenue, New York, New York 10016

First issued as an Oxford University Press paperback, 1992

Oxford is a registered trademark of Oxford University Press

Library of Congress Cataloging-in-Publication Data
Abelson, Elaine S.
When ladies go a-thieving / Elaine S. Abelson.
p. cm.   Includes bibliographical references and index.
ISBN 0-19-505125-4
ISBN 0-19-507142-5 (PBK)
1. Shoplifting—United States—History—19th century.   2. Female
offenders—United States—History—19th century.   3. Middle class
women—United States—History—19th century.   4. Women consumers—
United States—History—19th century.   5. Department stores—
United States—History—19th century.   I. Title.
HV6658.A24   1989
364.1'62—dc20   89-9379   CIP

2 4 6 8 9 7 5 3 1

Printed in the United States of America
on acid-free paper

For Hirschel

Acknowledgments

Writing a book is a singular process that cannot be accomplished without an immense amount of support. The debts are both intellectual and emotional, and it is often hard to separate the two. These pages are only an acknowledgment, not payment of an enormous debt.

Thomas Bender saw this project through. From the beginning of the dissertation to the completion of the book, Tom was my advisor, guide, staunchest ally, and friend. His careful readings of the various incarnations of the work enabled me to sharpen my own critical faculties and to rethink major parts of the analysis; his belief in the significance of the project provided me with critical direction and sustained me.

My work has benefitted significantly from the analysis and criticism of Barbara Balliet. A feminist scholar and a singularly talented editor, Barbara has the capacity (and tenacity) to wade through convoluted prose and sense its connections to the larger questions. When Barbara didn't understand a point I knew I was in trouble. She provided me with friendship and intellectual sustenance. Only by embracing the cat can I convey my true debt.

Daniel Walkowitz was an early supporter of this project. His insightful comments and criticisms were crucial to the success of the dissertation and still resonate in the book.

Molly Nolan and the Women's History program at New York University have been a source of encouragement and friendship, well beyond my graduate school years. My thanks are long overdue. Two seminars supported by the New York Institute of the Humanities at New York University have helped me to broaden the interpretive framework: The Sex-Gender Seminar and the Commercial Culture Seminar have both been forums for serious discussion of theoretical issues.

The contribution of Joan Jacobs Brumberg has been immense. Beyond reading and commenting on a number of the chapters, Joan has enlarged my thinking on the subject of the medicalization of behavior and the social and cultural reality of kleptomania at the end of the nineteenth century. Providing me with a lecture platform at Cornell University, Joan enabled me to test my ideas at a crucial stage in my writing. The sense of a shared intellectual framework has been enriching.

Susan Ware read the entire manuscript in painstaking detail. Her comments and critical judgment sharpened the text in many of the chapters.

William Leach has had great influence on all who write in the field of commercial culture. His work has helped give shape to the parameters of this field of study. Bill has been generous in discussing the world of the department store and in sharing his ideas and his sources. Without his enthusiasm and wide knowledge, I might never have dared to tackle the project.

Portions of the manuscript have been read by Steve Stowe, Susan Porter Benson, and Bert Hansen. I am grateful for their support and their willingness to tell me the hard truth when need be.

Various friends have become involved in this project. Claire Potter was always a supportive presence; Margaret Hunt sent me wonderfully arcane references from Elizabethan England and 20th century New York; Susan Yohn helped me to understand the significance of ministers' wives among the shoplifting sample; Rob Snyder's questions helped to clarify many of the issues discussed in this book, and he commiserated with me at various stages. It is impossible to calculate the contribution of Carol Reich. She questioned points of interpretation, vocabulary, and meaning woven into the definition of kleptomania and pushed me to refine my understanding of female behavior. An educator and scholar in her own right, Carol has been, above all, a friend. Archivists and manuscript librarians are the lifeline of academic research. Tom Horrocks and the archival staff at the College of Physicians in Philadelphia were particularly generous with their time; Florence B. Lathrop, Curator of Manuscripts and Archives at the Baker Library, Harvard Business School, introduced me to the range of material at the Library and culled the files for hard-to-find items in the R. H. Macy collection; Doris Carey in Special Productions at the R. H. Macy Co. in New York deserves special thanks for sharing her office and becoming an archivist for the two weeks I worked in the Macy archives. Thanks are also due to people at the various institutions which have housed and helped me: Eva Moseley, Curator of Manuscripts at the Schlesinger Library, Radcliffe College, the staffs at the New York Academy of Medicine and the American Antiquarian Society, and numerous research and reference librarians at Bobst Library, New York University. Librarians at the New York Public Library deserve special mention. During a period of almost continual construction at the main research branch at 42nd Street and at the distant annex, library personnel offered knowledge and assistance at crucial junctures. Dale Neighbors, Photo Archivist at the New-York Historical Society, and Bonnie Yochelson, Curator of Prints and Photographs at the Museum of the City of New York, were helpful in finding appropriate illustrative material during the final, rushed stage of manuscript preparation.

My family deserves special mention. They have lived with and been supportive of a long project, certainly as long as some of them can remember. I have encroached on their space and on their time with abandon, and I wish to thank Joshua, David, Adam, and especially Hirschel for their patience and their love.

Contents

Introduction, 3

1 Urban Women and the Emergence of Shopping, 13

2 The World of the Store, 42

3 The Two-Way Mirror, 63

4 Invisible Authority, 91

5 Dilemmas of Detection, 120

6 Shoplifting Ladies, 148

7 " . . . Disposition Shady, but a Perfect Lady", 173

Epilogue, 197

A Note on Sources, 209

Notes, 215

Index, 283

When Ladies
Go A-Thieving

Ladies, Don't Go Thieving

Oh, don't we live in curious times,
You scarce could be believing,
When Frenchmen fight and Emperors die
And ladies go a-thieving.

A beauty of the West End went,
Around a shop she lingers,
And there upon some handkerchiefs
She clapped her pretty fingers.

Into the shop she gently popped;
The world is quite deceiving
When ladies have a notion got
To ramble out a-thieving.

ENGLISH BALLAD, ca. 1867

Introduction

On December 10, 1898, the *New York Times* reported the arrest of two women in Siegel-Cooper, a large Sixth Avenue department store. Mrs. Sarah Raymond, wife of the manager of a safe deposit company, was charged by store detective George Bernard with stealing a bottle of perfume valued at one dollar. Mrs. Laura Swift, wife of a minister, was charged with stealing an umbrella and several other small articles valued at seven dollars. Mrs. Swift, Bernard testified, had hidden the umbrella in the folds of her skirt "when one of the clerks was not looking."[1] Described by the *Times* reporter as "well-dressed," of "unblemished reputation," "dutiful wife and mother," the two women were each arraigned and released by the court when Siegel-Cooper dropped the complaints. Only two of many similar incidents that Christmas season, the Sarah Raymond and Laura Swift episodes encapsulate the drama of ladies who went a-thieving in the late nineteenth century. Solidly middle class, if not necessarily well-to-do, and obviously respectable, these women entered the great dry-goods bazaars to shop and became enmeshed in a consumer world of seemingly unlimited dimensions. That they became shoplifters demonstrates the difficulties faced both by middle-class women and by Victorian society in the face of fundamental cultural and economic change.

3

Why look at the development of the department store in terms of the middle-class shoplifter? Because shoplifting was a major social fact in the emergence of consumer society in the United States in the period betwen 1870 and 1914. The actions of the respectable shoplifter become a vantage for exploring at once the development of consumer culture and its relation to a particular configuration of gender and class.

My initial intention was a straightforward investigation of the ways shoplifting related to urban change. Mary Ryan, in *Cradle of the Middle Class*, had indicated that shoplifting emerged as a problem in Utica in the 1840s.[2] There is some evidence to tie shoplifting to the dislocation caused by rapid urbanization, but what is more interesting is to look at who was doing the shoplifting and under what circumstances. The irrefutable fact that numbers of middle-class women regularly stole merchandise from the great stores forces us to rethink what we know of the public and private lives of these women. Literature about nineteenth-century urban women suggests patterns of domesticity and leisure that ignore the quasi-public world of the department store, yet it was in this arena that the relationship of women, gender, and class was vividly exposed.

I do not argue that shoplifting itself was new in the world. It is an ancient, if not honorable, art. Reports of thefts from shops and stalls appeared in Elizabethan England; Moll Flanders was sent to Newgate prison for shoplifting in mid–seventeenth-century London; in America, the notorious "light-fingered Sophie Lyons" became a detective story heroine during the Gilded Age.[3] But the shoplifting that seemed to appear so suddenly in the closing decades of the nineteenth century represented something entirely different: its context was the department store, it was a pervasive phenomenon, and it demonstrated, quite dramatically, a form of deviant behavior by a new group, the middle class. Under the rubric "kleptomania" this type of shoplifting was used to define gender as well as class notions of theft.[4]

The American department store was at the center of what may be legitimately called a culture of consumption.[5] After the Civil War, with vast increases in production and productive potential, and with a dramatic increase in the resources available to a new middle class, consumer values literally revolutionized society. The department store was the dominant institution in this transformation. With the ability to exploit a vast array of goods, the large stores educated people to want things, and they played a crucial role in determining the essentials of middle-class life and aspirations. The stores themselves served as showcases as they became part of a new urban, public culture. Marshall Field & Company was a sight to see in Chicago; no visitor to New York failed to visit Macy's. Dry-goods merchants, embodying the institutions, became merchant princes and members of a new elite. Hailed as "Modern Alexanders sighing for new worlds to conquer," the owners of the great stores wielded unparalleled influence. "Given a suffering world," a professor from the University of Chicago lectured, "there was no doubt that men like [Marshall] Field, who lessen the cost of living, would be of more value than men like Shakespeare."[6]

To look at the problems in the stores is not to be unaware of the possibilities: the excitement, the sensory stimulation, the profusion of goods, the crowds, the unnerving, often illusory, ambience that the large department stores still evoke. This side of department store culture has been emphasized in the new historical literature.[7] But there was a dark underside as well, which has not been explored. Glaring contradictions within the emergent consumer ethos are evident, and to ignore them would be to ignore the complexity of cultural change, and the price women had to pay for their days in the department stores. As the great bazaars became both magnet and danger to numbers of middle-class women, the shoplifter emerged as a significant social and medical problem.

This is a study of both response to change and of change itself. The great stores are the locale, the context of the action and an ineluctable part of the interpretation. It was in the department stores that middle-class women became shoplifters. Traditionally responsible for ensuring that family members were properly clothed and fed, women changed the location of these home-centered activities after the Civil War. Much of what was produced in the home in 1870 was a purchasable commodity a decade later. Assuming responsibility for consumption, women shopped. Notwithstanding its fundamental place in women's work, shopping was linked in the public mind with pleasure and personal freedom.

The association of leisured, urban women with shopping as a discrete activity dates from the early decades of the nineteenth century, possibly even earlier. In the antebellum period, well before the development of the great shopping bazaars, observers had damned the "perils of desire unleased by the vicious habit of shopping."[8] While this peripatetic shopping by the few in a limited market was quite different from the shopping that became a hallmark of middle-class life and identity in the Gilded Age, public anxiety about shopping persisted.

What drew women into the arena and how they responded to their new public role as shoppers cannot be understood apart from the particular environment of the stores. If the urban middle-class woman provides a window on the new experience of consumerism, the nineteenth-century department store illuminates the compelling reality of the social processes of consumption. The ideal realization of a materialistic age, the department store embodied a vision of trouble-free abundance. Aggressive merchandising, which intentionally made it difficult to leave a store empty-handed, combined with new middle-class notions of need to submerge traditional moral considerations. In the attempt to construct the boundaries of class via consumption, rational buying and restraint often gave way. "It is not that we need so much more, or that our requirements are so increased," one woman explained, "but we are not able to stand against the overwhelming temptations to buy which besiege us at every turn."[9] The central focus of the department store was the creation of desire. How well the stores succeeded was amply demonstrated in the increasing incidence of shoplifting.

Shoplifting was inseparable from other forms of department store life and shopping activity. The simultaneous participation of the respectable shoplifter in both legal and illegal forms of consumer behavior is evident. Many of the accused had legitimate purchases in their possession at the time of their arrest. While nineteenth-century shoplifting does not lend itself to either precise measurement or meaningful quantification, it is obvious that middle-class shoplifters were only a fraction of all women shoppers. The importance of their thefts stems less from the losses the stores suffered—though by all accounts they were considerable—than from the interpretation given this activity by medical and legal authorities, and, so far as we can tell, by women themselves. In the study and treatment of respectable thieves, the role of physicians (and scientific medicine) in developing categories of behavioral irregularity become vitally important. Women of the middle class took merchandise from the dry-goods bazaars, and doctors explained their actions not in terms of what the women were doing—shoplifting—but in the language of physical and mental illness. This language served not only as an interpretation of women's behavior, it established the meaning of their behavior as well. Labeling many of these women "Kleptomaniacs," doctors judged them to be fundamentally irrational, testimony to the "natural" constraints of the female sex. The result of the popular medical response was the creation of a new, representative female figure—the middle-class shoplifter—and her inclusion in the prevailing cultural definition of women.

Before Freud's insight into the development of the unconscious and the recognition of the problems associated with anxiety, neuroses, and psychoses, physicians explained various human behaviors in vague terms of internal "controlling mechanisms." Lumping together a variety of physical and mental ills, they described much of what they could not understand as the consequence of the imbalance of nervous energies.[10] For women, the imbalance was located in the stress of monthly menstruation, which exacerbated the effects of the so-called critical periods in a woman's life: puberty, pregnancy, and menopause. These natural processes of the female life cycle became the explanatory model for behavior. Was shoplifting without obvious indication of material need a disease? The answer for several decades was "yes." Letting cultural attitudes shape their diagnoses, physicians connected woman's mind and body in an analytical framework that, in its dependence on the organic absolutes of sexual difference and human nature, excluded other possible interpretations.[11]

Recognition of the way scientific views reflected and helped shape social definitions is central to understanding how and why kleptomania could become the most common explanation for middle-class shoplifting. When physicians suggested that the middle-class shoplifter was inherently unstable, lawyers, judges, merchants, and newspaper reporters were able to accept the diagnosis; ready to believe that many females were biologically inferior, shopping was a "mania," and women routinely succumbed to temptation. All women were affected by this new representation because all women shopping were seen as potential shoplifters. Part of the collective identity of middle-class women, the shoplifter legitimated existing notions of gender and the structural inequality of Victorian society.

By the 1890s the shoplifter-kleptomaniac (the terms were used interchangeably) had become an artifact of popular culture. A recognizable stereotype, even a joke, the "klepto" had become a character in a variety of legitimate dramas, vaudeville skits, popular songs, newspaper articles, novels and, by 1906, movies.[12] The portrayal had a number of variations, but relied on an understanding of the middle-class woman as someone who had an innate infirmity. Kleptomania was something women had, something they suffered from; it was also a disease that was inherent in their essential being. A sketch by comedians Weber and Fields in 1901 carried this understanding to its logically absurd conclusion. Mrs. Tankton, a wealthy, presumably respectable woman, "has been told by her doctor that she has kleptomania and was taking things for it."[13] Not infectious and not contagious, but endowed with unmistakable cultural meaning, kleptomania was popularly accepted as a natural, if eccentric, inclination firmly rooted in female life.[14]

Individually, the middle-class shoplifter eludes precise definition. Newspapers and trade journals created the sample and popularized the archetype, but the accounts dealt with women bereft of context. It is the male voice that we hear. The accused is rarely heard, and when she does speak it is only in the most formulaic language. Women either tearfully denied the evidence before them or begged forgiveness. What these women thought, what environmental stress or personal anxiety or domestic issues they may have been responding to in shoplifting, remained hidden. It is worth remembering, however, that gender definitions had validity for women as well as for men, and women used their socially defined roles to escape the consequences of their behavior. Illness became defense. As the sick woman found herself removed from moral judgment, the label often became its own justification. For many of the accused, "shoplifter-kleptomaniac" became an acceptable form of identity, even if it left them hostage to their own biology.

In a period of expanding possibilities for educated women, almost all the women in this sample were traditional housewives: home and family were their occupation. With neither economic autonomy nor power—and posing a very different threat to public morality than another group of women in public, working-class prostitutes—the middle-class shoplifters generated few exposés and only limited public discussion.[15] They were regarded as a class of actors, not individuals with different attitudes and motivations. Seemingly constrained by their own physical characteristics, their motives for actions were deduced from their physiology. Although they were not seen to be sexually out of control, these lady thieves represented, nevertheless, a powerful threat to the ideal of womanhood, and that threat needed to be contained.

While the middle-class shoplifter is the focus, the goals of this study are broader. The collective response to the shoplifter enables us to explore specific aspects of the process of consumption in America and to assess the tensions, even contradictions, within the larger culture. In the public figure of the shoplifter lay hidden concerns about gender and class.

Recovering the ambiguous world of the department store and the experience of urban middle-class women within that new institution involved the use of disparate sources. With little documentation from the department stores themselves, the search for the existence of a pattern of activity that was mentioned only in hushed terms and almost never fully prosecuted relied mainly on newspapers, trade journals, and medical texts. Because what was left out of the public debate was as important as the pronouncements of store managers, judges, and physicians, the search for evidence became a search for the unacknowledged implications of consumer capitalism.

Shoplifting by middle-class women had first entered public consciousness when, in December 1870, Rowland Macy, the owner of Macy's, arrested Mrs. Elizabeth B. Phelps, a well-known feminist and philanthropist.[16] While that incident created a furor in the popular press, in feminist organizations, and, presumably, in department store circles, such shoplifting attracted little obvious attention for the rest of the decade. By the mid-1880s, however, daily newspapers regularly contained articles about middle-class women detained for shoplifting in the dry-goods stores. Theft by this group was news, a decisive crossing of the barrier between public and private. While providing important basic statistical information—name, age, address, husband's occupation—the newspaper accounts, nevertheless, dealt with women as stereotypes. Ostensibly, they led parallel lives with little individual differentiation. Like much of the rest of society, reporters saw shopping as woman's natural occupation and shoplifting as the natural taken to the extreme.

Trade journals presented an equally narrow, oversimplified image of women. Unofficial spokesmen for the highly sensitive and competitive retail industry, their editors attempted to obscure the reality of shoplifting in the stores. While the New York–based *Dry Goods Economist (DGE)* and its Midwest counterpart, the Chicago *Dry Goods Reporter (DGR)*, rarely dealt directly with actual cases of theft, neither journal could ignore the ever increasing amounts of shoplifting by middle-class customers. In fact, the dry-goods journals became the source of advice to the trade about the baffling and seemingly intractable problem. The editors saw their role as that of education, and beginning in 1891 the *DGE* often served as a "how to" guide for the prevention of shoplifting.

The middle-class shoplifter became the focal point for a security consciousness that, in its essentials, has changed little in the last one hundred years. Spurred on by the trade journals, merchants acquired the most up-to-date technology for the display and protection of merchandise, hired detectives and created protection departments, but depended, ultimately, on salesclerks as the first line of defense. The response involved all levels of store operation.

Of immediate value were the firsthand accounts of police officials, private investigators, and store detectives. These gentlemen, and the occasional lady, were straightforward in acknowledging the extent of shoplifting by middle-class women and describing the ruses of many self-declared kleptomaniacs. Henry Blades, for example, the outspoken head of protection at Wanamaker's (Philadelphia) for thirty years, provided just that type of narrative, impressionistic documentation that augmented the statistical evidence. But even as these professionals accepted the existence of individual cases of kleptomania, they argued that most of the accused were simply lady thieves who were volitionally capable of *not* doing what they did.

The cultural meaning of shoplifting emerges most strikingly in the scientific literature of the period. Medical texts and papers and public statements by physicians constructed (or attempted to construct) a social and psychological reality: kleptomania. Women, the common argument ran, were at risk simply because they were women. There was no genuine consensus among doctors, as there was none among judges, but the accepted medical diagnosis of shoplifting was kleptomania—a female behavior disorder under the control of biology.

To look at the middle-class shoplifter through nineteenth-century eyes is to understand how class becomes consolidated. Appealing to rich and poor alike, the large dry-goods bazaars were, in fact, infused with the images and symbols of the aspiring middle class: the breadth of merchandise, the methods of display, the prices, the physical surroundings—each one proclaimed a similar message. Shopping had transcended functionalism, and middle-class shoppers were expected to want, if not to purchase, what was visibly arrayed all around them. While there was no universal motive, the woman who took merchandise from the department store was responding to the the calculated arousal of desire in an environment dedicated to sensory stimulation and unfettered abundance. In this sense consumerism and kleptomania were not in conflict. The common alibi "I couldn't help myself" was the appropriate reaction.

However logical, shoplifting by middle-class women was an unacceptable challenge to dominant values. Such unrestrained behavior seemed to imply a kind of moral chaos and to raise questions about the fundamental understanding of class and gender. The label "kleptomania" temporarily solved the problem. By defining the boundaries of the permissible it acknowledged the social constraints on women. Since ladies could not be called thieves, the medicalization of shoplifting provided an alternative and maintained the illusion of respectability. The individual became the focus; the crime was lost. Neither the excesses of the institutions nor consumer capitalism were indicted. The fault lay within women themselves.

1

Urban Women and the Emergence of Shopping

Women were part of the rising middle class in the second half of the nineteenth century, but, unlike their male counterparts, their role lacked an important degree of definition. It was often unclear just what it meant to be a middle-class woman. As domesticity expanded beyond the confines of the individual household and emphasis was increasingly placed on the new world of material possessions, shopping became woman's work and woman's recreation. Sanctioned by an older rhetoric of family, but taking place in a radically altered environment under the aegis of a changing value system, shopping and consumer spending emerged as an important component of urban middle-class identity in the decades after the Civil War. Women, who had been effectively excluded from significant economic activity, became, suddenly, central to that identity.[1] The tensions engendered by the convergence of the old and the new become apparent when we examine women's relation to the emerging culture of consumer capitalism in detail.

Clara Burton Pardee and Harriet Richards were two New York women who probably never met but whose lives were often mirror images. Born in 1859 and 1861, respectively, both women married in 1882; Pardee to a physician and Richards to a lawyer. Initially the two couples lived within walking distance, with Dr.

13

and Mrs. Pardee at 218 West 34th Street and Mr. and Mrs. Richards at 32 West 17th Street. Although the Richards family moved to suburban Orange, New Jersey, in 1889, and the Pardees remained city residents, the lives of these two women remained remarkably similar. The daily diaries these two women kept for more than forty years reflect their parallel interests, economic as well as social, and their common identity as middle-class women in the decades surrounding the turn of the twentieth century.

What stands out amidst the almost compulsive repetitiveness of the written record is the complexity of middle-class domesticity in late Victorian America. Amid timeless routines of keeping house and raising children, new manufacturing technologies and increased levels of industrial production changed the pattern of work in the home and enlarged the activities of the family as a consumer of goods. Many items that had formerly been of home manufacture were, between 1870 and 1880, manufactured elsewhere.[2] While home production did not cease in the post–Civil War period, its nature clearly did. In the cities, particularly, divers items of prepared food, ready-made clothing, household tools, and home furnishings appeared in the dry-goods stores and small specialty shops, and the link between these items and the home was the shopping woman.[3] In these decades the department store took its place as a permanent fixture in the commercial center of the larger cities, where it became both the focus of a new consumer ideology and a unique space for middle-class women. Shopping for new commodities in this new urban locale played a major role in the lives of these women, a role that signified opportunity along with status and economic power.

"Middle class" was a designation for growing numbers of urban residents. Not a class in a fixed, traditional sense, and no longer the self-employed artisans, shopkeepers, and gentry of the Republican era, by mid–nineteenth century the middle class was a group in the process of formation: mostly native-born and Protestant, white collar, salaried, commercial and professional men and their families. There were, however, successive levels within each of these categories, and many marginal people in economically precarious situations feared a social mobility that could go two ways.[4] Not limited to occupation and income, the working definition of this new middle class has a significant cultural component that must include the home and what went in it, residential location, levels and patterns of consumption, child-rearing strategies, and leisure activities. As a social class, this group has seemed to defy analysis.[5] George Ade, the Chicago journalist, offered perhaps the most vivid definition of this rapidly expanding segment of urban America when he described the middle class as those people who are "neither poverty stricken nor offensively rich, and who are not held down by arbitrary laws governing that mysterious part of the community known as society."[6] Appearing on the editorial page of the *Chicago Record* from 1893 until 1900, Ade's short stories and articles portrayed the vicissitudes of urban life and the ironies of class for men and women in social and economic motion. The essay "The Advantages of Being Middle Class" is a typical expression of his sense of social identity in a new milieu.

> The middle-class can take lake excursions on a hot summer night on a double-decked steamer with electric lights and a resounding orchestra . . . The upper class, except for a small portion that can afford private yachts, never enjoys a breezy moonlight ride . . . Lake Michigan might as well be a thousand miles to the east.

For Ade, the upper class alone was "fearful of mingling," fearful always of what others would think; and he celebrated the sometimes confusing, broad social possibilities accorded the middle classes. Writing in the same short piece about a couple enjoying a cool evening in Lincoln Park, Ade concluded:

> No Chicago millionaire has such a magnificent front yard, with such a large lake and so many stately trees around it. They must feel sorry for the millionaire, who cannot go to a public park in the evening to stroll or sit for the reason that so many other persons go there.[7]

Historian Stuart Blumin has suggested that in the nineteenth century the developing urban middle class was a self-conscious socio-cultural group.[8] The information on middle-class women detained for shoplifting supports this thesis. These women adhered publicly to the morality of their class and shared basic values and attitudes about social forms. Conscious of themselves

as women belonging to a particular stratum, they readily acknowledged that their behavior was inconsistent with accepted middle-
class mores. One young Boston woman confessed that "she could
not resist the temptation to steal . . . ," but added "between sobs,
'If only I could live the past year over again, I would not be found
in such a fix as this. It will kill my mother. As for myself, I am
disgraced. . . .'" "I can only say this," a Chicago woman said, "I
am well connected, and if this were to come out about me I would
be ruined and my family would be disgraced." Unable to account
for her shoplifting, a suspect from New York said simply, "God
only knows what I was doing."[9] Similarly, their husbands and
fathers, who were predominantly of the business class, shared certain economic expectations and social goals, and they viewed this
female want of self-restraint in the department stores as surprising
in the individual instance but consistent with their stereotyped
assumptions about women as a group.[10]

If not totally representative of the broader middle classes (they
were, after all, married to professional men), the Pardee and Richards women stand for an important and growing sector of the
middle class, and they are typical in their preoccupation with their
homes and families.[11] Maintenance of the home and maintenance
of the individuals in the home were the twin foci of their lives,
and functioned as full-time, unpaid jobs.

Most commentary on late nineteenth-century urban middle-
class women, by both contemporaries and modern historians, has
been concerned with reproduction of private social life and and
the hesitant extension of the domestic situation into an expanding array of predominantly female voluntary associations, societies, study groups, and clubs.[12] The Pardee and Richards diaries
support this traditional interpretation, but with a different
emphasis. To a far greater extent than earlier works would suggest, the diaries reveal women in public, acting purposefully and
autonomously on their own behalf as well as that of their families.
These two women and their contemporaries moved beyond singularly domestic confines and into an enlarged sphere of activity.
Whether we speak of them using the great urban parks, like New
York City's Central Park, taking day-long outings with their children to a still remote Coney Island, visiting the Museum of Natural History, or making repeated forays to the central commercial

and banking centers, we find these urban middle-class women comfortably moving about the city, populating public spaces outside of the feminized terrain of the shopping district. The assumption that these public spaces belonged to men is belied by the written evidence and the obvious physical presence of women in a variety of seemingly male preserves. Clara Pardee frequently attended to money matters "which are a great nuisance to us all," and on more than one occasion she attempted to shield her husband from financial concerns about their house.[13] Pardee's role was not unique. Women's diaries indicate that paying bills, if not allocating expenditures, was routinely within the wife's purview. Mrs. Caroline Dunstan's New York diaries, 1866 to 1870, mentioned successive trips to the bank and to Wall Street on "house matters"; presumably she took care of mortgage payments as well as household bills. Susan Forbes, wife of a prominent merchant in Springfield, Massachusetts, took care of a variety of economic transactions. Witness this excerpt from March 1874: "I walked down town to see Jeffrey at store about partnership. Called at Johnsons & paid society milk bill. Talked a minute with Buxton abt. money & called on Henry Lee about mortgage on place . . . also at Mass. Life Insurance Company."[14] Far from being disconnected from the public sphere, these women performed vital economic activities at the point where the family economy made contact with the larger economy.

Income data for the middle class are sketchy.[15] It is difficult to pinpoint how well off families designated "middle class" actually were in the closing decades of the nineteenth century. There is no indication of what Doctor Pardee charged his patients, nor whether the family had other sources of income. But they had at least two servants, their children went to private schools, and the family went to the shore for the summer. An observer would think them economically secure, certainly comfortable by nineteenth-century standards; yet financial uncertainty permeates Mrs. Pardee's diaries.[16] Though they were socially confident and appeared to be free from financial anxiety, in fact the Pardees often lived beyond their income.

Household budgets examined in the *Evening Post* (New York) in 1900 posited an income of $200 a month, or $2,400 a year, for a middle-class family of four (two children). Estimated expenses included wages for a servant at $16 a month, which was in line with the servant wages listed in both the Richards and Pardee diaries. The husband's personal monthly expenses "in the city" were estimated at $40, which, together with food, was the single highest monthly item. With insurance, rent, and clothes, the other major expenses, the total came to $151 a month. The remaining balance of $49 went for coal, wood, gas—fuels for heating and cooking—doctors' bills, and "extras." A woman who responded to this list of expenditures said $200 a month was "plenty," an excellent budget; a male respondant felt that it represented a necessary minimum.[17]

In a 1909 study of working-class families in New York City, Robert C. Chapin found that those families with yearly incomes above $1500 were no longer working class but were headed by white-collar workers and professionals. Chapin included clergymen, dentists, barbershop proprietors, railroad inspectors, and telegraphers among the new middle class. Those workers with incomes between $1,000 and $1,200 a year he placed at the lower edge of middle-class life.[18]

Apart from actual income (about which no two authorities ever agreed), a descriptive understanding of what it meant to be middle class in these decades is useful. Women were far more involved in the developing capitalist economy than conventional theories of nineteenth-century domesticity would suggest. Financial pressures and uncertainties were burdens for the women much as they were for the men; even well-established middle-class women confronted repeated cares about money. "Had one of our horrid money talks," Pardee complained in 1899, "but it will only react on Ensign [her husband] if I worry myself sick & I must find some way out of it."[19] Later in the year, after writing that her husband's medical practice was "slow," she privately lamented, "An unpleasant day because Ensign was cross ... I wish money was never known!"[20] Enmeshed in the maintenance of a way of life and a standard of living that demanded their active participation and propelled them into the public sphere, these active middle-class women belie the traditional notion of the isolation of the Victorian wife from the commercial world.

In those post–Civil War decades, when the ideology of the middle-class home emphasized the independence of the family unit from the stresses of the disordered and rapacious outside world, the woman, who was the theoretical center of this insular unit, was in fact thoroughly engaged in the public domain. Although rarely employed, she spent increasing amounts of time outside her home. It may be legitimately argued that women were acting in public mainly as agents of the family, and while much of their daily routine took place beyond the domestic confines, the domestic was omnipresent and usually took precedence. That may be the case, but it still suggests broad patterns of domestic social life and public activity that are more interesting for their interaction than for their presumed separation.

There is little support in these diaries for a portrait of female idleness. Clara Pardee, for example, often had more responsibilities than she could reasonably manage, and in 1894 she felt compelled to reduce her public commitments. "Mrs. Pardee does not think she can *possibly* retain the position she had last year," Alice Bartlett Stimson wrote her husband, the Rev. Henry A. Stimson. In a conversation Pardee had confided her intention to withdraw from some of her organizational activities in Stimson's Broadway Tabernacle Church. She simply had "too much work."[21] With three young children in 1894, the burden of maintaining the household, and "running up medicines" and sending out bills for her physician husband, Clara Pardee felt it necessary to pull back from over-involvement in other areas of her life. Similarly, when eleven-year-old Harold Pardee was hurt in a bicycle accident in October 1898, she immediately resigned from her active role in the Christian Missionary Society, explaining the necessity to "have my mind free and watch the boys."[22] Worried about her son and in an obviously agitated state of mind, Clara confided in her diary: "How fearful we are not doing right in every way."[23] By 1903, however, her children demanded less of her, and Mrs. Pardee was again fully occupied with missionary affairs.[24] Clearly, women were not "banished to the domestic circle," nor did they retreat there of their own accord.[25] Rather, they moved back and forth, defining their own complex pattern of involvement, which was always shaped, but never completely determined, by their primary domestic responsibility.

The Pardee and Richards diaries portray women moving in two worlds, preoccupied with the rhythms of their households, yet engaged in public activity compatible with, but not limited to, familial concerns. Both women went "downtown" frequently, as often alone as in the company of a friend or relative. They attended meetings of missionary societies, temperance organizations, and church prayer groups. They went to sewing school, art exhibitions, lectures, and concerts. They paid social calls, took rides and walks in Central Park, and regularly rode "down Broadway in the cars." These women were part of the urban throngs viewing the Statue of Liberty and Grant's Tomb and crossing the newly opened Brooklyn Bridge.[26]

Harriet Richards' description of "paying calls" in Brooklyn one January afternoon in 1884 revealed a woman moving alone and self-confidently in the urban environment. Public sanction for such new patterns of middle-class behavior was implicit in her words. "Left at 2:30 for Brooklyn; went over Bridge in cars." She made five brief calls and concluded the entry by tracing her return route. "Took Atlantic Ave. cars to S. Ferry and Elevated up. Home at twenty minutes to six."[27]

Even when there were unaccustomed and potentially unruly crowds in the streets, the two women seemed surprisingly unconcerned. On the day in August 1885 that General Ulysses Grant was buried, Pardee went out alone. "I never saw anything to compare with mighty crowd of people that thronged the streets. Went out in the morning, first alone and later with Ensign."[28] Rather than posing a threat to these women or their families, the city streets had become an arena for action. Pardee and Richards participated fully in urban life. "Not fearful of mingling," they moved out from their own "little islands of propriety" and were bound neither by neighborhood nor by locale.[29] Theirs was a new form of urban consciousness, accepting of heterogeneity and based very much on physical mobility and consumption.

As *Nation* editor E. L. Godkin observed in 1882, no longer were women sitting tamely at home. Women were now "in the streets, in horse-cars, omnibuses, excursion boats, railroad trains, and hotel corridors."[30] That they were in the dry-goods bazaars as well was evident. In short, "beautifully dressed women" were in public, seeing and being seen, often lending a certain panache by their very presence.[31] Female public life was conducted without the supporting ideology of masculine individualism, but these diaries demonstrate emphatically just how far social boundaries had expanded for urban, middle-class women.

Home and family provided the background in these meticulously kept diaries, but home was not the private retreat for the women that it was for the men. Quite the opposite. Because home was the female arena, it was also their battleground and workshop, and women sought "recreation and rest elsewhere."[32] Shopping was one such recreation. "A good shop" provided the context for divers forms of public and even cultural life, yet it was sanctioned by the demands of the private sphere.[33]

Shopping dwarfed all other activities. Women shopped constantly. There is no statistically accurate way to determine how often women shopped in the stores, but diaries indicate it was an ongoing process. In one nine-day period in the spring of 1885, Mrs. Richards "shopped" four times: March 31, April 2, April 4, and April 8. In May of the same year she mentioned shopping six out of eight days, generally at Macy's. Mrs. Pardee shopped just as often: in May 1893, she noted going downtown to shop both morning and afternoon on the second and again on the third, returning home for lunch on both days. She shopped once more on the eighth and again on the eleventh. When women did not go shopping, they cited often compelling reasons. Alice Stimson invariably mentioned the shopping she either did or should have done in her weekly letters to "My Dear Father" (1893 to 1895). In one such letter she described a meeting of the woman's club, Sorosis, in counterpoint to her usual chores: "It is positively a great refreshment to drop all thought of what we shall eat ... and where withal we shall be clothed for a brief period and exchange views on every other conceivable subject with a group of very bright women."[34]

For many of these women the stores provided a use for leisure time that necessitated neither rationalization nor apology. Trade journals promoted the idea that women could find a legitimate occupation in shopping. "When they have a few leisure hours they don't know how to occupy at home," the *Dry Goods Economist* suggested, women could say to themselves, "I guess I'll go down to A's and walk around their store a little. It's always so pleasant in there."[35] Much of the relentless shopping of women like Mrs. Richards did seem to be an attempt to deal with and coherently organize time. The *New York Tribune* captured the meaning of such activity: "To go about and see things, whether one wants them or not, to pick up a bargain here and there, to take a bite at one of the store restaurants, and to return home with stories of lovely things that are being sold. . . ."[36]

Undoubtedly, some women used the department stores to kill time and ease their boredom. "What do these women mean by such aimless shopping?" a woman asked rhetorically in a *New York Times* article on shopping and shoppers. "Why, my dear, it's a cheap entertainment," was the reply.[37] Not idle, despite the pervasive stereotype that men worked and women consumed, many women evidenced, nevertheless, a vague purposelessness. In a culture in which money translated into possessions and time had become a valuable commodity, the contribution of middle-class women was ill defined.[38]

The line between domesticity and female leisure was not clear-cut. The tension between the values embedded in the communal-domestic ideal and the reality of the new "shopping woman" participating fully in the commercial world was real, if publicly unacknowledged. More introspective than Harriet Richards, Clara Pardee recognized the balancing act in which she was constantly engaged. After days of sewing on her husband's dressing gown and cutting and fitting her own satin waist, all the while doing a good bit of her own housework, regularly working as her husband's pharmacist/assistant, and repeatedly going downtown to shop, she mused about how much was demanded and how little time she had. "It seems as if I accomplish but little, but days seem so full and business does take a great deal of time."[39] The repeated notation, "Hurried home to sew" was indicative of far more than congested days and the burdens of maintaining her family.[40] It spoke, indirectly, to the frustration and complaints of ennui voiced by many women of this generation, and to the male sense that the women were insufficiently occupied.

Pardee felt acutely pressured by the conflicts in her life, the very modern sense of either never having enough time to do all that had to be done, or of working all day in the house and for the family and having nothing to show for it. Author Abby Morton Diaz confronted this dilemma in her book *A Domestic Problem* (1875). Writing about women like Mrs. Pardee who "with an assistant or two do the work of the household," Diaz described a woman's day as devoid of "leisure, tranquility ... and culture." Nothing was ever quite finished in a day crowded beyond capacity: "Constant hurry," she wrote, "is a constant strain."[41]

"Making a middle-class home required work," and the work was primarily that of women.[42] While so-called idle dependence became an ideal of sorts, a sign of feminine delicacy and leisure and a mark of masculine status and prosperity, in practice most middle-class women were far from idle. A family role and a female role, "housewife" was very much a work role.[43] The duties of a woman, Diaz wrote, were "as innumerable as the stars," and as little valued.[44] Even the ubiquitous (but often unreliable) servant could do little to ease many of the diverse responsibilities and tasks involved in maintaining a middle-class home and family in the 1880s and 1890s.[45]

Certainly, some of the drudgery of housework had been eliminated for the middle-class woman—heavy cleaning and laundry for instance—but much time-consuming labor remained.[46] "I chored in kitchen and about house, A.M.," was a frequent notation in the diaries of Susan E. Forbes, wife of the owner of the Forbes and Wallace Department Store in Springfield, Massachusetts.[47] While "the atmosphere of the kitchen" may not have been deemed suitable for "Ladies," management of the kitchen and the maid-of-all-work was unquestionably the woman's duty. If they rarely cooked the meals, most women planned the menus and engaged in certain forms of food preparation, particularly baking, and canning and "putting up" large quantities of seasonal fruits and vegetables.[48] These women were not workers in any recognized sense—their labor was publicly invisible—but from the evidence of their diaries, reliance of middle-class women on others to attend to the real work of domesticity has been greatly exaggerated.[49]

Simultaneously an employer and a worker, the woman was responsible for domestic order and efficiency. Both the moral and the material home were her province, and how well she managed became a cultural expression of her own personhood as well as a sign of affection for her family.[50] Sewing, some cleaning and cooking, overseeing the children's education and spiritual life, tending the sick, and shopping were unvarying and unending obligations for the majority of middle-class women.[51]

The reformulation of housework around new tasks and new levels of sanitation required the full participation of all the females in the house, even with domestic help.[52] In fact, despite the new water and steam technology that became part of the middle-class home after the Civil War, the volume of household labor increased. In her study of housework and household technology, *More Work for Mother* (1983), Ruth Cowan has convincingly argued that some of the work was made easier, but the overall amount of work increased: there was more complex cooking, more laundry, more house cleaning, and quantitatively more clothes per person.[53] For instance, "refined women" were expected to have street and shopping costumes—special clothes, unlike those worn at home, that were subdued and suitable for the eyes of strangers—clothes in which one could present a public face and buy other clothes. Beginning in the 1890s, journals were full of advice about appropriate attire and advised merchants that "the success of every dry goods department depends upon whether or no women can be taught that different costumes must be provided for different occasions."[54]

By the early 1890s, as well, special clothing appeared for the new roles women adopted. The athletic woman, who participated in the growing number of sports available to middle-class women, found accessories and costumes adapted to her needs. Cycling, for example, a symbol of a changing culture as well as a fad, necessitated some modification in women's dress; but suddenly a whole industry revolved around "the wheel." There was a "cyclist corset for all athletic purposes," which came, so the ad said, "in all lengths and 100 different styles."[55] Similarly, there was the bicycle handkerchief in twelve designs for men and women; the bicycle suit, with and without divided skirt; the bicycle shirt, stock, hose, hat, sweater, collar, cap, vest, gaiters, and shoes.

Finley Peter Dunne, the Chicago journalist and creator of the popular sage, Mr. Dooley, homed in on the cycling craze and its attendant fashions with a column entitled, "The Divided Skirt."

> "Jawn," said Mr. Dooley, "did ye iver hear th' puzzle whin a woman's not a woman?"
> . . . Whin is a woman not a woman? mind ye. Whin's she's on a bicycle, by dad."

Not only was the well-brought-up woman riding astride on a bicycle, Dooley grumbled, but:

> "How d'ye suppose she was dhressed? In pa-ants, Jawn . . . In pa-ants. Oh, th' shame iv it!"[56]

The increasing specialization in the use of clothes, so evident in the late nineteenth century (and so quickly satirized by Finley Peter Dunne), meant that particular clothes were considered to be right and wrong for more and more occasions. The problem of not wearing the correct attire became one with not knowing how to shop and not understanding how clothes had been transformed into a new symbol of middle-class life.[57] Whether it was the "best and acceptable" dress materials for summer sports costumes, or the appropriate fashion for afternoon tea, the trade journals and the stores worked together to educate the consumer in the minutiae of dress: "The salesmen in the hosiery department," the *Dry Goods Reporter* instructed, "should be coached to urge upon the customer the different varieties which are correct . . . [they should] urge upon the customers the necessity of having variety of hose."[58]

The profound change in consumption patterns was the direct consequence of technological development and market expansion. The links between production and consumption were clear. Needs multiplied because there was more to be had and an increasing standard of living that made more things feasible. Social identity was established through the new possibilities of consumption. If we substitute "want" for "need," the nature of this critical change becomes apparent. People wanted more, wanted variety and costume and decoration, and wants are, by their very nature, both psychological and unlimited.[59]

Notions of what constituted basic necessities gradually expanded on all population levels, of course, but this was particularly true of the growing middle group of white-collar workers and their families. Though the Pardees were a professional family with no concern about their social position, their anxious financial situation, prompted as much by their consumer ambitions as it was by Dr. Pardee's fluctuating income, was symptomatic of the new middle class.[60]

The trade journals reflected the elaboration of "new needs" and a standard of life based upon consumer spending. Possession of the right product was part of the new ethos. In 1892 the *Dry Goods Economist* commented, "One must have so many shoes this season; high ones, low shoes to wear with spats, yatching shoes and some for tennis ... one becomes bewildered from the immensity of the choice."[61] The Chicago *Dry Goods Reporter* announced flatly, "The accepted standard of shoe needs today is that every person should have at least three pairs of shoes."[62] The same journal quoted a "notion girl" saying, "I never sell a woman one stock foundation, always two, and most always three; Women don't buy one thing at a time any more."[63] Style necessitated having more than one of a given item, and the stores overtly promoted such new buying habits in the name of middle-class respectability and progress.

What money could buy increased dramatically over the course of the nineteenth century. Vastly expanded productivity forced producers and their main retail outlets, the dry-goods bazaars, to cultivate and extend their markets. By the 1880s a wide array of new industrial products for the home and its inhabitants had become available. Not only was the home the "targeted destination" of an onslaught of consumer goods, as Mary Ryan writes, the shopping woman herself became a particular target.[64] But here, too, dichotomies may be misleading. New industrial products and older domestic traditions fit together in complex ways. It was not a simple matter of displacement.

Because sewing was a major occupation for both Pardee and Richards, as it was for most middle-class women in this period, the introduction of sewing machines into their lives did not pass without comment. Richards wrote of first using a machine in 1883 to make thirty cloth bags for a church fair.[65] Eighteen months later she hired a sewing machine for one week and made curtains for the family's new summer house in Litchfield, Connecticut.[66] Two years after that, in 1887, she finally bought a machine. "Had a lesson in the morning on the sewing machine," she recorded the day after its arrival.[67] Pardee, who at various times made every conceivable kind of garment for her children, her husband, and herself, in addition to repairing the upholstered furniture and sewing curtains and linens, waited until 1893 to buy her sewing machine and duly noted the purchase: "Went downtown and bought a machine." When it arrived three days later, she mentioned the event with evident satisfaction. "New machine came home & it is fine."[68]

Apart from practical use, domestic consumption of such items as cycling costumes and sewing machines provided a way of locating one's family in the class system and an immediate link between the middle-class housewife and the market. Housewives continued to be household workers, but the circumstances of much of their work were altered. The locus of traditional forms of productive activity shifted away from the home. Edward Bellamy called attention to the transformed content of household labor and the reapportionment of a woman's time in an article for *Good Housekeeping* magazine in 1889. Noting the widespread availability of many household necessities, Bellamy lamented what he saw as a lost American simplicity. Unlike forty years ago, he wrote, "independent existence is no longer considered advisable for a household; so constant is the shopping for household needs, one blizzard and the modern household is reduced to extremities."[69]

Leaving Bellamy's misplaced nostalgia aside, the increasing dependence of urban households on the goods and services industrial production provided changed the focus of the middle-class home. As the household began to consume the products of American industry, the orientation of the family became more outward looking. In the very middle decades of the nineteenth century, when the privatized middle class seemed to have reached its apotheosis, the pull of consumer capitalism provided a dialectic that never found satisfactory resolution. The intense and intimate social relations of the middle-class family were repeatedly challenged by an "avalanche of consumer goods."[70] Large-scale capital investment in new technology specifically adapted to home use placed the individual family in an ideological bind: While the private and self-contained family group was the theoretical center of the middle-class universe, there was "vivid evidence of worldliness and materialism" in the heart of the refuge.[71] "Things" became ascendant for the middle class, as ownership of new material objects was geared to the parallel assumptions of status and public display.[72] Diverse objects such as pianos and parlor organs, sewing machines, and gas stoves, while useful, also operated as social confirmation of class position.[73] Typical of the contradictions in Victorian society, many of these new consumer items were purchased in terms of an older, less self-conscious domesticity, but the goods themselves served to undermine the situation. By the end of the nineteenth century, respectability and the moral home were redefined; to be bourgeois took on new meaning, as consumption inside the individual home became a priority.[74] Created by industrial manufacture, with profit the immediate rationale, food and shelter, clothing and home furnishings all became commodities.[75]

It is within this understanding of family life and sex roles that the picture of the woman in the department store comes to life. Shopping became a main work activity of the middle-class woman and part of the new routine of urban life as well. By the closing decades of the century traditional female skills based on home production were replaced by the skills required to purchase factory-produced goods. Although men were certainly not excluded from consumption choices and often were active participants, women were the primary consumers, and it was specifically to them that department stores directed their appeals. The *DGE*'s "Wide Awake Retailer" presented the obvious as a fact, stating flatly, "Woman, Mr. Merchandizer, is the only proposition worth considering."[76] With a modicum of affluence and increasing amounts of unstructured free time, urban middle-class women integrated the dual roles of work and leisure into new patterns of behavior and became the "shoppers" so disparaged in much contemporary journalism.

Practically and symbolically, the woman shopping was just as engaged in the public "defense of home" as was her husband in his much more highly valued "work"; yet the woman, who made many of the major decisions and purchases quite independently of her husband, never achieved commensurate status in the market place. The larger community never regarded her as a substantive economic actor. With the household no longer the center of production, the position of the middle-class woman within that household was in a state of flux. Her unpaid labor was trivialized, if not ignored, and her public identity was cloaked in a domestic image—one of an undifferentiated throng of "shopping women." The "new woman" of the 1890s, harbinger of a future that promised greater equality for women within the existing institutions of education, marriage, and law, was subsumed under this heading along with her more-traditional sister.[77] So quickly did these women become objects of derision and moral condemnation in newspaper editorials, journal articles, and even the popular theater that if we are to understand either women's lives or their relationship to the emergence of consumer capitalism, it becomes necessary to recover the details of their public lives as shoppers.

Articles describing the shopping woman and detailing "Shopping as a Fine Art" were commonplace by the early 1870s, as shopping became an issue, part of the cultural iconography of womanhood, and a metaphor for the woman acting in the public domain.[78] Even the feminist *Woman's Journal* accepted the new role definition:

> Next to mental improvement, shopping is now the business of life, and a most bewildering and exhausting business it is. . . . Strong is the character demanded for wise shopping! Exalted are the Christian virtues needed to make that peculiarly feminine labor anything but anguish, mortification and a sad waste of money![79]

The "chief diversion of ladies," shopping became linked to the innate, natural characteristics of women; the department store, with the church, became part of their natural environment. The *New York Times* reported an incident in which an English visitor bemoaned the lack of spiritual sustenance in Philadelpia. "Whenever I was dull or cross," she said, "I used to run up to Westminster and go into the Abbey. A half hour spent in meditation would always make me ashamed of myself, and I would go home strong and happy." The American woman smiled and then said: "Why can't you do that in Philadelphia—there's Wanamaker's!"[80] While this may have been self-conscious parody, it had the ring of truth for an increasingly secular and commercial culture.

Women shopping were women working, but they were also women enjoying themselves. Shopping became a discrete activity quite apart from procuring necessities, and in nineteenth-century women's diaries we find repeated reference to their life in the stores. When Sophie Hall and her husband, the Reverend Mr.

George Hall, visited New York for three months in 1879, she arrived with a new diary and a list of the names and addresses of the prominent dry-goods stores in the city. Three days after her arrival from Wilmington, Sophie wrote, "Went out to find some shopping places to go to ... Got into Macy's Emporium ... and saw so many beautiful things there that we found it a *trying matter* to get out. . . then to Altman's, an extensive establishment on 6th Ave."[81] Shopping seemed to have been this visitor's main occupation. She recorded what she bought and what she did not buy, how much she paid, and sporadic incidents she found either amusing or disturbing. In one particularly revealing entry, she related how alarmed her husband became when she returned to their West 9th Street boarding house far later than expected one afternoon, having lost all sense of time wandering in the stores.[82]

Sophie Hall acted as she was supposed to act, as she had been socialized to respond to the world of consumer goods. People accepted the image of the middle-class woman losing herself in shopping as an accurate portrayal. The mid–nineteenth-century cultural stereotype of women like Mrs. Hall focused on their frailty and vulnerability, physical as well as mental, their irresponsibility, and their paradoxical moral sensibility. Had this woman been caught shoplifting, it would not have been out of character nor would it have been surprising.

Men could not view women in the department stores with any degree of equanimity.

> The awful prevalence of the vice of shopping among women is one of those signs of the times which lead the thoughtful patriot almost to despair of the future of our country. Few people have any idea of the extent to which our women are addicted to this purse-destroying vice.[83]

This introduction to a long and bitterly satirical article entitled "Shopping," which appeared on the editorial page of the *New York Times* in June 1881, was typical of a genre, and emanated in part from the irreducible conflict between earning and spending. Men worked but women shopped. The female "shopping habit" or "mania," as it was often called in those decades, was thought to originate in the inherent weakness of women and to rest upon the "savage passions"—vanity and self-indulgence. "The woman who is its victim will have fine clothes," one journalist opined. "If she cannot pay for them, she will go as near to stealing them as the conventions permit."[84] The writer was wrong only in degree. Middle-class women often went beyond convention, and their shoplifting made the moral crisis caused by the consumer revolution explicit.

The large department stores were for and about women, but primarily about women of the middle class. There were dry-goods bazaars that catered to a working-class clientele in all the major cities—shopping in the dry-goods stores was recreation for shop girls as it was for housewives—but the Macy's, Wanamaker's, Marshall Field's, and similar institutions appearing in this study are solidly middle class in appeal and outlook. While the poor still did much of their shopping in the street from pushcart vendors and sidewalk hawkers, most other groups found their way to the new dry-goods bazaars. Designed to serve the needs of middle-class customers, or, at the very least, the ideals and aspirations of this socioeconomic group, merchandising policy was framed within certain definite limits.[85] Every message communicated by the great department stores revealed the differentiation of markets, the assumption that the bulk of the customers were not drawn from the "shawl trade." A children's ditty commonly heard on Chicago's West Side in the 1890s underlined the common understanding of a socially and economically segmented society in which a high level of purchasing power was the expression of class and status:[86] "All the girls who wear high heels / They trade down at Marshall Field's / All the girls who scrub the floor / They trade at the Boston Store."[87]

The older American culture of self-denial, which the new department stores seemed intent on subverting, had always existed in uneasy juxtaposition with the allure of material things. The jeremiads of Cotton Mather and Charles Grandison Finney, the social criticism of James Fennimore Cooper, Mark Twain, and Thorstein Veblen sounded similar themes: collective misgivings about "sought after emblems" and erosion of strict social morality in an ever-growing material economy devoted to individual satisfaction. Protestantism traditionally had stressed inner control, and at the end of the nineteenth century personal self-restraint was still fundamental in defining the bourgeois character.[88] Yet even before the Civil War, in a far more limited capital market where the link between needs and available commodities was more clearly defined, observers noted an obvious tension between wants and possibilities. As secularization eroded a traditional value system and appearances seemed to count far more than reality, Americans feared the corrupting consequences of their own burgeoning materialism.[89] Much of the advice literature of the mid–nineteenth century spoke to the want of frugality and self-denial among young people and reflected inchoate fears of diversity and social disorder.[90] While there were important differences between the pre- and post-war decades, it is useful to remember that neither consumer society nor social criticism of that society arrived full-blown with the appearance of the dry-goods bazaar.

The descriptions offered in *A Peep into Catharine Street* (1846) could easily be a portrayal of the next generation of shoppers and shopkeepers. The unreasonable woman who demands "to see the entire quantity of which the assortment is made up," the crowds of shoppers "continually passing, jostling, dodging and buffeting" each other, the petty deceits and cheapening of goods to make people buy, appear as integral parts of the pre–Civil War urban shopping experience.[91] An even earlier title, *The Perils of Pearl Street*, written by Asa Greene and published in 1834, satirizes both dry-goods merchants and their customers. The instability of the trade looms large, and shoppers appear as benign scavengers who either exhibit the "shopping mania" and cannot stay away from the stores, or insistently "beg a pattern" and have no intention of making more than a token purchase. "Half his goods were disposed of in gratuitous shreds and patches," Greene wrote of the failed Joseph Smoothly. Among the perils of Pearl Street are the bargain hunters who cause a merchant to reduce his prices and ultimately lose his business. "He had acquired the reputation of selling cheap which is usually of great consequence to females because they pride themselves on buying bargains."[92]

After 1870, however, the process of commodification escalated rapidly. Filled with new manufactured items—many of them semi-luxuries that quickly became necessities and were replaced by new "luxury" items—the dry-goods bazaar acted as an enormous magnet. The very meaning of those categories, "necessity" and "luxury," changed with increasing material affluence and availability of goods and markedly influenced the behavior of women who entered the stores.[93] The transformation of perfume into a highly profitable consumer item is an example of the correspondence of technology, sales pitch, and the escalating popular demand for the trappings of the rich.

Once an expensive purchase with correspondingly limited appeal, perfume, along with toilet water and fancy soap, became more reasonably priced by the early 1890s and a leading attraction of notion and drug counters.[94] The torrent of technical changes lowered the cost of many consumer goods, including trivial things like scent, and made them widely available. Though merchants did all they could to push the new products, descriptions of women crowding the new toiletries departments lend credence to the repeated assertions by merchants and dry-goods publications that customers were, in fact, demanding the new consumer items. A push-pull effect operated in ways that are still not fully clear. As consumers wanted, or became convinced they required, more or better than they had been accustomed to, luxury and self-gratification came to enhance the everyday environment.[95] Four years into the new century, retailers could fully support the *Dry Goods Reporter*'s assertion that "20th century progress has played havoc with many an old hide bound proverb, among them, 'Never buy anything you can do without'."[96]

The concept of obsolescence ("outdated, not outworn," to quote Dorothy Davis, the author of the comprehensive *A History of Shopping* [1966]) became identified with the middle-class woman shopper and was part of the new, easier acceptance of consumption as a goal in itself.[97] The mass production of goods held out the promise of reducing class distinction based on objects, but in fact it seems to have fueled the passion for fad and fashion as a means of enforcing class distinctions. As money translated into possession, a new sense of class identity was forged, not in production but in consumption. The "right" purchases became signals, albeit temporary, of group cohesiveness.[98] Uniting as well as separating, consumption legitimated social difference. Novelty became a measure of social value, and (as was often the case) the *Dry Goods Economist* reflected social and economic reality: "The consuming demand follows fads until the limits of cheap trade have adopted the style in vogue; then something new or different is seized upon."[99] Taste was a communication system the middle class sought to monopolize. The stores thrived on the situation. "Any form of garment which permits of the remodelling of clothes of previous seasons to conform to the new lines is ruinous to business!!" the *DGE* warned its merchant readers. "Women must feel," the writer continued, "not to have new goods is to be far out of form." Not only did the new have to materially differ, but the old had to be "sufficiently déclassé by comparison."[100]

With developing means of mass production, the growth of national distribution networks, and new methods of advertising, the evolution of wants and tastes became an upward spiral.[101] Consumption became a dynamic concept in which the perception of an object became as important as its intrinsic qualities. In the race to keep up with fashionable appearances, the satisfaction derived from goods often depended as much on consumption by others, as long as they were the "right" others, as on consumption by oneself.[102] The new passion for "novelties," items that meant nothing or everything, were not remotely utilitarian, and literally sold themselves, added a feverish quality to department store shopping.

The Trilby "mania" is an ideal example. *Trilby*, a novel by George du Maurier, was published in London in 1894. A stage version appeared the following year; so, too, did a Trilby hat, a Trilby locket, a Trilby chatelaine purse, a doll, a shoe, and the game of Trilby.[103] Not even ministers' wives were exempt from the Trilby craze, as a letter from Alice Stimson in October 1894 to her husband Henry makes clear: "It is now Tuesday morning. I have been to market and down to Ehrichs where I bought 'Trilby' for 99 cts. A $1.75 book it is a 'special' for today only. But I got in *early* and bought a copy."[104]

Comparing buying habits for these instant "necessities" in New York and Paris, a reporter noted with only slight exaggeration, "a novelty will appear one day, be the rage in twenty-four hours and die from its own violence in a week."[105] Based on the endless redefinition of the emblems of class, needs often seemed to create themselves. "Every new article," the *Dry Goods Economist* editorialized, "must fill a demand that will, in all probability, be created after the article is shown."[106] The influential *DGE* was publicly telling merchants what had heretofore been the content of accusations: "In selling goods everything depends upon making a good impression"; quality and genuine value were secondary to the symbolic meaning of material objects.[107] The question of who created consumer demand remains. In the alliance between dry-goods bazaars and women customers, both sides could claim, with equal justice, that they controlled the situation and were responding to it.

It would be incorrect, however, to see the woman out shopping in the closing decades of the nineteenth century as a passive individual who had fallen victim to patently false or artificial wants.[108] Women had to walk a tightrope between real needs, defined by practical use, and stimulated wants created by a suggestive ambiance, lavish display, and, often, manipulated prices; wants that, the *DGE* reported happily, "caused many a dollar to burn a hole through its owner's pocket."[109] The categories were not clear-cut, they overlapped and collapsed into each other, and in a setting that was dependent on high consumption and quick turnover, confusion about what was in fact a real need or a symbolic need was encouraged. Shoppers, as William Leiss wrote in *The Limits to Satisfaction*, were "faced with the problem of continually reinterpreting 'need' in the context of a rapidly changing array of goods and services."[110]

The stores were capitalizing on a massive change in values just as much as they were promoting them. The transition to women's ready-to-wear clothes provides an illustration of the emergence of these new values and practices. A technical possibility by the 1870s, women's ready-to-wear became a growing element in store merchandising by the early 1880s.[111] However, well before mass production of women's clothing was a reality, merchants attempted to acclimate women to new modes of production, to displace their labor and skill from home manufacture, and to establish new categories of self-definition. Clothing became a commodity, and the department stores worked to create new patterns of consumer behavior (as well as new consumers) by touting the quality of the ready-made garments. Advertising ladies' and children's undergarments in 1875, Stern Bros. informed readers, "Upon critical examination will be found equal to the best home made garments at much lower prices."[112] Ehrichs, a well-known New York dry-goods establishment on Eighth Avenue, touted women's ready-made cloaks "cut and sewed and pressed by Journeymen Tailors, and hence they have a graceful shape and fit the form."[113] By insisting that ready-made garments were as good as or even better than homemade, the stores attempted to make it difficult for women, or anyone else, to justify the traditional feminine role in home manufacture.[114]

It should have been unnecessary to plead the cause of ready-made clothing. Home production of clothes was work, tremendously time-consuming, often fatiguing, and performed under inadequate physical conditions; good light was always a problem. The sheer burden of the kind of shopping that was necessary for urban home manufacture, the locating of the various components needed for fabrication of clothing, should in itself have been sufficient inducement for the change to ready-made. Abba Goold Woolson, an early feminist and advocate of dress reform, hailed the liberating possibilities of ready-to-wear. "Dress should be a convenience, and not a pursuit," she declared. "At present (her) life is spent in sorting ribbons and selecting lace; and as much time is devoted to matching a peculiar shade of olive-green as would go to the writing of an epic upon Jerusalem."[115]

Pardee and Richards were often preoccupied with matching colors and locating fabric, and they were constantly shopping for "pieces" to complete a particular garment. Typical comments read: "Shopped for buttons. No luck"; "Hunted up trimming and trimmed a hat"; "Hunted up velvet to fix Irving's [coat] but could not find it."[116] With ready-to-wear, the woman would no longer have to assemble patterns, dress fabric, matching lining, trimming, buttons, thread, stiffening, needles, and myriad other items that together enabled her to make a dress. Similarly, if a woman had difficulty in following the incredibly complicated new patterns, if she were an indifferent seamstress or could not hire someone to perform the work for her, she would often look better in the new ready-made clothing.[117] Thus Ehrichs' advertisement assured women that factory design and workmanship often exceeded the skill of a woman sewing for herself.

Although factory-produced clothing held the promise of easing a major burden of domestic life, the stores and trade journals had to overcome a great deal of resistence to such clothing. It was a new idea that touched the very heart of family roles and personal identity. There was also a social basis for the prejudice against ready-made goods. Factory clothing had previously been associated with poverty and war.[118] With the exception of men's shirts and vests, only uniforms and rough-quality garments had been produced under factory-like conditions until after the Civil War.[119] While men's suits and coats were readily available in the early post-war period in men's clothing stores and haberdasheries, only certain items of women's clothing, such as cloaks and shawls, gloves, handkerchiefs, corsets, and a few accessories were ready-made in any great number.[120] Once the techniques for factory production of women's clothes were perfected, however, stores aggressively marketed their new goods, seeking not simply a replacement market but a vastly expanded demand.

The pressure on women to increase their levels of consumption by buying new factory-made clothes was relentless. "New styles just landed," "Ladies' costumes ready-made—all trimmed in the latest styles," "Paris ready-made dresses, very elegant" were common appeals as early as 1875.[121] Immediately identified with European fashion, the new ready-made clothing for women heralded a fundamental change in domestic life. Between the mid-1870s and the first decade of this century, the pages of the daily newspapers and the trade press developed a rationale about clothes and styles that subtly denigrated the woman who sewed at home and made her feel old-fashioned. She was enticed by the lure of rationality and modernity. "You, too, can take advantage of technology," she was assured. Why continue your old and tedious ways when "modern mechanical devices are capable of reproducing even the finest and most delicate designs . . . only experts could tell the difference. . . ."[122]

The discourse of consumption had several threads, all seeking to render obsolete home manufacturing, self-sufficiency, and an ethic of restraint. The cheapness of ready-to-wear, particularly children's clothing, was a major appeal. The fatigue of overburdened women was another and was played on in various ways. American attachment to "progress" offered yet another approach in the relentless and successful campaign to sell women on ready-made clothes. Occasionally the themes were interwoven. "Why should a tired woman sew when children's clothes very often are actually cheap?" the *DGE* querried rather ingenuously. "At times mothers would make their children's clothes even when they left their own to the family dressmaker, but with American ideas of progression, we have changed much of that."[123] More up-to-date women bought their garments, easing the "drudgery" in their lives and "saving time sufficient to allow the proper devotion to other domestic duties."[124] Other appeals allotted the time saved to "recreation and amusement."[125] Good mothers were, by implication, progressive mothers who understood that the factory was ready to serve them and their children. Carried a bit farther, this line played on fears of not being a good enough mother. One article, for example, suggested that the manufacturers showed greater concern for children than their own mothers: "These little garments . . . have better and more conscientious work put into them than the average mother will put into a child's dress."[126] Why should mothers do for their children what manufacturers did better? Mothers were advised to let parental responsibility, freed from the burden of home production, take a new, modern form.

There was also a not very subtle appeal to status concerns, part of the massive process of identifying consumption with middle-class life. "Excellence of shapes and work" were consistently attributed to the new manufactured items. Although some women "still indulged in the home manufacture of underwear," merchants judged it "the exception to find women in the cities wearing any but ready-made garments of this kind."[127]

The message was multifaceted but essentially quite simple. Become modern and fashionable, buy ready-made: "The cut is more perfect and every detail is carried out with the greatest skill and perfection which cannot be accomplished in the home."[128] Old ways of life and domestic skills were devalued, while new ones were celebrated. "The bicycle, golf and tailor-made girl lets out her sewing these days to the factory girl . . . not only because women have no time for such work but because no such ties and waists could be gotten together at home."[129] Even the homemade bridal trousseau came under attack. "The bride is indeed foolish to try and make her own things when so many dainty and exqui-

site pieces lie waiting for her inspection in the lingerie departments of the stores."[130] So-called up-to-date women had no time,
no facility, and, it was suggested, no competence: "Today the
style and color are paramount . . . as women are less skillful
judges of quality and weave."[131] By the end of the century, wom-
en's ready-to-wear had become so significant a part of department
store merchandising that the *DGE* could assume that the majority
of middle-class women no longer either made their own clothes
or even assembled the components, and, as a result, could not
discern value in clothing.

While there is no direct evidence, it is probable that most
housewives were not unhappy to benefit from what surely meant
less physical labor and increased access to fashion. Part of the vast
extension of the scope and influence of the department store,
ready-made clothing allowed women to look and feel well dressed
as they kept up with the rhythm of ceaseless change demanded by
purveyors of fashion.[132] Middle-class women had to be convinced
that the new technology could produce clothing of a quality equal
to individually manufactured garments, but once that was successfully accomplished, the transition was inevitable. "I bought a
ready made dress coat and skirt," Clara Pardee confessed in May,
1898, and then added tentatively, "Hope I shall enjoy it."[133]

Women came into the stores for good reason: to avail themselves of the expanding array of commodities, to substitute ready-
made for hand-made goods, to participate in a new and exciting
form of consumption, and simply to enjoy themselves. But even
the large numbers who flocked to the stores were not enough for
a mass-production economy and retail profits that needed constant increases in sales. Women entered the stores on their own,
for pleasure and for necessity, but they were increasingly and
relentlessly courted as open-ended consumers. Spurred by competition, relentless expansion, and the requirements of ever-
higher sales volume for profitable operation, modern department
store retailing demanded throngs of shoppers and ever more
relentless consumption.

After ready-to-wear became widely available, women visited the
stores at increasingly shorter intervals. The department stores had
fostered an extravagant demand for clothes. There were more
choices, an "endless multiplication of merchandise" amassed all

in one place, and shoppers could instantly visualize rapidly changing styles.[134] "Fashion," the *Dry Goods Reporter* solemnly announced, "make[s] all the difference in the world . . . [it] is coming to be a most important fact connected with modern civilization and habits of thought."[135] Clara Pardee ultimately concluded she did little but shop. Exasperated beyond limit after an all-day shop with her daughter Gertrude, Pardee complained, "I am *so sick* of the stores and clothes . . . would rather the clothes grew on like feathers!"[136]

At a moment in time that can be fairly specifically dated, women's priorities changed; and they moved into a new relationship with the world of production, the so-called masculine world they were supposed to eschew. The *Dry Goods Economist* could invert cause and effect and write, "It is owing to the overworked condition of American women that the universal use of ready-made clothing came into vogue," but the facts belie the statement. Technological innovation and the marketing of new consumer goods worked together to persuade the great majority of women to abandon one tradition and embrace another; to become skilled, modern consumers. As part of a massive reorientation of values, women relinquished traditional skills but gained new ones, along with a degree of flexibility and leisure hitherto unknown.

Women and the new department stores became partners in a profound cultural transformation. Direct production of work in the family and for the family became even more peripheral, and images of satisfaction and plenty became associated with the world outside the home rather than the one within. Before the end of the century, "homemade" had become a term of reproach, while "factory-made" became an encomium.[137] It was a profound and highly significant inversion of values.

The department store was part of an inescapable current by the end of the nineteenth century. On her part, the woman shopper relied on the dry-goods bazaar to fulfill needs that grew along with the expanding array of commodities; on its part, the store successfully created an aura of authority and prestige that enabled it to push consumption as a route to individual satisfaction. Urban middle-class women found a new world in the department store, a world that in many respects was more acceptable than their own. The store was a sanitized, safe environment that catered both to their needs and to their fantasies and provided them with a quasi career in the form of shopping. "With all other calling denied her, she acknowledged the call of the shops."[138] So wrote one woman early in the twentieth century; and it is this environment to which we must turn.

2

---◆◇◆---

The World of the Store

Women were at the forefront of the gradual shift of middle-class values from prudent economy to guarded extravagance. But the stores played a large and hardly benign role in this process. In the closing decades of the century, as the department store emerged from the dry-goods bazaar, the experience of shopping changed considerably. Deploring what she called the "Napoleonic campaign against the middle-class pocket-book," English visitor Katherine Busbey charged that, beyond the profusion of consumer goods, the interior of the American department store furthered the campaign. The "amazing luxury" of decor, the important openings and promotions, the special holiday and seasonal attractions, the profuse displays of out-of-season flowers, the colorful caged live birds, the splashing electric fountains, and even the free samples of food provided an "unnatural tantalization" as they lent the stores a perennial air of festival and excitement. "What chance has. . . the call of thrift and a commonplace little home against such allurement?" Busbey wondered.[1]

The "Gala Shopping Week" organized by the Retail Merchants Association of Boston during the first week of December 1897 was just the sort of special occasion Busbey deplored. Supported by the press, which "boomed the movement far and wide," and the railroads, which reduced fares at stations leading into Boston, this shopping orgy was a successful, crowded prelude to the Christmas season. Boston merchants "woke the people up and demonstrated that Boston wasn't all history," the *Boston Globe* boasted, as store sales supposedly rose to record highs over the same period in 1896.[2]

It is not hard to recreate the wonder with which women viewed the dry-goods bazaars, for many observers have noted that special store atmosphere which took hold of all the senses. Descriptions of newly enlarged stores often began with the question: "Who does not remember his first visit to a department store and the feeling of wonder and bewilderment it inspired?" The department store was the ideal of a materialistic age, the lavish settings were free to anyone, and people remembered their early visits as an overwhelming experience.[3]

Turn-of-the-century store interiors used exotic locales to create romantic and exciting effects; some stores employed oriental motifs, others assumed the character of Turkish bazaars or the winter scene from the ballet *Swan Lake*. Zola's portrayal of a "white show" in the fictional *Au bonheur des dames* captured the effect of what historian Rosalind Williams has called the "inescapable spectacle of mass consumption."[4]

> There were the galleries plunged in a glittering blaze of light, a borealistic vista, quite a country of snow, revealing the endless steppes hung with ermine, the accumulation of icebergs shimmering in the sun. One found there the whiteness of the outside windows, but vivified, colossal, burning from one end of the enormous building to the other. . . . Nothing but white goods, all the white articles from each department, a riot of white, a white star, the twinkling of which was at first blinding, so that the details could not be distinguished amidst this unique whiteness. . . . And the marvel, the altar of this religion of white was, above the silk counter, in the great hall, a tent formed of white curtains which fell from the glazed roof.[5]

Even in the utilitarian pages of the weekly trade journal the *Dry Goods Economist*, we read of "wandering through galleries which seem to be built up of slabs of snow, or looking down into halls from the sides and roofs of which hang ice-like festoons of delicate webbing."[6]

Subtlety was not an attribute of merchants in the late nineteenth century, and descriptions of shopping emphasize the conscious involvement of all the senses as customers passed through the stores. If there was color used, it appeared in massive displays. Individual departments became a study in color and vied with each other in the dramatic uses of colors and combinations. Wanamaker's decorated the interior and all the windows in white to emphasize its white sale in early January 1900. The following week everything became a tricolor of silver, purple and white to advertise the annual silver sale.[7] Filene's in Boston was decorated in green "from basement to roof" in 1901.[8] One visitor's recollection had an surreal quality: "In a multicoloured dream I wandered through a maze of matter, labyrinths of glittering shapes."[9]

Colors became marketable commodities as the new uses and the multiplicity of colors created heightened awareness of fashion and style. A short excerpt from the French color card for the fall and winter season of 1893 is instructive:

> The new purplish old rose, or old pink shades are five in number—
> Aubusson, Walkyrie, Lotus, Diogene and Sigurd, the latter being
> sufficiently dark for a street color, the first-named suiting for evening
> wear and the other three answering for combination purposes. Ivory
> cream, a dainty yellow; Epis, a golden shade called Ceres, and the
> deep orange Toreador are the only shades of this kind represented
> in the 65 colors. . . .[10]

New choices of color and of color combinations were integrated into fashionable dry goods, ready-made women's clothing, and accessories. Lord & Taylor advertised "Ladies' cloth for dresses in nearly 200 shades" in 1892. Some trade spokesmen recognized the anxiety created by too many choices and the obfuscation of the vocabulary of color.[11] Which of the ten shades of reddish purple, for example, was the right shade? Colors that people had never before seen or imagined became central aspects of visual merchandising and appeared on walls and carpets, on counter displays and in show windows.[12]

By the 1890s there was a willingness to manipulate commodities, to reimagine them and reassemble them into flowers and castles and boats.[13] Repetition of commonplace items in display windows, on walls, floors, and even ceilings created an illusion of fantasy and distance from the mundane handkerchief, umbrella, rug, or parasol.[14] In the new toiletry departments the scent literally filled the air. "Keep the atomizer going," the *DGE* advised readers.[15] At the 1896 opening of Wanamaker's on Astor Place, the *New York Tribune* reporter was overcome by the display of silks in the great rotunda. "New weaves and designs of exquisite coloring and quality were on every counter, and the women who strayed into this spot were," like the reporter, "loath to leave it."[16]

While there was a never-ending barrage of journalistic ridicule and medical complaint about the dangers of novel-reading for idle women, there was little opposition to the stimulation of sensual desire within the public, theoretically more controlled and socially conservative, dry-goods world. An article that appeared in the *Dry Goods Economist* in March 1900 demonstrated the new standards of propriety, the highly suggestive and eroticized level of consumer appeal often found in the department stores. Comparing the new "dainty" feminine undergarments with "grandmother's serviceable, severe stuff," the writer noted how tempting this ready-to-wear lingerie appeared to the woman of small means but delicate taste.[17] Not confined to the woman with an elaborate wardrobe and a flexible income, sensually suggestive underwear was now on public display, part of the vast extension of what could be seen, but not always acquired.[18] Another *DGE* article describing sales aids for the perfume and toilet goods department described the "gaily colored little pamphlets" to be distributed to customers, "handsomely illustrated with pictures of ravishingly beautiful young women brushing their tresses before mirrors, powdering their dainty noses, and even peeping shyly over the rims of porcelain bath tubs, reaching out one alabaster arm for a cake of somebody's 'good morning' soap."[19] Seemingly it was appropriate to "fill a woman's head" with fantasy and suppressed longing in a public setting, but unwise, if not unhealthy, to do the same in the privacy of her home. Aided and abetted by the new dry-goods bazaars, the trend toward sensual expression made rapid inroads; the loosening of sensual boundaries gained legitimacy when acted out in the form of consumption.[20]

Late–nineteenth-century department stores became what one writer has called "a pantomime of gentility."[21] Continually bombarded by material objects and images of what money could buy, many women saw in the stores the possibility of authenticating their own social status and ambitions. The excesses that this illusion bred were obvious in the drama of the middle-class shoplifter.

A number of observers at the turn of the twentieth century— primarily in France, but in the United States as well—began to see links between women's apparently overpowering desires, the environment of the department stores, and the behavior that was alternately labeled "shoplifting" or "kleptomania." Paul Dubuisson's study, "Les Voleuses des Grands Magasins" (1901), is one of the first and among the best-known of the early investigations. While Dubuisson's multiple case histories are purely descriptive and rely on a preconceived notion of gender and female sexuality, he did consider the environment of the stores and concluded that there was something in the structure of the situation that provoked the behavior. Women were invited to participate in a sexually stimulating environment that often elicited behavior they felt unable to control.[22] The department store had become a social location in which the manipulation of various stimuli created an unreal world and led to behavior patterns that deviated from the range of either the desirable or the acceptable. Dubuisson concluded:

> Temptation is so strong, surging desire so powerful, so impervious, so irresistible that the act is accomplished before reason has time to plead its cause. Afterward, all the considerations of honor, reputation, and security will attack the unhappy spirit and bring forth remorse, but for the moment pleasure is everything.[23]

The explicitly sexual connotation of the above statement suggests that Dubuisson saw women in the stores living out a fantasy denied them in their daily lives. In this sense, shoplifting was not a single isolated act. If the stores were dream worlds, then the dynamics of the interaction created a tension between reality and women in the dream. The gratification of impulse became more pressing than any inhibitions of ego.

Some women caught shoplifting supported Dubuisson's thesis: they accused the stores of permitting too much freedom; they became "over excited" and over-stimulated in the large stores; they could not refrain from handling things, and no one bothered them. Surrounded with new sights, sounds and smells, and the lack of fixed boundaries, shoppers complained that everything led to temptation; the salespeople were either disinterested or too busy to be of real service, and there was a "deplorable liberty" to touch everything.[24] Quite often women found unexpected public support for these accusations. Justice Martin T. McMahon of the Special Sessions Court in New York, the police court where most shoplifting cases were heard, spoke out publicly on the plight of the middle-class shoplifter. "There is too much temptation in goods spread out for some people to resist," the Justice declared. "While I never knew socially a woman who was arrested for shoplifting, I believe I can discriminate between the professional thief and the one deserving of pity."[25]

The tension caused by the intersection of traditional values, particularly the postponement of gratification, with the newer, more compelling gospel of consumption, led already "nervous" women to higher levels of anxiety.[26] Many women admittedly (and realistically) feared their own impulses. With the removal of restraining props, the burdens as well as the delights of the new commercial culture became immediately apparent.[27] In creating fantasy, the stores encouraged an abandonment that produced behavior troubling in its implications for both moral and social restraint. One woman, accused of taking three pairs of gloves, calmly handed them back, explaining that she had taken them as a "present for her maid who was a great comfort to her. . . . " She offered no ready explanation and no excuse for her shoplifting except that "it was easy to take them and she had taken several articles before."[28]

As the quintessential institution of bourgeois consumerism in the late nineteenth century, the department store was supposed to uphold the moral order, not to threaten it; yet descriptions of the new shopping milieu suggest a latent menace in this social setting. While women in the stores did not have to buy, they could not escape an atmosphere that consciously involved all the senses; and it is easy to imagine the effect of this new and dazzling experience on the average shopper.[29]

In some extreme cases a Barnum-like atmosphere temporarily

prevailed. A popular Chicago department store featured a "repro-duction of a gold mine in active operation."[30] One large New York store put live lizards in a showcase to dramatize a display, and "the police had to interfere to disperse the crowds."[31] After the opening of its New York store in August 1896, Siegel-Cooper kept an elephant in the "animal department" for a month until it was purchased by a zoological garden in East 14th Street for a reported $2,000. Apologizing for the sale of this "large attrac-tion," a store spokesman explained, "she had to go the way of any other article for which a purchaser appeared."[32] Simulated gold mines, live lizards, and elephants may not have been what depart-ment store shopping was about for most women and for the majority of dry-goods merchants, but the new philosophy of retailing encompassed both novelty and hard sell.

Merchants experimented with various stratagems to entice shoppers. "A saucer of ice-cream to every visitor, whether she buys or not," was the summertime attraction of one Chicago empo-rium. Another offered a glass of soda water, and a third held out "a bicycle suit to the woman that looks the prettiest on her wheel." One New York store gave "cooking lectures for lady cus-tomers of the house," and Ehrich Brothers, a respected Eighth Avenue establishment, featured a complimentary "pink tea" between three and five o'clock each afternoon.[33]

At the turn of the century, Siegel-Cooper's "woman orchestra" was a favorite attraction. Playing popular music throughout the day in the monumental New York store, the orchestra was "con-tinually surrounded by a crowd of women," crowds so large that the reporter "found it rather difficult to get near enough to hear the music."[34] Acknowledged in the pages of the *Dry Goods Econ-omist* as both a magnet and a pragmatic device "to coax unwilling dollars from the purses of chronic shoppers," the female orchestra helped to fill the cavernous shopping bazaar and provided its own justification. With newspaper advertising and window displays insufficient to fill the big stores on a day-to-day basis, crowds had to be manufactured—if not to view specific merchandise, then to become involved in the aesthetics of the stores themselves.[35] Beyond the attraction of consumer goods and the pleasure of pur-chasing them lay the continuous spectacle that was the nine-teenth-century palace of consumption.[36]

As stores experimented with a variety of customer-pulling devices, a manager at Marshall Field admitted that "stores cannot wait for customers to come at their leisure . . . the goods must be sold at once."[37] Mullenmeister, the proprietor in Margarete Bohme's novel *The Department Store* (1912) understood this sort of pressure. Describing his plans for a monstrous new bazaar, he speaks confidently of the crowds of the plainly curious he expects to turn into eager shoppers.

> You would have to know the physiology of our houses to understand our methods of attracting great throngs. Believe me, of ten persons who enter an emporium with no intention of buying, at least eight will come out with a little parcel . . . they'll buy—depend upon it! The best and most effective advertisment is *attractions*, which perhaps seem to have nothing to do with the business, but which draw great streams of people into, or even only through the house. Once we get them in, the buying can take care of itself.[38]

Children became an important factor in merchandising strategy; directly or indirectly, they meant business for the department stores. Note this typical excerpt from the *Dry Goods Reporter* in 1905 advising merchants to "work the parents through the children."

> It would be a good thing to set aside one certain day or half day each week for the children. The children will not spend much money, but they'll spend some. The idea though is not to get them to buy things, but to allow them to see what they want. Then they'll go home and torment their parents to the limit until that thing is purchased.[39]

The *DGE* viewed children as potential allies. One article, aptly entitled "The Agency of Children," advised readers to "remember, the boys and girls often have a working majority of votes in the matter of where trading shall be done."[40]

Children were future consumers, and good merchants courted them assiduously, cultivating their good will and building up store recognition. Let children play with the toys, even when breakage occurs, the *DGE*'s "Wide-Awake Retailer" advised.

"The more you can interest them the more their mommas and pappas will come to you when buying time comes."[41] Less obvious ploys to get and keep young customers included essay contests, doll and book corners, displays of baseball paraphernalia, Christmas and Easter spectacles (including Santa Claus by the 1880s), and souvenirs for young shoppers during sale weeks.[42]

Manufacturers and merchants suddenly realized the immense fashion potential of children's clothing, "not only in the expensive markets," but in medium- and popular-priced levels as well.[43] Pressured to buy ready-made clothes for their children as both a matter of expediency and a sign of love, mothers were further pushed to see the store bought clothes as extensions of their own lives and expectations. Trade journals and women's magazines preached a similar line: Children's clothing should be "of equal consequence with that of the grown members of the family. The little daughter of the house must have her morning frocks, school dresses, visiting and dancing frocks, besides numberless frocks and outer wrappings for all sorts of weather."[44] By the 1890s, clothing for middle-class children was invested with as many status implications as was clothing for their mothers and fathers.

As the physical size of the stores increased after the mid-1870s, so did the array of commodities and services. When Siegel-Cooper of Chicago was planning its New York store in the mid-1890s, the intention was to "include as many departments as can possibly be put under one roof"; which in this case meant birds and animals (including, presumably, the elephant), wines and liquors, groceries, hardware, sewing machines, drugs, meats, a bank, a barber shop, a jeweler, a photo gallery, and an "intelligence office [an employment agency for domestic help]."[45] Given this sort of merchandising the carnival was implicit. With greater numbers of people having access to a wide range of commodities, "need" often became the need only of the instant and of the psyche.[46] The ability to change, via style or novelty, indicated the ability to spend, and spending stood as a symbol of middle-class identification and the up-to-date consumer.[47]

The importance and visible power of the large stores was evident in their extraordinarily rapid growth.[48] As they added departments and handled greater varieties of merchandise and ever larger numbers of people, they assumed a dogmatic stance vis-à-vis the components of family life and daily activity. The gradual accretion of authority over what constituted acceptable levels of comfort and possessions served to make the commercial institution an arbiter of social mores; the department store became the middle-class woman's best helpmeet in creating domestic happiness. It was no illusory power. Because the stores spanned the chasm between the producer and the consumer cultures in the second half of the nineteenth century, they became interpreters of the new for the masses of middle-class consumers.

In the attempt to cater to a burgeoning middle class, the department store consciously promoted a focus on the home. Along with fashionable dress, the domestic interior had become the primary cultural expression of the middle-class woman, and decorating advice appeared regularly in daily newspapers, women's magazines, and books. But it was the department store that stage-managed and gave immediate expression to home decor. The connection between home and store was such that one architectural historian has suggested that the housewife was encouraged to believe she could "buy a virtuous home," to see her moral universe as a purchasable commodity.[49]

In less than two decades, between 1870 and 1890, the big bazaars became far more than mere purveyors of goods. They moved from being selectors of merchandise to being judges, experts, and connoisseurs of the constituent parts of people's lives and aspirations. The stores assigned to themselves the role of new cultural authorities, creating and selling style and with it the distinctive signs of a new middle-class way of life.[50] Writing in the September 1911 *Woman's Home Companion*, journalist Anna Richardson summed up what other observers had also seen as the unique role of the large shopping bazaar in the education of the female consumer: "The department-store, more than any other element in her life, shows her the fallacy of mother's way in present-day environments and under modern conditions."[51]

As merchants worked to educate and form public taste, to help people visualize their conception of the good life, the home and its decoration became a trademark of the large dry-goods establishments. By 1901 the Chicago-based *Dry Goods Reporter* could state confidently, "It would be difficult to overestimate the work of the department stores in developing the taste of people for beautiful goods for personal wear and adornment of their homes, and their knowledge of the comforts of life."[52] A brief history shows the speed with which the stores appropriated the middle-class home.

Macy's carried some types of furniture and rugs in 1873, and Lord & Taylor opened a special furniture department the following year.[53] In the 1880s Marshall Field displayed the first model rooms.[54] Descriptions in the *DGE* indicate how elaboarate some of these so-called models had become by the late 1890s. One store showed not just a kitchen or a drawing-room but a "whole furnished flat."

> A reception room opening from a prettily decorated hall, a dining room, cosy room or smoker's den, drawing-room, bed room and nursery . . . the wall hangings, draperies, rugs, cut glass, silverware and china [were] all of the finest quality—each room was a different color but carefully matched with the balance of the draperies and furniture.[55]

The trend reached its climax just after the turn of the century. When John Wanamaker opened a second New York store in 1907 adjacent to the main retail store in the old A. T. Stewart building on Broadway at 9th Street, he included within it a twenty-two room private home called, appropriately enough, "The House Palatial."[56] This house within a store was meant to be a model of decorating styles and period furniture, but it was a model of tantalizing images for most of the 70,000 people who reportedly visited it on opening day.[57] Holding out the promise of democratized luxury, in fact Wanamaker's House Palatial linked countless women and their domestic environment with unobtainable aspiration and desire.

Admirer as well as critic of the modern department store, the French psychologist Paul Dubuisson articulated a sentiment widely held in this country: so wonderful and so well organized were the big stores that women could consider the large store as a second home, "only a home which is grander, more beautiful, more luxurious than the first, where she can spend all her time without caring for the interior, and where she will find around her only what she sees as pleasing."[58] There was, purposely, nothing in the store to suggest either the conditions of production or the difficulty of upkeep. In the new world of consumption, where commodities were removed from their source, the relationship was only between object and consumer. Often submerged in the domestic setting, the Victorian woman found a realm for individual action in the department store. New objects, wrote one historian, "defined and empowered a self which had not produced them."[59] Pretense and display became paramount. One American merchant captured the essence of Dubuisson's analysis by stating unequivocally: "A store should be planned and laid out in such a manner that at first sight on entering it a customer will feel this is, indeed, her Mecca."[60]

The dualisms and ambivalence of Victorian society were reflected in the emphasis on material possessions. On the one hand, merchants catered to the older ideology of gender asymmetry, female delicacy, sentimental respectability, and the moral home; while on the other hand, they prepared the bourgeois consumer for the new—new styles, new social strategies and new ways of life.[61] In a characteristic piece for the *Chicago Record*, George Ade grasped the absurdities that lay behind this new mentality of consumption with its restless, often antagonistic, search for both social mobility and middle-class validation.

> To-day the drawing-room is full of ladders and buckets. To-morrow the dining-room is having doors hacked through its walls and a new floor is being put down. The day after, carpets are being laid. The man of the house knows that after the week is finished, after every article of furniture is in place, the pictures hung, the rugs spread and the lamps lighted, it will be a snug and beautiful home, but no sooner is one spasm over than another begins, and he can never settle down to a quiet enjoyment of the comforts he has purchased.[62]

The obsessive need for change, which Ade so acutely observed, was played out in the stores as a form of modernization. There was a certain antagonistic strain in this development. Purveyors as well as arbiters of a particular meaning of class, department stores also held out the specious hope of symbolic social mobility, if not equality, through possession.[63] As was often the case, the *Dry Goods Economist* caught the temper of the moment when it reflected, "Your customers may not belong to the multi-million-aire class, but the biggest half of them like to pose as such occa-sionally.... They may have to go short somewhere in order to get full measure in other ways, but, depend upon it, the grocer and the butcher is more likely to suffer than the dry-goodsman."[64] Sig-nificantly, the writer failed to link this unquenchable desire for "things" to the shoplifting that was such a problem for the department stores.

In the attempt to lure shoppers and to respond to what they felt customers like Harriet Richards and Clara Pardee wanted, owner-managers devised increasingly elaborate amenities, and, between 1880 and 1900, made the stores into unique service institutions as well. Those stores that failed to provide tea rooms and restaurants, check rooms, information bureaus, free delivery, carpeted aisles, mirrors and bright lights, rest rooms and "retiring rooms" and libraries, as well as an ever-wider selection of stylish goods, found themselves with a different class of trade. In a series of articles on "The Ladies' Parlor" the *DGE* suggested that mer-chants make that space "the best known and most attractive place for ladies in the city, a real ladies' club." It ought to be a place "where women can meet each other down town, either for a shop-ping expedition or other errands of business or pleasure."[65] In-store restaurants were particularly popular. Richards mentioned taking her midday meal at Macy's Ladies' Lunch Room in 1884—a still-novel activity for a middle-class women that com-bined recreation and a degree of personal, if managed, freedom within the protective confines of the dry-goods store.[66]

For the middle-class customer, these expensive amenities quickly became necessary adjuncts to shopping. In 1902 in the new Marshall Field store, for instance, "customers could have their photographs taken or developed, their gloves cleaned, jew-elry or shoes repaired, or eye glasses ground."[67] The Fair, a pop-ular Chicago bazaar, built an in-store park and playground that could accommodate two hundred children while their mothers shopped.[68] Similar services were available in all the competitive department stores. Service, however, often contained a hidden agenda. During discussions about the new Filene store in Boston, one Filene executive suggested that "a nice dainty tea room" might bring more women in during the morning hours and prolong their shopping after they were in the store. "That," he added, "is the scientific theory of the tea room." In an article, "Display in the Ladies' Reception Room," the *DGE*'s 'Wide-Awake Retailer' advised merchants to seize the moment and "sell, sell, sell while women rest, wait for a friend or write a letter."[69]

But there was an even more important, if less easily documented, transformation under way. Commodities themselves became complex, value-laden objects.[70] With a plethora of choices and a continually changing drama surrounding the very act of purchase, consumers were encouraged to find meaning in material abundance. "A lady who takes pride in her home is never through buying," the *Dry Goods Reporter* counseled merchants.[71] Continually exposed to a world that seemed not to have significant limits, many shoppers found it difficult to resist the allure of things.[72] Nor were they expected to. Diaries, newspaper articles, and other firsthand accounts attest to the "overpowering effect" of the commodities on the customers. Suddenly, doing without became hardship rather than common experience. As many women shoppers chose not to do without, shoplifting and related forms of theft became common occurrences. "The standard of living has risen," one department store manager observed, "and the rage for lavish appointment seems to act as a stimulant to make morally honest people lose their heads."[73]

As the temptation to possess found instant expression on the department store selling floor, shopping itself became a dilemma—which did not pass without comment.

It is not that we need so much more, or that our requirements are so increased, but we are not able to stand against the overwhelming temptations to buy which besiege us at every turn. . . . We go to purchase something we want; but when we get to our shop, there are so many more things that we never thought of till they presented their obtrusive fascination on every side. We look for a ribbon, a flower, a chiffon of some sort or other, and we find ourselves in a Paradise of ribbons, flowers, and chiffons, without which our life becomes impossible, and our gown unwearable.[74]

With the new "glamorization of spending," and a world where seemingly everything could be bought, impulse buying had quickly become endemic and constituted a problem for many women and their families. Overbuying was routine, as many shoppers evidenced a compulsion to be involved with the merchandise. "When I was in the cloak department last winter," a salesgirl reported at a working-girls association meeting, "I was everyday sending off goods C.O.D. that did nothing but come back again. The ladies, when they said they'd take them, had no more idea of paying for them than I had."[75] There were endless journalistic discussions of the behavioral excesses of women who sent merchandise home with no intention of keeping it, and of women who ran up huge store bills and whose husbands refused to pay for the goods. The *DGE* related the tale of "a prominent citizen" who was sued by an unnamed store for $1500 worth of toilet articles, soaps and perfumes purchased by his wife. The man defended his action by denying his responsibility in the affair, saying his wife had become "possessed of a passion for such luxuries. . . ."[76] Such overbuying was obviously not shoplifting, but may be seen as behavior on the borderline of a permeable boundary.

In the new moral economy of boundless excess, rational consumption often had little place. One journalist noted that women shopping in A. T. Stewart "were unable to resist buying above their means. . . . They may strain their allowance and curtail their children's wardrobe, but they must have a French loomed camel's hair shawl."[77] Yet in a very real sense women were only following the rules of the game; successful retailing assumed female susceptibility, and merchants relied on their ability to break down rational patterns of behavior and self-control. In succumbing to the lure of the merchandise, shoppers were doing what they were expected to do, and stores were getting the results they wanted.

With the change from a philosophy of scarcity to one of abundance and the conscious seeking of pleasure, there emerged a new orientation toward standards of personal conduct and moral boundaries. Shoppers coped with the new environment in various ways. The historian Jackson Lears has identified the process of secularization as a disintegrative phenomenon in bourgeois culture. Lears is only partially correct. Not necessarily disintegrative, but evidence, certainly, of the breakdown of the vision of a unitary moral universe by the 1880s and 1890s, secularization was one way people came to understand the new material world. It was in the department store that this historical change made its most obvious impact.[78]

Christmas obviously, but Easter as well, lost its original framework of meaning and moved from religious occasion to "season," a blatant festival of commercial exploitation. Inaugurated in 1874, Macy's Christmas windows became the annual event that signaled the beginning of Christmas shopping, the arrival of Santa Claus, late store closings, and the frenzy that marks the modern holiday. Lent became little more than a preparation for spring and the Easter parade of fashion, and Easter became bunnies in store windows, giant eggs, flowers, and fashion openings that "marked the flood tide of the selling year."[79] Puzzled by the erosion of spiritual meaning and new hucksterism surrounding Easter, one Midwest merchant noted, "There is certainly something peculiarly American in this adoption of a prominent Christian holiday to commercial use." The pivotal importance of the Christmas and Easter seasons extended far beyond economic statistics. Contained by a traditional, if increasingly empty religious sensibility, these commercial seasons were the expression of abundant material wealth.[80]

While there is no direct link between a growing spiritual slackness and the decline of personal behavioral norms, it seems evident that this progressive secularization, coupled with the tendency to conflate material and moral progress, caused changes in the way individuals related to specific situations and environments. In a very profound sense, a deep moral ambiguity was inherent in this new economy of consumption as it expressed itself in the enticing world of the department store.

Testimony from "one of New York's very swell shops" neatly illustrates the moral dilemma in which customers and management were mutually entangled. A woman "in good social standing" and "a general customer of the house" sent home some hats for her husband to decide on. "It just happened that I knew Mr. B., a prominent lawyer, was in Washington that week," the merchant confessed, "but the 'bluff' was not to be called, so the hats went up." The next day the hats came back to the store. Mrs. B. carefully explained that "the pink hat didn't seem, to suit her costume," and she would return at a later date to make another selection. "She failed to state that she wore the $25.00 yellow bonnet without paying for it. In this way my lady easily has the use of, say, ten free hats during the season, not to say a word about cape sets, boas, flowers, etc. All are *carefully* worn but still show unmistakable signs to the adroit eye of the dealer, who, as a rule, does not care to speak."[81]

Incidents of this kind were not isolated. When Ella Castle, a wealthy American woman accused of shoplifting in London in 1896, was brought to trial, evidence was submitted that she would regularly send home clothes "on approval, wear them all and return them as not suitable."[82]

Shoplifting was similar to this type of appropriation, and while the levels of transgression are not the same, they both represent deviant consumer behavior. The woman who shoplifted did so at greater personal risk, but she was prompted by similar complex considerations of desire in an environment devoted to self-indulgence and enticement.

After the widely publicized shoplifting arrest of four women from Lynn, Massachusetts, in 1897, the *Boston Globe*, in an editorial, attributed "this distinctive and growing order of crime" among women of means and good connections to three factors: an uncontrollable "mania for pretty and elegant things," pride and vanity, and the necessity to maintain social appearances. The women themselves testified to their desire "to dress well," and to the overwhelming temptation of unwatched counters piled high with goods.[83]

Calculated temptation was built into the new form of retailing. Reading descriptions of the late–nineteenth-century department stores in women's magazines, trade journals, and newspapers, one is struck by the conscious and generally successful attempt to make the unwary succumb to the allure of the moment. "Her ostensible errand may be the purchase of a paper of needles, a few yards of lining or a few skeins of embroidery-silk," Anna Richardson wrote in the *Woman's Home Companion*, "but if she is a fairminded woman, she admits that, once these weighty problems have been disposed of, she will give herself up unrestrainedly to the joys of the great store itself."[84]

Little was left to chance; everything was planned, not only to make buying easier but to make it "hard to leave the store without making purchases other than [she had] intended."[85] Locating special sales on upper floors so the crowds of women "would filter through the store on their way out" was simply good business management.[86] A letter from Isidor Straus of Macy's to Mandel's, a large, popularly priced department store in Chicago, reveals how crucial such impulse buying was to profits. Straus was disturbed about the location of the china department Mandel's leased to the Strauses, and he voiced his concern. "The profit part of the china business arises, not from the sale of goods which people *must* buy, as much as from the sale of goods that are bought through the tempting manner in which they are exposed to the masses passing to and from in a popular establishment."[87]

William Titon, buyer and "taster" for the respected grocery and liquor department at R. H. Macy & Company, supported the thinking that underlay Straus' letter. Titon, who came to Macy's in 1897, told an interviewer that in the early decades of the twentieth century, groceries were purposely located on the fifth floor and not on the main floor. "She (the customer). . . may need other things, but she has to go the the fifth floor to get her groceries. Do you see what I mean. It was very important. She goes to the store, she does other things before she goes to the fifth floor or vice versa."[88]

The route to children's clothes steered customers, and, retailers hoped, their offspring, through lines of toys. Millinery and shoe departments flanked the latest model gowns. Merely to reach elevators and stairways, the shopper was required "to run a gauntlet of bargains, each snatching at her pocketbook." Even the placement of soda fountains was purposely calculated to tempt thirsty customers to make random purchases. Interior display literally forced customers to circulate throughout the store and see the merchandise. Management wanted shoppers to succumb and to let temptation be the basis of decision making. Having a variety of articles "loosely placed over the counters [to] add to the charm of an absolutely free and unrestricted choice of the assortment" was a frequently suggested selling technique.[89] Though at odds with any semblance of security consciousness, such inviting display was not the product of casual miscalculation. Merchants knew that accessible merchandise often disappeared, but they also recognized that it was "probably better to have the customers handle the merchandise and in this way increase sales and to put up with a certain amount of shoplifting."[90]

Merchants shamelessly pushed spending. An advertisement for women's capes in 1896 featured a bold headline shouting "Don't Worry!" The copy told shoppers what they wanted to believe: Don't worry about not being able to afford these capes. You can always afford what you need (read "want").[91] One store developed a scheme whereby "the woman whose credit stands the largest amount of purchases during a given period—say, one month" won a prize.[92] In its "Hints to Merchants" column in August 1897, the *DGE* ran a vignette entitled "The Great Benefit Realized from Tempting Displays." Not surprisingly, the benefit lay in profit for the store, but the last sentence reveals the tension within the new shopping environment. "I generally go out of here poor," one shopper admits to her friend. "I invariably see something that I can't resist buying, even though I had no idea of getting it when I started out."[93] Encouraging customers to spend more than they had anticipated was basic strategy, and yielding to temptation was merely acting the part of the good shopper. Shoplifting was often little more than a dramatization of these two strands.

Managers were not reluctant to acknowledge that the philosophy of the modern dry-goods store was one of both enticement and entrapment. A letter from an early graduate of the Salesmanship Class sponsored by the Jordan Marsh store in Boston reflected the deliberate policy of many department stores to push merchandise on customers. "Knowing your stock well and talking intelligently of your goods," the young woman wrote, "you can meet a customer more than halfway, and ofttimes influence her to purchase more than she had originally intended to buy."[94] *System*, the business magazine, estimated that in 1910, forty percent of all sales were made where customers had had no thought of buying.[95] The numbers may have changed over the years, but the concept of retailing had changed very little: fifteen years earlier, the *DGE* had readily admitted that successful retailing rested on the ability "to sell goods when a customer is supposed to be through with her purchasing; to sell a customer something she had not the remotest idea of buying."[96] A writer for the *DGR* seemed proud of the fact that the stores educated people to want things. "The great stores came and exploited their wares in such [a] manner that people who hadn't thought of wanting the things before came and bought them in ever-increasing quantities. People were educated out of their old frugal ways of living."[97] In this atmosphere, the old Franklinesque adage "Time is Money" was reinterpreted to mean the more time the shopper spent in the store, the more money the merchant made.[98]

In the context of the new ethic associated with the department stores, shoplifting and repeated "borrowing" of merchandise represented the disintegrative effects of the new consumer culture. While such behavior did not easily connect to standard middle-class considerations of right and wrong, the decline of personal moral responsibility was part of the general blurring of moral and cultural boundaries in the late nineteenth century.[99] At a time when the business ethics of men were notoriously bad, we should understand that many women, in their role as consumers, found it difficult, also, to define acceptable shopping behavior. The weekly journal *Living Age* professed to see in certain women shoppers a dangerous level of self-indulgence, "a certain lawlessness of disposition, an inherent dislike to live by rule, a breaking out of a wayward will at the point of least resistance." Life for such a woman, the writer concluded, "is hardly worth living if one is never to accede to a whim."[100] A judge of the Municipal Court in Chicago addressed the inability of many shoppers "to quickly and firmly decide the issue between right and wrong" in surprisingly similar terms:

> Most of them are women, wives and mothers who come from respectable, happy homes. They beheld something upon the counters which they desired, but could not buy. They debated with themselves the questions of right and wrong, and were lost. Not until the hand of the officer was laid upon their shoulders did they dream that they would ever be classed with thieves and robbers and burglars.[101]

It was not uncommon for a woman detained for shoplifting to state quite frankly that "she had seen others taking things, and did not know why she should not, too."[102] After her arrest in a Fulton Street dry-goods store, a "well-dressed Brooklyn woman," said "she had been given $12 by her husband . . . to purchase Christmas presents for the children and honestly intended to do so. 'But I saw other women taking lots of articles, and I was tempted, so I took some also, intending to save the $12.'"[103]

"Everyone stole from the shops," one woman explained in her own defense. "A woman friend told me to do it. . . . She said that she and all her friends took little things in the stores and never were caught. Besides, she told me that if I were caught I should get only a lecture and a warning."[104] This defense highlighted the moral confusion many women exhibited when confronted with the fact of their own shoplifting. New expectations and social patterns of satisfaction acted as corrosive influences in the individualistic, though feminine, department store world. Believing that in the generally crowded conditions of the dry-goods bazaars nothing was easier than to take something without being seen, and without its being missed, many shoppers seemed to be responding to what they knew others were doing. "Seeing someone do it" triggered impulses that some women did not bother to control. Not only did "respectable" customers steal with a degree of abandon, they did so in numbers that shocked merchants and caused serious problems in the "exotic wonderland" of the dry-goods bazaar.[105]

Merchants gave women what they thought they wanted, but also saw to it that these same women wanted what money alone could buy. Dollars and cents became the measure of social value. "It's all in the display," one writer contended. Anything that makes a home (or a person) beautiful is a temptation."[106] Middle-class shoplifting was inseparable from the techniques of "progressive merchandising" and the intense pressure to consume, but the price was high. The lust for things and the loss of any sense of proportion often overrode traditional moral considerations. Women shoppers were torn by an inability to redirect desire and to define themselves without material objects. All too often they gave in to unconscious impulse and stole what they saw and wanted. In the conflict between the "anxious excitement of spending" and the reality of restraint, there emerged a new individual and a new cultural stereotype, the kleptomaniac, the middle-class woman who shoplifted seemingly without need and without explanation.

3

---❦---

The Two-Way Mirror

If the dry-goods palaces represented "a pantomime of gentility," we must look beyond the physical appearance and surface amenities of these new institutions to the values and attitudes that governed their management.[1] Store owners and managers set out to challenge traditional notions of need and value. The special drama of the stores, the continual bombardment of sensual images, the new celebration of material goods, and the explicit refutation of an older ethic of self-denial and its replacement by one promoting self-gratification were the products of a conscious strategy. Geared to continual expansion and high profits, the staged luxury of late–nineteenth-century department stores encouraged consumption and desire beyond immediate need or means. It all prompted troubling conflicts in personal and social values for many women, and, as a consequence, the stores found themselves confronting a situation in which the relationship between the individual shopper and the new possibilities of possession became problematic.[2] Management was forced to defend itself against the very loss of a sense of proportion that it had in fact encouraged.

Hemmed in as the department stores were between the twin demands of high-volume sales and rapid stock turnover, and the equally pressing necessity to maintain control over the merchandise, management found itself in a paradoxical position. Only crowds of customers could provide sales and profits, yet these very customers became the source of constant anxiety. The evidence was everywhere—newspaper accounts of women arrested for shoplifting, retail groups' own estimates of losses, well-publicized court cases, and stores' internal memoranda. An editorial in the *Boston Globe* in December 1897, "The Shoplifting Habit," is as good an example of the extent of the problem as can be found.

> Shoplifting has become a distinct and growing order of crime. Each year the great shops became more and more crowded, and that the thefts have grown more and more frequent need[s] hardly to be stated. The startling feature of this crime is that its average exercise is higher up the alleged 'social scale' than any other. Women of means and good connections, when pressed for an explanation of their offenses, confess to a mania for pretty and elegant things which gets control of them when they are brought into close contact with them and the opportunity to purloin is at hand.[3]

Even as they were encouraged to shop—to linger within the confines of the department store, reading, writing letters, wandering around, viewing the store as a warm and welcoming, even intimate, place that desired only their well-being—the customers had to be closely watched.

Management was clear about its goals and its desire to provide a setting conducive to rapid sales, just as it was clear about the necessity to prevent public awareness of any problem, especially that of crime in the aisles and at the counters. In order to create and maintain an impression of total harmony in keeping with the fantasy world of the stores themselves, their public response to crime, particularly shoplifting, was decidedly low-key—virtually to pretend it did not exist—not in the hope that it would disappear, but to contain it and to keep the majority of shoppers oblivious to the darker side of consumption patterns. Faced with growing losses, merchants suffered in silence. "I wouldn't have it known that we are being robbed for a hundred dollars, as it would injure our trade," the proprietor of a Broadway dry-goods emporium confided to a *New York World* reporter in 1872.[4]

Forty years later, when shoplifting was a far more serious problem, merchants still maintained the fiction that it was no more than a minor annoyance. "No reputable establishment likes to have it be known that it is a frequent prey of the shoplifter; it might keep the good customers away," one store owner told the *New York Times* quite candidly.[5] Particularly toward the end of the nineteenth century, as their institutional image became an overriding consideration, merchants stifled, at least publicly, vigorous response. "The big store seeks to avoid embarassing the customers; [it] eliminates any method which in the least degree offends the customer . . . the department store is a vast machine of accommodation."[6] So great was the fear of antagonizing the shopping public and so far were they willing to go to "accommodate" the middle-class customer that the stores engaged in a vast deception. The daily press contributed to the pretense. Recipients of huge amounts of department store advertising, newspapers could not simply ignore the issue, but articles about shoplfting not uncommonly downplayed the extent of the losses and frequently omitted the name of the store, even when the name of the suspected shoplifter was prominently displayed.

In private, however, dry-goods merchants acknowledged the fact that shoplifting was widespread, rife even among their best customers, and they undertook a variety of countermeasures to inhibit the practice.[7]

Any examination of the department store's response to the increasing problem of shoplifting involves a number of disparate strategies: technological change, managerial reorganization, and an altered view of surveillance constitute the main categories for analysis. It must be kept in mind, however, that there is no neat chronology that encompasses the heightened response to shoplifting losses. Changes within the dry-goods bazaars occurred at different times and for very different reasons. Some vast transformations were the result of the widespread application of new inventions. For instance, both glass and light technology, which became the hallmark of all that was modern in late–nineteenth-century life, was rapidly introduced into these showplaces of the industrial age.[8] Other changes, particularly managerial ones, were the result of imperatives within the mass marketing and distribution systems, which were far different in their apparent application, if no less single-minded in their underlying rationale. Reorganization and rationalization accompanied physical expansion, and by the early years of the new century the large stores exhibited a highly centralized, often impersonal operation.[9] A formal hierarchical structure, incorporating functional divisions and multi-layered management, provided for tighter control of all operations on all levels. Protection became a major focus.

Protection itself has a checkered history in the department store, and the chronology of change that centers around spying on customer activities was far less visible than the introduction of mirrors into shelving or light into uninviting corners. From Macy's few detectives in 1870 to a formal protection department in 1902 is a leap more of organization than of activity. The real innovation, amounting almost to a revolution in thought, was the recognition and acceptance of the fact that many customers could not be trusted. Middle-class shoppers could also be thieves. The dimensions of the threat were multiplied by the simultaneous realization that the large number of clerks required by the enlarged physical operations and high volume of sales could not always be counted on to stand for the store's interest. Acknowledgment of their own high vulnerability brought a protective mentality to management, a security consciousness that went beyond direct surveillance and manifested itself in the intimate relations of buying and selling.

The radically altered physical environment of the dry-goods bazaars is the most obvious and perhaps the logical starting point for an examination of this new framework of understanding. The stores were among the early beneficiaries of the industrial advances of the nineteenth century, and technological innovation found many of its early applications in these new institutions. For a great many people, the first encounters with electric lights, elevators and escalators, expanses of plate glass, and even full-length mirrors came in the great bazaars of Macy, Marshall Field, and Wanamaker. Responding to a competitive psychology, the ever-increasing volume of customers, and the demands as well as the opportunities of physical expansion, the leading merchants incorporated change into store design as enthusiastically as they did style into their merchandise. Modernization became part of the competition for the consumer dollar, as stores tried to outmaneuver each other in their appeal to the shopping public. As the *DGE* editorialized, "The constant strife existing between the great department stores" did not end with prices, but extended to "methods of management, facilities for the convenience and comfort of customers and visitors, and alterations and improvements" of the physical plant.[10] Not only did the latest technology, particularly the modern uses of glass and light, provide new methods of creating desire as it protected the merchandise, it also simultaneously made the rapid applications of these methods possible.

Always the innovator in the dry-goods community, A. T. Stewart was the original American merchant prince. Stewart's dry-goods bazaar, commonly known as the Marble Palace, opened in in New York in 1846 at 280 Broadway, and was thought to be the first building in this country designed—architecturally and functionally—expressly for retailing. Featuring a white marble exterior (hence the name) and an elaborate, frescoed interior built around a broad circular staircase and a central rotunda capped with a glass dome, the physical aspects of the building were as remarkable as its dry goods.[11] Imported thirteen-foot-high mirrors adorned the walls and were the first such glass seen by the American public; the plate glass "French windows" were also a first and became an attraction in their own right to a generation of visitors and New Yorkers alike.[12] After inspecting the new establishment, Philip Hone, the cosmopolitan former mayor of New York, made this querulous entry in his diary:

> There is nothing in Paris or London to compare with this dry-goods palace. My attention was attracted, in passing this morning, to a most extraordinary, and I think useless, piece of extravagance. Several of the windows on the first floor, nearly level with the street, are formed of plateglass, 6 feet by 11, which must have cost four or five hundred dollars each, and may be shivered by a boy's marble or a snow-ball as effectively as by a four-pound shot.[13]

Four years later, during the enlargement and virtual rebuilding of the Marble Palace, Hone again remarked on A. T. Stewart's, boasting this time, "I certainly do not remember anything to equal it in London or Paris; with the addition now in progress the edifice will be one of the 'wonders of the Western World.'"[14]

But Stewart's was at once a prototype and an anomaly. In 1869, having moved uptown and expanded the retail establishment to cover a full square block between Astor Place and Broadway on 9th and 10th Streets, Stewart's became the largest and, for a short period, the best-known dry-goods store in America. New Yorkers were clearly impressed. Excitement ran high, as did sales, and descriptions of "Stewart's Store" filled the newspapers and magazines. A thoroughly modern, still white but now iron-frame building rising five stories above the street, this dry-goods palace contained even more glass than the Marble Palace—walls of plate glass windows on all sides, "so numerous and large that its four fronts can almost be said to be of glass."[15] The innumerable windows, however, were solely for interior light; they were high off the street and, according to a reporter for *Godey's Lady's Book*, "not even a tendril of enticement is outwardly put forth here."[16]

But for other retailers after the Civil War, the new plate glass windows were exploited in the interest of a new ideology. In the modernization process of the department stores, windows became primary selling tools.[17] Increasingly, merchants counted on the visual enhancement that plate glass provided. Windows were the initial step toward consumption, toward making it acceptable to buy beyond necessity. Promoting the merchandise within while creating unsatisfied desire, the display window embodied the modern idea of accessibility to all. An article in the *New York Herald* captured this new sense of the possible in an otherwise pessimistic discussion about shoplifting and the new breed of "supple fingered ladies": "The opulent spirit of the hour is in the air, and even if one goes along with the surging throng, purseless, . . . there is something in the democratic privilege of flattening one's nose against a five hundred dollar pane of plate glass and looking in at a ten thousand dollar layout of jewelry and bric-a-brac."[18] Demanding nothing from the pedestrian, shop windows seemed to promise everything.

Broadway store windows were described as "rich, beautiful and tempting" in 1872. "Jewels, silks, satins, laces, ribbons, household goods, silverware, toys, paintings, in short, rare, costly and beautiful objects of every description greet the gazer on every hand," James McCabe wrote in *Lights and Shadows*, his 1870 guide to New York.[19] Theatrical principles gave these windows part of their enormous appeal. Exploiting the new possibilities of plate glass and color, Macy's first holiday windows presented a spectacle that was as visually fascinating as it was novel.

> The large bay-windows present a very attractive appearance. One of these windows is turned into a scene where parties of richly dressed Paris dolls form a pretty 'tableau': It represents a skating-pond where dozens of lovely blonds and brunettes in seal-furs, velvet, rich silks, and exquisite boots, in tiny skates, are posing in the most coquettish manner to attendant admirers. These wonderful dolls are dressed in the latest styles, to the smallest detail. . . .[20]

After further homage to these splendors behind glass, the reporter for *Leslie's Illustrated Newspaper* commented, "Seeing the shops is one of the 'institutions' of the season, and around the windows where is displayed the tempting array of fancy goods, crowds gather to wonder and to admire."[21] Forty years later a Macy employee still remembered these windows of 1876 and the revolving figures that were such a "great sensation and drew large crowds."[22]

Trimmed windows became devices to catch the eye of the passerby, hold her attention, and induce her to enter the store. Window shopping became a new pastime.[23] The author of *New York Sketches* (1902) grumbled about the magnetic quality of shop windows "which draw women's heads around whether they want to look or not, causing them to run you down and making them deaf to your apologies for it."[24] "Men are subordinate in America only in shop windows," English visitor Katherine Busbey declared effusively. Shop windows, she added, were really "glass enclosed rooms," and like the model rooms within, this new sales medium was to educate as well as entertain the prospective customer.[25]

Significantly, this change of function represented far more an economic and psychological departure than a technological innovation. In the era of gas, stores still very much depended on windows to provide adequate light; but as the aggressive ethos of consumption gradually took over even heretofore neutral spaces, no area of possible profit was unaffected. "Window space is too valuable to be long empty," the *DGE* counseled.[26] Representing the freedom to look and the potential to possess, decorated windows articulated a particular social meaning. "Women see themselves in store windows as they resolve others shall see them," economist Bertha June Richardson observed, and added, tellingly, "to some it is a lesson well learned; to others it brings a wrong discontent."[27] The environment itself reinforced conformity to the existing system.

So, too, did large shop windows became part of an expanded urban consciousness. An example from Chicago serves equally well for New York: When the Chicago City Council sought to force Marshall Field to scale down their new show windows, which encroached on the sidewalk beyond the building line, the outraged editor of the *Dry Goods Economist* responded that far from being an impediment "the windows are an ornament to the street."[28] More than lures for potential customers, department store windows enlivened and embellished the streets themselves and became a legitimate part of urban culture. Conversely, as the stores grew in size and gained prestige and identity as fixtures in the urban environment, the streets, not infrequently, became "the corridors of the department stores."[29]

"Tempting" became the operative word for the successful window. "Who can walk the city streets without pausing," one journalist wondered. Windows "furnish the stuff that dreams are made of."[30] A magnet, and by the turn of the century a new art form, these sidewalk displays attracted so much attention that the a trade journal commented, only half jokingly, "There are many husbands, lovers, and brothers who would be all the richer if it were not for the window dressers."[31] Some proprietors created their own crowds. An article about "The Window Gazer and His Work," described a new profession that paid three dollars a day and demanded only that the person "impersonate a gentleman of wealth" standing transfixed before a display window.[32] Not even the sidewalks remained neutral. Competition, it seems, demanded that the exterior of a store be as crowded and busy looking as the interior itself.

The "resplendent temptations" of the shop windows were a staple for the new city guidebooks as well. In his 1892 *Handbook of New York City*, Moses King linked window decor to expanded consumer desire.

Ill fares the rural or provincial purse whose owner ventures before these attractive windows. . . . [They] present a perfect kaleidoscope of silks and velvets, laces and jewels, rich books and music, painting and statuary, rifles and racquets, confections and amber-like bottles, cloisonnée and cut-glass, everything imaginable for use or luxury massed in perfect affluence and displayed in the most attractive way possible.[33]

King's observation was accurate. Many of the women detained for shoplifting in the New York dry-goods bazaars were shoppers from the suburbs and visitors from small towns and cities.[34] Describing "The Modern Women's Paradise" for readers of the *Woman's Home Companion* in 1911, Anna Richardson unconsciously echoed King. Writing of the pleasure and conveniences that awaited the out-of-town shopper, Richardson told women that both the interior and the exterior of the modern department store endeavored "to give her a lovely day to make her spend the last penny in her purse."[35]

The development of the display window as a sales device was decidedly uneven, however. A. T. Stewart never did decorate his windows, and for many years Marshall Field followed suit, holding tenaciously to the belief that windows were for light. In his mind, selling from windows was a misuse of their function. Not until the 1890s would Field's expand its show windows beyond the two on either side of the main State Street entrance.[36] When the store hired Arthur Fraser away from a State Street competitor in 1895, "display was limited to doing fancy things with cheese-cloth."[37] Eulogized in *Women's Wear Daily (WWD)* at the time of his death as "the Greatest Displayman of them All," Fraser made window decor a commodity in its own right.[38] Joining Marshall Field and Company when window trimmers were considered "just a notch above store porters," he created the theme window, a miniature theater fronting on the public sidewalk. "Changing of the windows at Fields was like an opening of a new show," *WWD* commented.[39] So staged was the elaborate buildup of anticipation, and so compelling were the final presentations, that a single color scheme—red—in all six of the main Marshall Field windows launched fashion's "red epidemic" in 1897.[40] Fraser's innovative windows for Marshall Field were famous far beyond Chicago, and these "overpowering productions" contributed much to the store's prestige and elegance in the twentieth century.

The initial conservatism at Field's notwithstanding, the elaborately decorated display window became a common feature of most department stores during the 1880s. With profits uppermost in any calculation, windows had to bring shoppppers into the store. Like love letters, one trade editorial suggested, windows must arouse in women the desire for more.[41] Give a weak department a "liberal dose of window tonic," the *Dry Goods Economist* advised in its weekly column, "Wide-Awake Window Dressing."[42] Immediate rivalries developed between the window trimmers of the larger stores. During the 1889 Christmas season, for instance, "window artists" tried to outdo each other with the use of lights and mirrors and other "visual tricks" to make the windows seem more spacious and the merchandise more appealing. Similarly, there was a heightened use of color. A survey reported seventeen windows in stores on 23rd Street between Broadway and Eighth Avenue, and on Sixth Avenue between 14th and 23rd Streets, to be "quite remarkably" colorful.[43]

Changes came quickly in what became an important adjunct to an expanding consumer culture. By 1891 the *DGE* could write that only two stores in New York refused to make any window displays, one of which, the long-established and decidedly conservative Arnold Constable & Company, "rarely exhibited anything at all in their windows—occasionally a half-dozen umbrellas arranged in fan shape or perhaps a few lengths of dry goods."[44] The two hold-outs became news.

While some windows of the period showed "real laces" and rich, brocaded evening silks with flowers and feathers to match, by the turn of the century the windows demonstrated an opulence that deliberately overwhelmed the passerby. In an article aptly entitled "Windows and Temptation," the *DGE* noted:

Window space all over the city is given over to the goods that are rich, showy and expensive, with the result that there were never before seen such crowds of eager and envious-eyed women lined up along the store fronts . . . the gay colors added to the shimmer and sheen of gold and spangles make a combination that the average woman finds almost impossible to resist."[45]

The effect of these windows "all over the city" was obviously calculated. It was expected that window shoppers and other casual strollers would be caught up in the illusion of material abundance and move from the street into the store. Even the *Dry Goods Reporter*, a Chicago trade publication with nowhere near the sophistication and coverage of New York's *Dry Goods Economist*, advised window decorators to "study humanity," to understand the effects of lighting and display on the window gazer and learn the "psychology of human nature."[46] In other words, let fantasy and reality merge, let them become indistinguishable. This was exactly the complaint of many women shoplifters. "I had no intention of stealing," a tearful woman would confess, but "somehow the goods ended up" in her satchel, her bag, or her pocket.[47]

The articulation of the power of the new glass technology securely tied temptation to possession. "Goods should be so displayed," the *DGR* advised, "as to force people to feel that they really wish to possess them."[48] Chicago's Siegel-Cooper had two young men in one of their show windows demonstrating a miniature pool table. They played game after game in front of an increasingly large crowd on the sidewalk, and reportedly sold "a goodly number" of pool tables.[49] With the emergence of the window as the stage for the larger presentation within, the environment of the street itself reinforced consumer desire and the commodification of everyday life.

A substantial, observable transformation had taken place: windows had become part of the show and an integral component of the new consumer capitalism.[50] Though often muted, a certain tension accompanied the "progress in window display." Opposition to the emerging culture surfaced along with the constant popular acclaim. "Envy gnaws at your heart . . . till your mythical free will is down in the dust" and you enter a dry-goods bazaar, one resentful journalist wrote in an *Atlantic Monthly* article entitled "The Immorality of Shop-Windows."[51]

Margarete Bohme captured the intensity and complexity of the drive for consumption enacted through a shop window in her novel *The Department Store* (1912). Describing the dangerously packed crowd before the windows of a new store that displayed "a thousand radiant examples of the wonders within," Bohme then narrowed her focus to a single shop girl, Agnes, who was so transfixed by the displays in store windows that she "literally threw herself against the dazzling window of a lingerie shop . . . she pressed her face close against the panes that she might see it all the better, as if drunk with the color and beauty."[52]

The woman detained for shoplifting who complained, "I couldn't help myself," was, perhaps, no less dazzled.[53] The subliminal creation of insistent demand represented a conscious decision to manipulate the shopper on the sidewalk and bring her into the store with an insistent need to act. If buying was promoted as an irrational instinct, which "the average woman finds almost impossible to resist," certainly shoplifting was no less so for many.[54] While Bohme may justly be accused of exaggeration, physical reactions to visual display were tangible responses to the new art form, and, it can be argued, an important component of department store shoplifting. Confessing, as many of these women did, that she was "physically unable to resist the temptation to steal the things within her reach," the accused shoplifter was ensnared as Agnes had been. "The things were there," one woman admitted, and then added she "could no more control the action of her hands than she could fly."[55] Thoroughly imbued with a consumer mentality, the *DGE* unconsciously rationalized the impulse to shoplift. "The incentive to take things is particularly strong in view of the beauty and attractiveness of the holiday displays."[56]

The changing function of department store windows demonstrated the inherent possibilities in the use of glass. A neutral building technology that allowed natural light into Stewart's vast cornucopia of goods became itself a cultural form, expressing the ideology of consumption. Suggesting the promise of acquisition as they created desire, window displays drew shoppers into the stores and into even more dramatic encounters with the world of consumer goods. When Ellen Andrews visited her mother in Detroit in 1884, her letters to her husband James expressed the emotional confrontation between pedestrians and this new medium. "The windows are full of such beautiful things . . . you can imagine me standing in front of the windows, (which are arranged differently nearly every day) until I take everything in and then I go in and stand and look and look and then when I come home try to remember all I saw."[57]

Glass transformed store interiors to an even greater degree, for here we confront, directly, the complex interplay between enticement and security.

Traditional dry-goods store interiors had been less than inviting. Descriptions refer to them as uniformly small, gloomy, dusty, and cramped; many stores appeared rather dilapidated. Counters were of solid wood with enclosed shelving. Notions and the few ready-made goods remained hidden in boxes. Bolts of material, for everything from dresses and lingerie to blankets and sheets, occupied most available surfaces and had to be individually taken down or unwound for inspection. A customer had to know what she wanted and ask for it. Other than some stiffly draped fabric, very little was openly displayed, and there was almost no attempt to create demand.

Relatively light, large, and well managed, Stewart's Astor Place store was typical of many older establishments. However impressive it seems in the photos, with its floor-through glass-domed rotunda, layers of galleries, and open floor plan, the floors themselves were often wooden and bare, the two stairways were grand only if width counted, and the solid counters and shelving gave slight hint either of the extent or the variety of merchandise available.[58] Stewart made little effort to exhibit the stock: his skills apparently went into organization, not drapery. "Everything," journalist Edward Crapsey commented in an article for *Galaxy* magazine in 1870, "was done on a system, perfectly organized and perfectly administered," but instead of any dramatic exhibition of the stock, customers found placards on the counters listing the prices of the all-but-hidden merchandise. Crapsey noted the absence of "a tempting display of pretty fabrics to lure the money of the unwary from their pockets . . . one might go through the entire sales room without seeing anything very covetable unless one were especially looking for it."[59]

Interiors changed slowly. Big and prosperous as the dry-goods bazaars were by the early 1880s—"built by the purely feminine passion for shopping," according to E. L. Godkin, editor of the *Nation*—there was very little in the way of real display, of innovation, or of elegance.[60] Improvements were made haphazardly when stores added space, moved to new and larger locations, or felt their competitive position demanded the installation of new equipment and new amenities for their customers. Two "elegantly upholstered" steam elevators made their appearance at the new Field and Leiter store in 1879 and "sputtering arc lights" (powered by a dynamo in the basement) supplemented the hotter, if more reliable, gas lights.[61] But except for these mechanical improvements and steps toward greater customer comfort, such as a ladies' dressing room and lavatory in the basement, the look of the stores remained largely unchanged.[62]

The big innovation in store interiors came with the use of glass—for counters, for assorted cabinets, and for display cases. Although glass was available well before its acceptance, only at the very end of the 1880s did the "better stores" begin to change over to the distinctive glass-sided fixtures.[63] The initial appeal was to increased sales and profits. "Women don't ask for stock they don't see," ran one such line; another portrayed an ingenuous woman shopper commenting to a dry-goods merchant, "I thought that you had given up selling ribbons."[64] But glass was no gimmick. A technological advance of immense consequence, it enabled merchandise to emerge from opaque counters and boxes, providing a means to display both dry-goods and notions with some degree of control. To the old proverb "goods well bought are half sold" was added "goods well displayed are also half sold."[65] "No woman is going to get by one of these showcases," the Phillips Silent Salesman Showcase Company promised.[66]

Merchandise no longer had to remain either hidden or left heaped and unguarded on counter tops. The incentive to take things, the *DGE* warned merchants, "the kleptomaniac tendencies so often latent . . . are awakened by the tempting arrays and the too great opportunities presented by the free display of merchandise."[67] Mrs. Caroline Hobart would certainly have agreed. Picked up for shoplifting in a 23rd Street store in New York in November 1904, Mrs. Hobart (a fictional name according to the *New York Times* reporter) handed over the two pieces of jewelry to the detective with the rueful comment, "It's such an awful temptation."[68]

It was never entirely possible nor completely desirable to separate the shoppers from the goods. "To retain the interest of customers during unavoidable waits," the *DGE* advised, "keep a certain portion of the stock on the counter." While the editors cautioned merchants not to put out too many goods at a time, for goods will be soiled and lost, they warned, "but the loss sustained . . . will not begin to equal the increased sales made through liberal displays on the counter."[69]

It is obvious that a certain amount of shoplifting was tolerable if accompanied by ever-higher sales, but the piles of merchandise on tables and counter tops necessitated by the older wooden counters and vastly increased volume of customers, made it impossible to even begin to deter shoplifting losses. The *DGE* told merchants as much in July 1899: "If your notion and small ware counters are packed with all kinds of knickknacks, entirely unprotected, you must expect many dishonest customers at the store."[70] Store owners hoped, and manufacturers promised, that the transparent showcases would enable them to control the amount of merchandise on the counters and greatly reduce the "steady drain upon profits."

The new glass-sided fixtures revolutionized the look of store interiors as well as the psychology of selling. Glass made the stores look lighter and provided customers with an unimpeded view of the range of available merchandise, while erecting a transparent barrier between them and the goods. As the *Dry Goods Reporter* explained, exterior windows had created desire on the shopping street, and beginning in the 1890s glass showcases fulfilled that function within the store.

> The new glass combination case talks continually to any and everybody who ventures within seeing distance . . . it is a business creator in the fact that in forcing onto the attention of passing customers the goods, it creates wants which are immediately satisfied.[71]

> Any clerk can sell the customer the goods she came in and asks for, but it takes a "Silent Salesman" All-Glass Show-Case to sell goods that the customer never knew she wanted until she saw them displayed.[72]

Stores themselves became a spectacle, displaying goods and fueling new desires. For increasing numbers of people purchases were no longer governed by mere necessity or limited selection, but became a matter of choice, impulse, and decisions of the moment. The excitement of the environment itself was sufficient to produce sales. Customers were eager to enter the stores, eager to look, and eager to buy. The dry-goods palace of the 1880s and 1890s did not create the new consumer ethos, but it surely provided a "suitable terrain" for its elaboration.[73] Margarete Bohme's description of the secret longing and temptation that appeared on the faces of the women as they entered the Mullenmeister department store reflected a daily reality.[74]

The way these new fixtures were discussed is revealing. Here we see evidence, however indirect, of the problems store management was reluctant to publicize, along with the steps they took to protect themselves. "Goods can be exhibited in the most attractive form while being kept dust-free and free from handling."[75] This was the recurring theme. The very first advertisement in the *DGE* for a glass counter and showcase ran in the September 19, 1891, issue and read as follows:

> Just the thing for Dry-Goods Houses, who hate notions but must keep them: Everything displayed. Everything marked out. Everything kept clean. Everything protected from theft. Doubles sales on goods displayed over goods kept in boxes on the shelf. . . . The Drawers are drawn out from the back.[76]

Over and over again the articles and advertisements affirm the same truths:

> Goods can be displayed without risk from the nimble fingers of the Shoplifter[77]

> Blackledge's Upright Revolving Sectional Exhibition Cases—it sells twice as many sundries, it helps make the room look elegant, it prevents Shoplifting and fingering, it makes goods look finer.[78]

> Notion Glass Counter . . . always clean, nothing stolen, silent salesman, handy.[79]

> The Eureka Glove Case, A Silent Salesman and Up-to-Date Stockkeeper . . . it is an ornament, simply constructed, so that a salesper-

son or customer can see at a glance what is wanted, thereby saving time. It prevents Shoplifting, and prevents gloves from spotting and drying out. It will increase your sales.[80]

As more goods and a greater variety of goods came onto the market, the need to protect them became increasingly urgent. Shoplifting was already a critical problem in the stores by the 1890s; "a growing evil," wrote one reporter. Initially, the new fixtures seemed to solve the dilemma of the greater availability of merchandise and the increased incidence of casual theft. Descriptions of different display cases for individual departments and particular types of merchandise, each one promising to protect the goods from theft, seemed to flood the pages of the store journals in the early 1890s: leather goods, toilet articles, umbrellas, parasols, jewelry, "fancy" goods, gloves, handkerchiefs, shirts, suits, men's furnishings—suddenly, all required protective glass cases, allowing the customer to closely inspect but not to handle the merchandise—in sight but enclosed and definitely out of reach.[81]

George G. Hammond, a salesman in the black silk department of the R. H. Macy Company in the late 1880s, related the following incident during an interview many years later. His testimony seems to reinforce the claim that unprotected goods were at risk. "The buyer went downtown and bought a bolt of grosgrain silk which was put out on the counter at about 10:30," Hammond recalled, "and at noon [it] had disappeared, evidently stolen, as no one could tell what had become [of] it."[82] A *DGR* "interview" with an unnamed Chicago merchant sought to dramatize the same problem for its readers and point out the appropriate moral: The merchant related how he had placed a display of shoe findings ("blocking trees, shoe horns and the like") on a table in the front of the department, but found that, instead of the expected profit from the table, he "had to contend with a loss by persons helping themselves to these articles. Being on a table, many persons, not genuine thieves, of course, but absent minded, helped themselves to polish, laces, etc., on leaving the store. I saw after a time that the gain did not make up for the loss and I bought a show case. . . I placed it on the table and put my findings inside, so that people could not get at them readily. My findings sales increased, as many persons would stop and look into the case."[83]

Ribbons had their special cases by 1892: a glass front cabinet with shelves that slid out to one side, providing easy access for the saleswoman, but not for the customer. Before the end of the decade, advertisements for a more elaborate, revolving ribbon case assured the merchant that "no ribbons can be removed from [the] case except by [a] clerk."[84] An obvious nuisance, but an important fashion accessory, ribbons were a "must" for the stores: a valuable and easy-to-hide commodity, they were also a magnet for shoplifters. The problem seemed never to have resolved itself; for ten years later, fixture companies were still claiming that their particular ribbon cabinets were indispensable for "convenience in handling goods" and for "protection and attractive display of stock."[85] Handkerchiefs, too, were suddenly more effectively displayed in showcases. "The nature of their borders, whether self or fancy colored, can be seen through the glass, and when the customer desires to acquaint herself with the texture, the boxes may be taken out for inspection."[86] The implication was clear.

A *Dry Goods Economist* article on "The Millinery Department" presented a particularly interesting view of protection. "Everything," the article began, "must be displayed openly." But "openly" meant something quite different for differing grades of merchandise. The carefully drawn illustration showed trimmed hats (and it implied that they were expensive) exhibited in rather elegant, free-standing glass cases; untrimmed hats (obviously much less costly) lay about on a table top, unprotected.[87] Trimmings followed hats. Ordinary merchandise was often easily and openly available, while "a glass case . . . contained extreme and delicate novelties in this line."[88]

Even the commonplace hairbrush came in for its share of concern as trade journals advised merchants that "the modern woman brushes her hair every day and has several different brushes" for the ritual.[89] "The Improved Graves Brush Rack" eliminated "hair brushes thrown in a heap with marred backs and broken bristles" from constant "pawing" over. The Graves Rack promised to display "each one of 8 to 10 dozen hair brushes" and guaranteed to "do away with shoplifting, increase your sales, save your time and add to your profits."[90]

There was, suddenly, a whole industry centered on department store fixtures and the requirements of a new security consciousness. The advertisements of the Norwich Nickel and Brass Works of Norwich, Connecticut, illustrate the heightened interest in store interiors and the competing demands of visibility and protection. The company published an eighty-page illustrated catalog in 1891, and advertised it as "an arsenal" of display fixtures, counters, mirrors, and window dressing aids of every possible combination.[91] During portions of 1892 and 1893, Norwich ran a full-page advertisement every week in the *DGE*, each one differing from the previous week, and each one highlighting a particular store fixture. There was little subtlety in the Norwich copy; shoplifters were a given, and the copywriters simply pointed out the dual uses of the products, the opportunity offered both for profit and protection.

Émile Zola fully understood the connection between department store display and shoplifting. His 1883 novel, *Au bonheur des dames*, was an attempt to dramatize the materialism of late nineteenth century France and the moral implications of mass consumption as they were manifested in its quintessential institution, the large dry-goods bazaar. The power of the big store and the power of women within the store were the twin foci of the novel and the conflicting poles around which all action revolved. Not surprisingly, neither the tempo of life nor the realities of commercial seduction in the Parisian Ladies' Paradise were very different from those of a comparable American department store. The pressures to sell and to buy were equally intense. When an "aristocratic-looking" customer intimidated the salesclerk at the lace counter into showing ever more expensive samples, Zola captured the tension of the scene and the inevitable outcome: The counter covered with a fortune in Alençon lace, Mme. de Boves demanding to be shown still another sample, the clerk afraid to resist, yet hesitating, "for salesmen were cautioned against heaping up these precious fabrics, and he had allowed himself to be robbed of ten yards of Malines the week before." The salesman, Deloche, yielded, of course, and "abandoned the Alençon point for a moment to take the lace asked for from a drawer." A sample disappeared up the sleeve of Mme. de Boves, and Deloche was once again the ready victim.[92]

One doubts that many department store owners and managers read Zola, but one can bet they read C. G. Phillips, author of the influential "Wide-Awake Retailing" column in the *Dry Goods*

Economist. Throughout the 1890s, Phillips pressed for acceptance of glass cases and counters to prevent such incidents of shoplifting. Although new showcases were a capital expenditure like any other, stores were slow to convert. Some stores in the major cities replaced many of the older wooden counters with the new glass combinations, but even here there was an obvious reluctance to introduce a change that transformed the look of the traditional store interior. Again and again Phillips' articles touted modern fixtures as both a valuable asset and an indispensable protector of merchandise. The copy changed, but the message was always the same:

> Up to date showcases are worth their weight in gold . . . they sell goods, they preserve goods from injury, they prevent lots of mark downs, they are effectual protection against shoplifters, they give an air of brightness and general up-to-dateness to the store that makes business.[93]

Glass became an attraction in its own right and offered the merchant the money-saving advantage of a large quantity of goods in full view, theoretically safe from the ever-lurking shoplifter. "You save money by securing your goods against thieves, who are constantly operating in stores where the large quantities of easily concealed goods are lying about loose on the counters, not one in a hundred of these 'light fingered' people ever being discovered."[94] Phillips wrote this in May 1899; in July he upped the estimate: "For one so detected there are probably two hundred who go uncaught, the safe side is worth the necessary expense of showcases and glass counters."[95] "More money is lost annually," the Wide-Awake Retailer continued, "by having stock spread in open boxes and on counters than would pay for glass tops or glass show cases twice over."[96] Wide-Awake's final word for 1899 was marked by cautious resignation: "If you do not feel disposed to do anything just now, the *best plan* is to keep your counters as clear of goods as possible."[97]

As in the early days of retailing, the counter again became a sales mediator, a barrier between the customer and the merchandise. Merchants attempted to find a median between glassed-in stock, which meant slower service but a greater defense against theft, and open selling, which fostered impulse buying but also easier access and theft on a much broader scale. They were never very successful. There was no entirely satisfactory resolution of the problem, as the *DGE* recognized: "Either the custom of displaying goods promiscuously on table and counters without an adequate amount of help to watch them will have to be modified or the merchandise will have to be kept of of the reach of dishonest fingers in the boxes or in cases."[98] Sixty years later, a report by the National Retail Dry-Goods Association, "Controlling Shortages and Improving Protection," demonstrated how little progress had been made; the dialogue still revolved around the critical question of well-designed fixtures. "Merchandise on counter tops," the report contended, "was at risk"; only those counters free of merchandise were safe. The monumental problem of stock protection remained just that.[99]

By 1910 most department store displays were fully under or behind glass, and, as in the days of A. T. Stewart, customers were again forced to ask to be shown specific things. Management hoped the inoffensive glass barrier would stimulate purchases as it discouraged both "the general, almost unconscious habit of handling goods unnecessarily" and the tendency of far too many customers to pocket something on the sly.[100] But the great revolution in display seemed to have gone a full 360 degrees.

The mixed possibilities inherent in glass counters and showcases were duplicated in the newly extended use of mirrors. Although they had been used in stores since the 1860s, large mirrors were not manufactured in the United States before the 1880s and were still something of a novelty in the early 1890s.[101] A. T. Stewart had imported the first full-length mirrors from France in 1852 for his Marble Palace, and for the rest of the century "French plates" continued to be the quality reflectors.[102]

"Mirror, Mirror on the Wall" became more than an incantation; it expressed the newly discovered, essential role of reflection in the dry-goods bazaars. In the 1890s mirrors sprouted on walls and on columns, in showcases and in windows, and wherever customers might stop and look, indulging the sort of fantasies the stores sought to encourage. "Where is the woman," the *DGE* asked, "who is not satisfied on finding herself before a mirror?"[103]

Seemingly no function was too farfetched. A 1902 article suggested that "one of the best features of mirrors is the influence they exert on busy days. They put waiting customers in a more satisfied frame of mind and induce them to wait without complaint longer than they would ordinarily."[104]

As the psychological aspect of selling became more important, mirrors assumed a complex function. More than anything else, they changed the sense of dimension, "concentrating and heightening the light, sharply defining the articles displayed," making the window or display case seem larger and the material abundance even greater.[105] Mirrors doubled the stock without increasing the investment, one practical merchant pointed out. "Not an adornment," mirrors were an "absolute necessity."[106] In Zola's Ladies' Paradise, "mirrors, cleverly arranged on each side of the window, reflected and multiplied the forms without end, peopling the street with these beautiful women for sale."[107] They became an inseparable adjunct to the merchandise, a powerful "silent suggestor" which reflected the goods from a variety of angles and added to the illusion of unlimited availability of things.

The *DGE* maintained, however, that store personnel were unaware of the manifold possibilities of mirrors, and took upon itself the job of educating them. The journal argued that mirrors could be both "bait" to bring a woman into a store, and a toy to "entertain her" while she was there. Instructions told up-to-date merchants to place them—particularly the novel duplicate and triplicate ones—in strategic areas to enhance the merchandise while "they please the customers." They pay for themselves "over and over again during a season," the copy promised.[108] That a modern store could not have too many of "these look-at-yourself affairs about" became a commonplace.[109] With the increased availability of ready-to-wear, "our mirror sells more cloaks than a couple of salesmen," one mirror company advertised. "A customer can't doubt its reflection."[110]

What was implicit in this ongoing discussion was the corresponding use these same mirrors to provide a "judicious system of reflections" and scrutiny in an "unlimited multiplication of areas, objects and stock."[111] In the 1890s the Lazarus dry-goods store in Columbus, Ohio, had a mirror arrangement in the ceiling that could be observed from the elevated first-floor office of the owners, Fred and Ralph Lazarus. The mirrors "were at different angles . . . you really could see through brick and plaster walls by seeing around them, reflection after reflection," Fred Lazarus, Jr., recalled years later. Lazarus thought that shoplifting was not much of a problem in the 1890s but acknowledged that the mirrors were there to both "watch customers and see how salespeople were waiting on them, and they could see them."[112]

Some store architects made liberal use of mirrors at the back of shelving by the late 1890s. The object was far more than ornament: it was security.

> They serve as silent and unnoticed detectives. The clerk whose back is turned to a shopper while taking articles from the shelves or putting them back can observe every motion of the visitor. Many an act of shoplifting can thus be avoided and in the most graceful way. "Did you wish to take that article, Madame?" is quite sufficient to make the person examining it drop it like the proverbial hot potato. And there is no scene, no police station, no story in the papers.[113]

As with glass counters and cases, mirrors were charged with a twofold mission. While they reflected and enhanced the merchandise and the store itself, encouraging the fantasies of consumption, they simultaneously served for surveillance, reflecting the surreptitious and the illegal activities of a great many customers.

> One firm in Washington, D.C., protects what would otherwise be a most dangerous corner by a full-length mirror. It is in the book department where customers and shoppers naturally expect to rove unmolested from counter to counter and where an obtrusive watching of their movements would be impolitic. The mirror tells its silent tale: the visitor is watched but is all unconscious of the surveillance.[114]

"Sales people can watch the customers even when their backs are turned," became a vital selling point.[115] However, an article that appeared in the *Brooklyn Eagle* in the summer of 1901 was more persuasive than weeks of reasoned argument. Headlined "Alleged Shoplifters Caught," the piece described how a store detective "was looking at a mirror with his back turned to two shoppers when his attention was drawn to the movements" of one. He saw the customer "open one of the cases and take from it a garment." Until that chance look in the mirror, he said, the work "was so adroitly done that no one but an expert would have noticed them."[116] Far more than alert salesclerks or detectives, glass in its various manifestations became the primary safeguard for the merchandise.

The new uses of lighting furnish still another view of the continual dichotomy between display and protection. Proper illumination did not become an issue until technology provided the possibility of greater light at reasonable cost, and until the stores became large enough to require more than a minimum of interior illumination. By the end of the nineteenth century, "poorly lighted" stores came to mean "uninviting," and gloomy establishments drew only those women who entered out of necessity, not those who came to "shop."[117] Zola returned repeatedly to descriptions of the half-light in the old-fashioned shop of the dry-goods merchant Baudu: the funereal appearance of the store in which the goods were hardly visible and the customers only occasional visitors.[118] The failing Baudu was a relic of the past who exemplified everything the new bazaars sought to change.

Kerosene and gas were early methods of introducing light into the dry-goods bazaars, but both had the multiple defects of heating up the atmosphere, poor combustion, yellowish color, and limited capacity. Once electric light became feasible for large interior spaces, these other forms of illumination lost ground. Often a combination of the new and the old appeared side by side in the 1890s. Descriptions of stores of this period regularly mention the supercharged atmosphere, particularly in the afternoons when the growing crowds, the "glaring intensity of the light," and the heat of many hundreds of gas jets and electric arc lights made the stores stifling and even breathing difficult.[119]

Huge windows and a momumental center rotunda capped by a skylight characterized the Astor Place dry-goods palace of A. T. Stewart in 1870. Reflecting the best architectural and technological capability of its day, Stewart's used electricity, but only to automatically light the gas fixtures at a predetermined hour.[120] The result, however, was transforming. A description of the sudden metamorphosis of the store on a December afternoon when "suddenly, as if by magic, this vast pile became irradiated with a sea of light," allows us to appreciate the drawing power of illumination in the nineteenth century.[121]

The first stores to use electricity for light were, of course, the big, popular, highly competitive institutions. The R. H. Macy Company provides a good example of the progression from gas to electricity. A Macy's Christmas advertisement in the *New York Herald* in December 1875 mentions a "store beautifully illuminated outside and in." The illumination was gas. The first electric light, an electric arc light, appeared in 1878 outside of the 14th Street building, and although gas fixtures predominated for many more years, arc lights were used in the display windows and inside the store during the 1879 holiday season.[122]

A letter from Isidor Straus to the Manhattan Electric Light Company written in September 1888 indicated that Macy's wanted to fully modernize the lighting system at that time, but for some reason, probably the limited capacity of the lighting company, the store could not or did not. Only when they moved from 14th Street to 34th Street in 1902 was Macy's fully electrified.[123] The plant for lighting this extraordinary new store was said to be "the largest isolated lighting plant in New York."[124]

The pioneer decade for electric lighting in the big bazaars was the 1880s. "Well lighted buildings . . . always give people a sense of comfort, safety and security," Macy's advertised in 1881, and merchants and customers alike knew it to be true.[125] Light was still a beacon that represented safety and life and added to the already immense attraction of the dry-goods bazaars. Zola's descriptions of the "furnace-like brilliancy" of the Ladies' Paradise [which] "shone out like a lighthouse, and seemed to be of itself the life and light of the city" vied with *Dry Goods Economist* reports of Macy's ingenious use of "concealed incandescent lights and a powerful electric force above," which made the windows a "mass of sparkling jewels."[126] Nighttime window illumination produced spectacular results. Macy's brightly lit Christmas windows, "for the benefit of all New Yorkers," were an "instant, crowd-pulling sensation."[127] Diarist Clara Pardee was probably among the dense crowds, as she invariably noted "going downtown to see Christmas."[128] Although still only a seasonal extravaganza, the illuminated holiday windows were powerful symbols, which competitors quickly imitated. An article in *Outlook* in 1895 described New York shop windows "ablaze behind invisible plate glass barriers."[129]

However insufficient it was as a source of illumination, natural light had its adherents; there was a longstanding prejudice for daylight, which in the past had occasionally served merchants' interests. It was not unknown for merchants to pass on shoddy merchandise in the half-light of traditional dry-goods stores, and early discussions of good lighting often hinged on the problem of getting sufficient daylight into the cavernous interiors of the new bazaars.[130] Throughout the late nineteenth century, people still widely believed that natural light was healthier than any form of artificial illumination. Large windows and light-diffusing prisms, which magnified and refracted daylight but were insufficient for the acres of floor space in the larger emporiums, were compared favorably to the arc lamp systems, which theoretically produced a steady, even distribution of light but in fact often flickered and surged in intensity and were widely believed to be responsible for a variety of nervous disorders, headaches, and eye problems.[131] Many shoppers complained of the overheated atmosphere in stores. In *Au bonheur des dames* Zola linked the heavy, still air, the intensity of hundreds of gas jets, and the buying frenzy of the overheated crowds to an image of sensuality, covetousness, and moral flexibility.[132]

From the owners' and managers' vantage point these contradictions were only marginally important. A well-lighted store was both a "continual and most effective advertisement," and a store that provided a positive deterrent to the unyielding problem of customer theft. Incidents of customers' going to the door with merchandise "for better light" were commonly reported. In August 1887, Mrs. Julia Hershey was arrested in O'Neill's, a well-known Sixth Avenue dry-goods store, on charges of stealing an umbrella. Claiming that she was nearsighted and only wanted "to examine the silk of the umbrella more closely" in better light, Mrs. Hershey had walked out with the umbrella.[133]

Adequate illumination minimized shadows and diffused light "in all dark corners . . . behind posts, shelf fixtures and all other obstructions."[134] Fully lighted counters and showcases enhanced the merchandise but obviously made observation easier as well.

Managers assumed that with good lighting the fear of detection would inhibit many instances of impulsive shoplifting.

The Detective, the monthy "Official Journal of the Police Authorities and Sheriffs of the U.S.," described the effect of light on a potential shoplifting incident in its August 1899 issue. The woman in question used the excuse of poor light to move expensive material away from the direct supervision of the salesperson. The customer had repeatedly taken bolts of silk to the end of the counter, "ostensibly for the purpose of examining them in the light." When she had a number of such bolts at the far end of the counter and other women moved down to look at them, the shoplifter "slipped one whole piece into the pocket in her skirt."[135]

The *Brooklyn Eagle* reported a similar case. A Mrs. Cornelius Wigham was arrested in the Abraham and Straus store after six pairs of hose, a number of handkerchiefs, and an umbrella were found in her possession. "Liberated from jail" by her husband, Mrs. Wigham denied the charge of shoplifting and explained that she went to the umbrella counter to "make a purchase for her servant"; she took the umbrella to the door merely to see the material in a better light and was not aware that there were hose or handkerchiefs in its folds.[136]

The importance of light as a psychological factor in the attempt to prevent theft was unstated but implicit. What happened, however, was unpredictable. Illumination often aroused unmet desires and created the very conditions for shoplifting that management hoped it had eliminated. The "delight afforded to eyes eager to behold the new fabrics which glow under the brilliance of the electric pageant" was not simply advertising copy but a new reality.[137] Margarete Bohme's portrayal of a jewelry sale in Mullenmeister's Department Store on a Saturday evening near Christmas highlights the complexity of such stimulation, often amounting to a physical sensation.

Electric reflectors drew colored rays from the jewelry that lay on black velvet cushions ... the gazers seemed to be in a state of excitement verging on ectasy. A fat lady in furs was almost gasping.

"If I only had credit till the end of January! I should so like to have those emerald buttons," she said to her neighbor. "But at Christmas time . . . !"[138]

Frequently, temptation was a benign "silent salesman," but temptation of this sort was subversive to both the store and the woman customer.

By the early 1890s security was embedded in a variety of technological responses, all of which promised to protect the store and its contents. Security came to mean light and mirrors and glass. In these guises it functioned to invite customers into the store even as it provided a subtle barrier to the merchandise itself.

Unconscious surveillance, clear visibility without handling, illuminating engineering, an inoffensive barrier—these were the key phrases that pointed to a problem of wide dimensions, but one the stores took great pains not to publicize. Rarely was there direct or public comment on shoplifting, even as the owners and managers took concrete steps to keep the situation within tolerable limits. What these limits were was never clear, probably not even to the merchants themselves, but certainly the defensive mentality that was so evident was rife with ambivalence.

Store technology became a complex interrelationship between architecture and fixtures, and the imperatives of display, visibility, accessibility, and protection. There was never any doubt, however, that in the confrontation between the free entry principle, the democratization of luxury that the stores worked so hard to foster, and the exigencies of security, the former often took precedence. A degree of loss could be sustained if the aisles were filled with shoppers and the profits steadily increased.

Glass and light intensified the spectacle in the dry-goods bazaars and suported the carefully crafted illusion that anything was possible. By the late 1880s display was as important to sales as the merchandise itself. "Businessmen know," the *DGE* claimed with authority, "that the channel to the people's pocket is through the eye . . . no sane man will deny the selling power of display."[139] But the insoluble paradox of compelling display and the need to protect persisted.

Recognizing the limits of technology, merchants sought to exert more pervasive internal control over the employees, particularly those on the selling floor. Perhaps organization and technology could together sustain a fantasy of consumption without, as it was euphemistically called in the trade, "shrinkage."

Caricature of "The Dry-Goods Epidemic" on Broadway at 3:00 p.m., 1857. (Harper's Weekly, *Oct. 31, 1857, Museum of the City of New York.*)

Shopping on Broadway in 1870. (Harper's Bazar, *March 19, 1870, Museum of the City of New York.*)

Interior of unnamed New York City department store. *(Museum of the City of New York.)*

View of the rotunda from the fourth floor of Dennings Department Store, New York City. *(The New-York Historical Society.)*

Ladies ascending in the elevator on opening day at Lord & Taylor, 1872. (Leslie's Illustrated Weekly, *Jan. 11, 1873, Museum of the City of New York.*)

A new feature in shopping: the Reception Room at Lord & Taylor, 1875. (Scrapbooks of New York City, *views, United States History, Local History & Genealogy Division, the New York Public Library, Astor, Lenox and Tilden Foundations.*)

Engraving of merchant A. T. Stewart instructing a clerk to avoid misrepresenting merchandise, 1876. *(Museum of the City of New York.)*

Among "The Holiday Attractions of the Metropolis" in 1878 was the Lace Room at A. T. Stewart. (Leslie's Illustrated Weekly, *Jan. 4, 1879, the New-York Historical Society.*)

A. T. Stewart Building, Broadway and 9th Street, New York City, ca. 1876. *(Museum of the City of New York.)*

is new, and has a very pretty effect. In order to make this stitch, fasten the thread on the back of the canvas under which is laid the brown linen, then draw the thread through one of the holes in the canvas, wind it three times around the needle as shown in the illustration, put the needle again through the same hole as shown by the cross in the illustration, and bring the thread out again on the back of the work. In order that the knots may be of the same size, even in thread of dissimilar fineness, wind oftener around the needle in proportion as it is finer. The single knots are separated each by two threads of the canvas in breadth and two in width. To make a screen like the pattern, take a piece of canvas, according to the size of the frame; lay a linen lining under this, stretch it in an embroidery frame and work therein. The silk must be chosen of the colors given in the directions accompanying the pattern, but the leaves are very much worked in gray-green shaded silks. The foundation must make a border outside the design, as shown in the illustration. Border the still unworked edge of the canvas with a stripe of green silk, which must be laid in a fall at the corners. Sew five green silk cord over the seams between the embroidery and the silk, as also on the pleats of the corners. Line the back of the canvas with green silk, trim the edges of the different thicknesses of stuff, fasten them in a seam, and ornament this seam with green chenille. Then stretch the shade in the frame by means of fine green silk cord. This frame can be raised and lowered by means of a screw which is arranged in the stem.

Lingerie.

We give a number of illustrations of the following tasteful articles of lingerie, which our readers can readily copy or modify to suit their taste.

Lace fichu, edged with wide and narrow lace, narrow insertion, and grelots, and trimmed with loops and ends of pink ribbon.

Bavette collar and cuffs of fine double linen, trimmed with needle-work and Valenciennes edging in the manner shown in the illustration.

Collar with bow of needle-work. Swiss muslin insertion trimmed with a narrow needle-work frill and a Swiss muslin bow in front, which is also edged with the same frill. The sleeve terminates in a cuff of sleeved Swiss muslin, edged round the top with a narrow, and round the bottom with a wide needle-work frill.

Morning cap of Swiss muslin. The crown is formed of two puffs of figured muslin. Needle-work insertion, and wide and narrow Swiss muslin frills complete the trimming.

Morning cap of Swiss muslin, nec-

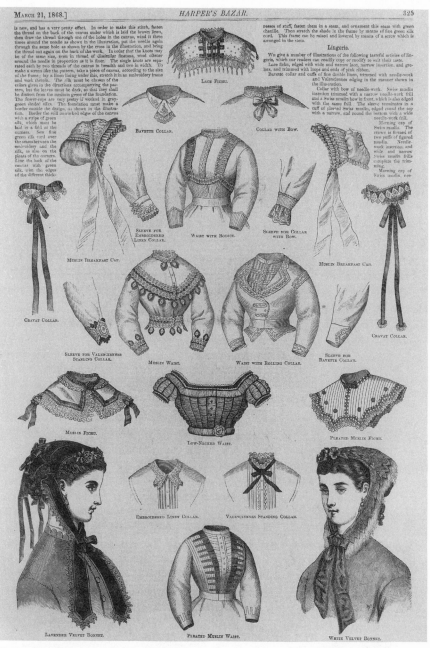

LACE FICHU.

BAVETTE COLLAR.

COLLAR WITH BOW.

SLEEVE FOR EMBROIDERED LINEN COLLAR.

WAIST WITH BODICE.

SLEEVE FOR COLLAR WITH BOW.

MUSLIN BREAKFAST CAP.

MUSLIN BREAKFAST CAP.

CRAVAT COLLAR.

SLEEVE FOR VALENCIENNES STANDING COLLAR.

MUSLIN WAIST.

WAIST WITH ROLLING COLLAR.

SLEEVE FOR BAVETTE COLLAR.

CRAVAT COLLAR.

MUSLIN FICHU.

LOW-NECKED WAIST.

PLEATED MUSLIN FICHU.

EMBROIDERED LINEN COLLAR.

VALENCIENNES STANDING COLLAR.

LAVENDER VELVET BONNET.

PLEATED MUSLIN WAIST.

WHITE VELVET BONNET.

Styles for the woman of fashion to copy, 1868. (Harper's Bazar, *March 21, 1868, Museum of the City of New York.)*

Engraving of a female shoplifter in 1872. (*James D. McCabe*, Lights and Shadows of New York Life, *the New-York Historical Society.*)

"Boozy Female Shoppers" of the 1880s being escorted from an unnamed dry-goods store. (*The Dorsey Collection, the New-York Historical Society.*)

Crowd on Sixth Avenue on the opening day of Siegel-Cooper, 1896. *(The New-York Historical Society.)*

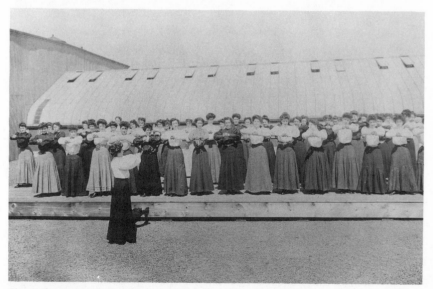

Siegel-Cooper saleswomen doing calisthenics on the roof. *(Byron Collection, Museum of the City of New York.)*

Siegel-Cooper saleswomen reading in lounge for female employees. *(Byron Collection, Museum of the City of New York.)*

Bargain Counter at Siegel-Cooper, "The Big Store," 1897. *(Byron Collection, Museum of the City of New York.)*

"Shopping in Broadway," 1870. (Harper's Bazar, *Jan. 22, 1870, Museum of the City of New York.*)

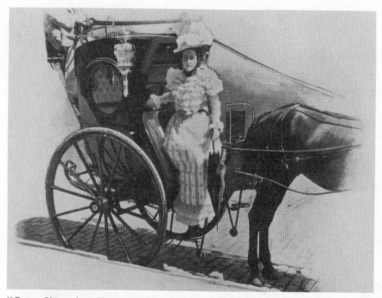

"On a Shopping Tour on Broadway," 1899. (*E. Idell Zeisloft, ed.*, The New Metropolis, *1899. United States History, Local History & Genealogy Division, the New York Public Library, Astor, Lenox and Tilden Foundations.*)

Saturday afternoon on Sixth Avenue just before the Christmas holidays, 1897. (Leslie's Illustrated Weekly, *Dec. 16, 1897, the New-York Historical Society.*)

Crowds viewing Macy's Christmas windows, 1880s. *(Museum of the City of New York.)*

A crowd of shoppers in front of the 14th Street Store (formerly R. H. Macy & Co. store), ca. 1905. *(United States History, Local History & Genealogy Division, the New York Public Library, Astor, Lenox and Tilden Foundations.)*

Bargain sale at the turn of the century. *(Museum of the City of New York.)*

Shop windows at Simpson, Crawford & Co., on Sixth Avenue, New York, 1905. *(Byron Collection, Museum of the City of New York.)*

Main floor counter at Siegel-Cooper, ca. 1908. Solid silver statue of Justice from the Columbian Exposition is at right. *(Byron Collection, Museum of the City of New York.)*

View of interior and grand staircase in unnamed New York City department store. *(Byron Collection, Museum of the City of New York.)*

4

Invisible Authority

Behind the glass façade lurked a disorder that reflected the essential paradox of these new institutions. No longer the familiar dry-goods emporium personally managed by a single individual and his assistants, the large urban department store generated a hierarchy of managers and employed a work force that, before the end of the century, numbered in the thousands.[1] Of necessity, the stores depended on a variety of new in-store roles and definitions of both authority and responsibility. The power relationships and strategies that developed in this framework allowed the bazaars to flourish, but, as several recent studies have shown, there was a variety of internal difficulties.[2]

Certainly department stores were not alone in facing the disturbing problems of unprecedented growth and change. As historian Alfred Chandler demonstrates, after the Civil War both the traditional firm and the developing modern business enterprise confronted the confusion of rapid economic expansion and social dislocation.[3] Like other businessmen, the new merchant princes responded with organizational innovation and rationalization of function in all spheres of store operation. They also attempted to substitute *esprit de corps* for the irrevocably lost personal knowledge and interest that had often characterized the smaller, more intimate organizations.[4]

The *Echo*, Filene's employee newspaper, published an article in 1911 that rather typically represented a nostalgic sense of loss:

> Years ago, when the store was small, everybody knew everybody else. The store was a little family circle. The people came into closer touch with the management and with each other. Mr. E. A. and Mr. A. [the Filene brothers] . . . met frequently with the people and discussed with them matters affecting their interests and the interests of the store. Since that time the growth of the store has been such that it has become impossible to continue this close personal relationship. . . .[5]

But neither *esprit de corps* nor nostalgia for the values of an earlier decade was guaranteed to protect the merchandise. Employers could exhort the sales force to be on their guard and watch "the customers' hands and their walk" when they left the counters, but there was no way to ensure or enforce this watchfulness.[6] Despite modern fixtures and better illumination, increasingly elaborate work rules and a new in-store watchfulness, the ubiquitous shoplifters multiplied. A letter from John Wanamaker to his son Rodman, manager of the Philadelphia store, recalls how reluctant managers were to acknowledge, even among themselves, the actual dimensions of the problems on the shop floor. Describing the shoplifting theft of some fur garments in the New York branch, the elder Wanamaker added ingenuously, "The curious thing about it is that all these things could be taken without any of our people having missed anything."[7]

An unwieldy army of salesclerks had become the pivotal ingredient in a profitable operation, yet the clerks themselves represented a weak link. Overwhelmingly working class and female by 1890, salesclerks were no more immune to temptation than the customers. Too often they cared little about safeguarding the merchandise.[8] The sales force straddled two worlds. They were forced to conform to a work ethic that supported restraint and personal self-control while working in an environment dedicated to self-indulgence and blatant materialism. While loudly supporting the traditional Protestant virtues of industry, sobriety and thrift for their employees, merchants, paradoxically, successfully challenged just such values in the larger environment of indulgence and fantasy they had created. In the contrast between the ethic of work and that of consumption, tension was never far below the surface and caused great problems in the operation of the stores as businesses.

People who witnessed the expansion of the large stores spoke of the "feverish speed of growth," and indeed their perception of the nearly total transformation of the dry-goods world was accurate.[9] From the small, rather specialized dry-goods emporiums of mid-century, to the seemingly gargantuan establishments that captured the imagination as well as the trade of New York, Philadelphia, Boston, Chicago and some fair-sized cities in between, was a change of such magnitude that observers found it difficult to describe or initially understand what they were witnessing. Benson J. Lossing's description of Macy's in his *History of New York City* (1884) gives the twentieth-century reader this sense of extraordinarily rapid growth and uncertainty about a new institutional form.

> Within the space of a generation a special kind of business has grown to enormous proportions in the city of New York. It is difficult to classify it. It may with propriety be called "variety," "fancy," or "general furnishing" business. The most conspicuous representative of this business is the house of R. H. Macy & Co.[10]

Advertising itself as the "Grand Central Fancy & Dry Goods Establishment," the Macy's of this period had diversified in ways unimaginable just a decade earlier. Lossing provides the timetable of expansion.

> In 1869 toys were added to the general stock, and subsequently house-furnishing goods, confectionary, soda-water, books and stationary, boys' clothing, ladies' underwear manufactured on the premises, crockery, glassware and silverware, dressmaking, dress goods, upholstery goods and lastly a ladies restaurant. The business house of R. H. Macy & Co. is the most extensive of its kind in the United States, perhaps in the world.[11]

In the last decades of the nineteenth century, management, like the dry-goods bazaars themselves, was in a period of remarkable transition. Alfred Chandler has cited the large department stores as unique examples of an entrepreneurial capitalism where, well into the twentieth century, "the owners managed and the managers owned."[12] Even as they created an elaborate administrative hierarchy and gradually moved to a more sophisticated form of corporate organization, owner-managers personally carried out top administrative functions and continued to involve themselves in day-to-day decision-making. Chandler is correct, broadly speaking, but he fails to take into account how structural transformation in the great stores exacerbated the problems and contradictions of the shop floor. Macy's is a quick case study.

Rowland Macy, the founder of the store, was a working proprietor who regularly interacted with his employees. In a series of interviews conducted in the early 1930s for the documentary history of Macy's, former employees recalled their early days in the store and the sense of identity they felt with the owners. H. M. Bowyer, one-time salesman and later superintendent, first met Macy in 1873, when the owner was "around the store all the time." A competitive, demanding man who often stood outside his office at the head of the stairs on Monday morning and announced who had the most sales during the previous week, Macy *was* the store to most of the employees.[13] He was the ultimate authority. "Macy did not worry about union hours at that time," Bowyer remembered, "everyone had to be in at 8 o'clock sharp and go home whenever Mr. Macy dismissed them." Bowyer related an incident that highlights Macy's close attention to the internal dynamics of a growing enterprise: "One day Mr. Macy was approached by one of his bold women (salesclerks) who told him it was impossible for her to live on her $3.00 a week salary and convinced him that he should give her an additional dollar, and the following week *everyone* in his employ received an increase of $1.00."[14]

Isidore and Nathan Straus, the second generation of Straus management at Macy's, and their partner Charles Webster, were very much like Rowland Macy in their personal, daily involvement in store operations; together, they represented the last of a type of dry-goods merchant. Although the Macy's of this period—the late 1880s and 1890s—was already a large and complex operation, functioning, like other the great stores, "as a mass marketplace for a mass society," the Straus brothers and Webster maintained an idiosyncratic, personal style of management.[15] Little interested in organization *per se*, Isidore and Nathan managed the entire enterprise "directly by personal oversight of operations and indirectly by supervision of department heads."[16] Lillian Kinnear, who started working at the store in 1882 and eventually became head of the prestigious book department, reported that in the 1890s either Isidore or Nathan personally saw every buyer on a weekly basis and received a detailed statement of each department as well.[17]

The weekly letters from Isidore in New York to Nathan and Webster at the Paris buying office have a twofold interest: they provide an intimate glimpse of the older social relationships of work still operative in the late nineteenth century, and they effectively illustrate the subtle nature of the contradictions operating within the dry-goods bazaars. One letter deals with a shortage of stock in the candy department.

> Feby 1, 1889.
>
> Dear Charlie,
>   We have investigated it and conclude that it lies in over weight to customers—giving more than 1 lb. (There was an overweight of 1 and 1/4 ounces in several pound parcels he examined, and the loss amounted to about 9% on the amount sold for the previous four weeks, or a loss in the department of $335 since the last stocktaking.) We will try to remedy this as far as possible—entirely it cannot be done as we *dare not* give skimpy weight and always must lean rather on the other side of the line.[18]

The managerial ethic of thrift here collided with the marketing ethic of consumption. Overweight of an ounce and one quarter per pound—the weight of hardly more than a piece of candy—entailed a loss both unnecessary and insupportable for a department. Yet overriding the older prescription in this letter and the concern for strict accounting was the consciously modern consumer ethic that spoke the language of generosity, even excess. If the customer was encouraged to be extravagant, so the store must be willing to make a similar gesture—and never risk even a suggestion of having shorted a customer. In this explicit confrontation between thrift and extravagance, management became entangled in a morally and practically ambiguous situation that reverberated throughout the operation and was very much its own creation.

Modern, rational management at Macy's appeared with the entry into the firm of Jesse and Percy Straus, the Harvard-educated sons of Isidore who entered the store in 1896 and 1897, about the time that Charles Webster retired.[19] One employee recalled that "Mr. Jesse and Mr. Percy came in fresh from College and fussed around causing lots of trouble."[20] Years later Percy Straus spoke about this transitional period. In a lengthy interview in 1930, Straus, or "Mr. Percy" as he was always referred to in Macy circles, said that management only "became a separate function shortly before the move to 34th Street (1902) . . . They had little concept of the development of scientific retailing . . . Nathan was a man of hunches, of feminine intuition. He did not believe in checks, in doing training, or in the function of management. He could never see why an inventory was necessary. 'What difference does it make? You have what you have. . . .'"[21]

The obvious conflict, at once ideological and tactical, was between the new college graduates with their studied, pragmatic views of institutional structures and those who relied on older patterns of order and authority without benefit of formal credentials or technical skills.[22] While the overarching concern of both groups was management of an enterprise that in 1900 only vaguely resembled the original model, the twentieth-century owner-managers operated within a radically altered definition of organization and in-store relationships.

A comparison between generations—between the concept of personal response and control and the organizational charts of rational, bureaucratic management of twentieth century—is instructive. When Abigail Golden, Macy's chief cashier in the late 1880s, brought the plight of a poorly paid older employee to the attention of Isidore Straus, Straus acted: he called in the superintendent, checked the details, and told the man to remedy the situation.[23] Conversely, when a distraught woman wrote to Jesse Straus in 1910 to plead for his intervention in allowing her husband to resign from Macy's rather than be fired for "carelessness" when a coat was missing from the men's clothing department,

Jesse replied formally, "I know of nothing I can do regarding the matter of which you write, as it is entirely in the hands of the Manager."[24] There was no question of blame or even of loss, merely a disassociation from involvement in a departmental matter. What Chandler calls "a phalanx of managers" had replaced any semblance of personal involvement. In 1915 Percy Straus, Jesse's brother, elaborated the reasoning behind this kind of decision making: "In a large organization it is not the individual who counts but it is the position he fills."[25] While remaining a family firm, a formal hierarchical organization had replaced the more direct relationships of the nineteenth-century entrepreneurs.[26]

It was no coincidence that the problem of theft increasingly occupied merchants as they personally grew more remote from the customers and employees alike. Management could try to convince the salespeople that their interest and that of the store were identical, but there was no way to disguise or rationalize the great changes that affected those who worked and shopped in the late–nineteenth-century department stores. Stealing from Macy's was not the same as stealing from Mr. Macy, and watching what belonged to an employer you know, however remotely, was far different from caring about the goods of a department whose manager might not even have known your name. The "Department Store Investigation" undertaken by the National Civic Federation in 1913 voiced its concern that the gulf between executives and department store workers was so great. "The general management is unknown to the shop girl," an investigator wrote. "The management knows the girl as little as the girl knows the management."[27] The nervous, excited behavior of Macy salesgirls whenever a member of the Straus family passed through a department made it clear to observers that upper-level management was hardly more than a name to the clerks.[28]

Increase in physical size and numbers of daily customers were obviously important, but they did not account for all the changes. At the very period when the bazaars were experiencing their greatest expansion, the influence of scientific management "transcended the narrow sphere of the factory" and strongly affected the operation of the large stores. Well before Frederick Winslow Taylor published his *Principles of Scientific Management* in 1911, the term had become common in the retail lexicon. By the mid-

1890s, store journals espoused a popular version of the new dogma, and the expression appeared wherever efficiency, system and organization were required.[29] Typically, the *DGE*'s message would begin, "In this predominantly scientific age every successful business is conducted on a more or less scientific basis. . . ."[30] It was not only in the office that the factory model caught on. Throughout the store, so-called scientific management received homage; it became the context for shaping the stores' response to the paradox of thrift amid materialism and protection amid the lure of open display. The advertising manager of John Wanamaker's in Philadelphia addressed the issue in the common military imagery of the decade: "System is to mistakes," he wrote in 1896, "what a big navy is to war—a preventive!"[31] A "leak in the route," the new rationale made clear, was "usually due to carelessness of proper business methods."[32]

Though they insistently attacked the longstanding problem of shoplifting theft in the name of efficiency and service, many owner-managers never were able to feel in control of the situation or cut the depredations in any substantial way.[33] Twice removed from participation on the selling floor, they could do little more than admonish store personnel to exercise greater control over the merchandise and hope that the one or ten detectives would be able to "keep losses down." As the "not real thieves" surfaced in ever-increasing numbers, management's inaccessibility fed its own apprehensions and did little to effectively discourage the shoplifters. As if to reassure themselves, however, that control of selling and the people who did it was ultimately possible, merchants promised that "the store of the future will be organized on *so* scientific a basis that the many losses which they formerly experienced will be avoided."[34]

Management tried to mask the new impersonality of organization with a paternalism based on welfare secretaries and employee newspapers, picnics and summer outings, clubs and choruses; but it remained a fact that the large majority of store personnel had become replaceable hands, important not as individuals but only in their function as cogs in a complex machine.

There are countless indications of just how serious the question of the salesclerk had become, but an editorial in the October 1905

Chicago *Dry Goods Reporter* described the situation accurately and poignantly.

> In the typical city department store as the public understands it, the clerk has become little more than a mere machine—a talking machine, perhaps, capable of answering questions, but the questions must not be too hard, for if they are the clerk cannot answer them. . . . They are very poorly informed . . . their knowledge of merchandise is superficial and also their experience in life and with people is nearly as superficial. . . . Anyone studying the clerk life of the city department store must be conversant with the condition which obtains there, namely the elimination of individuality in a clerk. . . . This is one of the most destructive features of the department store.[35]

The strongly disillusioned tone of the *Dry Goods Reporter* goes far toward identifying a basic problem of the late–nineteenth-century dry-goods bazaars. At once "the most important factor," without whom "the other conditions of trade are worthless," the majority of salesclerks in the large stores were without recognizable skills: they were young, female, and poorly educated, with no long-term goals beyond marriage and family.[36] Their relationship to management had become similar to that of a factory worker to a manager: impersonal, hierarchical, and class-bound. Expected to perform a public function and embody the values and judgments of owner-managers, department store clerks found it difficult to overcome either the limited valuation of their abilities or the often demeaning conditions of work found in the artificial community of the department store.[37]

While stock shortages often became the focus of management's efforts to force the clerks to higher productivity and greater care, there was no single definition given to the problem of clerks. Carelessness, lackluster salesmanship, internal theft and shoplifting were the different layers of concern and were equally important at any given time. Dependent upon their sales force as they had not been when the stores were smaller and the owner met both customer and employee face to face, department store management sought to transcend the difficulties posed by rapid expansion by developing strategies that would solidify worker allegiance. In a twofold effort to promote sales efficiency and provide greater defense against escalating theft, store executives attempted to mitigate the vast distance between top and bottom, hypocritically promoting the store as a moral community in which the lives of the employees and the goals of the organization intersected. Convinced of the necessity to enlist employees on its side, stores undertook to project the idea of a voluntary association of interest between workers and management.[38] Even the *DGE* acknowledged the problem: "[The] unfriendly feeling between the sales force and their directors detracts from all attending to the best interest of the house, with all eyes open for their employers' interests. . . . A House divided against itself cannot stand."[39]

There are innumerable indications that loss of merchandise was a conscious factor in much of the social welfare work that stores undertook. Competition with other stores and a much-heralded "new spirit of the age" were powerful influences that, when combined with the demand for stepped-up internal vigilance, forced employers to consider conditions on the shop floor.[40] In fact, by the end of the century, welfare work became little more than the practical application of good business technique. Mutual self-interest was tied to increasing efficiency, security, and profits.

For the big stores the goodwill value in both advertising and potential employee loyalty easily overrode the cost.[41] The tangible benefits of a day's outing were obvious: free advertising for the store, "an excellent impression made on the public mind," and a "closer feeling of comradeship and union among the employees."[42] A former chief clerk and floor superintendent at Macy's, Mr. Schoenfeld, spoke this very language. Schoenfeld, who came to the store in 1889, told interviewers, "The firm was very good to its employees, [it] gave them May picnics in Central Park, for instance. No other store did that."[43] When Abraham & Straus set up a lunch tent for employees during the hot weather because it was impossible to properly ventilate the basement lunch room, a store spokesman explained, "Mr. Straus thought in this way the lunch hour would be better enjoyed and be more beneficial to the employees. Prior to the erection of the tent a number of cases of fainting of the salesmen were reported daily."[44] The image of the store was uppermost in any calculation: the customers would think such beneficence the mark of a good store; and the employees, grateful for the demonstrated personal interest, were potentially better workers, loyal to the interests of their employers. So prevalent was this particular form of paternalism that merchants could be quite frank about their motives. One unnamed store owner reminded investigator Pauline Goldmark that his store was not a charitable enterprise.

> It is a solid business proposition and every cent pays. Not only does it pay to advertise a model establishment, but it pays to supply employees with comfortable surroundings so that neither illness nor physical discomfort may interfere with their efficency. . . . "Esprit de corps" that is created among employees distinctly enhances their value.[45]

Managers expected the positive feelings generated by welfare work would extend to the sense of belonging to the store as an institution, or, as the *New York Times* so aptly phrased it, "Identity with the store helps the saleswomen to bear unpleasantness."[46] More than just a place to work, the store would link the public and private, appearing as a benefactor to the employee and a contributor to the well-being of the employee's family. "Let it be 'our opening' or 'our sale,'" the Wide-Awake Retailer advised, "and not something of a private or mysterious character concocted and engineered solely by the firm and a few of the 'heads,' and with which the rank and file have not interest or concern."[47] With the risk of shoplifting high and the fear of collusion between the shopper and the clerks always present, if "*the* store" became "*our* store," if welfare measures could foster an identity with the institution, theft would, managers hoped, be mitigated. Employees would be less likely to pilfer and would "exercise more care" with the customers. Shoplifting would be a common concern of workers and owners. "Loyalty is proof against all persuasion and temptation," the *DGR* preached, and merchants hoped it was true.[48]

When Siegel-Cooper of New York launched *Thought and Work* in 1903, one of the earliest department store newspapers for employees, trade publications applauded it as an important way of bringing management and workers closer together. One writer reasoned that an intelligently edited store paper would "increase the effectiveness and prestige of the store . . . [be] a direct benefit and profit to the store"; but, more to the point, the paper would "be sure to inspire greater loyalty to the store, making it more difficult to leave the employ of the firm."[49] Articles and 'Letters to the Editor' stressed how much fun it was to be a "Siegel-Cooper girl," how very privileged were the women who worked there. They were able "to do a share of the work which keeps the great world moving onward and upward toward a more worthy perfection."[50]

Bombarded with clichés about their value to the store and to the nation, salesclerks were set up for their role as guardians of the best interests of others. Management's self-interest intersected with the new imperatives of welfare capitalism, and together they sought to provide employees with a focus and a sense of significance for what in fact was typically unskilled, demanding, and poorly paid work. By tying consumption to nationalism, the editors of *Thought and Work* provided the clerks with a symbolic importance, and thus were able to exhort them to ever-higher levels of performance and responsibility. In "A Word to Clerks" during the 1903 Christmas rush, the editors told them that, by their efforts, they "market the productions of the factories. You must *sell*, and *sell* a great deal, in order that the artisan and the manufacturer may prosper. . . . You are important in the highest degree to the nation's prosperity."[51] Part of the common idiom of the day, such patriotic pep talks allowed employers to propagandize baldly about the significance and challenge of department store work.

Siegel-Cooper realized that the employees had to feel that *Thought & Work* was their paper, and indeed it was, up to a point. Solicited from the different departments, articles leaned heavily on heartwarming fiction, current jokes, and gossip: store romances, marriages, and babies were important and constant sources of news. The editorial direction of the monthly publication, however, was not in the hands of the employees. A variety of anecdotes, moralisms, homilies, and sermons appeared in each issue and were unquestionably the voice of management; the paper served as a painless way of getting the official line across, and store rules and regulations found wide publicity through this medium. In setting out the aims in the very first issue, the editors said the paper aspired to be interesting and uplifting, "to tell us those things which are best for us . . . to encourage thought in connection with work."[52]

As the modern department store became more of an abstraction to the employees, a principal goal of management was the creation of a high degree of unity of purpose in which the greater good of the institution stood above all. Not only were department store employees to participate in maintaining an ideology that often had little connection with their own personal interest or welfare, they were to legitimate the position of management, protect its claims and interests. "Don't allow your employer to suffer loss when you can prevent it," the Wide-Awake Retailer preached in the summer of 1895, and he continued with this theme in following issues. "The success of the clerk should be bound up in the success of the merchant. . . . If this could be the ruling spirit of the store, customers would be better served . . . more and larger sales would be made . . . and waste and small losses that amount to huge ones in the course of the year would be carefully guarded against."[53] In the setting of the modernizing department store, where profits depended upon high volume and rapid turnover, indifference and neglect amounted to real dollar losses.

Not every observer found salesclerks wanting. A reporter for the *New York Herald* attempted to put shoplifting losses in the context of a chaotic sales floor and morally weak female shoppers.

> The clerk's duties are generally manifold . . . take down and sort his wares for customers . . . answer a thousand idle queries . . . puff up the goods, summon the cash boy and see to the account and change, while all that time the throng are whirling past him, and he has no eyes for an individual lounger. Women who, above all others, infest these places cannot but see how ample are the chances offered them, and such as are of the light-fingered community and even some who are simply not strong in resisting the temptations to which their sex are most subject are only too liable to pick up some stray trinket or bundle they have been handling and walk away with it.[54]

Despite such sporadic public support, buyers, department managers, and floorwalkers laid the problem of shoplifting theft at the feet of the salesclerks. They demanded of clerks a personal efficiency within the impersonal efficiency of the institution, and urged "the girls" to act as responsible agents.[55] The Filene's *Buyers' Manual* of 1910 specifically instructed executives to train the salesclerks in "responsibility."[56] The manual did not indicate what this meant or how it was to be accomplished, but it was very clear that the buyers were to make their employees "become cooperators in the burdens of the business."[57] Often frustrated in their designs, owner-managers constantly complained that the "merchant's severest loss today is from carelessness on the part of the clerks."[58] What these complaints seem to have overlooked was both the diversity of outlook and expectation that emerged with the extreme fragmentation of the work force, and the demanding, often difficult conditions on the shop floor.[59]

Division of labor in the department stores succeeded in creating many detail workers with only rudimentary skills. Yet even without increased specialization and fragmentation of function, regulation of in-store life was inevitable. Susan Porter Benson has analyzed the constraints as well as the possibilities of this work culture, and she has concluded that elaborate rules and regulations served a dual function—greater service and efficiency, and removal of signs of working-class origins in the salesclerks.[60] Some of the change simply represented the necessity for greater organization in a situation where employees began to be numbered in the hundreds, and then thousands, and the number of daily customers often reached the one-hundred-thousand mark.[61] If executives could no longer grasp a large dry-goods operation in its entirety, there was certainly a general "decline of any chance for the employee to see and understand the whole operation."[62]

In the 1880s and 1890s, technology seemed to offer a partial solution; the cash carrier systems for packages and change, pneumatic tubes, and the cash register, all products of the period, were a response to the size of the great bazaars. While it did not change the nature of sales work, the emerging business technology made the processes of work smoother and, as a side effect, made closer surveillance of the clerks possible.[63] But the only answer to the twin demands of increased sales and control of merchandise lay in influencing the behavior of the salespeople. Selling was the "defining feature" of the department store, and productive work for the clerk meant selling, "converting shoppers into buyers and buyers into customers."[64] It was upon the shoulders of the saleswomen and men that management laid the burden of proving the store to be a well-run, profitable organization.

W. F. McCurdy, superintendent of Siegel-Cooper in New York at the turn of the century, said quite bluntly that "the help of a department store is a commodity . . . which can add to or undo a world of advertising; they can virtually make or unmake the store."[65] The clerks had to serve both the business of the store and the pleasure of the customer, protecting the former while waiting on, deferring to, and watching the latter. The sales force not only had to develop new work attitudes and habits, they had to become willing accomplices in management objectives; and in this lay an essential contradiction. While theoretically holding themselves (or, more to the point, being held) to an ascetic work ethic, aloof from temptation, salespeople had to communicate the pleasure of consumption to a myriad of potential customers. "Shoppers will surely part with their money if tempted a'right," became the sales-clerks' gospel.[66] The customer was to be tempted, but a clerk was never to desire "what was beyond her purse."[67] Store work neces-sitated frugality, self-control, and perseverance on the part of the employees; while the stores themselves promoted a consumer ide-ology predicated upon the very opposite qualities.

In an effort to ensure strict adherence to its agenda, manage-ment became preoccupied with discipline. Clerks at R. H. Macy & Company recalled only a few strictly enforced rules in the 1870s, and those concerned sitting down or having unnecessary conversations behind the counter.[68] Marshall Field & Company printed a folder of rules for its employees in 1871 that covered store policy and general rules of behavior. With almost five hun-dred clerks in an establishment covering five floors, the company was large, and management quite accurately perceived the neces-sity of ensuring consistent behavior by employees and providing uniform service to customers. The rules concerned courtesy and deportment, cash refunds, a strict prohibition of the misrepresen-tation of goods, and the handling of complaints. Field's prided itself on guaranteeing satisfaction and recognized in the early stages of its phenomenal growth that salespeople were the crucial element in the implementation of this policy.[69] Over the next two decades, however, Field and its competitors established increas-ingly thorough regulations that moved away from the concept of customer service and became an attempt to control the lives of the employees, from arrival and dismissal times and procedures to hygiene and personal behavior both on and off the selling floor. The huge department store with many thousands of workers became a world of its own, and store journals campaigned for "printed rules posted in a conspicuous place," precise instructions "to which employees should strictly adhere."[70]

Because of the special nature of the department store—simultaneously a shop floor and a selling floor—it was important that customers not see the rules. Customers had their own ideas of appropriate behavior and might not understand the need for certain rules, some of which applied to them. Invoking the old republican image, managers piously reminded themselves that a just government "requires certain rules to obey."[71] But "don't be arbitrary," one writer cautioned. "Americans love liberty . . . and it is decidedly un-American to flaunt arbitrary commands before the guise of every stranger. Post the rules in an out-of-the-way place . . . [and] make rules requests rather than commands."[72] Whether managers were being warned not to be dictatorial or not to let "others" see the dictates is unclear; what is unmistakable is the injunction to post rules yet have them appear to be self-imposed and noncoercive.

As in the army, which in the 1890s was often cited as a comparable institution, rules and regulations sought to deprive the clerks of initiative and to ensure only one type of behavior in any given situation:[73] "Employees of every description must be governed by well known rules so that few occasions will arise where there is any uncertainty as to the course to pursue."[74] The Fair, a popular Chicago store, promoted "regulations governing every phase of business," and in an orgy of bureaucratic regimentation issued separate and different instructions for "sales people, floor walkers, cash girls, inspectors, tube wrappers and ushers."[75] Managers hoped to force the clerks to take an active interest in their work, to instill in them a sense of the seriousness of their jobs. The rhetoric would have had the clerks mutely accept discipline and willingly replace their own individuality with that of the store.

Part of the increased discipline and hierarchy of in-store life, dress codes for sales help were the norm in most of the larger establishments. As a general rule, women had to wear black or, at the very least, navy blue from September 15 to May 15; summer costumes were often relaxed enough to permit "neat shirt waists" (white preferred) and dark skirts. Short sleeves were forbidden as were "artificial complexions," exaggerated hair styles, and "all but the most simple jewelry."[76] Men were universally relegated to dark suits, winter and summer.[77]

As with most store rules, these dress regulations conveyed a number of contradictory messages. The more the sales force was in uniform dress, the more they stood apart from the customers and the process of consumption. (Similarly, uniformly dressed clerks made a customer behind the counter immediately visible.) Uniform regulation was to effectively prevent employees, particularly the salesgirls, from "foolishly aping the dress of the rich. . . ." Not only did the black dress make "a defined and appropriate class distinction," which many managers thought "very pleasant to the average lady shopper," but at the other extreme, uniformity carried with it a sense of authority. The uniform made clerks and shoppers alike conscious of their relationship to each other and to the store.[78] One large (and, unfortunately, unnamed) New York store suggested that floorwalkers might wear a kind of uniform, a "dark navy, military undress coat buttoned close to the neck with black braidings in military style . . . which would lend a pleasing air of official appearance to the individual."[79] A number of quasi-military, quasi-police-looking officials on the selling floor could only act as a positive deterrent to various forms of antisocial behavior, but particularly to shoplifting. In the most benign yet transparent manner, customers were to feel the constraints of institutional authority. The plan was abortive, however, and floorwalkers continued to look officious rather than official.

Management's prescriptions on day-to-day life in the store were voluminous, and they bring us directly to the class tensions played out daily on the selling floor. Clerks not only had to be taught the essential discipline of the "system," they also had to be weaned from their own working-class culture.[80] One trade journal gave wide circulation to a list of sixty-four "Don't's" that covered every possible situation but were rationalized as beneficence toward employees. Rules may serve as "an education in manners" ran one justification; another held that there was "no degradation in living up to certain rules, but in fact it was in the clerk's own best interest" and did not mean "loss of self respect."[81] *Thought and Work* informed Siegel-Cooper employees that the department store provided a "practical education in discipline, order, method, business customs, obedience and a strict adherence to the truth."[82] Rarely did explanations go deeper than these self-serving platitudes, and never did management seem to acknowledge the contradiction between such rigid work rules and the publicly indulgent, often sensuous atmosphere that it worked so hard to promote.

Clerks were the first line of defense against shoplifting, and rules, as these examples suggest, were also warnings about the "light-fingered ladies."

> DON'T think all customers are honest or give might-be thieves a chance to steal.
>
> DON'T fail to remember that customers frequently hand you a $2 bill and when you hand them the change they declare they gave you a $5 bill. Call back the amount every time. It's easy when you get used to it.
>
> DON'T be disloyal to your employer.[83]

Salespeople worked on the floor and generally knew what went on, at least in their own department. Consequently, many of the rules that governed their working lives focused on the ever-present reality of stock shortages. Rule #19 in one New York store was quite specific: "You are the custodian of your stock and responsible for it. Be continually on the alert to see that it is not injured or stolen."[84]

Pointedly cautionary humor supplemented the voluminous regulations. For instance, the "Medical Column" in an early issue of *Thought and Work* contained this piece of advice: "Dear Doctor: I feel like thirty cents, what shall I take?" [ans.] "Be careful of what you take or Detective Bernard will grab you."[85] The message was unmistakable: Clerks were to "be constantly on their guard" against the many possibilities for dishonesty, their own as well as that of the customers. There was a poorly veiled assumption that neither group could be trusted. Citing the frequency and costliness of constant small leaks, W. H. Cooper, general manager of New York's Siegel-Cooper at the turn of the century, insisted that safeguards "could not be too complex or too rigid."[86]

A change had taken place that reflected far more than the size of the work force. Management viewed control over the employees as control of what went on in the store; and by fostering a watchfulness among them, managers thought they could curb the material losses that plagued the stores. Fears about the honesty of the sales force became fused with apprehension about dishonest customers. Not only were clerks encouraged to monitor each other as they watched both customers and merchandise, but professional shoppers watched the clerks. The hierarchy of surveillance duplicated that of responsibility.

On the surface the professional shopper was just what the title implied: an employee, almost always a woman, hired to quietly "shop" other stores and report on prices and retail trends. Competition among the stores was fierce, and no store felt it could operate without knowing what similar institutions were doing. The Macy-Hearn 14th Street price wars were famous, as was the short-lived rivalry between Siegel-Cooper and Macy's or the later one between Macy's and Gimbel's.[87] Big stores employed as many as fifteen professional shoppers each, but as secrecy was endemic, none of them were identified as such. "She is seldom known to anyone connected with the store excepting the manager," was all one publication would divulge.[88] "There is hardly an employee of the store who knows any of these shoppers," commented another.[89] It seems evident that the reason for the large number of such "shoppers" and the elaborate precautions to conceal their identity was the work they performed in their "home stores." "Not only is the shopping force valued in the respect of watching competitors," the *DGR* reported, "but much important information concerning the home store is procured from this source. In fact the shoppers are made to spend considerable time in their employer's establishment merely to report on the general discipline and conduct of the sales-people."[90] It was an ill-kept secret that one Broadway store "employed ten employee-detectives whose business it was to go about as clerks in the several departments and work themselves into the good graces of the sales people in order to discover their method of home life and if they are honest."[91]

The professional shoppers made their appearance in the mid-1890s, possibly earlier.[92] By the twentieth century the existence of "espionage on the sales staff" had become public knowledge and was defended by owner-managers as an essential adjunct to the store detective. In her novel *The Department Store*, Margarete Bohme described these women in "the secret service of the firm . . . tracking and spying, listening and watching," unknown women who were a symbol of management's invisible authority and a source of persistent anxiety for the shop girls.[93]

In testimony before a Senate Investigative Committee in 1911, Hilda E. Svenson, an early organizer for the Retail Clerks Union, condemned what she and the other saleswomen called the "spy system" in the stores.

> The girls never feel they can trust anybody. They always feel somebody is up next to them to *spy* on them. Little things are always reported back, and they don't know whether the girl sitting next to them, or the buyer, or anybody around there, is not going right to the employer always with every little thing.[94]

The almost continual observation by a combination of decoy customers and peer informers had a terrible effect on the morale of the employees, Svenson said.

Benjamin Gitlow, President of the Retail Clerks Union, testified that the spy system actually encouraged theft because the spies, also known as "shoppers," "had to have a good book to show just the same as the clerks on the floor had to show a good amount in sales . . . these shoppers don't particularly care whether the girls are honest or not—but they are out for business just the same as a saleswoman, and if they don't get dishonest persons they will be discharged." Gitlow implicated the store detectives along with the shoppers: both, it seemed, had to produce, and both "tempted honest people into crime."[95] He cited an example that he said was from his own experience at Bloomingdale's. It was a scheme that involved a "shopper" not waiting for her change. The employee, usually a new one, was tested to ascertain if she would keep the change and wait to see if the customer would discover the loss, or immediately report the incident as she was supposed to do. "I went and asked one of the old help on the floor," Gitlow testified, "and she says, 'By all means return that money to the floorwalker; that change has been left by a spotter, by a "shopper," and if you keep that change you will be blackballed and dismissed as being dishonest.'"[96]

From the discipline required to run a large department store smoothly and efficiently with a minimum of friction, to spying on employees to make certain they were doing their job and actually entrapping them in questionable situations not of their own making, was a leap prompted by estrangement and fear. No longer tied by any semblance of personal relationship or understanding, employers and employees were adversaries on a fundamental level. In his testimony before the U.S. Commission on Industrial Relations in 1914, John Wanamaker called his store of seven thousand employees a "large village," but Wanamaker was speaking only of size; the affective, reciprocal ties of community life were missing, and in its modern application the village analogy was merely a hollow phrase. Stores were huge financial operations whose goals were "nothing less than industrial efficiency and (maximum) profits," but the profits, along with the store's reputation, very much depended upon the work force.[97] As one merchant pointed out, "The dry-goods store is for distribution of goods not for storage."[98]

There is no way accurately to judge the losses the stores sustained. By the 1880s it was common knowledge that shoplifting was widespread in the big stores. The situation at the then-popular Ehrich Brothers in 1883 was not unusual, nor was the merchant's reaction.

> We lose more than I care to say every year by small undiscovered thefts, though every care and diligence is used to protect ourselves . . . but in a store as large as ours, how can you help articles being stolen. . . . Of course, like every other large house we have a private detective constantly on the watch. But I tell you it would take half a hundred detectives to begin to catch all who filch little articles, generally of personal adornment, and who are generally well-dressed and respectable people. In fact the majority of those caught are really rich people.[99]

Judging by newspaper reports at the turn of the twentieth century, customer thefts of merchandise had increased significantly. Articles purporting to appraise the situation used the analogy of an epidemic to suggest the uncontrolled nature of the scourge.[100] But documentation is sparse, and nineteenth-century methods of bookkeeping and stock taking were simply not able to provide neat, verifiable figures. Controllers only slowly became important in store management, and inventory control procedures were still wildly inexact. As late as 1915 the R. H. Macy Company could describe the shrinkage problem to the J. L. Hudson Company of Detroit as unfathomable:

> Insofar as we know there is no accepted rule of percentage of shrinkage in a department or departments. We endeavor to keep a record . . . but at the end of a season there is always shrinkage. . . . This of course varies in departments according to the nature of the goods, and about the only guide we have is our previous records and judgement.[101]

Stores were painfully aware of their losses but had little sense of just where they were most vulnerable or how to take effective defensive action without offending the customers. According to one textbook on department store organization and operation, the management of a large store was interested in knowing whether there was much shoplifting. "An empty box was neatly wrapped and placed on a counter unwatched. It disappeared in a few moments. Another box was put in its place and this also disappeared. In a day, a dozen boxes were stolen."[102] The story may be apocryphal, but the point was unmistakable. Management could only guess at the extent of shoplifting.

In 1914, merchants roughly estimated shoplifting losses in much the same hit-or-miss fashion as they had in the 1870s. The *New York World* published a long article on "New York Shoplifting" in 1872 and quoted one Broadway merchant as saying, "These petty losses make up a large amount in the aggregate. At the time of the German Jubilee an entire box of kid gloves worth $120 was taken from the counter and never recovered. . . . I make an allowance of about two percent for such losses."[103]

A Simpson, Crawford & Simpson manager expressed an almost

identical assessment of loss due to shoplifting when he told a reporter for the *New York Tribune* in 1883, "Though I cannot pretend to estimate the amount of our yearly loss it must be something considerable. Professionals! Well, no. We manage to spot *them* by means of our detectives as soon as they come into the store."[104] What the manager meant but did not say was clear; the stores saw the middle-class shoplifter as the source of the problem.

Woodhull and Claflin's Weekly quoted Rowland Macy in 1870 as saying "he lost tens of thousands every year through petty pilferings."[105] This may have been a wild guess to justify his Christmas-time arrest of Elizabeth Phelps, the well-known philanthropist and feminist, and four other middle-class women; but given his claim of having arrested over one hundred people for stealing in less than three years, the figures may not be much of an exaggeration.[106] Surviving Macy bookkeeping records from 1875 and 1876 show "shorts" of from 2.5 to 5 percent of potential profits. The figures, which reflect sales and estimated profits, are really just a crude attempt to determine overall shortages. Certainly, some of these losses came from sources other than shoplifting—shopworn, unsalable merchandise, breakage, over-measuring, clerk theft, and carelessness—but even in these years the customers were thought to be the major reason for such shorts. Merchants were just coming to grips with the problem of shoplifting, and these Macy figures—estimates all—are early confirmation that such conditions existed.

While merchants in the 1870s could only guess at the percent of loss due to shoplifting, they were never in any doubt that the figures were high and that it was a real and proven business expense.[107] However, a *DGE* article in 1899, "Stock Taking," concluded with the rueful assessment that there had been little improvement in pinpointing the source of shortages: "In stock taking there are conditions which prevent the inventory account from tallying accurately . . . it is impossible to take account or even to estimate with any degree of accuracy the pilferings of employees or the drains upn department profits by the ubiquitous shoplifter."[108]

A nostalgic but nevertheless accurate article about "Shopping and Shoppers" in the *New York Daily Tribune* considered the problem of shoplifting and the losses suffered by the big stores in 1901 in much the same vein as the *Dry Goods Economist*. The voice was that of a floorwalker who had been a shopkeeper himself "away back in the '70s." What he had to say captured the essence of the contradiction inherent in the modern bazaars:

> Formerly shoppers were watched to see that they did not get away without making a purchase. Those who are watched nowadays are shoppers who we fear may get away with something, for shoplifting is one of the ills from which every large establishment suffers. We catch them once in a while, but between them and the dishonest clerks they rob the stores of great quantities of goods every year. That is a drain which cannot be estimated. We know what our rent, our help, our advertising and other big items cost us, but what Mr. and Mrs. Thief take from us we can estimate . . . and it is a big amount.[109]

A similar article written at about the same time by an "Ex-Superintendent" in the "most important but not the largest department store in New York City," made a similar claim.

> At each stock taking inexplicable shortages were discerned in the stock sheets . . . I tell you the owners of the department stores today haven't the faintest concept of the amount of money they lose each year from peculations and theft; they have no idea of the extent to which stealing is carried on.[110]

Shoplifting seemed to be a byproduct of the new form of merchandising, and by the 1890s no department store left the salespeople to deal with shoplifters without specific guidelines. "Employees are cautioned to look out for Shoplifters and Kleptomaniacs" was the usual warning, and from this broad admonition, stores individually defined their procedures. Siegel-Cooper used guilt by both omission and association in an attempt to forestall the problem. They cautioned all employees that if they failed to report "anything dishonest or against the interests of the house," they were "in a measure guilty" as well.[111] Most other stores were satisfied simply to lay down specific rules of behavior, as in this example from The Fair in Chicago.

> If at any time you detect or suspect a person stealing, notify your floor walker immediately, taking care to do it quietly, so that your

conversation will not be over-heard. In no case and under no circumstances accuse or detain any one yourself. Your business is simply to keep track of the person and to report; take no action personally.[112]

Marshall Field offered clerks a reward for detection of shoplifters—five dollars if the theft did not exceed that amount and corresponding amounts for more expensive "catches."[113] In all cases employees were to act as the eyes of the department but take no definitive action on their own.

So strict were the warnings against direct employee interference, even in incidents of flagrant shoplifting, that it is evident the stores preferred to sustain the losses rather than have salesclerks intervene. Was there a class dimension to these injunctions? Possibly, but it is far more likely that management felt it necessary to mask any suggestion that the clerk and the customer were adversaries. Painstakingly built up, the whole ambience of shopping, the fantasy world of luxury and indulgence, would have been shattered if the customer thought the salesclerk might suddenly turn on her. Moreover, false accusations and mistaken arrests had received wide publicity, and concern about keeping "good" customers and the store's image was added to the fear of lawsuits.[114]

When a Miss Kirkpatrick was publicly accused of shoplifting and arrested at Macy's in December 1904, Macy's found itself in a difficult position. The woman was, apparently, innocent. While her lawyers recognized the store's "desire to avoid publicity," they pointedly suggested that such false accusations could affect "the attitude of courts in dealing with shoplifting cases and would affect the conduct of your business in other respects."[115] Macy's quickly apologized to Miss Kirkpatrick, "regretting the mistake," and the managers understood that the store had gotten off lightly.

The rationale behind the insistence on employee vigilance was understandable, however. Saleswomen who were watching for potential customers were theoretically in the best position to watch the goods in their immediate care. According to the accepted creed, a bright, alert sales force was the best defense against shoplifting. Far better than detectives, they were the ones who would "be quick to note a suspicious action."[116] Only the clerks could police the counters adequately. "If the store is a big one, two or three or a dozen detectives cannot be everywhere at once," was the explanation of one merchant for the reward he gave to employees who detected shoplifters. "The reward serves as an extra inducement to salespeople and others to be on the alert."[117] It also served to protect the interests and claims of management.

Rationally, store managers understood that the "faithful service" they expected was often a myth. Philip Farley, a detective turned writer, felt that the clerks actually overlooked most instances of shoplifting. Clerks were so poorly paid they "had no interest in looking after the goods," Farley wrote in his sensational *Criminals of America* (1876).[118] Although he was describing the professional thieves who plagued the shopping bazaars, the problem of the clerks' not caring about shoplifting losses, whether by professionals or amateurs, persisted. As early as 1872, there were complaints about the clerks' lack of vigilance and concern. "I tell the clerks," one merchant reported to a *New York World* investigator, "they are not half sharp enough, for they let the thieves steal before their faces. . . . We have offered our clerks a reward if they would detect a shoplifter, but it doesn't seem to do any good, and so we suffer in silence."[119] The merchant was speaking for many dry-goods proprietors.

It was problematic just how much salespeople did care about shortages and how far they were prepared to go to protect the assets of the store. Using words practically identical to the less scientific conclusions of the 1870s and 1880s, the New York State Factory Investigation Commission reported in 1913 that salesclerks had little personal attachment to the big stores and were understandably indifferent to much of what occurred around them.[120] In Margarete Bohme's novel, *The Department Store*, published at this same time, a department superintendent loudly berated a young apprentice when an Irish lace blouse on a sale table was unaccounted for. "Where were your eyes? What are you put at the table for? Not even for that are you any good!"[121] In noting the indifference of the salesclerks, Bohme reflected a common complaint.

But many clerks scrupulously guarded their counters without extra inducement. Often it was the saleswoman who noticed a would-be shoplifter and signalled a detective. A Miss Collins "proved herself a good detective and plucky" when she observed shoplifters in Bloomingdale's and intervened.[122] Numerous articles in the New York daily newspapers specifically noted that salespeople were frequently involved in detection and apprehension of shoplifters.[123] Miss Collins could have been one of any number of saleswomen.

Department managers and buyers urged salesclerks to be aware of how much merchandise they took out to show customers and how much they returned to stock. Saleswomen at a jewelry counter in a large New York City department store were paradigms of management success. These clerks called the store detective when they discovered a ring missing: "They knew that there were eight rings of a certain pattern in a tray on the counter when Mrs. Morris stopped to price them and there were only seven rings in the tray when she turned away." Although it was clear to the saleswomen that the woman had stolen the ring, they had not *seen* her do it, so the detective could do nothing about the loss but caution them "to keep a look out for the woman and notify him if she came into the store again." She did, the saleswomen alerted him, and the story repeated itself—except this time, the shoplifting was observed and the woman arrested.[124] Deloche, the salesman in Zola's novel, on the other hand, lost his position at the Ladies' Paradise because he showed too many things at the same time, let too much pile up on the counter, lost track of his stock, and thus "allowed himself to be robbed." Persistent shoplifting dictated defensive salesmanship. "When a box of gloves has been opened to show a customer some of the assortment it contains," the *DGE* advised, "replace the rejected pairs and put on the cover before any other gloves are shown."[125] Salesclerks were to be alert, to be "on their toes." Under these conditions work took on a very different meaning.

The warnings about shoplifters emphasized a variety of tricks to be aware of and a number of possible defenses. The chief danger seemed to be that of turning away from the customer.

If one is retiring from an audience with a royal personage one must never turn the back in going out, but is required by court etiquette to 'back out' face toward the Queen. . . . This custom would be a good one to observe—to never turn your back on the store enemy.[126]

Presumably, if it was impossible to keep one eye on the customer and look for goods with the other, the mirrors embedded at the back of the shelving would serve as advertised, as "silent detectives." Diana Hirschler, an early leader in welfare work and educational training for department store employees, warned her student-salesclerks to "be so familiar with the location of the different stocks that you could put your finger on them in the dark; you often do this practically if you keep your face turned to the customer, as your should do, both to be polite to her and also *not to subject her to the temptation of appropriating your goods* without paying for them."(Italics mine)[127]

Nowhere was the ambiguous nature of sales work and the subtly antagonistic relationship between salespeople and customers more evident than in these repeated cautions and admonitions. The customer-salesclerk-management relationship exposed the "web of contradictions" that underlay the operation of the department store. By not showing goods properly, "by pulling one pair of hose or one piece of underwear from the lot and leaving the box on the shelf, instead of putting it on the counter to show the customer, [she] would be justified in thinking that her honesty was questioned."[128] So fearful were managers of not satisfying the shopper and "turning away trade" that the merest suggestion of customer displeasure or minor annoyance was sufficient to overturn all previously implanted caution. "Even if we can show pretty good evidence of guilt, our employers won't take our word against that of a customer," one New York saleswoman complained.[129] Yet responsibility for customers' behavior, including shoplifting, was laid at the feet of the salespeople. Untutored working-class shop girls were held accountable when the enticed middle-class shopper turned into the enemy.

Management feared salesclerks' alienation and sought to counter it both by explicit rules and by the attempt to manipulate the sales force into identifying with the store. The salespeople were to be cautious and responsible for their stock and to understand that what was good for the store was "in the long run" good for them. Self-interest was the final line of defense. One store even suggested that if shoplifting losses were less, their salaries would be higher.[130]

The contradictions inherent in the department stores negate

any easy understanding. Neither clerks nor customers could be trusted. "It is much to be regretted," one merchant confessed, "that the firm has so far lost all confidence in human nature that every employee is branded as a suspect."[131] But when the customer, the *raison d'être* for the new status drama of shopping and the primary source of profit, became the nemesis, the paradoxical nature of the big bazaars stood out as their essential feature. Merchants knew that exposed merchandise was an invitation, but they chose to ignore the implications, trusting that increased sales production would offset inventory shortage. As merchants themselves admitted, they could afford to put up with "the pecularities of women, as long as they show a disposition to fall victims to the gorgeousness of [their] displays."[132] With profits so very high in these decades and the image of the stores all-important for their continued success, owner-managers were easily able to rationalize losses from shoplifting, many of which were either hard to pinpoint or difficult to prosecute.[133]

Salesclerks were in an untenable position. They were asked to master the complex variables that allowed them to meet the shopping woman on her terms while treating seriously the thefts the stores themselves often dismissed with a slap on the wrist. Department store salespeople were thus charged with the success of management objectives.[134] "Shortages," whether by routine employee theft or the far more serious and shocking customer shoplifting, were contradictory at their core, making ambivalence and surveillance a part of daily store life.

5

———❦———

The Dilemmas of Detection

At the moment the dry-goods emporium became a department store, the detective became part of the store's labor force. But until the sensational arrest of Mrs. Elizabeth B. Phelps and four other "respectable women" for shoplifting at Macy's in December 1870, the store detective remained a shadowy figure, an invisible member of the supporting cast. The notoriety and public indignation accompanying the Macy arrests placed store detectives in an immediate spotlight and, as we shall see, very much determined the response of the dry-goods bazaars to the complex problem of middle-class shoplifting. The reverberations from the Phelps case persisted into the twentieth century.

Elizabeth Phelps, Mary Bryant, Sophie Eisner, Elizabeth Claussen, and a Miss Nielson were arrested in the Macy store on the day before Christmas, 1870. Taken to the central police station for booking, each woman was tried in the Special Sessions Police Court, and in each case the charge was dismissed.[1] Because of the social position of Mrs. Phelps and the unmistakable respectability of the other women, the arrests became a *cause célèbre*. Macy and his employees were denounced in the strongest possible terms in newspaper articles and in letters to the editor by a public unwilling to believe that any of the arrested women could be guilty of theft. Special Officer Woods and "the other detectives in atten-

120

dance" were singled out for particular abuse, denounced as "unfit for their business" because of their manifest "stupidity."[2] The women may have been "indiscreet," the New York *Commercial Advertiser* admitted, but that was no reason for charging "innocent ladies" with theft.

What the reporter meant by indiscreet can only be surmised, but it seems obvious that, whether or not Mrs. Phelps and the other women who were arrested in this two-day period were actually guilty of shoplifting, they occupied a social position beyond the reach of Rowland Macy's claim of self-defense.[3] Citing an insupportable increase in the number of holiday thefts, Macy said he acted to protect himself. The thieves were all women who "were dressed like ladies and looked like ladies, too," he explained to a reporter for the *New York Sun*. Unable to distinguish between "real thieves" and middle-class shoppers, his employees watched everyone, and while he regretted the arrest of any innocent person, Macy defended the arrests.

The very idea that a Mrs. Phelps could stand accused of so tawdry a crime was inconceivable. "Lady" and "shoplifter" were not yet synonymous terms, and so disturbed were the editors of one New York newspaper by this overt challenge to the class position of these women, and by the disclosure of secret surveillance in the showplace of emergent consumer capitalism, that they feigned surprise at the lack of violence by male relatives of the four women and predicted retribution in the form of economic sanctions. "[Macy] must do something," the *Commercial Advertiser* warned, "to give assurance to the public that ladies visiting his place of business will be safe from arrest. . . . No lady can visit his premises under the present management with any sort of security against being branded as a thief. . . . Mr. Macy owes it to himself to change his system of spies and detectives."[4]

The woman who was the centerpiece of this morality play based on class and gender was Elizabeth B. Phelps, a wealthy New York City philanthropist. A vice president and member of the executive committee of Elizabeth Cady Stanton's National Woman's Suffrage Association, Phelps was a major benefactor of the newly organized Woman's Bureau in New York.[5] Charged with stealing a small package of candy and summarily arrested, Phelps was just as quickly "honorably discharged" by Special Sessions Judge

Dowling. Mrs. Phelps, the judge announced, was "a lady widely known for her high character and benevolence and it was evident there was a mistake."[6]

The Phelps arrest was exhaustively reported in four New York City daily newspapers. The *New York Daily Tribune* ran the case for four days, the *Sun* and the *New York World* for three days each, and the *Commercial Advertiser* for one day. The case did not die with the new year. *The Revolution,* the weekly organ of the National Woman's Suffrage Association, carried articles on Mrs. Phelps and the indignity she had suffered at the hands of Rowland Macy for two consecutive weeks in January of 1871. Sorosis, the prominent woman's club that had been organized only the preceding year, adopted a resolution at its first meeting following the incident, unanimously condemning "the unjust and vexatious treatment received by one of our members at a well known place of business in this city." The membership offered Mrs. Phelps friendship, sympathy, and support and further pledged themselves "to avoid purchasing anything whatever, hereafter, at the place where she received such hurtful treatment, from which she is still suffering in body and mind."[7] *Woodhull and Claflin's Weekly* kept the story alive; for two months later, in March 1871, it published an article about the arrest of the four women, dramatically entitled "The Felon's Dock."[8]

The reaction to the Macy's incident was extraordinary. To the *Woodhull and Claflin* editors it was beyond belief that "wives of leading citizens of high standing and repute" were seized as shoplifters. The arrest of these "innocent women" was a scandal and a threat to all women of this class, the more so because explanations, proffered while the women were still in the store, "ought to have been sufficient to satisfy any reasonable person" and clearly they were not. The fact that Macy would not accept the word of a lady was taken as proof of his malign intent.[9]

Not content to castigate the well-known merchant for his presumed mistake, newspaper and journal editors were unanimous in their condemnation of the Macy employees who had precipitated the events. A shrill, class-based rhetoric pitted working-class detectives and salesgirls against middle-class customers. Detectives, *Woodhull and Claflin's* protested, were employed "to look after thieves and keep order" in the Macy store—not to pounce upon unsuspecting shoppers. It was a common assumption at this time that thieves were not ladies, and ladies did not create disorder. The "promiscuous arrest of a large number of ladies" was unheard of and signalled the breakdown of this unwritten but widely understood social code. The *New York World* charged that the women were not simply arrested, they were "seized by a policeman, insulted and dragged away."[10] Another publication characterized the detectives in the case as "so ignorant and besotted as to be totally wanting in discrimination." Only a boycott of the Macy store, "emptiness and desolation reigning in his wide halls," could redress "the insult to the best class of customers."[11]

The outrage that gripped the popular press after the Phelps arrest was directed at both detectives and clerks, but the denunciation of the Macy saleswomen, popularly known as "waiter-girls" in 1870, seemed especially vituperative and became condemnation of an entire class. The editors of the feminist journal *The Revolution* were especially humiliated by the knowledge that it was the saleswomen (whom they angrily labeled "female spies and detectives") who pounced upon the "innocent women and delivered them into the hands of policemen."[12] "Respectable matrons, young wives and beloved sisters" were pitted against working-class women described as "possible frauds, imposters, thieves and perjurers." *Woodhull and Claflin's* accused the Macy saleswomen of dressing above their station ("dressing like a duchess" the article claimed), being less than pure, and of questionable honesty; their morality seemed as dubious as their character. It appeared far more likely to the reporter that the clerks, rather than "women of our best families, should sink into a moral cesspool all of a sudden. . . ." Furthermore, the paper charged, "the waiter-girls were not immaculate, like vestal virgins of old time . . . they go to theatres, balls and operas of an evening *like any Mrs. Phelps* . . . they dress too well and put on airs . . . they are not unused to a little cheating and some of them a considerable amount of lying." (Italics mine.)[13]

The author of this article, which was signed "J. S.," went even further in displaying indignation and bitterness, accusing the saleswomen of making up the accusations "to serve a purpose— whatever that purpose may have been." J. S. saw waiter-girls' subjecting "many excellent ladies to the dreadful and humiliating indignity of arrest and imprisonment" for motives that were certainly suspect. The inference was unmistakable: either the sales-clerks were thieves themselves, or these working women derived satisfaction from placing upper and middle-class women in a situation where, at least for a brief period, the power of money and position were useless. When the "character of the customers were so completely at the mercy of these flaunting waiter-girls, any customer, may at any time, by their wickedness or malice, be arrested for a crime they would rather die than commit; therefore what protection for women frequenting this store is left?" For *Woodhull and Claflin's*, class bonds overrode any claims of gender solidarity.

Although it was suggested that her court appearance and the degradation of being compelled to swear that she was not a thief "must have crushed Mrs. Phelps almost to madness," Judge Dowling was spared in the general condemnation of the proceedings. "Whose word should the judge take," *Woodhull and Claflin's* demanded, "the waiter-girl and the detective or Mrs. Bryant?" Mrs. Mary Bryant, one of the other women arrested at the same time as Mrs. Phelps, was accused of stealing a small match safe. The wife of a publisher/dealer in law books who was listed in *Phillips Elite Directory*, Mrs. Bryant was unmistakably "a respectable lady," and her arrest aroused an equally indignant response. Judge Dowling obviously understood that class resentment was the underlying issue and made the only possible decision: he released both women from the charges preferred against them and dismissed the case to the "considerable applause" of those in court.

The Macy-Phelps confrontation had lasting repercussions. The torrent of adverse publicity surrounding the arrests served to change subtly the balance of power in the merchant-customer relationship: after 1870 merchants rarely ignored the question of class in deciding whom to charge with shoplifting.

The questions about the legitimate jurisdiction and proper role of private police, questions that were infused with such anger in the Macy arrests, demonstrated an understandable confusion. Historically, people had protected their own property. The right of shopkeepers to defend what was theirs and to detain people suspected of shoplifting was never in doubt.[14] When Rowland Macy complained of his inability to stem shoplifting amid the throngs of people in the store, the public, objectively, deemed it "natural and even laudable" that he "should endeavor to detect these culprits and bring them to justice."[15]

The problem arose with the appearance of the "ladylike and gentlemanly pilferers of the city."[16] Macy had ignored the question of class. Claiming to have lost "quantities of valuable goods" —tens of thousands every year through petty pilferings—he was "compelled by the circumstances," he explained, "to secure the services of a skilled police detective."[17] The arrests followed. However, in this first public confrontation between working-class salesclerks and detectives and middle-class shoplifters the issue was framed and acted out in explicit class terms.[18] A letter to the editor of the *New York Tribune* revealed the various strands of meaning in the case as it expressed doubt about the authority of a detective, policeman, or employee "to arrest, or cause the arrest of a lady of gentleman for removing or handling articles exposed on a counter where no intention has been indicated to carry them from the store."[19] Focusing as he did on the social position and presumed innocence of respectable shoppers, and ignoring the question of store employees acting as legitimate surrogates of the proprietor, the letter writer, along with the *Woodhull and Claflin's* editors and others, denied that department store detectives had the right to "catch ladies in and make thieves of them."[20]

Because the middle-class shoplifter was not supposed to exist, the issue was never fully resolved. After the Phelps incident the department stores used great caution in challenging suspects, even as the need for a more systematic, fixed protective presence became obvious. Although department stores were private property, these crowd-attracting institutions had quickly become "public places in need of policing."[21] By 1881, newspaper articles detailing "unaccountable shoplifting" by middle-class women also noted the presence of the special detective in virtually all the dry-goods bazaars.[22] Without detectives, one observer asserted, "the show counters would be systematically looted and many customers, deterred by the knowledge of keen but secret surveillance, would become dishonest."[23]

Urban crowds were not new, but in the past they were impermanent, formed for discrete causes, and had their own logic of organization.[24] The new institutions—the hotels, theaters, amusement parks and museums, but particularly the department store—invited and even created a new kind of crowd: a crowd of women. An Italian visitor complained to one journalist of being forced to walk in a Boston street because of the "solid, unmovable congestion of femininity" on the sidewalk. The journalist then added her own observation: "The whole world of women in the city and from the suburbs betakes itself to the shops everyday . . . the shops are stifling, the street cars jammed, the sidewalks impassable."[25]

For some observers the crowd was the quintessential expression of the urban experience. "The city is the center of the mass," Gerald Lee wrote in the *Atlantic Monthly* at the turn of the century.[26] Crowds of things and crowds of people, the defining features of the department store, were for Lee simply "the crowd principle in commerce," an inevitable and positive component of late nineteenth century "crowd civilization."[27]

The big stores quite obviously depended upon the crowd, upon hordes of daily shoppers; so much so that the size of new additions and buildings became a numbers game. At the opening of the new James McCreery & Company building on 23rd Street in 1895, the owners boasted that "ten thousand people can move comfortably at one time in the store."[28] Much as any showman, these allegedly conservative merchants who catered to the wealthy women of New York understood the seductiveness of a crowd, the importance of having a busy-looking store with "plenty of people entering and leaving"; even if "the people were piled up like logs in a giant jam" (as they were in the larger, more theatrical bazaars), and a given store was actually "inadequate to the rush of the crowd."[29] One woman's words were unconsciously revealing of the comfort she took in the collective behavior of throngs of shoppers when she explained her dislike of an uncrowded store: "One feels as if under a microscope when walking down one of those broad aisles under the eyes of a few floorwalkers and a double file of clerks."[30] The feeling of being watched, of being conspicuous and not being able to lose herself in the crowd, unnerved her.

Store openings and special sales attracted massive crowds—traffic-stopping crowds both in the stores and on the streets—and the police were regularly on call to protect property and prevent disorder. So serious did the crowding become in Boston in 1897 that the *Boston Herald* reported on a plan for double-decker sidewalks on Washington Street, the main shopping thoroughfare. The crowds were so compact in front of the large department stores, the paper noted, that "every now and then . . . women were obliged to hold their paper boxes above their heads to keep them from being crushed."[31]

As the bargain counter became a fixture in many of the large stores in the late 1880s, it contributed to the throngs within the stores and came to represent the best and the worst of modern retailing. Dry-goods journals touted the development as a boon to trade and to the innate shopping hunger of women, but these same journals simultaneously evinced concern about crowds of "unruly ladies" and elbowing, scrambling rushes such as the one in which a woman had her shoulder dislocated at a crêpe-de-chine counter.[32] Unmanageable crowds of bargain-hunting women became a basic ingredient of department store humor, a sure sign that the stereotype had become a permanent fixture. This squib from the *Boston Sunday Herald* in 1897 is typical.

IN THE DEPARTMENT STORE

PROP: We thing [*sic*] of opening a hospital on the 6th floor.
FRIEND: A Hospital?
PROP: Yes, Customers injured in bargain rushes will be treated free.[33]

The image of a formless crowd "losing itself" was given sharp focus in fictional representations of the dry-goods bazaar. Margarete Bohme returned to the crowd theme repeatedly: "Huge crowds surged before the windows . . . dangerously packed crowds before windows which displayed a thousand radiant examples of the wonders within . . . police were needed to regulate traffic near "The House."[34] Zola, too, seemed preoccupied with the crush outside and inside the Ladies' Paradise. He described counters jammed "as if there were not enough shopmen to suffice for all the greedy outstretched hands of the customers," and aisles so packed with the immense crowd that it took a woman shopper ten minutes to get to the silk counter.[35]

While the newly discovered crowd was a necessity, it posed difficult, unanswered questions for merchants. Large numbers of unknowable employees and amorphous, pushing crowds of shoppers and visitors heightened the difficulty of responding to the middle-class shoplifter. Professional shoplifters and merchants were old adversaries. With the enormous proliferation of things to see and to buy, however, the seemingly innocent housewife rapidly proved herself a possible thief and became a new opponent.[36]

An ordinary news story about a shoplifter in the *Brooklyn Eagle* in 1896 illustrates the basic triad: the crowd, established definitions of class, and the increased opportunity for casual theft. Headlined "Police Arrangements to Prevent Stealing and Panics," the article described the usual "refined looking and well-dressed woman" who entered a popular Brooklyn store and was subsequently arrested for shoplifting merchandise ranging from silver-plated spoons to spools of cotton thread. "This is no unusual occurence," the reporter wrote of the arrest of the apparently well-connected "Jane Doe," and in an attempt to explain the particular circumstances he added, "Never before in the history of Brooklyn have there ever been such enormous shopping crowds. In spite of the extraordinary increase of clerks and saleswomen, the stores . . . find it next to impossible to cope with the growing trade."[37]

The link between the crowd and its psychology and shoplifting was real. The crowd helped to loosen ingrained controls; it acted as a shelter, and women who otherwise led blameless lives, who never would have consciously admitted the temptation to steal, did in fact walk off with merchandise. In a long article on "City Shoplifters," the *New York Herald* elaborated on the components of the problem without providing an answer: "The general exposure of the goods of the house on counter or on floor, the throng which is ever stirring about, the constant diversion for the eye or ear of watchers—all serve to prepare an easy way for the shoplifter."[38]

Merchants tried to see the individual faces in the crowd and determine who was the would-be thief, but it became obvious that in a crowded store a public sort of privacy was possible. A woman might be both visible to others and isolated from them; she could "walk in and out and around without attracting the least observation."[39]

Merchants were trying to control a social situation in which both the crowds and the behavior of women were still unusual. Detectives seemed to be part of the answer, yet the role of the store detective remained an anomaly. Like the floorwalker, with whom s/he was often confused, the detective was an employee of a special sort: one who unquestionably represented management but was not of management; one who spied on the employees even as it was necessary to cooperate with them to protect the interests of the employer; one who was empowered to detain middle-class shoppers, yet was constrained by social convention.[40]

Throughout much of the nineteenth century, Americans were suspicious of police power and feared private detectives, those "secret agents," as a potential danger in a democratic society.[41] In New York in the 1870s, and probably in other large cities as well, there was protracted discussion in the daily press about "The Private Detective System and Its Abuses."[42] Describing the detectives at Macy's as "that demoralized and demoralizing section of the police force," the editors of the *New York World* were merely echoing a common understanding.[43] With the difference between "rogue" and "detective" obscure for many observers, the legitimacy of private detection in almost any guise was problematic. Such was the situation when unknown and unsuspected detectives at Macy's arrested Mrs. Phelps late in 1870.

There were three categories of detectives working in the stores in the last decades of the nineteenth century. The first and most prevalent was an employee merely acting as a detective. Floorwalkers quite often acted in a dual capacity; adding to the confusion, however, detectives at Macy's were referred to as "shop walkers" in newspaper accounts of the Phelps arrest.[44] Marshall Field & Company hired no outside detectives, using only their own employees, "people brought up in the store" and of unimpeachable loyalty, except for special occasions such as seasonal openings and the Christmas rush.[45]

The second type was a detective from a licensed detective

agency, such as the Pinkerton Agency or the Theil Detective Service, which specialized in department store work and was one of the over thirty licensed agencies in New York City by the end of the century. All these private detectives—and they were women as well as men—held nominal police power, but in most instances had no greater power of arrest than the ordinary citizen.[46] They could merely detain suspects until the police intervened.

The third category of store detective, generally designated as a "special," was often a regular police officer. Hired in a private capacity and paid by the store, specials were used regularly for department store security. Special Officer Woods, so castigated for the arrest of Mrs. Phelps, may have been, in fact, a policeman. Specials were obviously popular with merchants, for many of the newspaper articles about women arrested for shoplifting document their presence, and Macy's used them well into the twentieth century.[47]

Theoretically, the detective watched everyone, "keeping an eye on every person at or near the counter or tills," and it was exactly this comprehensive nature of the position that often resulted in the customers' misunderstanding and the employees' fear.[48] In a situation of great social fluidity, detectives very often found themselves stranded, supported neither by the salesclerks nor by the customers. An article about female detectives that appeared in the *New York Evening Post* at the turn of the century outlined the dimensions of the problem: "In spite of safeguards the disappearance of stock persists and the detective is constantly alert to discover the means of its disappearance. She watches from balconies, cash desks, stairs and other elevations and makes a point of learning the character and habits of each individual in the store."[49]

The use of women in store detection emerged as a specific line of defense in the late nineteenth century. If they considered them at all, the shopping public thought of store detectives as rather dim figures, shadowy men. Policemen were men, most "private eyes" were men, and so were a high percentage of store detectives.[50] But women had held a place in store protection from the initial development of the shopping bazaar. Beginning with the lone woman on the Macy force in 1870, the number of women in detection gradually increased until they comprised ten percent of the protective departments in some stores, and even more in large stores like Macy's.[51] Because women comprised the vast majority of the customers, women detectives were far less noticeable than were men. As in so many other aspects of the department store world, appearances meant everything. "Women detectives can go everywhere. They can work their way into crowds . . . at the women's underwear counters, women's hosiery counters, and in the fur and jewelry departments, they are invaluable."[52]

Male detectives simply stood out at a bargain counter. Consequently, men in protection and selling alike were relegated to specific areas, much as women were in the management hierarchy. A *New York Tribune* interview in 1905 with the chief of detectives at one of the large New York stores unconsciously revealed the continuing prominence given to class as well as gender differences in the stores. Detectives, the chief said, "are always dressed in street clothes . . . in thoroughly up-to-date style, the idea being that their appearance shall not serve in any way to give a clew to their calling."[53] Had working-class detectives dressed in the clothes they normally wore, they would have stood out among the customers. Appearing to be what they were not, detectives, in turn, had to judge shoppers by their appearances.

Detection was as a new role for women, and the daily press called attention to it whenever possible. An advertisement for female store detectives in 1901 asked for a "bright, intelligent woman," gifted with a large amount of tact and intuition, as well as a quick eye and a level head. In commenting on this advertisement, the *Tribune* added that the woman detective must not be troubled with nerves or be imaginative or easily excited, but she must be ladylike in dress and manner and appearance.[54] The requirements were a demanding amalgam of so-called feminine virtues and masculine skills. An article in the *New York Evening Post* appearing at just about the same time called women's detective work in the department stores "a difficult profession" and said it was hard to get women for this work because of its association with the "seamy side of life." Nevertheless, the *Post* supported this type of work for women; feeling, perhaps, that their feminine role-playing skills equipped them particularly well to be store detectives. Traditionally nonconfrontational, women had the ability to blend in and pass unnoticed among other shoppers. Although the women had to be be "worldly wise" in judging human nature, according to the reporter, those gender-related attributes of tact and "a fund of patience" were the prime qualities, "for detecting is often slow work."[55]

Descriptions of women detectives, like descriptions of female shoppers, were cast in the common idiom of the late nineteenth century. In that *New York Tribune* interview of 1905, the unnamed chief of detectives praised his female operatives in these terms:

> "I want to say right here that they are the slickest in the business. Why, this little woman here," and he indicated an active little person who had just entered his office, "is worth a whole bunch of some male detectives." The object of the chief's praise made a pretty grimace and with an airy toss of her head proceeded to report on a case. . . .[56]

Some of the women who became store cops attained a modest notoriety. Helen Parsons was a respected professional who was in great demand in New York City department stores in 1905.[57] Mary Plunkett, another well-known store detective, spent her entire career at Macy's. Plunkett's work history was a familiar one. She went to Macy's in 1879 and became a detective in 1888. "When I was a little girl in the store," Plunkett told the *New York Times* reporter, "I was detained to spy around. Now little girls do this for me."[58] She was so competent in her employee-*cum*-spy role that management decided to use her particular skills on a full-time basis. By 1895 her expertise as an antishoplifting dynamo was regularly reported in the newspapers, although there is no suggestion that it was thought to be more seemly for a woman to arrest another woman within the decidedly feminine confines of the late nineteenth-century department store.

An account of one of Plunkett's successes detailed the familiar story of a wealthy women arrested for shoplifting who carried a bank book in her own name showing a Dry Dock Savings Bank account for $1,231. The arrested woman became only the pretext for the story about "Mrs. Plunkett's clever work." Plunkett was patently a whiz at her job—"extraordinary tact and success . . . seldom mistaken" were the descriptions. Added to these encomiums, however, was this portrayal of Plunkett as she stepped up to the witness stand: "a youthful little body, with classic features, pale complexion and snooded brown hair, garbed in black to Quakerish simplicity, with dainty, flat-brimmed head gear."[59]

The stores and the newspapers patronized female detectives along with female customers. Although the "lady detectives" were professionals, with the authority that accompanied the position, their gender became paramount when they became the center of interest. Detection was outside woman's "natural" sphere, so even as they placed themselves in a man's role, women detectives had to appear as ladylike creatures who somehow made the job seem more humane.

Detectives did not advertise themselves, but employees knew, even if customers did not, that management anticipated dishonesty and relied on secret surveillance to combat it. Feeling, with some justification, that the use of private police was primarily directed against them, many clerks "distrusted the basic premise of detection."[60] For their part, detectives viewed the clerks as a group growing weary of "plodding honesty" and ultimately "pliant to temptations and tempters."[61]

The danger, of course, was that of a self-fulfilling prophecy. Benjamin Gitlow's testimony to the Senate Committee in 1912 was substantially accurate: ultimate success for many detectives meant proving a client's suspicions, whether about customers or employees, well founded. A contemporary description of William Pinkerton as "he wandered the aisles of the great State Street emporiums [in Chicago] watching for pickpockets and shoplifters" was certainly mirrored in the behavior of detectives in New York, yet the surveillance of employees and customers presented different problems.[62] In employee theft the emphasis was on prevention. Shoplifters did not steal from the stock room, but they presented even more difficult problems of detection and apprehension.

The surviving *Time Books* of the New York office of the Pinkerton Detective Agency cover the period from late 1873 through the end of 1920.[63] The agency offfered a "store inspection service" that promised "protection against shoplifters, pickpockets and other criminals; thefts by employees detected and dishonest schemes exposed." Pinkerton's clients included almost all the major New York City department stores at one time or another:

H. B. Claflin, H. O'Neil & Company, R. H. Macy, Siegel-Cooper, Arnold & Company, Stern Brothers, Ehrich Brothers, Bloomingdale Brothers, James A. Hearn & Son, and F. Loeser & Company in Brooklyn.[64] Detailing dates, account names, types of operation, operatives, time worked, and daily charges, the *Time Books* provide a picture of local Pinkerton operations for much of these forty-seven years and reinforce and extend the knowledge gained from more ephemeral sources.[65] In 1876, for instance, two operatives each spent from one-half to a full day "watching employees" in H. O'Neil & Company between September 24 and October 3. In December 1881, five different operatives spent a total of forty-one days on the lookout for shoplifters and pickpockets at Ehrich Brothers. Macy's hired Pinkerton detectives to combat "petty robberies" over a nineteen-day period in February and early March 1883, and the popular Brooklyn store, Frederick Loeser & Company, employed three different Pinkertons to guard against shoplifters for eighteen days before Christmas in December 1889.[66]

Pinkertons worked only a few consecutive days on a particular job, although an operative's name often reappears in the *Time Books* days or even weeks later at a given store. Engaged in an ongoing game of cat and mouse, detectives and shoplifters sought anonymity, each trying not to look the part. Often they succeeded. "It is about equally difficult to spot a detective and a shoplifter," the *New York Times* explained in a full-page spread on "Shoplifting in the Great Stores" in April 1908.[67]

December was a month of increased shoplifting, and the Pinkertons in Ehrich's and Loeser's probably beefed up the stores' regular protection during the Christmas season.[68] The normal Wanamaker contingent of four or five detectives became thirty between Thanksgiving and New Year's 1901.[69] According to Henry Blades, chief detective at Wanamaker's at this time, the deterrent was aimed particularly at the professional shoplifter. Managers privately conceded they could effectively do little to reduce the problem of the amateur shoplifter during the holiday rush, but with the professionals they were more sanguine. "Word gets out," Blades told a *DGE* reporter. "Let it once be known that this or that department store is well policed and half the battle is won." Similarly, Macy's employed more than fifty detectives during the 1906 "season," reportedly both to watch the customers and to guard them against pickpockets.[70] In the topsy-turvy department store world, everyone had dual roles to play.

Each December the *Dry Goods Economist* felt compelled to advise increased vigilance and caution in the stores. "It is advantageous to have a 'stock watch' behind the counter during the holiday season or at a special sale," was the typical warning.[71] In his column "Beware of Light Fingers," which appeared in early December 1892, the Wide-Awake Retailer reminded his already security-conscious readers that "this is the shoplifters' harvest time, and it behooves every clerk to keep his eyes open and his wits about him, . . . save profits and avoid annoyance!" Of particular concern was the woman shopper who purchased trivial articles and was "nearly all the time desirous of having something 'back there' shown to her." An editorial the same month suggested the use of a special "detective number" whereby the clerk could shout out a number and "call the attention of the floorwalker or store detective to suspicious actions at his counter without, at the same time, putting the shoplifter on her guard."[72] In a later decade Filene's instituted this very system. Calling out "212" was a signal for immediate assistance, very much akin to the "Hey, Rube" call at the circus.[73] Clerks, even though under suspicion themselves, were to be alert and cooperative; they were to make themselves into "effective auxiliaries to the detective force and from them, [it was hoped] will come many, if not most, of the valuable clues."[74]

As with detectives, the distrust of saleswomen as a group gradually lessened. Wanamaker's often used clerks to supplement their in-store police force. Detective Henry Blades proudly recounted how one of his best detectives was formerly a salesgirl at the fancy goods counter. "She gave our sleuths so many excellent clues as to suspicious shoppers—clues that we successfully followed—that we persuaded her to join our staff."[75] Clerks and detectives were cast as a team. Together they were to "see the person," to understand the involuntary disclosures of personality and character that would give important clues to shopping behavior.[76]

It seemed vitally important to be able to read human nature from physical clues, such as the shape of the head or the placement of the nose, and phrenology had a strong following in the last decades of the nineteenth century among those entrusted with policing the department store.[77] Long after it was discredited as a pseudo-science, phrenology remained an important part of the mystique of selling as well as protection. The job of the stores was handling people, particularly women; and the idea that salespeople, floorwalkers, and detectives could judge the character of those they dealt with was an assurance that success was possible. "Each man is a sealed book [which] will repay careful study," was a commonly held assumption.[78] An Arnold & Constable manager told a reporter for the *Daily Tribune* that they rarely had much trouble with either shoplifters or kleptomaniacs, "for we believe in the old adage, that 'an ounce of prevention is worth a pound of cure.' We, therefore, have a private detective, who is a skilled physiognomist . . . and who watches everyone that comes into the store."[79]

Both clerks-as-detectives and the bona fide detectives were thought to have a better than average understanding of human nature, body language, and the human face. It seemed to be part of the dry-goods mythology. A. T. Stewart always felt "the best clerk is a reader of human nature."[80] The manager of one large Sixth Avenue emporium reportedly insisted that good store detectives had to be good judges of people and of faces.[81] And J. N. Daggett, the superintendent of Wanamaker's at the turn of the twentieth century, held firmly to the belief that "guilt is self conscious."[82] Convinced that an individual's "temper" was reflected on her face, Daggett thought a suspicious or startled look often gave the first clue to the possibility of shoplifting, and the keen clerk or detective ought to be able to spot it. The vast amount of casual and undetected shoplifting proved the Daggetts wrong, of course, but store officials continued to believe that the undereducated salesclerks and private cops possessed intuitive skills that fitted them for particular aspects of their jobs. Wanamaker chief detective Blades explicitly supported this way of thinking in the interview he gave to the *Tribune*. He declared that the store rarely recruited from the police, but looked instead for those in the store with the detective instinct. "Good detectives are born not appointed. God makes them, not a boss. If a man hasn't the detective instinct he can't be inoculated with it."[83]

A leader of the movement for practical vocational training for saleswomen in the early twentieth century, Lucinda Prince classified the thirty-six types of customers floor personnel were likely to encounter.[84] Her popular notions of personality offered catchy formulas and levels of explanation that students at The Union School for Salesmanship in Boston could easily grasp and, they hoped, employ. Central to Prince's analysis was the widely disseminated idea that both clerks and detectives could "see" and thus "understand" the customer. Even the well-known and respected Diana Hirschler (welfare manager at Filene's in the early years of the twentieth century and author of *The Art of Retail Selling*, a textbook for salespeople) warned her students that they dealt with a mind "hidden by an exterior which you must learn to interpret . . . you deal with that which you cannot see and yet must understand."[85] Part sales psychology, part defensive reaction, Hirschler's instructions were a response to the ambiguous, often chaotic department store environment.

The importance of these diverse formulations lay in the belief (and hope) that store personnel could in fact control the situation on the shop floor. If what lay behind the mask was in fact written on the face and discernible to the keen eye, clerks and detectives would have had immediate and valuable clues to behavior. Such knowledge might even have ensured that all who left the store with merchandise had paid for it.

Police detectives were divided on whether or not a potential shoplifter unconsciously revealed herself. William B. Watts and Benjamin Eldridge, two high-ranking officials of the Boston Police Department, wrote a comprehensive survey of crime, which was published in 1897. While dealing primarily with the professional criminals of the late nineteenth century (whom they jocularly dubbed "rascals"), Watts and Eldridge included a fair amount on that "constant nuisance," the amateur shoplifter. Citing the detectives, floorwalkers, and "other employees of the establishments" who were "instructed to keep a sharp lookout for those thieves," they confidently concluded that such random shoplifting was all but a dead issue. The system of store detection was "so extended and complete that none except the most sly and expert shoplifters can steal any considerable amount before they are arrested." The professionals received summary dismissal as well. "They are so well known," Watts and Eldridge wrote, "that they are rarely suffered to enter the stores."[86] The two detectives never made clear what they based these wildly inaccurate perceptions upon, but it was not on the ability of store personnel to unmask the potential shoplifter "through an understanding of the size, shape and general appearance of the head and face."[87] Watts and Eldridge maintained that there were "no phrenological signs that enable us to distinguish the criminal from the non-criminal. If malefactors betrayed themselves by their faces, the police would have less trouble."[88]

In any case, many detectives were fooled by the appearance of the new breed of shoplifter. Because the strongly held prejudice about intuitive perception merged with the tendency to judge women on their bearing and appearance, particularly the outward manifestations of class, store detectives too often forgot the well-worn maxim, "the good is not always the comrade of the beautiful."[89] Recounting a thirty-year career that began in 1899, former New York City policeman and detective Cornelius Willemsc described how shoplifters regularly misled store detectives, and he related what he said was a typical case history:

> Catherine had the manner that makes department store managers bow on sight. Hard boiled store detectives would give her a glance of respect whenever she appeared. She *looked* to be exactly what she represented herself to be, the wife of a rich and distinguished citizen. . . . Her expensive clothing, her cultivated voice, her treatment of department store staffs were just what might be expected from a matron of the "400."[90]

Value-laden language and description preserved the dominant social ideology of class; yet Catherine Bolch was a shoplifter who operated successfully in Siegel-Cooper, Macy's, Wanamaker's, and Abraham & Straus.

Normally there was no discernible interaction between detectives and store customers. Many, if not most, women were oblivious to surveillance by ubiquitous floorwalkers and clerks and were unaware of the presence of private detectives. Only occasionally did the antagonism between the two groups surface; but when it did, it was bitter.

However the store detective perceived the customer, theirs was a naturally antagonistic relationship, full of complex undertones of class, and often of gender, which surfaced only when the detective was doing his job—preventing theft. Placed in the department stores to maintain the rights in property of the owner, the police became surrogates of the class from which the large majority of the shoppers came. Almost always of the working class themselves, the store police were employed to protect the privileges of the propertied middle class, but this often meant interfering with members of this group—detaining them, searching them, and when necessary turning them over to the city authorities. It was a social situation that subtly precluded action.

The furore in the aftermath of the Phelps arrest at Macy's demonstrated to the stores just how vulnerable they were. Not only was there the sudden and very real possibility of legal action for false arrest, there was the almost greater threat to the public image of the stores.[91] Owner-managers looked upon newspaper publicity and the "accompanying notoriety attached to such proceedings as undesirable and harmful."[92] A year after the Macy brouhaha, a member of McCreery & Company told a reporter for the *New York World* that their managers never had anyone arrested unless their guilt was irrefutable: "the arrest of an innocent party would be a terrible mistake to make and it has never been *our misfortune* to make such an error in judgement." (Italics mine.)[93] Macy management took refuge in publicly denying that any problem existed. After the plague of shoplifters that culminated in the arrest of Elizabeth Phelps in 1870, "one of the firm" told a *Daily Tribune* reporter in 1883:

> We have not prosecuted more than a half a dozen cases in the last five years and those were all regular thieves. . . . Now and then there is an unpleasant scene in this little office when some richly dressed customer is brought before us and accused by our detective of secreting some of our property. The story is always the same, a "sudden impulse, no necessity, will pay twenty times the value of the stolen article, only for Heaven's sake do not expose me!" As it is we can rest assured that the experiment will not be repeated twice.[94]

Merchants were understandably reluctant to make indiscriminate arrests or to challenge customers. And for their part, customers were not to suspect this dark underside of consumption.

Arrests were usually made as discreetly as possible and with as little fuss as the detained customer permitted. It was the announced wish of one house "that matters of this sort be conducted as secretly as possible . . . a high class store had rather lose hundreds of dollars than be associated in the public mind with police court trials and sensational arrests."[95] Zola described an incident in the Ladies' Paradise that captured the anxieties surrounding the arrest of a casual thief. A woman was caught shoplifting and taken to a dressing room to be searched. There were raised voices and threats of sending for the police while "three or four customers buying gloves stood looking on frightened." The scene ended quickly, for the assistant manager realized what was happening and removed the suspect, the saleswomen searching her, and the detective to another part of the store.[96] Any possible commotion or hint of scandal damaging to the reputation of the store or the respectable woman was to be avoided in this world of fantasy. With image uppermost in their minds, managers were afraid of the attendant publicity and possible loss of trade; they were worried about offending the customer, her family, and her friends even when she was caught stealing!

Wanamaker chief detective Henry Blades gave the *DGE* a revealing interview in 1901—thirty years after the Phelps incident—and described the almost excessive "caution and discrimination used in making arrests."[97] Detectives had to be absolutely certain of finding hidden articles on a suspected shoplifter and even more certain that these articles had indeed been stolen, that there was no other plausible explanation. Seeing a woman take something was not enough; detectives had to exercise what Blades euphemistically called "judgment." Merchants obviously did not encourage random arrests of women who looked to be wealthy and well connected. Blades acknowledged that overzealousness was one of his chief problems: detectives "imagine that they are not making a showing—not earning their salary—unless constantly dragging offenders up to the office. So anxious are they to show results that they are apt to overdo it." The problem at Wanamaker's, Blades acknowledged, had reached such serious dimensions that he had to instruct new detectives never to make an arrest "without calling my old staff for consultation."[98] The situation appears to have completely reversed itself; enthusiastic detectives now had to be restrained, rather than shoplifting customers.

Blades was not alone in recognizing the explicit class bias exhibited by cautious merchants. Macy detective Mary Plunkett told a *New York Times* reporter of the "dreadful temptation and tantalization . . . when you're morally certain, and even more, that a customer has stolen and has the plunder in her possession." For her part, the fear of being wrong, "the barest possibility of a mishap," controlled the impulse to act. Slow and deliberate action was the only way to be absolutely certain of "what you think you see." Plunkett charged that "some stores, or rather their detectives, appear to plume themselves on the arrests made." This forthright woman concluded with a puzzling warning: "It is not well to try to make a record of arrests; that in time might develop zeal, and zeal is dangerous."[99] Commenting on a widely publicized suit for false arrest, a Boston merchant supported Plunkett's assessment: "I never allow a detective to arrest, or even accost a suspected shoplifter in my store. If he thinks he has caught one, he must immediately send for me. I politely invite the suspected one to kindly step into my office. By her actions at this invitation I can generally tell whether she is guilty or innocent. . . ."[100] This merchant's solution to shoplifting carried with it an ovbious defense of class interests. Unquestionably, the reverberations from the Phelps incident lingered, influencing the reactions of detectives as well as managers.

The steps merchants took to control shoplifting were part of a numbers game; expanded surveillance during the Christmas holidays was just one element of a constantly increased level of vigilance. New methods of retailing and display required new levels of careful observation. Special sales and promotions and seasonal openings also became occasions for strengthened protection and often remained a permanent part of the store's defensive posture. The new glass counters, better lighting, and strategically placed mirrors could forestall some of the depredations, but only large numbers of watchful employees and detectives could even begin to thwart the more determined shoplifter. Calling shoplifting "this growing evil," the *Dry Goods Economist* wrote of the necessity of "a special service in the large retail stores and a more positive recognition of the problem."[101]

Stores that had had a single detective in the 1870s and 1880s had full-blown protection departments of ten to fifteen employees by the early twentieth century. Only Lord & Taylor was reluctant to concede any need for such employees. A member of that firm told a *New York Tribune* reporter in 1883 that they were always on the lookout for the professional shoplifter, but most of those women were known to store personnel. "We employ no regular means of detection, for a detective's time would be wasted utterly in our store." The Lord & Taylor man added, rather smugly, "The amateur shoplifter is rarely found in the rank of life from which we draw the majority of our customers."[102] For the remainder of the century, Lord & Taylor continued to deny that their customers could also be shoplifters.

Barring Lord & Taylor's disclaimer, virtually all department stores employed detectives as a permanent part of their labor force. In an 1883 survey of a group of New York dry-goods stores, Arnold & Constable; Simpson, Crawford & Simpson; Ridley & Company; and Ehrich Brothers all admitted that they had hired detectives in an effort to curb shoplifting.[103] Macy's, of course, had them in their employ, and although a member of the firm denied that shoplifting was much of a problem in the 1880s, he acknowledged the presence of "a policeman stationed on the sidewalk outside, a plain-clothes man inside and a corps of many hundred watchful detectives in the shape of our sales people. That's the secret. Our own people are continually on the watch."[104] If newspaper reports of shoplifting arrests were correct, Altman's, Stern's, and Bloomingdale's employed in-house detectives as well.[105]

By the late nineteenth century, the stores were rapidly losing ground to the shoplifters. With more of everything—more services, more goods, and more sophisticated and elaborate displays in new buildings designed to sell both merchandise and the image of the "House" itself—the dry-goods palaces had enough daily customers to populate a medium-size city.

While not typical of many establishments, Siegel-Cooper represented the trend of development at this period. Advertising that it was "A City in Itself," the New York store was gigantic by any measure. Fronting on an entire Sixth Avenue block between 18th and 19th Streets—the center of what came to be known as the

Ladies' Mile—Siegel-Cooper encompassed eighteen acres of floor space and was nearly twice as large as any other establishment in New York City.[106] What people remembered, however, was the main aisle; "a broad central avenue" (forty feet wide) leading to a fountain under a rotunda surrounded by twenty-two marble pillars. In the middle stood an exact thirteen-foot-high replica, in marble and gilded bronze, of the Statue of the Republic from the Court of Honor at the World's Columbian Exposition.[107]

Such grandeur and monumental size does not explain why shoplifters seemed to be getting the upper hand, but the carnival atmosphere found in some of the new department stores must certainly have contributed to the sense of rules' being suspended and normal inhibitions' being cast off in the anonymity of the crowd. Shoplifting thrived in the "buzz and excitement" of a busy store; and even after the turn of the century, when merchants were willing to publicly acknowledge the seriousness of the losses, the courts viewed the first-time shoplifter as "a woman who has simply yielded to temptation," and treated her accordingly.[108]

Throughout the 1890s there were greater stock shortages and, for a while at least, more publicity if not more arrests. Articles in all the important trade journals highlighted the problem and discussed possible ways to effectively combat it.[109] Technology had progressed as far as it could for the moment. Descriptions of the new Lord & Taylor store on Fifth Avenue in 1914 mentioned an electric push-button under each counter, but this was the only novel antishoplifting device until the middle of the century. The button was to alert the store's chief detective, who would then "flash a signal to a section in which he knew a detective was stationed. The detective immediately phoned to the chief and was told to get busy and where to do so."[110] It seems a cumbersome process but probably worked better than shouted codes or hurried whispers between saleswomen.

In the decades of their rapid growth, the major dry-goods bazaars confronted many similar problems, notably those of personnel, in-store organization, and application of technology; but none of the problems associated with growth were as intransigent as that of shoplifting. Hindering the stores' response to the increasing incidence of customer theft was their inability to speak with any sense of consensus. A possible answer to the problem seemed to lie in combined policing efforts among an associated group of stores. The formation of the Retail Dry-Goods Association of New York in 1895 was both a practical solution and a utilitarian response that signaled the first change in the individualistic stance of the stores.[111]

Association did two things for the protective posture of the department stores: it enabled them to make, if not enforce, common policy, and it gave them an added measure of clout with municipal governments. Through the efforts of the Retail Trade Board of the Boston Chamber of Commerce, for instance, an attorney was hired to represent the larger stores in shoplifting cases in the courts. Individually, the Boston stores promised to toughen their stance against shoplifters—all shoplifters: store detectives would be less hamstrung in carrying out their primary responsibilities, and management would follow through on prosecutions.[112] It was hoped that an attorney who worked for all the stores and specialized in prosecuting shoplifters would be less susceptible to the combined pressures of class and social status, and that the court, in its turn, would more readily punish those brought before it.

The Boston Municipal Court heard 638 cases from the sixteen member stores that first year, 1909: a record 516 received some form of punishment ranging from jail to probation; 18 were "put on file"; of the remaining 104 there was no mention.[113] Just who the shoplifters were, professionals or first-time amateurs, remains unclear; nor is it clear whether the determination to prosecute continued, but there is no doubt that association pushed the stores and the courts to view shoplifting as a problem on a par with other forms of theft. Such small numbers, however, suggest that either most shoplifters were not detected or that many cases were handled informally, as in the past.

Years before the formation of any such organized defense, New York City merchants, speaking through their new trade organization, had mutually pledged arrest of any and all shoplifters, "without prejudice or favor," alleging it was not in the interest of any store to allow a shoplifter to escape punishment. Though stores, thereafter, could place the onus on the trade association, "thus avoiding offense to the customer," at no time were they actually committed to the arrest of shoplifters unless they were known to be professionals.[114] Collectively and abstractly, merchants wanted shoplifting checked; on an individual basis, none wanted it stopped at the price of adverse publicity.

Two examples, both from 1896, suggest the typical, unchanging attitude toward "respectable shoplifters" by New York stores in the decades under consideration. The case of a fifty-three-year-old widow, Julia Furlong, was typical. Described as a "very respectable looking woman, past middle-age," Mrs. Furlong was seen by the detective at Namm's in Brooklyn "to take a table cloth and a pocket book and secret them." She must also have taken articles from Loeser's because the article concluded with the comment, "Mrs. Furlong will probably be discharged as neither the superintendent at Namm's or at Loeser's cared to make a charge against her." When twenty-three-year-old Margaret Johnstone was arrested in Liebman's dry-goods bazaar on Fulton Street, with "cloth enough for two dresses, a white shirt and two ostrich feathers (which she said she had purchased) under her wrap," the proprietor pleaded with the court for a suspended sentence. "This young woman comes from a respectable family, and I am sure that she did not intend to steal but was overcome by the opportunity presented and a sudden dishonest impulse."[115]

After the turn of the century, cases involving so-called impulsive amateurs were usually hushed up, much as they always had been; and, according to one retail journal, "the inference is that one is quite safe in stealing from a store if reasonable precautions are used."[116] While merchants rationally understood that arrest and prosecution and intensive newspaper coverage might eliminate many of the losses, they were not prepared to act in any consistent way. Only the fact of the problem and its scope were examined within the trade organizations; there was little change in the stores' internal policy.[117]

Although the National Retail Dry-Goods Association (NRDGA) hired the William J. Burns Detective Agency in 1910 "to provide for its members a more thorough protection from shoplifters and those who make a practice of filching from department store counters," this caused little forward movement within individual stores.[118] Affiliation meant three things for the NRDGA members. First, it meant the installation of a metal plaque stating that the store was "A member of the NRDGA, Protected by the William J. Burns International Detective Agency Inc." Burns naïvely assured the stores that the sign alone would act as a preventative. "The Detective Agency," he wrote, "is known and feared by criminals throughout the country who, at the sight of the sign, do not know how many operatives of the Agency may be watching them."[119] Second, it meant the issuance of monthly "Protective Department Bulletins" beginning in 1912. These bulletins contained "Most Wanted" photographs of professional shoplifters, and feature articles with titles such as "Shoplifters and Store Thieves," "A Talk to Employees," and "Beware of Pickpockets." Third, it meant procuring the services of Burns detectives "skilled in retail and department store work in the capacity of salesmen and women, floorwalkers, house detectives, shipping clerks and others," which provides confirmation once again of bogus employees in the "secret service" of the firm, watching and reporting.[120]

The association with Burns meant very little in the apprehension of the middle-class shoplifter. Burns was geared toward catching the professional thief. Though the agency recognized the problems the stores faced with the amateurs, they said very little about them, relying on the knowledge that the store was under their surveillance to deter the more aggressive variety. As had been the case since the time of Rowland Macy, it was left entirely to the stores themselves to deal with the problem, if they would.

Detectives, clerks and floorwalkers, and an occasional assistant manager were charged with preventing shoplifting. They had to produce, but they had to exercise infinite judgment while protecting the store and its merchandise. Never at any time did management "go public" with the problem; other than the occasional newspaper article about shopping in the stores or about the occupations of detectives, there were only the infrequent reports of unaccountable arrests of well-to-do women for shoplifting. Like abortion in the late nineteenth century, shoplifting was something about which few women would admit any awareness. Unless it happened in the family or to a close acquaintance, knowledge of this sort was something people preferred not to have. The stores downplayed the problem to such an extent that, publicly at least, it did not exist.

If management had advertised the fact of shoplifting by the

noncriminal class, they would have had to acknowledge surveillance, and this they were not prepared to do. The aura of shopping would have been marred by the knowledge that someone was watching. Detectives, and later protection departments, were perpetually and historically "cloaked in mystery." Marshall Field & Company was so reluctant to admit that there were detectives in the store that they called them "special service" personnel; the chief detective was the "special service chief."[121]

Although a protective philosophy was essential, there was resistance to acknowledging it. It was at this ideological level that store detectives often ran into difficulty. When they intervened, when they stopped a woman from leaving a store and accused her of shoplifting, detectives were doing what they were hired to do: protecting the property of the institution. Leaving aside the question of over-zealousness, which unquestionably was a factor in the proliferation of suits for false arrest, it is evident nevertheless that store detectives were in a particularly precarious position. To do their job with any degree of thoroughness required interacting with many shoppers. Store owners wanted shoplifting controlled—there was never any hope of eliminating it—but they did not want to interfere with customers. Management did not really want the store detective to act, if in doing so, the customer reacted. They would rather lose the merchandise than create a scene or alienate a patron over a two-dollar pair of stockings. Censoring the problem materially increased shortages, of course, but owner-managers seemed more than willing to accept stock losses in return for high profits and good will. The possibility of scandal or a repetition of the Phelps-Macy incident was sufficient to inhibit the most determined of managers.

In that first widely publicized incident of shoplifting by a middle-class woman the onus rested on the merchant and his employees—clerks, floorwalkers, and detectives. The issue of class was paramount. It was to remain so. But as the public grew accustomed to the idea that respectable women did in fact take merchandise from the stores without the formality of payment, the blame shifted, subtly, to the women themselves, but not in a way that would hold them accountable. Explanations now centered on their physiology: it betrayed them and became the culprit.

6

―――――•∞•―――――

Shoplifting Ladies

The Kleptomaniac, Edwin S. Porter's 1905 silent movie, gave powerful definition to the late nineteenth-century female shoplifter. Dealing directly with the pattern of relations that had developed within class, gender, and consumerism in America, Porter told the parallel but very different stories of the thefts committed by two women. The story is simple. A wealthy woman is arrested for shoplifting in Macy's. In court the elegantly attired defendant is accompanied by her husband and a frock-coated lawyer. She is treated with sympathy and given a chair. The two men are treated with deference; they are obviously important. The Macy detectives who argue the case have no chance; the woman goes free over their strenuous objections. In the same courtroom, a poor woman who has stolen a loaf of bread for her starving children goes to jail. Justice, Porter says in this biting social commentary, is not blind, but blinded by money and power.[1]

What made the movie work so well, what made such a blunt point seem more subtle and compelling, was the popular acceptance of a stereotype. American audiences recognized the kleptomaniac instantly. The nineteenth-century women who went "a-thieving" in the department stores had quickly become a type of cultural artifact, remarkable for the very fact that they were "Ladies." Far removed from the subculture of crime—the professional women shoplifters, pickpockets, and sneak thieves who, traditionally, had plagued merchants—these late nineteenth-century thieving women were from an entirely different class and background.[2] The new breed of shoplifter seemed to fly in the face of all previously understood relations of crime, class, and gender.

In April 1908, after years of reporting on shoplifting by the "fair fine ladies," the *New York Times* still wondered at the phenomenon.

> It seems impossible that these beautifully gowned, gracefully moving creatures, all polish and delicacy and poise, should harbor among them all one single thief. The word seems absurd, an affront to their well-bred faces and their well-filled purses hanging on jeweled chains. And yet it is indeed from this class that the army of shoplifters is largely made up.[3]

A highly visible paradox to merchants and the public alike from the time of the Elizabeth Phelps–Rowland Macy furore in 1870, the middle-class woman shoplifter became the reverse image of the ideal woman shopper. Key elements of the nineteenth century's definition of "female" were worked into an image of female weakness that made sense of the shoplifting phenomenon. But this cultural construct, however serviceable to consumer society and middle-class respectability, profoundly undermined the self-respect of women as individuals and as a group, even while freeing them of the onus of criminality.

The problem of shoplifting exposed the contradictions at the heart of department store consumerism. Middle-class women were the backbone of the stores' clientele, and the shoplifters among them, who seemed to appear so suddenly and in such great numbers in the dry-goods bazaars after 1870, were indistinguishable from other shoppers. But they represented a new category of crime as well as a new social danger. The controversy was not simply over arresting shoplifting suspects. Definitive action would have meant action against the very group merchants were loath to accuse, and in many instances dared not accuse. The interrelation between the store and the middle-class customers was such that there was a widespread reluctance to make demands on the customers even when they were acting against the interests of the institution. Management preferred not to "catch" many of these women, and given this reluctance, the problem ultimately proved insoluble.

Obviously, a few middle-class women were arrested and some names were published in the daily newspapers. Personal embarrassment and family shame must have been high in these instances. However, because of the special characteristics of the crime and of the group committing the crime, there was no immediate moral isolation of the arrested women and little in the way of harsh or judgmental pronouncements by the stores. Merchants were well aware of the fact that exposure of shoplifters fascinated the public, and too often publicity meant sympathy for the thieves.[4] After the well-publicized arrests of four respectable women in Lynn, Massachusetts, the *Boston Globe* commented on the "many . . . expressions of sorrow and sympathy heard for the women who had been tempted and fell."[5] Newspaper articles about the four women dramatized just how ensnared late nineteenth-century men and women were by the phenomenon. At the bail hearing, the reporter for the *New York Times* described a scene bordering on hysteria. A mob of women filled the court room, the corridors, and the streets in the vicinity of the court.

> Some of the best known and most highly respected women in this city came in carriages or walked and stood with their sisters outside the doors waiting anxiously for the signal to enter. . . . When finally some of the accused women were allowed to depart, the waiting crowd surged around them, endeavoring to get a glimpse of their faces which were concealed by thick veils and even tried to look into the carriages in waiting to drive them away.[6]

The reporter concluded that "such a scene was never before witnessed here."

The Lynn shoplifters wondered what their friends would say, and, according to the *Globe*, one of the women "broke down," but there is little evidence that there was any social ostracism of such women; quite the contrary. Newspapers, magazines, and fiction in various guises all suggest an intense curiosity about and a sentimental attachment to such "unfortunate women." The object of gentle and generally silly satire in a variety of literary forms, the lady shoplifter was a nonthreatening figure, often seen as irresponsible, more childlike than adult, unable to resist momentary temptation and ready to succumb to the "lust of possession." The popular image of the middle-class shoplifter, sometimes called a kleptomaniac, was that of victim.[7]

Beyond periodic determined pronouncements about the scourge by retail trade groups by the 1890s, only in the occasional newspaper editorial was there ever any serious condemnation of the woman herself.[8] The *Boston Globe* took note of the public's fascination with the massive shoplifting caper uncovered in Lynn and warned that "education and social position" should not make these women exempt from the fullest penalties of the law. The excuse of "pride and vanity" must not mark their escape from such punishment as would be meted out to the humblest working girl in Boston guilty of a similar offense.[9]

Despite their ovbious reluctance to act, in the face of substantial losses department stores were forced to confront the problem of the middle-class shoplifter. The Retail Dry-Goods Association of New York offered one solution—prosecution—but the member stores never consistently supported such a hard line.

The situation in New York during 1904 and 1905 demonstrates the ambivalence of the stores toward the middle-class shoplifter. A spokesman for the association announced in the *New York Times* that shoplifting losses for 1905 had increased significantly and were expected to reach an astonishing $500,000. This was followed by the claim that the stores were fully prepared to deal with the depredations during the Christmas season already under way. Headlined "Harvest Time of The Shoplifter," the article was in fact a report on the state of the art in New York City. In what was to become a perennial threat/promise, the Dry-Goods Association declared, "No mercy is to be shown to shoplifters, all are to be punished to the limit of the law, no matter what 'influence' there may be behind them."[10] Obviously the prospect of such huge dollar losses demanded a tough stance, but in fact such pronouncements remained little more than that. There would be a spurt of selective shoplifting arrests accompanied by an occasional jail sentence, but it was a hit or miss situation at best, and publicity, which might have deterred some of the thefts, was kept to a minimum.[11]

A perfect example of this contradictory attitude towards shoplifters was revealed in the account of the arrest of a socially prominent woman in November 1904. "Lawyer's Wife Accused" ran the headline in the *New York Times*. Mrs. Caroline Hobart, a name everyone agreed was fictitious, was arrested after being observed taking several pins from a jewelry counter in a well-known 23rd Street store. Coming at the height of one of the sporadic efforts by the New York Retail Dry-Goods Association "to restrict as much as possible this form of theft," the arrest of the woman became a real problem for the judge, store detectives, and managers alike. Special Sessions Magistrate Martin Whitman made his feeling very clear in the overblown prose typical of the period. "This is one of the saddest cases that has ever come to my attention. Here is a woman who is the wife of one of the most respected members of the bar of New Jersey and a mother of some very promising children." But prodded by the determination of the Dry-Goods Association to pursue these cases, Whitman felt compelled to hold Mrs. Hobart for trial, "much as I would any other person."[12]

The store manager appeared in Whitman's court the next day and attempted to withdraw the charge. "We have made an investigation and have learned that this woman is a member of one of the best families in the city and, moreover, that she has been suffering from severe illness for three years. We believe that in this instance she committed the theft under stress of some sudden mental defection."[13] Here was the essential contradiction: A socially prominent, wealthy woman had given patronage to a store, and even when the woman was caught stealing, management did not want to jeopardize that relationship. Here, too, was the basic confrontation between the courts and the medical profession. Was this theft or disease? Was the woman who called herself Caroline Hobart suffering from a physical or mental disorder, or was she simply a shoplifter who relied on the court to treat her as it had countless other middle-class women? Was this form of shoplifting to be exonerated as a disease or prosecuted as a crime?[14] In this case the ambiguities and unanswered questions remain. Apologizing that he had a duty to perform as a public official, Judge Whitman remanded Mrs. Hobart for trial in spite of the manager's attempt to withdraw from the case. There is no further mention of Mrs. Hobart in any of the newspapers.

Occasionally judges were determined to prosecute. When John Wanamaker attempted to drop charges against a customer arrested for shoplifting in December 1882, the judge was adamant. Wanamaker asked his lawyers to intervene and stop the procedure.

> I wrote a note to the Magistrate on the 25th of December saying that I did not desire to prosecute the case; but I am informed that he refused to be governed by my note. . . . I do not wish to prosecute the case and wish you could withdraw the Bill before it is called by the Grand Jury.[15]

Faced with a typical action in 1893—wherein a genteel young woman "from one of the best known families in the city" was before him on the charge of stealing a piece of silk and two pairs of gloves at Stern Brothers—a Judge Voorhis displayed his skepticism. "I suppose," he said, "this is *another* of those respectable family cases."[16] The judge interpreted the situation perfectly. When Stern's discovered the woman's identity, they withdrew the charge and the case was dismissed.

When Siegel-Cooper detective George Bernard arrested two middle-class women for shoplifting, one who, it was charged, stole a bottle of perfume, and the other an umbrella, which she unsuccessfully attempted to hide in the folds of her skirt, the store quickly withdrew both complaints the following day: the explanation was that "restitution had been made."[17] The judge in the case was clearly unhappy with the situation, but felt he had little room to maneuver. "I don't see what I can do in the matter," Judge Olmsted said regretfully. With no complaint there could be no case.

These cases of shoplifting by the middle-class and socially prominent were replete with contradictions. Judges routinely faced instances of stores' backing off from prosecution, and without strong pressure from an interest group comparable to that which Whitman confronted, most judges felt they were left with no choice but to discharge the prisoner.

In May 1900, after presiding at yet another non-case, in which a store had withdrawn the charge against a young woman upon her father's personal appeal, one magistrate spoke out publicly on the situation, saying there were "altogether too many cases of this kind coming before the courts of late and an example should be made."[18] The magistrate agreed with his fellow judges that the indulgence of the courts made an already compromised situation that much worse, and he wanted to see more rigorous standards of fairness. "I have no sympathy with these women," another magistrate commented to the court the following year. "My sympathies are entirely with the storekeepers. I do not see how they manage to exist at all. They do not catch one in a hundred of the offenders, and as soon as an arrest is made the proprietor is besieged with requests to withdraw the complaint."[19]

Many judges were openly resentful of a system that forced them to participate in such visibly class-based justice. Whitman responded like many magistrates in Special Sessions who heard the shoplifting cases: while he maintained an unconcealed class alliance with many of the suspects, as a judge he was frustrated by a system that resolutely discriminated in favor of the middle class. But with stores rarely willing to prosecute, and defendants able to marshall doctors and lawyers to plead extenuating circumstances and friends to attest to their unblemished respectability, cases of shoplifting by middle-class women were routinely dismissed. Throughout this period it was generally accepted that the poor had simple motives for these crimes, while the rich had complex explanations that required sympathy and understanding.

One further example will demonstrate how a number of these strands interacted and temporarily worked in the woman's favor. Louisa Schloss was arrested for shoplifting in the Siegel-Cooper store in New York in December 1908. Caught leaving the store with a variety of small trinkets in her possession, the woman challenged the arrest on the ground of its absurdity. She was, she said, the wife of a respectable merchant, and she had credit accounts in all the big department stores. Her lawyer, Daniel Blumenthal, produced an affadavit from her physician, which read: "This is to certify that Mrs. Schloss is a patient of mine; that she is a very nervous woman, and I feel that it would be very injurious to her health if she had to go to court tonight. She is very subject to nervous shocks." In spite of the strong objections of store detectives David (Daniel) Kash and Rose McCauley, who swore in court that the woman was a thief, and that they had witnessed her repeated shoplifting, the woman went free. Siegel-Cooper overrode their own detectives and decided that "a mistake had been made." Indeed it had; the mistake was the arrest of a well-connected woman.[20]

Lawyers were obviously aware of the dual system in effect in the Special Session courts. In 1905, counsel for a woman suspected of being a professional shoplifter challenged the magistrate on this very issue; he demanded the same show of "mercy" for his client that the court had shown when it released a wealthy woman convicted of shoplifting the preceding week.[21] The plea, of course, failed. While Judge Whitman could refuse to dismiss the case against Mrs. Hobart, maintaining that "there should be no discrimination, and there will be none in this court whether the accused be poor or rich, socially prominent or unknown," other judges, feeling there was no strong public support for such a position, shied away from prosecuting the middle-class shoplifter.[22]

The severity toward shoplifters briefly apparent in 1904 and 1905 did not persist. Magistrates could agree with the Retail Dry-Goods Association and say that "shoplifting in New York [was] getting to be so bad that something must be done to stop it," but, like many other anticrime campaigns, their efforts were halfhearted and lacked the momentum to continue without constant pressure.[23] Much as stores seemed to agree that "none should recommend mercy in any case of the kind," in fact, they rarely supported this particular line. Their customers, honest or not, were much too important.[24]

Between the defiant pronouncements of the Retail Dry-Goods Association and the absolutely muted public posture of the stores themselves, the newspapers provided the only even halfway accurate accounts of the situation in the department stores. "Shoplifting is costing the stores thousands of dollars a day" was the message, but it was difficult to see just what the stores were really doing to defend themselves. In spite of official pronouncements by retail trade groups of forthcoming "wars on shoplifting" and "arrests without prejudice," no common policy was ever enforced for any extended period of time, and no two stores seemed to follow the same procedures. While they varied widely in their approach to the amateur shoplifter, rarely did any store prosecute the first offender, the faithful customer, or the woman of recognized social position. An unnamed detective succinctly summed up the situation: "Often they're so rich and influential—fine social standing, husbands in public life and the rest of it. You see it would be out of the question."[25]

The situation remained constant into the second decade of the twentieth century. Secrecy remained endemic. While acknowledging that stolen merchandise represented "sums sufficiently large to constitute a source of real anxiety . . . it is impossible to estimate accurately how much is lost in this way." The editors of the influential *Merchant's Record and Show Window* despaired of reducing the losses. Without publicity, the journal said, without the stores' determination to prosecute, the amateur shoplifter seemed to be in very little danger. In the few instances where the stores did act decisively, "pressure is generally brought to bear through friends of the culprit, nothing appears in the papers about any shoplifters being punished, and those who have a propensity for casual thievery [think] that none are ever detected."[26]

A letter in October 1917 from Frederick Kernochan, Chief Justice of the Court of Special Sessions of the City of New York, to Jesse Straus of R. H. Macy & Company, illustrates the accuracy of the observation. "I am indeed aware of how much the department stores suffer from the depredations of shoplifters," the judge wrote.

It is a problem in which myself and my colleagues are deeply interested, and I should be delighted to take the matter up with the Retail Dry-Goods Association. Undoubtedly, many people may think that we treat shoplifters with undue consideration. I should be glad to inform you of our reasons for so doing. We do feel that the complaining witnesses in these cases have a just ground for demanding severity, and it always has been a surprise to me that more pressure has not been brought upon the court from the standpoint of the complainants—urging severity.[27]

Margarete Bohme captured the fundamental impasse in her semidocumentary novel *The Department Store* when she wrote,

"Pilferings were not seriously regarded—so long as they were kept within reasonable bounds. The management took into consideration the 'suggestion' of tempting opportunities offered by the emporiums, and when the long-fingered ladies *were* caught in the act by the female house detectives, they were always allowed to go scatheless for a first offence."[28] Merchants knew their losses were not decreasing, just as they knew the amateur shoplifter was not a momentary aberration, but they seemed paralyzed by their own inability to come to terms with the situation. The contradictions of the new consumer ethos demanded expediency, and merchants and judges ultimately defined in terms of their own class interests who had committed a crime and who had not.[29]

The group of women who were the cause of the escalating losses and the object of all the concern were neither as rich as the stereotype would have us believe, nor poor in any observable, material way.[30] While the exact dimensions of the problem are unclear, the vital statistics of the women accused of shoplifting in the New York City department stores between 1870 and 1910 lack any distinguishing features. Assembled from reports in daily newspapers, the profile of the women who were caught and whose names entered the public record appear to represent the middle-class shopper.[31]

Popular understanding underscored medical "fact" to connect many important characteristics of shoplifters with the female life cycle, particularly the onset of middle age and the beginning of menopause. Yet of the ninety-seven women whose ages are given, the average age is thirty-six and a half, an age without any particular significance in the reproductive cycle. Many of the ages are probably estimates; occasionally the reporter guesses "between forty-five and fifty" or simply settles on "middle-aged." Of the 190 women in the sample, over one hundred women were "married"; a few were widowed, some were listed as "Miss," but for others there is no indication of marital status. All were white; only two were foreign born, and they were both wealthy Cubans.

Whatever their exact ages and specific nationalities, the largest number of women were in the middle stages of life—set in their domestic, housewifely roles, responsible for home, children and husbands. Age was significant not in its connection to the reproductive cycle but in what the women were doing: shopping. The overwhelmingly female presence in the department stores represents both the strength of conventional gender boundaries and the "social changes which had occurred in the day to day functioning of the urban middle-class home." Shopping denoted freedom from one sort of labor and signified, as well, the intricate texture of women's lives in which domestic work and leisure were often confused.[32]

A great many women were out-of-town visitors: Chicago; Dayton; Philadelphia; New Orleans; San Francisco; Canton, Ohio; Charlestown, Massachusetts; and Corning, New York, were a few of the more distant permanent addresses. Many of the women were from various parts of New Jersey, southern Connecticut, Westchester and Rockland Counties, and Brooklyn, and appeared to be in the city on legitimate shopping expeditions that culminated in their arrest for shoplifting. For women from the the more remote suburbs and smaller cities—such as Sophie Hall, the visitor from Wilmington, Delaware—the atmosphere in the large department stores must have been particularly intoxicating. The unusual crowds of women, the profusion of merchandise and choices, and the routine overselling contributed to what all observers agree was often an over-stimulating environment. We tend to forget that both the size and the special atmosphere in the stores were unique to large urban centers at the end of the nineteenth century.

The occupations of only three alleged shoplifters were specified: one woman worked as a milliner, another was an insurance agent, and the third, the wife of a suburban minister, was the superintendent of the primary department in the Sunday School of the Church of the Puritans in New York City.[33] Presumably, some of the other women, particularly the unmarried women, were employed; but statistically, most of these middle-class women, married or single, would not have held paying jobs. They would have been engaged primarily in the domestic sphere, and shopping was one of their major domestic roles. "The task may be a pleasant one or it may be a trial," the *New York Tribune* explained to readers in 1901, "but it is one of the duties connected with housekeeping."[34] Women had become the purchasing agents for the family; men were the primary wage earners, but women were the unchallenged wage spenders. Even the masculine trade often came through the women in the family. They were "the natural and regular customers in the department stores."[35]

The occupation of the husband or father, the public badge of female identity, was mentioned often enough to give us a good sense of the economic circumstances of the family. While there was wide variation in employment patterns, in no case was the male a common laborer or a factory worker, or unemployed. In only one instance was the husband described in a way that might suggest working-class status: Mr. Lynch, the *New York Times* reported, was "a respectable, hard working mechanic."[36] Of the other men, three were Protestant ministers, two were described as engineers, four were in insurance, one was an artist, and one a town official in Newton, New Jersey. One man was a conductor on the New Jersey Railroad and another was a superintendent on the Jersey City Railroad. The largest number of the husbands (and the father of one woman) were in a range of businesses: produce merchant, liquor dealer, shoe dealer, contractor's supplies, hardware merchant, grocer, and representative of a large machinery house. There were three lawyers, a judge from Sandusky, Ohio, a retired physician, and a Republican politician from Brooklyn. A number of these men were simply described as "an influential man," "well connected," or "wealthy retired businessman." The most important-sounding title was that of Mr. Russell Raymond, who was secretary and manager of the American Safe Deposit Company and a trustee of the American Savings Bank.[37] These men were, with few exceptions, solidly middle class, more often than not from the professional, managerial, and business ranks.

What conclusions can be drawn from this sample? The women do not appear to typify the "new woman," the college-educated social worker or the woman prominent in local community or national affairs who has been studied in this period.[38] While there were, undoubtedly, some club women and active feminists among them, the women arrested for shoplifting epitomize the traditional nineteenth-century domestic model, that vast majority of women who were enmeshed in what what some observers demeaned as the "idle busyness" of housekeeping.[39] Certainly the middle-class status and respectability of the women is evident. They belong to that broad, amorphous, middling group of women whose role lacked a degree of definition and whose contribution, in a culture that valued hard work and money, was ill-defined.

The scenario of arrests had certain common features. The drama began when the suspect was stopped and told the manager wished to see her.[40] Detectives generally waited until the women were leaving the store—in fact they often stopped suspects on the sidewalk—both to minimize possible disturbance in the store and to ensure that the intention to steal was unmistakable. In most instances the woman apparently made little objection to this part of the routine and quietly followed the detective to the manager's office or special room used to question suspected shoplifters. Creating a case was the next step. Away from crowds and curious eyes the suspect was asked about the unpaid merchandise thought to be on her person. At this point she was usually charged with shoplifting by the manager or the detective, often in the presence of the salesperson.

Virtually all the women became indignant, loudly denying they had stolen merchandise in their possession, and frequently insisting a mistake had been made for which the store was going to be very sorry! If she consented, a search of the woman usually followed; invariably it yielded hidden articles. This discovery often produced hysterical weeping, occasionally even fainting, followed by impassioned pleading, desperate promises, and a variety of excuses for "what must have happened." The drama was enacted at a high emotional pitch; it was a scene that obviously had to be played out just as it was played up.

There is always the question of how to analyze such scenes. Were the excuses true, or were they created on the spot in self-defense? It is entirely possible that a woman picked up for shoplifting could not have described what provoked her particular response to the store environment, but true or false, more or less fanciful, the explanations would seem to be part of the play.

Store managers readily acknowledged that every effort was made to "hush up the cases." Shoplifters were routinely allowed to give back the goods, sign a release admitting the theft, and promise never to enter the store again; refusal could mean arrest and exposure.[41] If there were a prosecution, the store had sufficient leverage that its name was "usually withheld," even when that of the suspect became public knowledge.[42] Hesitancy to arrest the amateur shoplifter may have fallen within the concept of store service. Managers were protecting themselves and the image of the store, but they were also concerned with the broad circle of potential customers. "To ruin the reputation not only of a possible unwilling offender but also her family, throwing a stain upon the fair reputation of all connected with the accused, is too serious a subject for the average merchant, or man for that matter, to carelessly handle."[43]

Not only was there a distinction drawn between "the shoplifter who deliberately and willfully 'lifts' things for a living" and the "unfortunate beings who just happened to take it because inclination and impulse got together"; lenient treatment was a service to the reputation and social status of husbands and families, society, and especially the stores themselves.[44] With people generally unaware of individual instances of shoplifting, the trouble-free, dream-world image of the store remained intact. Detective Daniel Kash felt many shoplifters were so skillful that "the next neighbors of the shoplifter who is caught in the act never know anything about it."[45] Henry Blades, the chief detective at Wanamaker's, readily admitted that "no good end can be served by such exposure. Moreover it would be a *bad advertisement* for the house, for such cases would receive extended newspaper comment, to the the detriment of the firm exposing the culprits."[46]

Repeat customers who were suspected of shoplifting by store detectives were, not uncommonly, left alone just because they were recognized as good customers. Daniel Kash, a former New York City policeman and a well-known detective at Siegel-Cooper at the turn of the century, recalled "accidentally" finding an expensive handkerchief in a wealthy charge customer's muff. Although the woman had been suspected of shoplifting for some time, Kash took no action, merely commenting, "Why Mrs. B. you must have picked this up by mistake with your bundle." We let her go, he told the reporter, and "she continued to trade at the store, as there was no apparent reason for stopping her charge account."[47] The repeat shopper was a mainstay, and one that the stores assiduously cultivated. Management interpreted store loyalty as a signal that the store was providing the material and psychological satisfaction customers were thought to require. But this very constancy often made shoplifting arrests difficult. When such shoppers were stopped or finally arrested, the store often declined to prosecute. "Caution and discrimination" were essential in making arrests of this kind, warned detective Henry Blades.[48]

Newspapers made regular mention of this aspect of the shoplifting problem. When Laura Little, "a handsomely dressed young woman" and a regular customer of Stern Brothers in New York, was arrested by the store's detective, the firm decided not to prosecute.[49] Stern's made this decision despite testimony from their own detective that she had seen the woman take two silver pins and some goods from the silk counter. Moreover, another store detective testified that he had been suspicious of Miss Little for some time. The excuses were legion, yet the story was always the same: a respectable woman of a good family with good connections and important, persuasive friends. . . . Headlines such as this one told the story: "Rings in Her Handkerchief. Mrs. Jane Morris Was Not Prosecuted Because Influential Friends Settled Her Case Quietly."[50]

Shop floor personnel were obviously aware of management's reluctance to confront good customers. An incident that occurred at Koch's, a popular department store on 125th Street, was typical. A wealthy woman who had been a customer of the store for eight years and was "well known to members of the firm and to the clerks," was detained only after repeated indications she was stealing. Reportedly dressed in sealskin and diamonds, the shoplifter was accused of taking a pair of shoes valued at five dollars.[51]

In January 1899, another shoplifting suspect, "a woman who buys regularly in the store," was finally arrested when her thefts became too blatant. The woman detective acknowledged that she had suspected the woman for some time, but "she knew the woman she trapped was very wealthy, and she acted with great caution as the defendant was a frequent customer."[52]

The *New York Times* reported an offshoot of the problem of the repeat customer as shoplifter. In this instance a "well-dressed woman" shoplifter was caught but not arrested because another customer intervened. The woman who interceded on the shoplifter's behalf did so purely for personal reasons, but the superintendent felt, pragmatically, that he could not deny her refusal to become further involved: "Being one of our best customers, we could not afford to offend her by pushing the matter."[53]

Many of the detained women gave false names and addresses; the police knew it and so did the courts, and neither group seemed unduly alarmed by the practice. A case with a fictitious name was the stuff of cheap novels and daily newspapers alike; such a case might appear in the *Times* or the *Tribune* two or three times under such tantalizing headlines as "Who is the Mysterious Shoplifter?" "Mystery About a Shoplifter," "Keeps Her Secrets Well," or "She Gave the Wrong Name."[54]

There was a special kind of anonymity in the central city. In an age where personal documentation was not a necessity, women could give any name they wished, and without a good deal of investigation their real identity need never be known. Lawyers even stood up in court and swore they did not know their client's true name.[55] Mrs. Caroline Hobart was patently a "nom de guerre," as were the names of at least thirty to thirty-five other women in this sample. The excuses were of a kind and seemed, in part, to be a response to the reporting of the arrests in the daily press. Some of the women were frankly afraid of their husbands' reaction.[56] In 1880, for example, Mrs. Catherine King refused to reveal her legal identity when arrested for shoplifting in both B. Altman and Arnold Constable, claiming, "she did not want to disgrace her family; her husband is a well known businessman of Newark." In court nine days later, she still maintained her silence, refusing to give any clue to her identity "on account of her family and connections."[57]

The rationalization changed little over the years. Annie Smith was the name given in Special Sessions Court by a "handsome, matronly woman dressed in black silk . . . and wearing expensive diamond earrings."[58] The justification for the pseudonym (for there was no pretense that the name was bona fide) lay in the fact that the putative Annie Smith was a respectable, well-connected lady. "Why should I disgrace my family?" asked a woman who called herself Maria Miller.[59] One woman said she was Jane Doe, and another, who called herself Mary Brown, was paroled to her husband, John Doe.[60]

Mary Smith was a commonly used fictitious name, but other, far less ordinary, names were used: May Hues, Josephine Durand,

Emma Webster, Adelaid Martin, Louise Bryson, Leone Greenberg, Gertrude Price, and Nellie O'Brien are just a few. The list goes on, the names becoming more or less fanciful, but the attempt to protect the family, and obviously themselves, does not change. These women had something tangible to lose—their reputation and, with it, their self-esteem.

There is evidence of moral confusion in these attempts to hide behind fictitious names. Attempting to cope in the Gilded Age environment of rampant commercialism and speculation, some women found traditional virtues and inhibitions ineffective tools. Momentarily submerging the distinction between right and wrong, the women had taken what they thought they wanted from department store counter tops. When caught, they found that what they really wanted was the facade of middle-class respectability. They coveted "things" and seized the opportunity to take them, but when arrested they held tenaciously to the security of class.[61] On another level, however, these explanations shed light on certain cultural understandings of the period. In refusing to be named, women seized control of their own stereotype; they remained non-actors, non-participants, who hoped thereby to escape the consequences of their behavior.

Often, of course, the real woman emerged despite the fictions, and notwithstanding any attempt to dissociate the actions from the person one really was. Maria Miller turned out to be Mrs. W. D. Burnett of West 124th Street, New York City, whose husband was "entirely at a loss to understand his wife's actions."[62] Similarly, one Jane Doe was in fact a Mrs. Cornelius I. Wigham, the wife of a retired and quite "astonished" liquor dealer in Brooklyn.[63] It is a mark of this woman's presumed social position that the court papers continued to carry the pseudonym Jane Doe.

Whatever the repercussions and personal shame, it was not felt by the women alone. Shame attached to these men as well. The untoward notoriety threatened their status, community standing, and possibly their jobs. The newspaper statements of the men who were dragged into the situation were strikingly similar in tone, expressing concern with the implicit threat to their own position.

Dr. Swift (The Rev. Dr.) said he was "dumbfounded" when the telegram arrived; he was sure there must be some mistake. . . . Mr.

Swift further declared in court that "it stands to reason that my wife would not stoop to take an umbrella and disgrace her own and my good name."[64]

He was at a loss to understand his wife's actions. She was very absent minded but. . . .[65]

Mr. Guinzberg stated that there was *no* reason for his wife to steal. They have a fine residence and Mr. Guinzberg is well-to-do.[66]

Her husband took the stand to testify "his wife was given plenty of money and did not *need* to steal."[67]

These denials of motivation or of need denied, as well, the possibility that social and material ambitions spurred the behavior.[68] But given the uneasy economic position of many middle-class families in the decades following the Civil War, one can assume that wives felt the twin pressures of money and status as keenly as their husbands did. The department store gave concrete expression to these pressures, tying the aspirations of class to material objects. The very existence of the grand bazaars suggested that commodities had redemptive power, and that their possession signified individual worth.[69] Thorstein Veblen understood this. In his language, reputation and status rested on the strength of the outward manifestations of success. Symbols replaced reality. Conspicuous consumption, or at least emulative spending, even at the risk of economic strain, was a necessary concomitant of social standing.

The quartet of middle-class women from Lynn, Massachusetts, who amassed "Trunkfuls of Booty" before they were caught in 1897 had no hesitation in giving their reasons for shoplifting: "They saw things they wanted, could not buy them, so took them from the counters when they were not watched."[70] Because we are aware that there is no necessary correlation between income and class in the late twentieth century, we should not be too quick to dismiss the possibility of economic motives in some of these cases. In a mobile society, in which appearances meant so much, the appearance of not being able to afford "things" was a threat of serious proportions.[71]

Obviously, no husband would ever say of his wife's shoplifting, "I suspected it all along." Husbands insisted that because their wives had an established social position, based of course on *their* wealth or position, and had what they considered to be a suitable allowance, the possibility the wives might shoplift did not exist. There seemed to be a growing distance between what men and women thought necessary to maintain the apearance of class. It was the woman who spent, "largely to bring about fulfillment of some idea or other of what [the] conditions for a pleasant environment should be for herself and for others."[72]

Most middle-class men had little firsthand knowledge of the realities of day-to-day consumption. Their understanding of what things cost was probably vague, and they were unlikely to take into account what having enough money meant in the social context of the department store. This was the first generation for whom material abundance was an everyday possibility. "The question today," Bertha June Richardson wrote in her 1904 study of women's economic function, "is not what shall be produced to supply my needs, but *how shall I spend to satisfy my needs*." (Italics mine.)[73] There was an infinite variety of things to buy, a push by the stores and their advertisers to buy them, and, increasingly, a society in which one's social position was tied to material possessions.

For the middle-class woman, financially dependent, without income or economic position of her own, having sufficient money did not necessarily mean freedom or control over spending. Even as they turned over part of their salary to their wives, husbands still regarded it as their own. It was *their* money. In an early feminist tract, *Fettered for Life, or Lord and Master* (1874), Lilly Devereux Blake observed that women had to justify and account for everything they spent, including ordinary expenses.[74] Echoing Blake, the author of an 1889 treatise on domestic economy demanded, "Let women have money to spend as *they* see fit [and] avoid annoying explanations as to *why* they need to buy another spool of thread today when they just bought one yesterday!"[75] Years later a woman reminisced, "In my girlhood we spoke with awe of my contemporary, Louise de Koven, who had a bank account and could sign checks!"[76] Empowered in the domestic arena as mothers and homemakers, women dominated the consumption process—there was little division of labor here—yet they had virtually no control over money. A woman's allowance or pocket money was generally a gift bestowed, not something to which she was entitled. Dismissed as "pin money," a woman's allowance reflected the explicit power relationships within the family.[77]

Feminists were aware of the problems surrounding money. "The Poor Little Rich Girls" was how the *Business Woman's Journal* described unmarried girls of comfortable families who were expected to "keep up" but either were never given money of their own to spend (Daddy paid the bills), or were given a wholly inadequate allowance. From their sheltered economic position many of these young women resorted to various strategems to get what they felt they needed—and wanted; a "demoralizing" state of affairs that, columnist Ella Wheeler Wilcox charged, "leads the weak and irresolute to shoplifting and petty larceny. . . ."[78]

An article in the *Boston Herald* in September 1890 tackled the problem of women and money head-on. The author, a Mrs. Ives, declared the failure of men to see that their unwillingness to allow their wives a discretionary income left them often "unable to meet the demands laid upon them by the social conditions surrounding them." Unnamed "social tragedies" were the result: "Women lie and steal and resort to all sorts of questionable expedients in order to obtain the spending money which they require for their own private purposes."[79] There was a reality to Mrs. Ives' argument. Many of the women had legitimate purchases in their possession and money in their purses when they were caught. Their shoplifting was that extra something that they felt they could not afford or possibly could not justify buying.

Women generally took things for their personal use, citing needs, or perceived needs, that often exceeded their ability to pay. Purchasing some things—most things—and stealing others, many women seemed to use shoplifting as a kind of budget-stretching device.[80] To many shoppers, the stores seemed so rich, so large, and so impersonal that it was a simple thing to maintain the illusion that what they did was not really theft; theft was something someone else committed. Women who would never steal from an individual took merchandise from the department stores and denied the implications of the act. For these women, shoplifting was a form of consumer behavior. Contrary to all logic and to the evidence, more than one woman rejected any conscious motive and adamantly defended herself with the assertion, "I am an honest and respectable woman."[81]

This level of denial was pervasive. If suspect Maria Miller had thought herself to be a shoplifter or had let others brand her "shoplifter," she would have had to question why she knowingly violated her own ethical precepts; and, even more troubling, she would have had to face the moral implications of her lapse. She would have been guilty of something more than irresponsibility. Aware of the normative distinctions between stealing and not stealing, these women were seemingly incapable of sensing emotionally that their shoplifting was wrong. They told themselves they were innocent, and, however fragile their defenses, they did not think of themselves as thieves.[82]

How, then, did these women see their own actions? Some women were quite frank about their reasons: like the quartet in Lynn, Massachusetts, whose "motive for stealing was the desire for fine apparel which they could not afford to buy." Others cited the example of women they had observed or had heard about— these women were imitators; they did what they knew other women were doing.[83] The more difficult responses to interpret were those of the women who readily acknowledged they could pay for what they wanted, but stole the merchandise just the same. The Brooklyn woman who decided to shoplift instead of spending the twelve dollars she had been given to buy Christmas presents suggests the taking of a calculated risk, a conscious level of action quite different from that of the woman who was at a loss to explain what had happened.[84]

Many of the women described the overwhelming temptation, the "physical inability to resist" the magnetism and lure of the displays. This was a common defense, and one that store personnel and magistrates came to expect. Although this routine explanation quickly became a cliché, it fulfilled social expectations. Women were expected to succumb to temptation. The claim that she had "no recollection of taking the articles found on her person," was a variation of this common defense.[85]

These stories, with their close relationship between truth and plausibility, become evidence for the mentality of the group.[86] It is not unlikely that some women were genuinely confused by their own actions. Their shoplifting was a spur-of-the-moment act, and their shame emerged as total denial. Even when a suspect pleaded guilty, as Mrs. Abbie Long did in 1898, it was not unusual for her to implore the judge to understand that "I did not mean to take the articles, indeed I did not. I had money and I could buy them. . . . I did not do it. I *could not* have done it."[87] For Mrs. Long, the wife of a clergyman, the expanding material economy posed choices even more difficult than those faced by other women. Hers was a public role and her conduct was minutely scrutinized. Expected to embody traditional values, the minister's wife was supposed to eschew the more blatant manifestations of the material culture.[88] That she often did not is evident. Mrs. Long's refusal to believe what she had done was the shocked reaction of a woman for whom the stakes were high.

The available cultural stereotypes focusing on woman's weak state of mind and frequent episodes of irresponsible behavior played into these explanations. In one highly publicized case in 1893, Dr. W. Gill Wylie, a prominent New York gynecologist and Professor of Medicine at Bellevue and Polyclinic Hospitals, appeared on the scene and posted bond for a suspected shoplifter. The doctor, who had a private sanitarium at 215 West 43rd Street, explained that he had been treating the woman for "seven or eight years for a reflex nervous trouble which rendered her at times unaccountable for her actions."[89] "Reflex nervous trouble" was a pervasive, if ill-defined, female symptom, and Dr. Wylie was probably saying little more than that his patient was hysterical. In providing this excuse for shoplifting, the doctor thus reinforced the common assumption that the female was often unstable, ruled by her nervous system and her emotions.[90]

Many times the woman's unconscious became the culprit. "I had no intention to steal anything," the putative Mary Smith told the judge, "[I] took the things unconsciously."[91] Mrs. Eladia Rubria protested that she did not know what she was doing when she took the candies, needles, kid gloves, silk scarves, and a comb, which were all jumbled together in a Gladstone bag she carried on her arm.[92] Laura Little's defense was classic. Not only was she described as "one of those apparently inexplicable cases of a young woman [she was thirty-one years old and unmarried] of respectable parentage being detected in shoplifting," but she, too, confessed that "she did not realise what she was doing when she took the fichu and other articles." She said she felt "possessed of an impulse to seize things and walk off." A variation on this theme was replayed with dismaying regularity.[93] The women used it to explain themselves, their lawyers used it to justify their clients' actions, and doctors used it to legitimize their diagnoses.

What they were describing, of course, was the pathology of consumption. Modern merchandising was geared to self-gratification, to the impulsive purchase, the irrational desire. Merchants wanted to make shoppers feel the propriety of such responses. Whetting the consumer's appetite with their emphasis on spending and material possessions, merchants, paradoxically, helped to promote the legitimacy of wants over needs, and "wants," sociologist Daniel Bell writes, "by their nature are unlimited and insatiable."[94]

Laura Little's case had one other paradigmatic aspect. After protesting her good intentions in spite of the accumulated evidence, she tearfully pleaded for the court's indulgence. "Oh, I have been punished enough, Your Honor, please let me go!" Little's cry was exactly what people wanted to hear, and it fully vindicated the pain of exposure as a sufficient punishment for middle-class women. Shame and remorse became recurring themes in these shoplifting cases. From the *Woodhull and Claflin's* article in 1871 bemoaning the "dreadful and humiliating indignity of arrest and imprisonment" for Mrs. Phelps and the other three women, to the *New York Tribune*'s description of arrested women begging to be spared the disgrace of arraignment in 1905, the middle-class shoplifter was seen as a special case. Her class prohibited her being viewed as an ordinary thief. Lawyers pleaded with judges to keep these clients out of jail, claiming their penance was the irretrievable loss of their good name. "They are ruined now!"[95]

The plea of extenuating circumstances became almost as common as "I could not help myself." This statement is from a woman in 1883: "She supposed the bonnet had become fastened to the bead trimmings on her sleeve and that she had dragged it under her circular [cape]."[96] A particularly fanciful but not uncommon defense was offered by Mrs. Peter Horen who explained that she had fully intended to pay for the articles, but "she had taken a glass of beer at her luncheon, and the liquor had dazed her so that she hardly knew what she was doing."[97] The alcohol, if she indeed drank it, may have facilitated Mrs. Horen's inclination to steal, but within the indulgent atmosphere of the department store her lack of will power probably needed very little prompting.

A Mrs. H. A. Hornig ascribed the whole affair to a "desire for notoriety by the female detective."[98] Placing blame on the detective was still common in the 1890s. Two years later another woman accused detective Eva Peyser of planting the merchandise on her after she left the store. "Miss Peyser," the accused shoplifter said, "had tried to put her hand in her pocket on the street" as she was forcing her to return to the store.[99] Not unlike the situation in the wake of the arrest of Mrs. Phelps in 1870, these women were attempting to shift the onus onto the detectives. They, not the respectable middle-class shoppers, were to be the culprits.

Even if a few of these excuses were legitimate, most of the explanations reinforced the stereotype of middle-class women and placed responsibility somewhere other than on the suspected shoplifter. Women and their lawyers told of buttons falling into the folds of a shawl, recurrent absent-mindedness, a ring getting caught in a handkerchief, a belt catching on the ribs of an umbrella, fainting while examining a cloak, having a headache. . . .[100] These women seem to personify what Nina Auerbach has called "the many faces of a single image."[101] While the excuses allowed the individual to escape the consequences of her actions, they served to confirm the commonly held view of women as passive and incompetent.

In most cases the likelihood of being detected seemed never to have occurred to the women, for the general absence of caution was a hallmark of their behavior. On the other hand, some suspects probably did mean to get caught. For these women shoplifting was possibly a rational act of defiance to punish others— husbands and families—by punishing themselves. It is also possible that some women were reacting against their own dependence and economic powerlessness. As women began to move from the limited framework of domesticity and into a different self-definition, they might have been reacting to a crisis internal to the middle-class family. In shoplifting they were exercising both power and control, even if it was also what one psychiatrist has labeled a form of "moral suicide."[102] The four women from

Lynn certainly were rational and aware of what they were doing and why they were doing it. Respectable women, who were ostensibly dedicated to the maintenance of middle-class values—which included the prohibition, "Thou Shalt Not Steal"—the Lynn shoplifters seemed not unduly burdened by such standard moral values until they were caught.

Although the source of the behavior was located in the individual and the changes taking place in the middle-class family, the relationship between consciousness and activity can never be fully charted. Valid reasons many not be operative reasons.[103] But whether the opportunity was there, or whether the women created it, the ease of shoplifting in the modern department store made it seem like an invitation. The culture of the big store, the divers stimuli within the shopping milieu, created the environment that affected the behavior of so many women. Given the free entry, the immense and almost seductive display of all kinds of objects, the "freedom to pass unnoticed in the middle of a crowd" that constantly pressed on all sides, and the possibility of touching whatever she found pleasing—given all these factors and the virtual assurance that her class position protected her—it is entirely probable that the middle-class woman shoplifted without thinking seriously of the consequences.

There is no dearth of evidence that the impact of these middle-class shoplifters was substantial. A relatively specific form of activity that became as much a female symptom as a crime, shoplifting was decisively important because of the meaning placed on it by physicians, the legal profession, the stores, the individuals involved, and the larger society.

7

————⚬————

"... Disposition Shady, but a Perfect Lady"

At the forty-first meeting of the Association of Medical Superintendents of American Institutions for the Insane in 1887, Dr. Orpheus Everts, Superintendent of the Cincinnati Sanitarium, delivered a paper that recounted the case of a thirty-nine-year-old widow with children and of "good society." Admitted to the asylum as hysterical, with a history of kleptomania, this woman proved to have "womb disease mania," which the doctor labeled, in turn, "larceny and eroticism with hysteria."[1] The case served to answer the question posed in the title of the paper: "Are Dipsomania, Kleptomania, Pyromania Etc., Valid Forms of Mental Disease?"[2] Everts' answer was a qualified "yes." These manias existed, he said, but only in a dependent relationship with other symptoms. In respect to kleptomania, he argued that it was really a "natural desire to accumulate exaggerated by disease," and that this combination of desire and disease amounted to a valid mental disorder.[3]

With the hindsight of one hundred years we can look with a combination of horror and some bemusement at this and similar late–nineteenth-century medical diagnoses, but we must also keep in mind how these explanatory models, which built upon the science of the day, served to reinforce accepted gender roles and definitions. On the surface a relatively benign label, the diagnosis of kleptomania was in fact a heavily value-laden, demeaning judgment about women and female sexuality. While the medicalization of shoplifting implied a search for treatment and held out a hope for cure, there was a mixed message in the diagnosis of such behavior as disease. It suggested, on the one hand, that older moral judgments of "bad" behavior were inappropriately simplistic; but on the other hand, it served to put the reproductive functions of women in a medically questionable category. If these so-called manias could be located in the womb, as Dr. Everts implied, the sexuality of women became one with disease and behavioral irregularities. There was a dialectic in operation. Just as medicine had a distinctive role in shaping definitions of gender, so, too, did it reflect gender values in the society at large.[4] Even as it became a socially and medically credible diagnosis, kleptomania became another proof of the inferiority of women.[5]

Both symptom and disease, kleptomania had multiple meanings. As a concept about gender and female sexuality, it was a social construct. Women "suffered from" or were "victims of" kleptomania because they were female. Victorians saw men and women as fundamentally different: argument upon argument supported the idea of gender inferiority with its supposed hereditary limitations of women's place in nature. The concept of women as the lesser sex, at once romantic and derogatory, neatly fit the picture of the kleptomaniac, prone to invalidism, neurasthenia, and the "periodic ordeal."[6] Internalizing the definition, many women, wittingly or not, accommodated themselves to the model.

As a medical diagnosis, kleptomania rested on physiology, but this was a post-hoc diagnosis. With no coherence or any discrete symptoms it was never typically a full-blown disease. The social construct provided the intellectual framework for the medical diagnosis, and shoplifting became disease. Sexuality and morality substituted for more specific medical indicators. Save for the class and sex of the afflicted individual, there was little diagnostic unity.[7] Only in behavior was the vague term given any definite meaning: Kleptomaniacs were shoplifters; shoplifters were kleptomaniacs. Middle-class women suffered from kleptomania; lower-class women who stole from stores were classified as thieves.

The well-documented and at times sensational shoplifting case of Mrs. Ella Castle is a revealing case history. It highlights the social and cultural value system that underlay the diagnosis of kleptomania in the late nineteenth century and illuminates the entanglement of medicine and law in the interpretation of the shoplifter. Most significantly, perhaps, the case demonstrates how women accepted the label "kleptomaniac" and the dependency it implied. Indeed, coming as it did in 1896, at the height of the development of the modern department store, the Castle case may be seen as a textbook discussion of the myriad and often conflicting strands of social, medical, and legal thought on kleptomania.

On October 5, 1896, Mr. and Mrs. Walter Castle, wealthy and socially prominent American tourists, were arrested in London for shoplifting. Temporarily remanded to Holloway Prison, the Castles were released on bail but forced to undergo the ordeal and spectacle of a public trial. American newspapers had a field day with the case. The *New York Times*, for instance, ran nineteen separate articles and editorials on the incident between the arrest on October 5 and the release of the Castles from English jurisdiction on November 13.[8] The *Times* and the *San Francisco Chronicle*, the couple's home-town paper, covered the proceedings in a style that can be fairly compared to the coverage of the arrest and trial of Jean Harris in 1980 for the murder of Dr. Herman Tarnower— shoplifting was a crime under English law, but medical interpretations along with assumptions about gender and class overshadowed the simple act of stealing a sable muff from a fashionable West End establishment.[9]

Mr. and Mrs. Castle were brought to trial four weeks after their arrest; her behavior and past history were minutely scrutinized and became the focus of the case. Although Mrs. Castle ultimately pleaded guilty to the shoplifting charge, both in the weeks before the trial and in court, she appeared not as a thief but as a mentally unstable, physically ill woman who, from the onset of puberty, it appeared, had evidenced mental "troubles incidental to female life."[10] Again and again press reports described her virtual physical collapse and spoke of her as subjected to a "disease which may have temporarily turned her mind."[11] The attending physician of Holloway Prison called her a woman of "highly nervous temperament and disposition."[12] The prestigious English legal journal, *Law Times*, seconded the diagnosis, referring to the "diseased condition of the moral nature" in this particular case.[13] An affidavit from the Castles' family doctor in California cited "her excessive nervousness since the birth of her child," and testimonials from American friends recalled her disordered state of mind, which had been a "pathetic secret . . . for many years."[14] English medical specialists summoned in to examine Ella Castle were united in the opinion that she was neither mentally nor morally responsible for the offense.[15] Admitting his client's guilt before the trial, Mrs. Castle's English lawyer defended her as a pitiful kleptomaniac:

> I have had her examined by some leading specialists in mental diseases, and have no doubt that the judge will admit that her symptoms are such as to warrant the defense of kleptomania. She suffers from pain in the head, from complete loss of memory and from other irregularities, which according to medical science, are known to be frequently associated with delusions. There is no reason in life why she should have taken these few trumpery bits of fur. . . . She has a well-to-do husband, who was willing to satisfy her every want.[16]

On November 7, the day of the trial, Mrs. Castle made her court appearance, sobbing, half-swooning, and supported by two uniformed nurses. Dr. William Chapman Grigg, specialist in diseases of women at Queen Charlotte's Lying-In Hospital, testified that:

> . . . after repeated examinations of Mrs. Castle he had formed the opinion that the disease from which she was suffering was one of those which are almost always accompanied by great mental disturbance causing different manias, as kleptomania, religious mania, etc., in different women. He asserted that Mrs. Castle was clearly unaccountable for her actions and not able to distinguish the consequence of her acts.[17]

The eminent Dr. George Henry Savage, Lecturer on Mental Diseases at Guy's Hospital and author of a widely read text, *Insanity and Allied Neuroses*, seconded Grigg's testimony.

It is not inconsequential that Mr. Castle, who had been arrested and indicted *with* his wife on the shoplifting charge, was subsequently "exonerated from all responsibility for her pilferings."[18] At the bail hearing a week after the arrest, when the prosecution still considered this to be "a regular case of shoplifting," it was revealed that "a part of the property was found among the husband's clothes."[19] Now, three weeks later, the prosecutor declined to offer any evidence against Walter Castle, arguing that even though Mrs. Castle's trunks at the Hotel Cecil "contained a museum of articles" taken from various London stores, "in not a single instance was she detected in taking anything, so that she must have done her work so skillfully that even her husband, who was beside her, was unable to see what she was doing."[20]

A tea importer from a wealthy and prominent San Francisco family, Walter Castle was the source of his wife's spending money, and it is not unreasonable to wonder, as did Police Inspector Arrow who was in charge of the case, how Castle could have failed to take note of what in fact was a vast accumulation of stolen merchandise.[21] The decision to attribute the thefts to Mrs. Castle seems to have been prompted in part by pressure from U.S. Embassy officials, but was facilitated by medical expertise. The availability of the kleptomania diagnosis, coupled with the deep-seated but unspoken assumption that "men don't act this way," made Mr. Castle's innocence easily rationalized.[22]

A repressive medical argument that relied upon woman's supposed physical and mental instability, kleptomania was part of a complex pattern of psycholgical tension between Victorian men and women.[23] While Mr. Castle quickly became the long-suffering, understanding husband to both prosecutor and judge, Mrs. Castle was neatly packaged as a mentally unstable woman who, in the throes of her illness, was a skillful shoplifter.[24] Her defense revolved around the plea of kleptomania based upon "her suffering from a woman's ailment which would account for her mania"; his rested on "his reputation for honor and integrity."[25] Walter Castle was defended and deferred to rather than suspected because he was not subject to a biological determinism that saw insanity lurking in the female sexual organs.

Pleading guilty to the charges and convicted on seven counts of shoplifting, Ella Castle was deemed mentally and morally irresponsible for her actions and speedily released by the British Home Secretary "on her husband's promise to take charge of her."[26] The couple sailed immediately for New York.

The case assumes even greater interest in its second phase, for upon her return to the United States Mrs. Castle went directly to Philadelphia to consult doctors at the Philadelphia Polyclinic Hospital. A team of senior physicians examined her, and their detailed report on the patient allows us to appraise mainstream medical and gynecological thinking about the relationship between women and kleptomania at the end of the nineteenth century. At a conference in February 1897 entitled "The Relations of Nervous Disorders in Women to Pelvic Disease," the Polyclinic physicians discussed their findings and the specific medical procedures initiated in the case.

Dr. S. Weir Mitchell, who had been lecturing and writing about diseases of the nervous system in women for two decades, was called in on the case for "assistance and counsel," and he became the chief spokesman for the medical team. Citing his "long experience of many forms of neuroses associated with pelvic disease," Mitchell wrote:

> I do not believe that Mrs. C. had any clear notion of the nature of her acts, or of their consequences, and I am of [the] opinion that very positive and long-neglected uterine and rectal disease had much to do with the disorder of mind from which she has suffered, and which is apt to be associated with hysterical conditions. . . . I think her hysterical, weak, and unbalanced, but not criminal. It is characteristic of her form of mental disorder that she should show no other obvious signs of insanity than the overwhelming tendency which belongs to her form of monomania.[27]

Not surprisingly, Mitchell's diagnosis supported the conclusion of Dr. William Chapman Grigg, one of the trio of specialists who had examined Mrs. Castle in London, testified at the trial, and reported the following to the Home Secretary:

> She is intensely neurotic. The condition of things—a disease of the upper portion of the uterus—is a very common accompaniment of various forms of mania in women, such as melancholia, religious mania, nymphomania, and I have seen it in several cases of klepto-

mania. It is invariably coupled with much mental disturbance. The condition I discovered is quite sufficient to account for any form of mental vagaries which are so well known to affect a certain class of women (neurotic) with disordered menstruation. Her bowel condition would aggravate this.[28]

Dr. Solomon Solis-Cohen, the physician in charge of Mrs. Castle's medical care at the Polyclinic Hospital, identified her specific medical symptoms as disordered menstruation, hemorrhoids, and uterine irregularities. And, the doctor reported to the assembled conference, from physical problems such as these, "various forms of mania in women," including kleptomania, commonly appeared.[29]

The diagnosis of kleptomania was part of the ongoing discussion of insanity and the female reproductive system. Shoplifting was perceived as an insane act for this woman, yet she could not be held morally culpable. Identifying her as a kleptomaniac was a way of resolving the problem.

What historical meaning ought we to give to this drama, at once intensely personal and broadly social? That Mrs. Castle was playing a culturally sanctioned role after the arrest seems obvious. Her exaggerated symptoms of hysteria, accompanied by the appropriate props in the form of concealing black veils, smelling salts, and uniformed medical attendants, may read like stage directions in a second-rate play; but they conformed to an appropriate behavioral norm for a certain class of woman in the late nineteenth century. Had the medical and social institutions acted consciously and in concert to produce an archetypal kleptomaniac, they could not have been more successful. Featured prominently in English and American newspapers for over a month, the actor, labeled Mrs. Ella Castle, exhibited every symptom a respectable kleptomaniac was supposed to possess: frequent nervous episodes, pains in the head, loss of memory, and menstrual problems. Furthermore, she was married to a well-to-do merchant who was said to be "very generous" with his wife. Mr. Castle, in his turn, professed the proper ignorance of his wife's shoplifting and said the evidence came as a "frightful revelation," even though he was aware that "she had been subject at certain periods to mental delusions and loss of memory."[30]

The drama's implications extended well beyond the panoply of female symptoms and complaints. The diagnosis of kleptomania implied a social concern about middle-class conduct. In this sense the incident was part of an ongoing struggle between the medical profession and the courts to determine whether kleptomania was a vice or a disease.[31] Mrs. Castle's doctors used their expertise to encourage the courts to dissolve a criminal act into a medical problem.

Dr. Arthur Conan Doyle captured the twin elements of the case in a letter to the *London Times* imploring the editors' intervention on behalf of Mrs. Castle: "If there is any doubt of moral responsibility the benefit of the doubt should certainly be given to one whose sex and position . . . give her a double claim to our consideration. It is in the consulting room and not to the cell that she should be sent."[32] In this public appeal for leniency, the creator of Sherlock Holmes lent his prestige to the medical interpretation of kleptomania. Doyle ignored the questions of motivation and responsibility, focusing instead on the imperatives of sex and class.

Beyond whatever obvious role-playing she was engaged in, Mrs. Castle's elaborate portrayal of the hysteric may have been a protective device as well. One senses in this incident the sort of issue Helen Lynd described in her classic book *On Shame and the Search for Identity* (1958). Shame, she observed, can be characterized by the unexpectedness of the sudden sense of exposure, "of being unable to deal with what is happening."[33] Mrs. Castle's intensely personal drama shook her assumed identity. That her husband would have no significant part in the prosecution's case was clear almost from the beginning; but she was exposed, revealed in public as a woman vastly different than any previous image she had had. What the newspapers reported was not simply the transgression of prescribed boundaries in a shopping, or many shopping situations, but the hitherto unrecognized aspects of a woman's personal life.[34] And in this vulnerable state, she found herself intensely alone. What identity was available to her? She was, because of her class position, spared the label of criminal, but because of her sex she could be labeled a kleptomaniac.

We have little evidence of how women responded to this medico-sexual language that relieved them of criminal identity at the price of trapping them in another, quite problematic one. Mrs. Castle's voice and those of other women detained for shoplifting are not heard; we have to rely upon the public record, and beyond the occasional stereotyped, ready-made response, there was no publicly acceptable outlet for the voices of these women. But if text provides access to social context, and if sexual ideology mirrors social relations as several historians of women have suggested, their silence helps to clarify their role, and is also an element that functions as an integral part of what was said by doctors, husbands, and judges.[35]

Ella Castle may not have been a totally representative figure—she was wealthier and more socially prominent than most women detained for shoplifting—but physicians made the same connections between her mental and physical condition as they did with other women labeled "kleptomaniac," and the various surgical procedures she submitted to under the guise of alleviating these mental and physcial disorders were well within the prevailing medical standards of the period.[36] While we have to believe that the Polyclinic doctors found legitimate physical ailments, nevertheless, they operated because she was a shoplifter. This is a perfect illustration of the confusion of psychological and somatic disorders by physicians in the late nineteenth century. By treating her pelvic disease, doctors hoped to cure her kleptomania.[37]

While we may caution ourselves not to confuse nineteenth-century medical rhetoric with either social or physical reality, the thinking surrounding this case of kleptomania forces us to consider the role of medical discourse in society at large. Science was the new authority, the preeminent voice in the second half of the century, and the coherence of its world view gave support to Victorian ideas of sexual polarity and sexual conduct.

Traditional views of the static, "eternal" nature of women, which fit in so easily with the concept of kleptomania, were given an unexpected boost by Charles Darwin. By the early 1870s, Darwin's theories had already begun to be absorbed into the collective consciousness and imagination of educated men and women. In *On the Origin of Species*, but, more particularly, in *The Descent of Man*, published in 1871, Darwin had given scientific authority to Victorian ideas about innate sexual difference, as well as support to the popular belief in the paramount importance of biology in defining sexual spheres.[38] We must be precise here. There was certainly nothing new in the assertion by doctors and disparate "experts" that the condition of the uterus could affect a woman's mental state; but Darwin's influence, deriving in part from the neutrality of his methodology, gave signficant scientific support to this traditional belief.[39] Even when the "new woman" was beginning to push against a purely domestic role and the concept of monomania was losing scientific credibility, the understanding of kleptomania, principally a disease of women, changed very little, remaining firmly within medico-psychological boundaries and supported after 1870 by the logical implications of Darwinian theory of biological determinism.[40]

While the new theories of biology and social evolution never stifled debate on the true nature and proper place of women, they provided the framework and the idiom within which social questions were examined, and they certainly reinforced a conservative interpretation of woman's sphere.[41] Faced with the bizarre and unsettling phenomenon of respectable women's stealing merchandise from the dry-goods bazaars, physicians used new scientific explanations to reinforce older cultural dispositions. Where religion had once provided clear moral absolutes, science, with its more rational understanding of human behavior, introduced a relativism that made it possible to be a "partial" thief.

The linkage of ideas of the scientist and the layman had serious implications for women. In their attempt to explain what was deemed to be irrational behavior, doctors and the general public alike embraced a view of women that limited them to biological dependency, to prescribed social roles, and to actions governed by the emotions. The medical and legal reaction to the Castle shoplifting incident illuminate this "close association between popular ideology and medical fact."[42]

However, in the contest between the Queen's prosecutor and the newly professionalized doctors, class was the hidden issue. If the medical construct of female sexuality made kleptomania a possibility, class identity motivated it. Class and sex together produced the outcome. What in another instance and with another couple would surely have been criminal conduct became disease.

American doctors, if not merchants and lawyers, certainly were aware of the diagnosis of kleptomania by the French physician,

C. C. Marc, which had appeared in 1840. Distinguished in this its earliest interpretation as the impulse of a diseased imagination and characterized by the absence of economic need, kleptomania, the so-called thieving mania, was widely accepted in France, Germany, England, and the United States as the impairment of the individual's voluntary powers.[43] A diagnosis that was not initially gender-specific, kleptomania quickly attached itself to women, specifically to the female reproductive economy.

Most shoplifters were women—almost exclusively so—but to hinge shopping behavior on biological processes, as was so dramatically demonstrated in the Castle incident, was a cognitive leap that was deeply rooted in the intellectual assumptions of the Victorian period. Kleptomania became an explanatory model for the excesses of untold numbers of middle-class women, as physicians found a comfortable fit between this form of moral insanity and their *a priori* understanding of gender. Medical textbooks, clinical lectures, and journal articles all supported an interpretation that placed kleptomania solidly in the category of female disease.

The work of the French was of primary importance in the early–nineteenth-century definition of mental illness. It was French physicians who developed the concept of monomania that became the foundation for the derivative notion of kleptomania. French theory divided the mind into independent mental and moral hemispheres, and recast certain types of impulsive criminal activity within the moral framework. Pyromania, dipsomania, and kleptomania, for example, were not the outcome of willful behavior, but were the result of "distempered imagination," the partial or complete transformation of conventional morality. "Persons thus affected are led by an irresistibility of feeling, to the commission of acts which they know, and often confess, to be wrong."[44]

Beginning with the description of homicidal mania that appeared in 1838 (which in turn built on earlier work), Jean-Étienne Esquirol and his most well-known disciple, C. C. Marc, based the theory of monomania on an understanding of behavior that saw a single cause for a complex of symptoms. Deviant forms of behavior, designated "manias," became "illness," evidence not of moral depravity but of mental disease.[45]

This represented a significant change in social assumptions. Until the end of the eighteenth century, individuals who committed crimes were "considered mentally ill only if they were in a state of actual delirium or dementia."[46] Insanity and even lesser forms of mental illness were thought to be physical diseases of the brain that manifested themselves in a variety of emotional and behavioral aberrations.[47]

The new analysis, which was developed and refined simultaneously in Europe and in the United States over the middle decades of the nineteenth century, claimed the individual no longer had to be in an active and continuing state of delirium; partial delirium, or what English physician James Prichard labeled "Moral Insanity" in 1833, could account for temporary loss of reason and "extravagant behavior." An individual could be mad in one respect and unimpaired in other areas of life. Certain actions resulted not from a lesion of the brain, Prichard reasoned, but from one of the will. Moral Insanity was "reasoning madness" or *manie sans delire* in French terminology, which might, but did not necessarily, involve the intellect. The afflicted were aware of what was acceptable behavior but were unable to act accordingly. "He is drawn away from his accustomed course to the commission of acts," Esquirol wrote, "which neither reason nor sentiment determine, which conscience rebukes and which the will has no longer the power to control. The actions are involuntary, instinctive, irresistible."[48] Though entirely different clinical conditions, homicidal mania, pyromania, nymphomania, and kleptomania were all ultimately presented as perversions of moral sensibility; impulses that were "instantaneous, unreflective and stronger than the will."[49]

There were strong criticisms, of course. The social and legal consequences of accepting moral insanity as a legitimate mental illness appeared to be dangerous to many observers: "A dubious apology for misconduct," said John Gray, superintendent of the New York State Lunatic Asylum at Utica and editor of the *American Journal of Insanity*, in 1858.[50] "Folly and wickedness," not "irresponsibile lunacy," wrote English physician James Hendrie Lloyd twenty years later.[51] Gray's distrust of the claim of moral insanity was evident in his testimony at the trial of Charles Guiteau, the assassin of President James Garfield, in 1881.[52] Gray was an expert witness for the successful prosecution of Guiteau, and his thinking was consistent with a position he had elaborated years earlier in the *American Journal of Insanity*: "Disease is not to be inferred from the act, but the act must be shown to be the result of the disease."[53] The theory of diminished responsibility was, in his view, a dangerous license.

Critics—particularly lawyers fearful of putting crime on a footing with disease, but physicians as well—saw a phantom in the concept of monomania and maintained their traditional support for facts, not "intellectual subtleties" of uncontrollable impulse or "paralysis of the moral sense." They were were hostile to insanity pleas; concerned, as was John Gray, that formulations based on such vague concepts would become "dubious apologies for misconduct," and responsibility for action would shift away from the individual.[54]

These fears were, in fact, justified. The unmotivated and irrational act was coming under increasingly sympathetic scrutiny, and the idea that individuals could be temporarily in the throes of mental disorder was accepted by many doctors. Elaborating the legal understanding of kleptomania for a medical publication in 1879, Ernest H. Crosby explained: "Kleptomania . . . is a very common form of moral insanity. The acts of theft are often of the most unreasonable character." Exemplary in all other respects, Crosby asserted, such women were literally "forced to steal."[55] The doctrine of monomania, particularly in its application to kleptomania, did remove the onus from the respectable shoplifter and had a decidedly softening effect in the courts.

The Castle incident falls squarely within the ongoing nineteenth-century moral and medical debate about the relation of insanity to the female reproductive system. Over the course of three decades many formulations and criticisms jostled for hegemony at medical meetings and in the pages of various internationally recognized medical journals. But for all the differences evident in these debates, there was a construction of gender that showed little variation across national boundaries and cultures.[56] Mrs. Castle was arrested and tried in London, but doctors in Philadelphia evaluated her condition in terms identical to those used and understood by their English counterparts. In both countries, medical descriptions of the celebrated shoplifter emphasized "the diseased condition of her moral nature," her highly nervous temperament and disposition, and the temporary insanity "occasioned by disease of the important pelvic organs."[57] While many of the arguments hinged on "whether madness was at root an organic disease or a psychic disorder," the construct of the kleptomaniac invariably located the site of the disease in the physical distinctions of female sexuality.[58] Tied directly to the expansion of the dry-goods bazaar, kleptomania emerged and established itself as a new disease entity in the transatlantic context of a new scientific empiricism and a burgeoning consumer culture.

The relationship between menstruation and insanity, a key element in explanations of female behavior, became integral to the debate over kleptomania. Seeking to understand apparently motiveless theft and the possible physical causes of nonvisible mental impairment, doctors tended to emphasize menstrual disorders. What they designated "ovarian insanity" was discussed in terms familiar in the more specific discourse on kleptomania. In the widely read American edition of his textbook, *Clinical Lectures on Mental Diseases* (1884), Scottish physician T. S. Clouston singled out disturbed menstruation as a "constant danger to the mental stability of some women. . . . It is often hard to determine," he explained, "whether disordered or suspended menstruation is a cause or a symptom." Clouston concluded on a note of resignation: "Some of them were most estimable Ladies, whom it was impossible not to pity, the whole thing was so contrary to the tenor of their lives. . . ."[59] When Dr. Solis-Cohen identified disordered menstruation as a contributing factor to Mrs. Castle's kleptomania, he was well within this accepted medical paradigm.

Neither Clouston's lectures nor his conclusions contained anything startling. His morally and mentally unstable women were medicalized versions of a more general cultural construction of gender. His definition of female illness fit easily into a whole storehouse of assumptions and prejudices. Weir Mitchell's diagnosis of Ella Castle's shoplifting as the result of uterine disease was textbook-perfect: the physical constitution of female sexuality was the root of female behavior.[60]

Meanings became interwoven. Sometimes kleptomania was cited as the reason for a moral lapse, at other times an "affliction with a disease which rendered the woman unaccountable for her actions" was both the diagnosis and the excuse.[61] In either case, the defective inhibition that characterized kleptomania was linked directly to a woman's physiology: pregnant (or recently delivered), lactating, ovulating, menstruating (or irregularly so), and, especially, menopausal—women were deemed at risk at most stages of their lives. They were effectively pigeonholed, diseased by their own sexuality.[62]

With some pathology of the reproductive system expected and often found, the localization of the disease in this period of still uncertain and speculative gynecology seemed beyond doubt. If kleptomania was under the control of biology, doctors reasoned, the kleptomaniac was physically defective, but not evil.[63] Not unlike hysteria, "uterine disease" became a diagnostic catch-all.[64] This explanatory model removed responsibility from the afflicted individual and made moral judgment of behavior inappropriate. In a period where self-control was the ideal, such dysfunctional behavior was easily classified as disease, "the symptom of which is crime."[65] The diagnosis of Mrs. Castle was revealing for the clarity of this point.

Doctors labeled Mrs. Castle a kleptomaniac because in their minds she had lost the powers of reason—she suffered from hysteria triggered by specific physiological malfunction; an extreme diagnosis in our eyes, but perfectly understandable to the courts, reporters, the newspaper-reading public, and department store owners of the late nineteenth century.

These scientific and medical discussions were far removed from the general public, yet they reflected a common cultural understanding about middle-class women and new patterns of consumption associated with the rise of the department store. While neurologists and asylum superintendents were working out meanings and classifications of specific forms of mental disease, the popular understanding of kleptomania (also known as shoplifting) was framed in terms consistent with commonly held stereotypes and social needs. Struggling to understand the phenomenon of shoplifting by those not in need, writers of every ilk used the term "kleptomania." This example from the *New York Evening Post* in 1903 is typical: "It is not an unheard-of thing in the shops to discover a thief in a wealthy customer. Such a person is called a kleptomaniac, of course, and she is sometimes allowed to go home with her loot."[66]

The public discussion of the mania, not unlike the scientific, was an extended commentary on women, on class, on role definitions, and on the questions of sickness and health. Had shoplifting, defined as a form of female delinquency, not been interpreted as illness, it would have to have been understood as crime, and the possibility of respectable middle-class women's falling into such a "moral cesspool" and forfeiting "the esteem and love of their best friends for a bottle of cosmetic" was unthinkable.[67]

French interest in the problem of kleptomania persisted. Between 1896 and 1911, French psychologists returned repeatedly to the question of kleptomania and enlarged the picture of the kleptomaniac considerably. Using the new device of the case study in their attempt to understand and systematize the relationship between illness and theft, French investigators—notably Paul Dubuisson, Roger Dupouy, and Pierre Janet—drew an explicit picture of the department store environment at the turn of the twentieth century.[68] What Dubuisson said he wanted was proof of the existence of "that special folly which seizes a woman the moment she crosses the threshold of a great department store."[69] But these arguments, which suggested an unconscious sexual content to kleptomania, merely rationalized traditional behavior patterns and defined a narrow base of feminine activity. Within this highly restrictive model, women and department stores were seen in a symbiotic relationship, in which the stores filled an elemental need for women. Shopping had become women's life and women's work. Not that they needed to buy anything, Dubuisson wrote, but they needed the atmosphere and the sight of "all those beautiful things."[70] Even the most honest and respectable women, it seemed, were fallible. In all essentials these clinical studies lapsed into conventional gender stereotyping but corresponded to what less scientifically informed American publications had also been suggesting: beyond the weaknesses that were commonly attributed to women, there was something in the environment of the stores themselves that activated "this curious and frequent form of theft."[71]

The inventiveness of the French contribution to the understanding of department store shoplifting was unmatched and quite probably was little known in the United States. Yet much of what the French theorized about this "curious and frequent form of theft" had, without all the theoretical elegance, become part of American department store lore.[72]

> Kleptomaniacs were principally women, very often rich, well brought up women who needed nothing and whose thefts left judges and store owners equally astounded.
>
> Such women stole only in the big department stores; outside of the stores their existence was irreproachable.
>
> Kleptomania was a sickness by women not really in possession of themselves, whose actions were so absurd they could not be explained by ordinary motives; thus one had to look to pathological motives.

Free access, the freedom to look with no obligation to buy, was the initial element in this formulation. Perhaps for the first time, a woman could "circulate on her own, unattended, without interference from anyone and without rendering account to anyone."[73] Dubuisson observed this in Paris, and it was an accepted feature of the American dry-goods bazaars. There was a freedom within the store situation that was not often duplicated in other areas of a woman's life. What the French scientific theorists grasped was equally understood by pragmatic American merchants. The *Dry Goods Economist* cited an unnamed store assuring women customers in 1902, "You may roam our floors unquestioned, without being urged unduly to buy ... our place is to entertain you."[74] Many of the accounts of shoplifting women describe their wandering aimlessly through the stores, killing time, going from counter to counter and floor to floor, seemingly without any particular destination but fixated by the "new wilderness of goods."[75]

In Sophie Hall's "Diary of a Visit to New York City" (1879) there is repeated mention of "looking in" at various stores, not buying but simply "shopping" for diverse items, including silks and "elegant lace curtains." One Saturday she noted: "Left Ridley's, walked up to 2nd Ave. where we took the cars and came up to 9th St. Got out, walked as far as Stewarts ... where we went in and stayed a good while." Leaving Stewart's, Sophie Hall and her companion went to another store where they "whiled away some more time."[76] Merchants were acutely aware of this new phenomenon and obviously encouraged it; ultimately they became dependent upon it.

Observers of these women, seeking a way to explain and understand shoplifting, called them, almost unthinkingly, kleptomaniacs. Doctors seized upon the concept in their effort to justify what they understood to be woman's essential nature and allotted social role. Many lawyers "came around" to kleptomania. Some seemed intellectually persuaded; others, quite obviously, adopted it as an acceptable defense. Store managers, detectives, and the courts all worked within a framework that understood kleptomania both as a disease and as an autonomous type of behavior by women of a certain class. Casual references to kleptomania became part of the daily vocabulary in department stores, police stations, and courtrooms.[77] Women often called themselves kleptomaniacs when they spoke of irresistible temptation, and their physical inability to bypass an object, a counter, or a particularly attractive display. Seeing a way to explain themselves that removed the threat of criminal prosecution and maintained the respectability of their husbands and families, women adopted the available cultural label. Unspecified feminine weakness was an accepted syllogism.

Mrs. Dora Landberg, a wealthy widow and a frequent customer in the store that finally had her arrested, claimed to be "suffering from Kleptomania."[78] A twenty-seven-year-old woman, Sarah Dengler, told court authorities that she was a kleptomaniac and "vainly sought to resist the temptation to steal." She added that "she had pains in her head at times during which she was subject to the disease." The report ended with the notation, "The police were inclined to believe Miss Dengler's story."[79] Fannie Lendrum, forty-five and from "respectable family" in Brooklyn, was defended in court by her husband, who said that "her mental aberration lately had been due to her physical condition. She had no reason to steal and never before had developed any dishonest characteristics."[80] The attorney for another suspect, arrested in a Sixth Avenue department store in 1904, described her as "a very studious girl. She has studied art and is somewhat literary. She has long suffered from a nervous trouble. Her father is heartbroken and has done everything to cure her. She spent the summer in a sanitorium, and has been to Bermuda. . . ."[81]

Stores lost merchandise from many sources, but only the middle-class shoplifter was recognized as acting out of a medical disability. A large proportion of these women were excused either because of a straightforward plea of kleptomania or an explanation that cited general malaise and physical debility without using the label. When Sarah Dengler complained of pains in her head at the very times she was subject to fits of kleptomania, she was, not unlike Mrs. Castle's lawyer, defining the disease for the layperson, conflating female illness and shoplifting.

More than gender was involved here. If kleptomania was a concept constructed upon cultural assumptions about gender, particularly about the irresponsibility and generative phases of women, it was also a class concept. Only the middle classes seemed to suffer from it; stealing by other classes was simple theft. One Paris newspaper suggested, not altogether facetiously, that a new dictionary of definitions was needed. The definition of *thief* ("vol") was to be a "a kind of kleptomania, but of the lower social class," while the definition of *kleptomaniac* was to remain as it had always been, "a kind of thief, but of the better class."[82]

It was not that insanity bypassed the poor—quite the contrary. After 1840 there seemed to be a high incidence of mental illness and functional nervous disorders among immigrants and the working class.[83] But middle- and upper-class men and women seemed to be more prone to neurasthenia and other rather "imprecise disorders"; their nervous systems were more "sensitive," possibly because they had the time to be sick and the money to afford it. The well-known neurologist George Beard, no doubt reflecting on the patients who sought his help, thought that "neurasthenia was principally a disease of the comfortable classes."[84] Doctors and laymen alike thought middle-class women had a predisposition to certain moral weaknesses and were vulnerable in ways that presumably less genteel women were not. While no one said that less refined women were immune to the broad-spectrum hysteria and neurasthenia that plagued middle-class women, there was no question in either the professional or the public mind that the lower-class or working woman was constitutionally far stronger and far more able to set aside the "evils of bodily organization" than was her more fortunate sister.[85] It was thought to be unlikely that a shoplifting charge, with its possibility of the shame of public exposure, would have crushed a working-class woman almost to death as it was feared might be the case with Mrs. Phelps.[86]

As an operating concept in American department stores, kleptomania took hold only gradually. Probably because of the reluctance to bring the problem of shoplifting out in the open, there was little public discussion and few exposés.[87] In the uproar which followed Rowland Macy's arrest of the socially prominent New York feminist and philanthropist, Mrs. Elizabeth Phelps, in December 1870, the question of kleptomania was virtually ignored. That dispute was not really about shoplifting but about class: working-class salesclerks and detectives versus middle-class customers.[88] Denying any wrongdoing, neither Mrs. Phelps nor the other women arrested utilized kleptomania as a rationale. Newspaper reporters, however, latched onto the concept and used it indiscriminantly. The *New York Daily Tribune* headlined its first story on the multiple arrests, "Macy's Alleged Kleptomaniacs, The Case of Mrs. Phelps."[89] The *New York Sun* reported, erroneously, that Mrs. Elizabeth Claussen, one of the four arrested women, and a "highly respected and wealthy resident of 113 West 13th Street, was tried in Special Session Court on a charge of kleptomania . . . [but] the testimony against her was very slight, and she was discharged."[90]

There are few instances of shoplifting in the 1870s that refer to kleptomania or excused shoplifting because of unspecified female illness. Ten years later, when shoplifting by the middle-class woman had become a widespread phenomenon, so, too, did the plea of kleptomania. In 1882 Ellen Sardy, a "well-dressed middle-aged woman of respectable appearance," was caught shoplifting in the Sixth Avenue store of Simpson, Crawford & Simpson. Her loot was three pairs of stockings and five pieces of silk, a considerable haul for the 1880s. Sardy was released when her lawyer admitted the larceny but "asked clemency on the grounds that the prisoner for some time past had been of weak mind and was not always responsible for her actions."[91] The Sardy case was probably not the first such plea in New York City, but because it came when it did, at the beginning of the 1880s, it was in its own way a milestone. Whether the accused woman was actually weak-minded and occasionally irresponsible as her lawyer pleaded is irrelevant; what is important is the court's readiness to accept the excuse and the definition of the middle-class shopper.

The following year the *New York Tribune* ran a long article entitled "Tricks of Shoplifters," and, while not specifically examining the twin issues of class and medical definition, the editors made it clear that they were aware of them. The article questioned whether kleptomania was a legitimate plea, and whether "moral obliquity is to be *less* severely punished when its possessor is habited in brocaded velvet than when a gingham gown and a battered bonnet compose her outer garments."[92] The *Tribune* decided it was not its role to argue the merits of either side, but it is clear from the question that the image of the middle-class shoplifter acting not out of economic necessity but from an inherent weakness was already fixed. Here we have the essential contradiction— the Victorian woman who was thought to be more moral than the man, "yet less in control of her very morality."[93]

Doctors and lawyers in the 1880s defended these women by saying little more than "she is a respectable, well-connected lady, but evidently a kleptomaniac."[94] A woman from Sandusky, Ohio, who was picked up for shoplifting in Ehrich's, appeared in court with a Dr. Augustine Daussé of West 22nd Street, in New York City. The doctor claimed she was "a reputable woman, the wife of a judge . . . and at present under his care for special medical treatment." The woman contended she had no recollection of taking the merchandise as charged and "no object for taking them, as she is able to pay for everything she wants." The implication was clear; the lady was a kleptomaniac. The case was dismissed.[95]

In a case that was international news in 1887 and appeared on the front page of the *New York Times*, "Two titled Russian ladies" belonging to court circles were picked up for shoplifting in the Louvre, a large and popular department store in Paris. The alibis were the familiar mixture of temptation and irresistible magnetism of the displays, but the reporter, in a gratuitous aside, added that "certain sort[s] of weak-minded females" were prone to derelictions of this sort.[96] What he meant, of course, and what his readers immediately understood, was that women who shoplifted with two thousand francs in their purses were most certainly ill, suffering from a type of moral insanity or kleptomania.

Chief Inspector Thomas Byrnes of the New York City Police Department fully supported this broadly based, yet narrow class definition of shoplifting. When two well-dressed women of "apparent respectability" were arrested for shoplifting in McCreery's and brought to central police headquarters, Byrnes interviewed them. Why they ended up at central headquarters instead of the local precinct is a mystery, but in seeing them, Byrnes may have wanted to verify his own understanding of this type of theft. Three years earlier, he had written *Professional Criminals of America* (1886) and in it he had singled out the middle-class shoplifter, whom he called a kleptomaniac, for special notice. "These women," he wrote, "were so carried away by admiration of some trinket or knicknack as to risk home, honor, everything to secure it."[97] Such unthinking, illegitimate behavior by respectable women clearly baffled, yet still fascinated the inspector, and he indicated that his view of middle-class shoplifting had not changed in the intervening years. He made a public statement defending the arrested women in their plea of kleptomania. "He believes," reported the *Times*, "they are kleptomaniacs and are no more legally responsible for these thefts than a lunatic would be for assault and battery."[98] Byrnes' understanding of kleptomania was, by this time, shared by a wide segment of the public.

The explanation offered at the trial of a Mrs. Henry von Phul, a wealthy fifty-two-year-old woman from New Orleans, was part of this understanding. A spokesman told the judge that "the family has been subject to insanity, and Mrs. von Phul only left the asylum a few months ago. When in one of her fits of mental derangement, she has no control over her actions."[99] It was made clear to the court that the arrested woman was of unsound mind; her moral perversity in this instance taking the form of shoplifting or kleptomania. Given the subjectivity surrounding the whole question of heredity as well as a woman's health and normal mental condition, neither this woman's behavior nor the interpretation was exceptional.[100] She was tyrannized by heredity and subject to her own moral perversions. Whether mentally healthy or truly insane, Mrs. von Phul was part of a socially determined view of women and madness. Dorland's *American Illustrated Medical Dictionary* defined kleptomania in its 1900 edition as "an insane impulse to steal; insanity marked by a desire to steal."[101] The case of Mrs. von Phul was dictionary-perfect: insanity and kleptomania were inextricably linked.

In 1900 the *Dry Goods Economist* called kleptomania a "favorite plea."[102] Women detained for shoplifting and their professional advisors, trade journals, and store personnel were using the term in a consistently referential pattern. The alibis and explanations all relied on a definition of middle-class women that said many of them were in more or less disordered mental states: "Respectable ladies . . . found with bits of lace or ribbon tucked away in their sleeve or muff were the victims of kleptomania."[103]

One young woman, described in the *New York Times* in 1905 as a "literary lady," explained that her bag full of assorted stolen merchandise was nothing more than material for a story showing how easy it was to shoplift. The reporter placed this alibi under the heading of "Kleptomaniac Excuses."[104]

Everyone seemed to know about kleptomania. There was public acceptance, if not belief in the framework of the behavior, but most people successfully ignored its implications. With the exception of Edwin S. Porter's 1905 movie, *The Kleptomaniac*, serious discussion of the phenomenon was limited to the French medical journals.

In the cultural climate of the late nineteenth century, the excessive behavior patterns of a few middle-class women were deemed representative of the constitution and fragility of the group. The diagnosis hinged on a distortion of the female image, a gendered view of woman totally ruled by her biology. Disease became an explanation and a defense. Weir Mitchell understood this perfectly when he wrote of Mrs. Castle's guilty plea in the English court: "She is now under a stigma from which it will be difficult to escape . . . this [guilty plea] involves long explanations; the plea of insanity would have involved none."[105]

Because nineteenth-century doctors saw women as prey to their own periodicity, they were believed to be inherently unstable, never totally "self governing." Whatever the plea, and however dramatic the symptoms, the words were symbols that meant very much the same thing, both to the women who invoked them and to the the men who sat in judgment. Middle-class women eagerly embraced negative female stereotypes in their own defense. Building upon the diminution of personal and moral responsibility, their excuses relied heavily on acceptance of masculine standards for female behavior. This was not a conscious strategy by any means, but a ploy to exonerate themselves, to invoke sympathy and understanding, and to justify their days in the department store as a legitimate activity.

The legacy, of course, was a sacrifice of gender to class. Middle-class women continued to be seen as "other." Letting themselves be defined in negative biological terms, and sacrificing the possibility of a positive gender identity, they were imprisoned even as they went free. Illness, kleptomania, mental derangement, obsession, feminine weakness—one was understood to be no different from the others. Popular wisdom embraced a view of these women acting the way they did in the department stores simply because they were women—shopping as they were supposed to do, behaving in an appropriate fashion much of the time, but too often letting themselves collapse under some temporary aberration of the mind. If instability was thought to be rooted in woman's nature, it is easy to see why kleptomania found such ready acceptance. Testimony to the successful stimulation of consumer desire, it served as both explanation and excuse. Not consumer capitalism but middle-class women were the fundamental problem.

Epilogue

Shoplifting by middle-class women did not decrease over the course of the twentieth century. Long after the nineteenth-century understanding of kleptomania lost credibility, shoplifting was still described by one female store detective as "a battle of woman against woman."[1] But with the emergence of a new scientific language, the terms of debate changed. The biological image of a specifically female disease gave way to Freudian psychiatry. In this new language, as in the old, women still provided the model of the shoplifter as patient; even though men as well as women, adolescents as well as the elderly, made up the army of casual shoplifters. Only in recent decades has the singular association of shoplifting and women weakened.

French psychologists Pierre Janet and Paul Dubuisson had suggested a link between kleptomania and repressed female sexuality in the late 1890s. With the advent of Freudian modes of analysis, this view was was given a dramatic new framework and achieved considerable force. As in the nineteenth century, American doctors borrowed heavily from European intellectual developments, and in the first two decades of the twentieth century many psychiatrists moved from understanding "the shoplifting mania" as an activity dependent upon the passive, automatic processes of female biology, to "a new conception" that tied kleptomania to the dynamic variations of individual sexual psychology.[2] If the reproductive system alone was no longer the source of the disorder, the disorder's cultural meaning remained rather constant. Freudians sought to explain the activity of middle-class shoplifters as the product of the unconscious; it was the mind that governed the behavior. These women, they felt, were acting out a host of personal emotional dissatisfactions. Shoplifting was a palliative for individual psychological and sexual distress.[3]

In his article "The Sexual Root of Kleptomania," which appeared in the July 1911 issue of the *Journal of the American Institute of Criminal Law and Criminology*, Dr. Wilhelm Stekel, a Viennese "psycho-therapeutist," described first the temptation— the "unknown power [that] suddenly compelled" a patient "to touch some object and *put it in her pocket*," (italics Stekel's)—and then the amnesia, shame, or revulsion that often followed the act. Calling "the temptation to commit a sin" the culprit, and using the new tool of "psycho-analysis," Stekel's account left no doubt about the origin of this behavior. "The root of all these cases of kleptomania," he wrote, "is ungratified sexual instinct."

> These women fight against temptation. They are engaged in a constant struggle with their desires. They would like to do what is forbidden, but they lack the strength. Theft is to them a symbolic act. The essential point is that they do something that is forbidden, *touch* something that does not belong to them. (Italics Stekel's.)[4]

Stekel's conclusion, that shoplifting is specifically sexual in nature, leaned heavily on the new authority of psychiatry to define women. He effectively deconstructed the act of shoplifting: the theft gets lost in the quest for the forbidden.

Acceptance of the theory of unconscious motivation, with its implication of diminished moral responsibility, signalled no sharp break with late nineteenth-century explanations. When accused nineteenth-century shoplifters had described the physical inability to resist the temptation that assailed them in the drygoods bazaars, their excuses were generally understood in terms of female hysteria and mental degeneration. Women seemed to have accepted this interpretation, as well as the popular medical dogma that viewed the female body as the basis of social behavior.

By the second decade of the twentieth century, this form of temporary insanity had a new look, if not a new label. Still occasionly called kleptomania, such shoplifting was now attributed to individual female psychosexual disturbances.[5] Women's accounts of their shoplifting, however, were connected to those of a generation earlier. "I was compelled to take the objects," a young female patient explained. "I had to take them, I had no peace until I did."[6]

Both interpretations, that of the nineteenth and that of the twentieth century, were grounded in the immutable fact of sexual difference, but twentieth-century medical explanations of kleptomania replaced biology with psychology. Organic disease was all but eliminated as a cause; female sexuality became an active force, blindly pursuing its own ends, outside of the normal rhythms of the female body. Connections to menstruation, pregnancy, and menopause were still frequently heard, but uterine disease was no longer an unexamined, "natural," causal factor.

By the 1920s, doctors defined kleptomania in a new language: it was now "the neurotic impulse to steal." Psychiatrist Karl Abraham explained that kleptomania was often traceable to the unremembered experiences of childhood.

> A child feels injured or neglected in respect of proofs of love—which we have equated with gifts—or in some way disturbed in the gratification of its libido. It procures a substitute pleasure for the lost pleasure, and at the same time takes revenge on those who have caused it the supposed injustice.[7]

As Abraham and his colleagues sought to unravel the persistent problem of shoplifting by the middle-class woman, their explanations, like those of Wilhelm Stekel a decade earlier, focused on thwarted emotional gratification. The sublimated anger and aggression implied by the desire for revenge can also be seen in the image of the nineteenth-century female hysteric.[8]

"Inseparable from kleptomania is the pleasure of the forbidden," psychiatrist Fritz Wittels observed in a leading medical journal in 1929. Kleptomaniacs, he later noted, took "a masochistic pleasure in [the] dangerous consequences" of their actions.[9] Pleasure tinged with the titillation of possible exposure accounted for the motive and made an incomprehensible act comprehensible. Wittels' analysis posited a sharp distinction between women and men: women, he felt, were more subject to kleptomania than men were, and those men who did steal repeatedly "always present feminine characteristics, physically or psychically."[10] So subjective and far-reaching were the social and cultural meanings given to gender difference that when a man was labeled "kleptomaniac" he lost his masculinity in the process. In the twentieth century as in the nineteenth, the debate about kleptomania was based on the ingrained cultural perception of middle-class women. The underlying, gender-based image of the kleptomaniac remained unaffected either by scientific developments or by intellectual trends.

Thirteen years later, Dr. Wittels was still seeking to demonstrate a close connection between kleptomania and female sexuality. In a paper presented to staff psychiatrists at Bellevue Hospital in New York City in 1942, he told his audience of doctors that sufferers from kleptomania were generally women who were *really* taking love (italics mine). For these women kleptomania was the re-creation of the sex act "in a shape adequate to their libidinous understandings." He used the testimony of a woman patient to make his point.

> When I have taken an object in a department store I thrust it in my bosom under my blouse, hide in the next doorway and wait with my heart beating. When I see that I have not been noticed I feel a wild triumph, a lust the like of which nothing else can offer.[11]

For Wittels these words came "as close to a description of sexual orgasm as a seemingly non-sexual act can."[12] While not supporting an explicitly functional interpretation of kleptomania, the doctor certainly skirted the edges of such an interpretation in his emphasis on the domination of physical desires and the disruptive power of female sexuality. Such ladies come to doctors begging to be cured, he said. Wittels identified thwarted sexuality as the root of kleptomania. His message was clear: Repressed female sexuality is fundamentally dangerous, a source of social disorder.[13]

Until recently, when the term "kleptomania" has largely fallen into disuse, discussion of the middle-class shoplifter/kleptomaniac never moved beyond this gender-coded representation of disease. Elaboration of sexual difference remained crucial.[14] As in the nineteenth century, professional journals in the twentieth century continued to carry articles posing the question, "Is There a Relation between Kleptomania and Female Periodicity?" Opinion was divided. If occasionally it was the general sense of medical practitioners that there was little clinical data to support an affirmative answer, just as often they found a link between kleptomania and tumultuous female sexuality.[15] In a study conducted in five midwestern cities in 1933–1934 among "specialists in nervous and mental diseases," for example, few respondents saw a direct relationship between kleptomania and menstruation, *except in neurotic women*—obviously a key exception susceptible to endless definition and one with many pitfalls for women. While there was no consensus, other than in defining kleptomaniacs as neurotic, no respondent in this study disavowed the use of the term "kleptomania," nor was there any suggestion that it was an irrelevant or meaningless diagnostic category. Many of the physicians felt kleptomania was neither well defined nor adequately diagnosed, but none questioned the assumption that the malady was primarily a female disorder.[16]

After mid-century the terms of the debate changed once again. "Kleptomania" fell out of fashion. Medical professionals and department store personnel stopped using the word, feeling perhaps that on the one hand it was old-fashioned, and that on the other hand it lacked precision.[17] Doctors, particularly, began to see kleptomania as the name of a symptom or a constellation of symptoms rather than as a definite medical condition.[18] Yet the underlying meaning assigned to such shoplifting changed hardly at all.

Stealing for "symbolic needs of sexual gratification" or for the need to be caught to alleviate unconscious guilt were the two explanations for shoplifting offered in a report of the National Retail Dry Goods Association (NRDGA) in the 1950s.[19] The terminology at mid-century was more self-consciously Freudian, and the diagnosis was more complicated—less a simple matter of cause and effect—but the central figure remained the same. Women were still the majority of shoppers and of shoplifters, and the author of the report, Dr. Fabian Rouke, fell into a familiar pattern. He validated, once again, existing medical and cultural stereotypes and demonstrated the tenacity of traditional modes of reasoning about women and shoplifting.

Entitled "The Psychology of the Retail Criminal," the NRDGA study posited categorical distinctions between the three types of shoplifters: the professional thief ("or business criminal who steals for profit"); the casual pilferer ("the person who takes things for his own use or for gifts to give his friends"); and the neurotic thief ("whose stealing is symptomatic of a deep-seated emotional need").[20] The second type—the casual pilferer—seemed to be Everyman; vague as this was there was no additional clarification. Only the last type, the neurotic thief, merited elaboration; for Rouke presented a series of vignettes to demonstrate his understanding of this particular cultural construct: "She was home for the holidays. Her parents were down in Florida for the winter season, but she was left a generous allowance . . ." begins the first of these descriptions. "One woman who came to me had stolen a small article . . . and at the time she stole it she had over $100 in cash in her purse. She had an open charge account in good standing at the store. . . " begins another. The neurotic thief had replaced the kleptomaniac, but the gender association remained firmly in place. The four examples of this new type were all women, of varying ages as in the past, and all but one were securely middle class.[21]

The larger cultural shifts that were emerging in American society were the focus of an article that appeared in a 1967 issue of *Life* magazine. "One Out of Sixty Is a Shoplifter," *Life* announced in a banner headline.[22] A photo essay, which demonstrated that shoplifters were less exclusively female underscored the statistic: two teenagers pocketing lipsticks, a mother stealing crayons, a drug addict (male) swiping a sweater. Tricks of women and tricks of men were differentiated and photographed, but, according to the editors, few men regularly shoplifted: "most of the 'snitches' were respectable housewives." Such women, who *Life* said were neither kleptomaniacs nor professionals, accounted for 95 percent of all shoplifting.[23] Why did they steal?

One criminologist interviewed for the article felt that some housewives shoplifted "to pick up luxuries which could not be rationalized within their budgets"; but a more important motivation, he felt, was "a desire for the thrill of getting something for nothing." These women wanted to feel alive, and the act of shoplifting was one way to achieve this. That so few shoplifters were caught, and even fewer were prosecuted, added to the attraction.[24] The specifically sexual content had dropped out of the interpretation, but the sense of displaced sexual energy lingered. Shoplifting now was an exciting game, but it was the same game Fritz Wittels had noted in 1929 when he wrote of the pleasure kleptomaniacs took in the dangerous consequences of their actions.

Another criminologist in the *Life* study moved away from a distinctively Freudian interpretation. His response analyzed the elaborate process of rationalization that allowed "normally law-abiding people" to turn into shoplifters. Based on a sense of victimization (Macy's cannot possibly be victimized, and the shoplifter is or has been), such stealing became "justifiable retaliation."[25] One woman's description of her own repeated shoplifting, which appeared some years after the article in *Life*, echoed this analysis: "The physical universe and I were at war, or at least not feeling connected."[26]

A suspect at the turn of the century claimed that "everyone stole from the shops," but her ingenuous defense that everyone did it differs markedly from the modern contention that stealing from the department stores is explainable and is not inherently a bad thing. Middle-class shoplifters in the nineteenth-century had operated within a moral economy that took a dim view of theft (even though they, paradoxically, were rarely prosecuted), and these women felt compelled to justify their actions to themselves and to the authorities. The mid–twentieth-century model justifies her actions as well, and in language often quite similar to that of her Victorian counterpart, but the underlying meaning of her response is quite different: she is more contentious, ready to see her actions as a form of resistance to a situation that is consciously manipulative, and she is less willing to accept social criticism. One bejeweled woman explained that her theft of a candy dish was "just for kicks."[27] Another acknowledged, "If I thought shoplifting was hurting somebody, I wouldn't do it."[28] These explanations reflect a major shift: although the voices are still female, the accounts make no reference to gender; reflecting a decisive repudiation of Victorian culture in the 1960s.

Articles imitating *Life*'s photo essay but painting a far grimmer picture of the situation in the department stores have become commonplace.[29] A new twist, however, is the television program, radio talk show, or newspaper or woman's magazine article based on interviews with self-proclaimed shoplifters. All middle class, generally college educated and working, these women—and they are all women—employ a True Confessions model. They capitalize on the fact they are shoplifters and have no problem admitting what they do, though they have a variety of motives that valorize their actions. "I had been losing things ever since I was a little kid," one shoplifter admitted; and added, "now I was tipping the seesaw in my direction."[30] Another woman stated flatly, "The art of shoplifting is born of thrill not of necessity."[31] A third explained, "It was control of my life, I was in control of what I was taking and what I was doing."[32]

Women's public voices were muted in the nineteenth century, and we cannot know with any certainty what shoplifting represented for the Victorian woman. But the voice of the middle-class shoplifter *is* heard in the late twentieth century, and what she says suggests that material need is not a conscious factor: "No one needs any of the things they sell in Bonwit's," one shoplifter commented wryly. "The entire seven floors had [*sic*] nothing to do with need whatsoever."[33] Many shoplifters speak of their thefts in frankly sexual terms, while others employ the language of drug use: they like the thrill; they get an edge and a high when they are stealing.[34] There seems to be a pervasive rebelliousness and sense of entitlement in much of this testimony. Some shoplifters admit they want to achieve a "certain look"; others speak of loss and emptiness.[35] "Want" is still translated into "need," but need has become the urgency of relieving depression or the demand for excitement. Shoplifters in the nineteenth century went along with the diagnosis they were given: twentieth-century women define their own behavior and, thus, themselves. Though their explanations are often based on current therapeutic vocabulary, these women fashion language in their own way. They do not passively allow it to define them.

Despite how self-confessed shoplifters interpret their behavior, physicians and psychologists diagnose middle-class female shoplifters as victims of stress and their "unmet or unresolved emotional needs."[36] Lack of sexual fulfillment, anger, or depression are the meanings assigned to shoplifting and the common denominators used to describe these women. The term "kleptomania" may be heard rarely in professional circles, but the link between shoplifting, female sexuality, and thwarted emotional gratification—vestigial remnants of an older age—remains strong.[37] In 1987, psychologist Janet Markowitz echoed a diagnosis offered by Karl Abraham sixty years earlier: "It's difficult to know what is being played out . . . but the closest I can come is that shoplifting arises from a feeling of not being given to."[38] Fritz Wittels' patient who thrust stolen objects into her bosom finds an echo in the woman who admits to shoplifting for the risk and excitement it brings.[39] But is it the same? Are "risk" and "excitement" only code words for repressed sexuality, or are they (like skydiving or ski racing) representations of modern possibilities for women? There is no conclusive answer, but the salience of Victorian assumptions about gender seems remote in the late twentieth century.

Shoplifting has changed the way America shops. In the second half of the twentieth century, shoplifting and its prevention has emerged as a major industry. Security consciousness is no longer a secret: stores want customers—all customers—to understand that everyone is suspect. With the boundary between legitimate and illegitimate behavior often flexible, and a widespread cynicism about business institutions and methods, merchants are trying to combat the notion that it is "okay" to shoplift. "We as a society put up with shoplifting because it is an impersonal crime," a consumer psychologist told a *New York Times* reporter. "Nobody is hurt, there are no bodies scattered about . . . no evidence of corruption in high places, and . . . we put up with it because we have all done it, most of us as children."[40]

Shoplifting prevention has become a business in itself. The state of the art includes electronic surveillance devices that require neutralization or removal, metal cables that secure merchandise to display racks, and hidden television cameras. One large Washington, D.C., department store employs one-way mirrors to monitor the customers.[41] While the shopper is looking at herself, on the opposite side of the mirror, security personnel are watching her.

A tribe of security experts has emerged as well. Security consultants, specialists in consumer psychology, and a generous supply of in-store detectives and guards all seek to deter the ubiquitous shoplifters. Class no longer provides protection. And with inventory shrinkage increasing year by year, security has become a problem beyond the confines of a single store.[42] One retail consultant publishes a series of newsletters geared to specific levels of retail operation, sponsors management seminars on the "five-finger discount," and advises individual retailers on prevention techniques. This same consultant, apparently working both sides of the fence, also runs a rehabilitation service for first offenders.[43]

Behavior modification is the newest kind of shoplifting prevention. Self-help groups, such as Kleptomaniacs Anonymous and Shoplifters Anonymous, are part of a broad movement of mutual aid organizations that provide emotional support and practical assistance in dealing with this recognized and admittedly common problem.[44]

In 1988 a market analyst noted that "shoplifting is becoming the great American pastime."[45] If we accept this statement as hyperbole with a jarring ring of truth—and, given the relentless escalation of shortages in retail outlets, there seems no reason not to accept it—then the question of why women still provide the model of the shoplifter remains.[46] More women than men shop, and more women shoplift—this is as true in the late twentieth century as it was in the late nineteenth century—but to focus almost exclusively on female shoplifters, as has been the case in the recent spate of publicity about retail theft, is to continue to associate shoplifting with women beyond any claim of temporary social anxiety about class, female roles, and sexuality.

The female kleptomaniac is figure from the Victorian past. Articles about shoplifting, which now appear regularly in daily newspapers and financial publications, take care to mention the wide assortment of casual amateurs who grab merchandise in the large stores: "a kid, a student, a housewife, a cop, even a nun," according to one New York security consultant.[47] Yet many news reports still rely on old stereotypes and terminology. A security guard in

Macy's felt confident that 90 percent of the current batch of shoplifters were women.[48] A report in the *New York Times* referred to modern-day kleptomaniacs as "psychologically deformed."[49] While everyone is suspect in a society besieged by crime, the social construct of the shoplifter remains largely and curiously static: a middle-class woman, not in obvious need, who steals merchandise from department stores and (most recently) specialty shops. Only female adolescents have been added to this skewed, yet persistent image.

The medical image, however, has undergone substantial modification. In the nineteenth-century definition, any middle-class woman was susceptible by virtue of her sex; in the late twentieth-century definition, the middle-class woman who shoplifts is a woman with a problem. The difference seems slight but is, in fact, signficant. Although a shoplifter is more likely to be female, no longer is any woman seen as a potential thief simply because she is female. Although the situation in the stores is as bad as it has ever been, shoplifting is now part of a general pattern of an affluent and post-Victorian society.

A Note on Sources

This is a bibliography of the primary and secondary sources that figured prominently in my thinking about this book. Since I have drawn upon a wide variety of material, the footnotes provide a far better indication of the scope of the bibliography than a short essay can.

There is a growing literature on middle-class formation in the nineteenth century. Two excellent reviews of such sources are the bibliographic essay in John S. Gilkeson, Jr., *Middle-Class Providence, 1820–1940* (Princeton, N.J.: Princeton University Press, 1986), and Stuart M. Blumin, "The Hypothesis of Middle-Class Formation in Nineteenth-Century America: A Critique and Some Proposals," *American Historical Review* 90 (April 1985), 299–338. For both primary sources and recent work on budgets, spending, and the concept of a "new middle class," see notes for chapter 1.

The domestic world of middle-class women has received such intense scrutiny in the past two decades that it is difficult to single out specific works. Divers studies of housework, the woman's club movement, education, health, voluntarism, leisure activities, household economics, and feminism have charted the changing roles of Victorian women. Here again, for a complete list of sources, see notes for chapter 1. The "widening sphere" of the middle-class housewife was evident to contemporary observers as well. Emma Churchman Hewitt, *Queen of Home: Her Reign from Infancy to Age, from Attic to Cellar* (Philadelphia: Miller-Megee Company, 1889), is a good starting point. A few of the more suggestive primary sources include Abba Goold Woolson, *Women in American Society* (Boston: Roberts Brothers, 1873), Abby Morton Diaz, *A Domestic Problem: Work and Culture in the Household* (Boston: J. R. Osgood and Co., 1875), Kate Gannett Wells, "The Transitional American Woman," *Atlantic Monthly* 46 (December 1880), 817–23, and Margaret Deland, "The Change in the Feminine Ideal," *Atlantic Monthly* 105 (March 1910), 289–302. Women's diaries are often the best indication of the transformation in women's lives. Some of my clearest insights came from reading the private musings of late nineteenth-century diarists. Often trivial, repetitive, and formulaic—for example, daily weather reports and the state of the writer's health—diaries can also be historical treasures. They throw fascinating light on gender relations and the pace of change in the individual household. Most useful for my purposes were diaries by Marguerite Delavarre DuBois (1907), Caroline A. Dunstan (1866–70), Susan E. Forbes (1841–1908), Sophie C. Hall (1879), Clara Burton Pardee (1883–1938), and Harriet Richards (1883–1901).

The world of the department store has become an arena for serious historical inquiry. Beginning with Michael B. Miller's book, *The Bon Marché: Bourgeois Culture and the Department Store, 1869–1920* (Princeton, N.J.: Princeton University Press, 1981), the nineteenth-century department store has emerged as an ideal locus for the study of consumer culture, labor relations, and the development of modern business methods. For a list of the important new works on department stores, see endnotes for chapters 3 and 4. Studies on the great stores prior to the 1980s were, by and large, business histories that had either been commissioned by the stores themselves or were written with the active cooperation of the stores. I refer to such seminal works as Ralph M. Hower, *History of Macy's of New York, 1858–1919: Chapters in the Evolution of the Department Store* (Cambridge, Mass.: Harvard University Press, 1943) and Robert Twyman, *History of Marshall Field and Company: 1852–1906* (Philadelphia: University of Pennsylvania Press, 1954). A title that suggests numerous lines of inquiry for any study of department stores is Alfred D. Chandler, Jr., *The Visible Hand: The Managerial Revolution in American Business* (Cambridge, Mass.: Harvard University Press, 1977).

Trade journals occupy a special place for anyone attempting to enter the world of the nineteenth-century department store. The *Dry Goods Economist*, the *Dry Goods Reporter*, the *Merchant's Record and Show Window*, *System*, and the *Merchant's Trade Journal* provide a unique record of the development, organization, and thinking that was characteristic of the operation of the stores and their owner-managers during the late nineteenth and early twentieth centuries, the decades of greatest growth. While they rarely elaborated on specific instances of shoplifting, the trade journals recorded the defensive mentality that became central to department store operation. With almost weekly advertisements and commentary on the most effective methods to foil the shoplifter, these publications demonstrate just how serious and widely recognized the problem of shoplifting had become in the modern department store.

A number of studies helped me to refine my thinking about the issues involved in a study of consumerism, material accumulation, and commercial culture. Among the most valuable were Daniel Bell, *The Cultural Contradictions of Capitalism* (New York: Basic Books, 1976), Fred Hirsch, *Social Limits to Growth* (Cambridge, Mass.: Harvard University Press, 1976), William Leiss, *The Limits to Satisfaction: An Essay on the Problem of Needs and Commodities* (Toronto: University of Toronto Press, 1976), and Richard Wrightman Fox and T. J. Jackson Lears, *The Culture of Consumption: Critical Essays in American History, 1880–1980* (New York: Pantheon, 1983). Daniel Horowitz has included an insightful bibliographic essay in *The Morality of Spending: Attitudes Toward the Consumer Society in America, 1875–1940* (Baltimore: Johns Hopkins University Press, 1985).

Many of my impressions of late–nineteenth-century department stores were garnered from contemporary newspapers and magazines. Journalists were fascinated with this new institutional form and devoted endless columns to it. While it is difficult to pinpoint any single piece, a good place to begin is Samuel Hopkins Adams, "The Department Store," *Scribner's Magazine* 21

(January 1897), 4–27. Articles about the stores, the wonders and the delights of shopping, but also criticism of the stores' methods and environment, appeared regularly in a variety of publications. The *New York Times* and the *New York World* are valuable sources, as is *Everybody's Magazine*, *Outlook*, the *Nation*, and the *Ladies' Home Journal*. At the turn of the twentieth century a number of investigative reports and exposés provided useful primary evidence about conditions in the stores. I refer specifically to such studies as Annie M. MacLean, "Two Weeks in Department Stores," *American Journal of Sociology* 4 (May 1899), 721–41, Anne O'Hagan, "Behind the Scenes in the Big Stores," *Munsey's Magazine* 22 (January 1900), 528–37, and "Facts About the Department Store," the *Nation* 97 (July 1913). Government documents were helpful as well. See, for example, the 1914 *Department Store Investigation* of the Committee of Fourteen in New York City and the *Report of the Industrial Commission of the Relations and Conditions of Capital and Labor Employed in Manufactures and General Business*, 56th Cong., 2nd sess. (1901).

The primary concern of this book is shoplifting, and in this category documentation was far more diffuse. In *no* area were the stores less willing to go public than in the question of shoplifting. They skirted the issue, they talked around it, they took defensive measures, but only rarely did they publicly confront it. Newspapers, magazines, and journals, however, did. References to shoplifting by middle-class women appear regularly in articles about the stores, shopping, the new consumerism, and crime. Full pages were devoted to exposés such as "Harvest-Time of the Shoplifter," which appeared on page one of the Sunday magazine section of the *New York Times* on December 11, 1904. Footnotes throughout the book are the best source to mine for these citations. Novels about department stores provide corroboration for the primary documentation. Émile Zola's *Au bonheur des dames* (Paris: F. Bernouard, 1884) and Margarete Bohme's *The Department Store* (New York: D. Appleton and Company, 1912) have graphic descriptions of "respectable" shoplifters.

I did not discuss the involvement of drugs with shoplifting, though it might have been a possibility in some cases. Henry Blades, chief of detectives at Wanamaker's in Philadelphia, felt it was a problem, but he offered no evidence. There was no indication from Blades or any other source that middle-class women shoplifted in order to support a drug habit. A number of sources discuss the prevalence of drugs and the issue of female addiction in the late nineteenth century. For example, see J. B. Mattison, "Morphinism in Women," *American Medico-Surgical Bulletin* 8 (November 15, 1895), 1399–1400. Two useful secondary works are David T. Courtwright, *Dark Paradise: Opiate Addiction in America Before 1940* (Cambridge, Mass.: Harvard University Press, 1982), and Sarah Stage, *Female Complaints: Lydia Pinkham and the Business of Women's Medicine* (New York: W. W. Norton and Co., 1979).

Kleptomania is a huge topic. The best guide for understanding the scope of the medical concern with kleptomania in the nineteenth century is the *Index-Catalogue of the Library of the Surgeon General's Office, United States Army*. This is a thorough and endlessly fascinating compilation of medical periodical literature published worldwide. Public concern with the kleptomaniac was no less intense. For a full list of sources, American as well as English and French, I refer the reader to the endnotes for chapters 6, 7, and the Epilogue.

Similarly, the literature on the real and perceived physical condition of women in the late nineteenth century is voluminous. A good place to begin is with two articles by Carroll Smith-Rosenberg, "Puberty to Menopause: The Cycle of Feminity in Nineteenth-Century America," and "The Hysterical Woman: Sex Roles and Role Conflict in Nineteenth-Century America," in *Disorderly Conduct: Visions of Gender in Victorian America* (New York: Oxford University Press, 1985), 182–216. Two other secondary works that suggest the broader cultural changes in the relationship between Victorian women and medical practitioners are John S. Haller, Jr., and Robin M. Haller, *The Physician and Sexuality in Victorian America* (Urbana: University of Illinois Press, 1974), and Charles E. Rosenberg, *No Other Gods: On Science and American Social Thought* (Baltimore: Johns Hopkins University Press, 1968). A worthwhile study of a different sort is George Frederick Drinka, *The Birth of Neurosis: Myth, Malady and the Victorians* (New York: Simon and Schuster, 1984). For primary sources I again refer the reader to the notes in chapters 6 and 7.

Shoplifting was a female crime no less than a disease. A good twentieth-century introduction to the relationship between women and crime is Frieda Adler and Rita James Simon, editors, *The Criminology of Deviant Women* (Boston: Houghton Mifflin Co., 1979). Though not dealing with women *per se*, David Greenberg, editor, *Crime and Capitalism: Readings in Marxist Criminology* (Palo Alto: Mayfield Publishing Co., 1981) is an informative and provocative analysis. For a nineteenth-century interpretation see Ely Van de Warker, "The Relations of Women to Crime," *Popular Science Monthly* 8 (November 1875–January 1876), 1–16, 334–44.

Notes

Introduction

1. *New York Times* (Dec. 10, 1898), 3:2.

2. Mary P. Ryan, *Cradle of the Middle Class: The Family in Oneida County, New York, 1790–1865* (New York: Cambridge University Press, 1981), 149.

3. A. V. Judges, ed., *Elizabethan Underworld* (New York: Octagon Books, 1965), 170–71; *Autobiography of Sophie Lyons,* files, Pinkerton National Detective Agency (New York: Star Publishing Company, 1913).

Margaret Hunt found a definition for shoplifting in 17th-century England that sounds surprisingly similar to its 19th-century counterpart: Women would tuck up their own gown and "boldly go into a mercer's shop, and there pretend to lay out a great deal of Money; whereas her [*sic*] whole intent is to convey into her nap some piece of silk or satin. . . . She is commonly well-clad." *The Ladies' Dictionary: Being a General Entertainment for the Fair Sex* (London: John Dunton, 1694), 477.

4. There is a continuing debate among historians on middle-class formation during the 19th century. For examples of these discussions, see the following: Stuart M. Blumin, "The Hypothesis of Middle-Class Formation in Nineteenth-Century America: A Critique and Some Proposals," *American Historical Review* 90 (April 1985), 299–338; Arno J. Mayer, "The Lower Middle-Class as Historical Problem," *Journal of Modern History* (Sept. 1975), 409–36; Karen Halttunen, *Confidence Men and Painted Women: A Study of Middle-Class Culture in America, 1830–1870* (New Haven: Yale University Press, 1982); Daniel Horowitz, *The Morality of Spending; Attitudes toward the Consumer Society in America, 1875–1940* (Baltimore: Johns Hopkins University Press, 1985).

215

5. By linking culture and consumption I do not mean to dematerialize consumption, but to indicate the totality of consuming behavior, its products, and its institutional form; see Helen Lefkowitz Horowitz, *Culture and the City: Cultural Philanthropy in Chicago from the 1880s to 1917* (Lexington: Univ. Press of Kentucky, 1976), 88.

6. *Dry Goods Economist* (Nov. 5, 1896), 49; Hugh Dalziel Duncan, *Culture and Democracy* (New Jersey: Bedminster Press, 1965), 92–3. One New York newspaper concluded, "Probably a better candidate for President could not be found than the successful head of a dry-goods and furnishing house." *New York World* (March 31, 1872), 2.

7. For a sample of current literature, see Susan Porter Benson, *Counter Cultures: Saleswomen, Managers, and Customers in American Department Stores, 1890–1940* (Urbana: Univ. of Illinois Press, 1986); William Leach, *True Love and Perfect Union, The Feminist Reform of Sex and Society* (New York: Basic Books, 1980); Michael B. Miller, *The Bon Marché: Bourgeois Culture and the Department Store, 1869–1920* (Princeton: Princeton University Press, 1981); Rosalind H. Williams, *Dream Worlds: Mass Consumption in Late 19th Century France* (Berkeley: University of California Press, 1982).

8. Asa Greene, *The Perils of Pearl Street* (New York: Betts & Anstice and Peter Hill, 1834); Caroline Kirkland, *The Evening Book or, Fireside Talk* (New York: Scribner, 1852), 64; Horowitz, *Morality of Spending*, introduction.

9. M. Jeune, "The Ethics of Shopping," *Fortnightly Review* 63 (Jan. 1, 1895), 124.

10. Cushing Strout, "The Uses and Abuses of Psychology in American History," *American Quarterly* 28 (1976), 325; Charles E. Rosenberg, *No Other Gods: On Science and American Social Thought* (Baltimore: Johns Hopkins University Press, 1978), 5–6.

11. George Frederick Drinka, M.D., *The Birth of Neurosis: Myth, Malady and the Victorians* (New York: Simon & Schuster, 1984), 13.

12. Mark Melford, "Kleptomania," A Farcical Comedy in 3 Acts in *French's Acting Plays* 138 (London & New York: T. Henry French, ca. 1888); Margaret Cameron, "The Kleptomaniac," A Comedy in One Act, Oct. 30, 1901, reviewed in the *New York Dramatic Mirror* (March 29, 1902 and April 15, 1905); Gus Edwards and Will D. Cobb, "Mamie, Don't You Feel Ashamie" (1901), in *Song Hits from the Turn of the Century, Complete Original Sheet Music for 62 Songs*, Paul Charosh and Robert A. Fremont, eds. (New York: Dover, 1975), 162–166; Edwin S. Porter, *The Kleptomaniac*, 1905. Edison film.

13. Felix Isman, *Weber and Fields: Their Tribulations, Triumphs and Their Associates* (New York: Curtis Publ. Co., 1924), 280–81.

14. T. J. Jackson Lears, "The Concept of Cultural Hegemony: Problems and Possibilities," *American Historical Review* 90 (June 1985), 589.

15. Barbara Mell Hobson, "Sex in the Marketplace: Prostitution in an American City, Boston, 1820–1880" (Ph.D. diss., Boston University, 1982).

16. New York newspapers were full of news and comment about the arrests. See, for example: *New York Daily Tribune* Dec. 26–29, 1870, *The World* Dec. 25–28, 1870, *The Sun* Dec. 26–28, 1870.

1. Urban Women and the Emergence of Shopping

1. Patricia Branca, *Silent Sisterhood: Middle-Class Women in the Victorian Home* (Pittsburgh: Carnegie-Mellon University Press, 1975); Hugh Dalziel Duncan, *Culture and Democracy* (New Jersey: Bedminster Press, 1965), chaps. X, XI.

2. Siegfried Giedion, *Mechanization Takes Command: A Contribution to Anonymous History* (New York: Oxford University Press, 1948).

3. Arthur M. Schlesinger, *The Rise of the City, 1878–1898* (New York: Macmillan, 1933), 132. Schlesinger quotes a *Good Housekeeping* article of 1887 in which a woman, rejoicing at the new prepared foods, says, "House-keeping is getting to be ready-made as well as clothing"; see also Adna F. Weber, *The Growth of Cities in the Nineteenth Century: A Study in Statistics* (New York: Macmillan, 1899), 219–20.

4. Margaret Gibbons Wilson, *The American Woman in Transition: The Urban Influence, 1870–1920* (Westport: Greenwood, 1979), 9–11, Sinclair Lewis defined the aristocracy of Gopher Prairie as "all persons engaged in a profession, or earning more than twenty-five hundred dollars a year, or possessed of grandparents born in America": Sinclair Lewis, *Main Street* (New York: Harcourt Brace Jovanovich, 1948), 76. Because of the repeated economic crises one writer noted that "women should be able to work if necessary . . . [it is] a melancholy fact that 'ladies' are at times unexpectedly obliged to support themselves (and even those around them)." See Emma Churchman, *Queen of Home* (Philadelphia: Miller-Megee Co., 1889), 404.

5. Daniel Horowitz, *The Morality of Spending: Attitudes toward the Consumer Society in America, 1875–1940* (Baltimore: Johns Hopkins Univ. Press, 1985), 68–69. William Dean Howells concluded that the middle class "eluded analysis." See Stow Persons, *The Decline of American Gentility* (New York: Columbia Univ. Press, 1963), 119.

6. George Ade, *Stories of the Streets and of the Town*, from the *Chicago Record*, 1893–1900, Franklin J. Meine, ed. (Chicago: The Caxton Club, 1941), 176. Ade was a contemporary of Finley Peter Dunne, whose Mr. Dooley stories appeared in the *Chicago Journal*.

7. Ibid., "The Advantages of Being Middle-Class," 5–79; Karen Halttunen, *Confidence Men and Painted Women: A Study of Middle-Class Culture in America, 1830–1870* (New Haven: Yale Univ. Press, 1982), 29ff.

8. Stuart M. Blumin, "The Hypothesis of Middle-Class Formation in Nineteenth-Century America: A Critique and Some Proposals," *American Historical Review* 90 (April 1985), 309, 337; see also the suggestive essay by Arno J. Mayer, "The Lower Middle-Class as Historical Problem," *Journal of Modern History* 47 (Sept. 1975), 409–36.

9. *Boston Herald* (Dec. 5, 1897), 1:6; *New York Times* (Dec. 1, 1896), 3:5 and (Dec. 19, 1880), 8:1.

10. Eli Zaretsky, *Capitalism, the Family and Personal Life* (New York: Harper & Row, 1976), 135; Warren Susman, *Culture as History: The Transformation of American Society in the Twentieth Century* (New York: Pantheon, 1984), introduction.

11. For discussions of the "New Middle Class" and its development in the 19th century, see: Mary Ryan, *Cradle of the Middle Class: The Family in Oneida County New York, 1790–1865* (New York: Cambridge University Press, 1981); John G. Cawelti, *Apostles of the Self-Made Man* (Chicago: The University of Chicago Press, 1965); Paul Boyer, *Urban Masses and Moral Order in America, 1820–1920* (Cambridge: Harvard University Press, 1978); C. Wright Mills, *White Collar: The American Middle Classes* (New York: Oxford University Press, 1951); Blumin, "Hypothesis."

12. Catharine W. Beecher and Harriet Beecher Stowe, *The American Woman's Home, or Principles of Domestic Science* (New York: J. B. Ford, 1870).

13. Clara Burton Pardee, *Diaries,* 1883–1938 (N-YHS), entry, June 3, 1885.

14. Caroline A. Dunstan, *Diaries,* 1866–1870, New York Public Library, Mss Division NYPL, entry, ca. June 19, 1866; Susan Forbes diary—*re* household bills, March 25, 1874. For an article ridiculing women's role in financial affairs, see Annette Austin, "When Woman Buys," *Good Housekeeping* 49 (Dec. 1909), 624–32.

15. There is little precise information about middle-class budgets. Edgar Martin, *The Standard of Living in 1860,* concluded: "There is hardly enough information to justify and general statements about the salaries paid to members of the executive and professional classes before the Civil War" (408). According to Stuart Blumin, Martin was "unable to make many useful distinctions between the levels or patterns of consumption of different income groups." Blumin, "Hypothesis," 330, fn 65. This lack of accurate information about incomes also held true for the Tenth Census, 1880. Wage series for a small number of factory occupations appear in this census but it is unclear how close these wages come to minimum middle-class levels: Superintendents/Foremen across the country in different categories earning about $100/month in 1880. Wages vary; some lower, many higher than $100. Although income data remain sketchy, Daniel Horowitz examines the standard of living and attitudes toward consumption between 1875 and 1940. Horowitz cites both the study in *Harper's Bazar,* "The Increase in Household Expenses, 1906–1907," and the work by Robert C. Chapin, "The Standard of Living among Workingmen's Families in New York City, 1909." Horowitz, *Morality of Spending.* 51–61, 72; see also Robert Grant, *The Art of Living* (New York: Charles Scribner's Sons, 1895), 7–28.

16. Pardee, *Diaries,* entries from 1899–1903.

17. *New York Evening Post* (Sept. 22, 1900), 16; see also Robert Grant, *Art of Living,* 7.

19. Pardee, *Diaries,* March 7, 1899.

20. Ibid., Dec. 12, 1899.

21. Alice Bartlett Stimson Papers, New-York Historical Society, Folder 3, Oct. 12, 1894. For a catalog of the upper middle-class woman's day, see Grant, *Art of Living,* 182, 184, 192, 195.

22. Pardee, *Diaries,* Oct. 28, 1898.

23. Ibid., Oct. 25, 1898.

24. Ibid., Dec. 29, 1903.

25. Ryan, *Cradle of the Middle Class,* 190; Martha H. Vergbrugge, *Able-Bodied Womanhood: Personal Health and Social Change in Nineteenth-Century Boston* (New York: Oxford University Press, 1988), 67, 92.

26. Harriet Richards (Mrs. George Richards), *Diaries,* 1883–1893, 1900–1901, New-York Historical Society; Pardee, *Diaries.*

27. Richards, *Diaries,* Jan. 25, 1884. For a description of a "call" that another woman made with her daughter, see Caroline Dunstan *Diary,* Oct. 15, 1870: "Mag and I took car to 59 St. 8 Ave. car to 125. Steam car to Inwood, walked to Mr. S. Left at 4½ [*sic*]. Carriage to Inwood. Steam to 30 St. 7 Ave. car home, about 6."

28. Pardee, *Diaries,* Aug. 8, 1885.

29. Both women, generally without their husbands, would "engage the crowd." They often took excursions to Coney Island during the hot weather, and occasionally went to Asbury Park. Viewing Christmas in the stores was an annual rite for Mrs. Pardee, and one or the other of them usually witnessed the special events that mark urban life. "Put up lunch and went to Dewey Parade with Ensign and children. Had fine seats." Pardee, *Diaries,* Sept. 3, 1899. See Ira Gerstein, "Domestic Work and Capitalism," *Radical America* 7 (July–Oct. 1973), 101–28.

30. E. L. Godkin, "Stewarts," *The Nation* 34 (April 20, 1882), 332; In his *Suburban Sketches* William Dean Howells describes life on the horse-cars between the suburbs and Boston, the "intimate associations of velvets and patches," and the obvious "contrasts of splendor and shabbiness." Middle-class women shoppers were "strap hangers" as much as anyone else in the "indecently crowded" cars. William Dean Howells, *Suburban Sketches* (Boston: Osgood and Co., 1872), 105–11.

31. Howells, *Suburban Sketches;* Neil Harris, "Museums, Merchandising and Popular Taste: The Struggle for Influence," *Material Culture and the Study of American Life.* Ian Quimby, ed. (Winterthur, 1978), 154.

32. *Appleton's Journal* 51, "A Further Notion or Two About Domestic Bliss" (March 19, 1870), 328–29.

33. Pardee and Richards diaries; Ann Douglas, *The Feminization of American Culture* (New York: Avon Books, 1977).

34. Stimson Papers, Oct. 1894. The diaries of Harriet Hanson Robinson also reveal her shopping habits. Living in the suburb of Malden five miles north of Boston, Robinson had access to the city on the Boston & Maine Railroad or on the omnibus line that crossed the river via ferry. Specific shopping expeditions took her to the city approximately twenty-five times in 1870 and 1871 respectively. She made other trips into Boston for cultural and social events. "I enjoy this running into Boston—it refreshes both body and soul, and relieves the monotony of everyday life," she wrote in 1871. Claudia L. Bushman, *A Good Poor Man's Wife: Being a Chronicle of Harriet Hanson Robinson and Her Family in Nineteenth Century New England* (Hanover: University Press of New England, 1981), 19. I owe this reference to Barbara Balliet. Shopping was obviously not a new activity for many women. See Mrs. John Farrar, *The Young Lady's Friend* (Boston, 1836), cited in Douglas, *Fem-*

inization of American Culture, 323: "The women visit the dry-goods store every week, perhaps oftener. . . ." *Dry Goods Economist* (Dec. 1, 1894), 69.

35. *Dry Goods Economist* (Sept. 1, 1900), 85.

36. *New York Tribune* (July 21, 1901), (S) 1:4.

37. *New York Times* (Dec. 6, 1885), 4:5.

38. Churchman, *Queen of Home,* 57. Churchman emphasized the importance of labor-saving devices in kitchens. The sense of time was as important for women as for men. "Can women afford to lose time?" she asked. Michael K. Marrus, ed., *The Emergence of Leisure* (New York: Harper & Row, 1974), 94.

39. Pardee, *Diaries,* March 11, 1885.

40. Ibid., April 16, 1898. In their preoccupation with daily accomplishments, women like Clara Pardee had begun to adopt a male model and to see themselves as workers. So common an activity was sewing that diarist Susan Forbes felt it necessary to note a day without it: "I did no sewing today." *Diary,* March 12, 1874; see also Lillie Devereux Blake, *Fettered for Life; or, Lord and Master* (New York: Sheldon & Co., 1874), 378.

41. Abby Morton Diaz, *A Domestic Problem: Work and Culture in the Household* (Boston: Osgood & Co., 1875), 43–44. Churchman also noted the "constant strain upon women," *Queen of Home,* 210.

42. Joan M. Seidl, "Consumers' Choices: A Study of Household Furnishing, 1880–1920," *Minnesota History* (Spring 1983), 183–97.

43. Thorstein Veblen, *The Theory of the Leisure Class, An Economic Study of Institutions* (1899) (New York: Viking, 1931); Daniel Rodgers, *The Work Ethic in Industrial America 1850–1920* (Chicago: University of Chicago Press, 1979), 202; Ann Oakley, *Women's Work: The Housewife Past and Present* (New York: Vintage Books, 1976), 1.

44. Diaz, *Domestic Problem* 10.

45. Grant, *Art of Living,* 192; The employment of a full-time maid was a *sine qua non* for the middle class in the 19th century, yet this aspect of home life was a source of constant complaint, comment, and anguish. See Pardee, Richards, and Forbes *Diaries* and Ruth Schwartz Cowan, *More Work for Mother: The Ironies of Household Technology from the Open Hearth to the Microwave* (New York: Basic Books, 1983), 121–22. This unquestioned class symbol was visually portrayed in all sorts of product advertising after 1880. In an article for the *Philadelphia Public Ledger,* Simon Patten suggested that middle-class women should do their own housework and not try to "ape those who are wealthy" (Nov. 2, 1907), 8:5–7. This "solution" to the servant problem elicited heated controversy in the *Public Ledger,* Nov. 2–3, 1907.

46. David Katzman, *Seven Days a Week: Women and Domestic Service in Industrializing America* (New York: Oxford University Press, 1978); Cowan, *More Work,* 100ff; Oakley, *Woman's Work,* 49ff.

47. Susan E. Forbes, *Diary,* American Antiquarian Society, Nov. 26 and Dec. 24, 1879, and May 10–22, 1880.

48. Pardee, *Diaries,* Sept.–Oct. 1887, July–Sept. 1888; Richards, *Diaries,* Sept. 1883, various entries from 1887–88; Harriet Richards never cooked dinner. *Diaries,* May 12, Nov. 19, 1888; Susan Forbes did.

49. Douglas, *The Feminization of American Culture,* 76.

50. Cowan, *More Work,* 177; Bonnie Smith, *Ladies of the Leisure Class: The Bourgeois of Northern France in the Nineteenth Century* (New Jersey: Princeton University Press, 1981), chap. 4.

51. Pardee, *Diaries,* 1885, 1887, 1893. Ensign Pardee seems not to have belonged to the church and did not participate in the religious activities of his family. Clara was admitted to Communion. She organized the christenings, instructed the three children, took them to Sunday School and prayer meetings, and was the religious force in their lives. The situation was similar in the Richards family. Harriet Richards took the lead in the moral and religious training of the children although George Richards attended church on Sundays. In 1886 he taught in the Sunday School. In the Forbes household both adults were active in the church: Various entries: 1872, 1874, Jan. 17, 1880; Branca, *Silent Sisterhood,* 46.

52. Barbara Ehrenreich and Deirdre English, "The Manufacture of Housework," *Socialist Revolution* 5 (Oct.–Dec. 1975).

53. There is a great deal of evidence about the increasing complexity of household cooking; for instance, the number of cookbooks proliferated after 1870. Jillian Strang, "Recipe for Success: Six Culinary Entrepreneurs, 1870–1900," unpublished paper, *Facing the Future,* Graduate Student Conference on Scholarship on Women, Yale University (April 13, 1985). For a contemporary discussion of the need for "distinct utensils for cooking," see Churchman, *Queen of Home,* 56–57; Cowan, *More Work.* 62–66, 89, 99.

54. *Dry Goods Economist* (Feb. 21, 1891), 32; (Feb. 18, 1893) 25, editorial; (July 6, 1893), 5; and (March 10, 1900), 28. Cowan, *More Work,* 98; Ehrenreich and English, *Housework,* 7; *Our Manners at Home and Abroad* (Harrisburg: Pennsylvania Publ. Co., 1883), 87–89. Many sources cite the importance of elaborate mourning costume. For mourning ritual and special street attire, see Nathalie Dana, *Young in New York: A Memoir of a Victorian Girlhood* (New York: Doubleday, 1963), 28, 95, 118. Also *Dry Goods Reporter* (Sept. 15, 1900), 47; *San Francisco Chronicle* (Dec. 20, 1896), 15; *Business Woman's Journal* IV (Jan. 1892), 18.

55. *Dry Goods Economist* (Feb. 11, 1893), 13 and (Dec. 19, 1894), 116; *Dry Goods Reporter* (Jan. 22, 1898), 13. What was true for bicycling was also true for ice skating, although to a lesser degree, see *San Francisco Chronicle* (Dec. 6, 1896), 6, "What Eastern Women of Fashion Wear When They Appear in the Rinks." For a discussion of variety and style, albeit in food, see Sidney Mintz, *Sweetness and Power: The Place of Sugar in Modern History* (New York: Penguin Books, 1986).

56. Finley Peter Dunne, "The Divided Skirt," in *Mr. Dooley: In the Hearts of His Countrymen, The Chicago Journal,* 1898 (Rprnt. Greenwood Press, 1969), 154–57; *Dry Goods Economist* (May 4, 1895), 55. Richards took lessons on the bicycle, see *Diary,* Nov. 25, 1889. Alice Stimson also rode a bicycle and described a trip she took. Stimson *Papers,* Oct. 1895.

57. Quentin Bell, *On Human Finery* (New York: A. A. Wynn, 1979); *Dry Goods Reporter* (Oct. 19, 1901), 39.

58. *Dry Goods Economist* (March 28, 1891), 32, (May 30, 1891), 37, and

(April 7, 1894), 10; *Dry Goods Reporter* (Sept. 15, 1900), 47 and (March 3, 1906), 23. In December 1897, fashion advertisements in the *Boston Globe* spoke to the specific uses of clothing, e.g., "Street Gown from Paris," ". . . The very latest Gown for Church and Promenade," "Morning Costume from Paris," "House Gown from Paris." *Boston Globe* (Dec. 4–5, 7–9, 1897).

59. Daniel M. Fox, *The Discovery of Abundance: Simon N. Patten and the Transformation of Social Theory* (Ithaca: Cornell University Press, 1967), 109ff. In the same vein, see "The Ethics of Shopping," *Fortnightly Review* LXIII (Jan. 1, 1895), 124–45. See discussion of true and false needs in Herbert Marcuse, *One Dimensional Man: Studies in the Ideology of Advanced Industrial Society* (Boston: Beacon Press, 1964), chap. I; see also Daniel Bell, *The Cultural Contradictions of Capitalism* (New York: Basic Books, 1976), 22; Mintz, *Sweetness and Power*, 58–59.

60. Veblen, *Theory of the Leisure Class.*

61. *Dry Goods Economist* (June 4, 1892), 37.

62. *Dry Goods Reporter* (Jan. 23, 1904), 73.

63. Ibid. (April 11, 1906), 62. In an article on perfume and cologne the *DGE* asserted no dressing table was complete without one or more atomizers. *DGE* (Aug. 11, 1894), 43. Similarly, women were expected to own and use a number of different hairbrushes. *DGE* (Sept. 28, 1901), 53.

64. Roland Marchand, *Advertising the American Dream: Making Way for Modernity* (Berkeley: University of California Press, 1985), 160ff; Ryan, *Cradle of the Middle Class*, 199.

65. Richards, *Diaries*, Dec. 22, 1883.

66. Ibid., May 18, 1885.

67. Ibid., March 8, 1887.

68. Pardee, *Diaries*, Sept. 22, 25, 1893.

69. Edward Bellamy, "A Vital Domestic Problem," *Good Housekeeping* 10 (Dec. 21, 1889), 76.

70. Ryan, *Cradle of the Middle Class*, 199.

71. Gwendolyn Wright, *Moralism and the Modern Home: Domestic Architecture and Cultural Conflict in Chicago, 1873–1913* (Chicago: University of Chicago Press, 1980), 35.

72. Veblen, *Theory of the Leisure Class.*

73. Ryan, *Cradle of the Middle Class*, 203; Kenneth Ames, "Material Culture as Non-Verbal Communication: A Historical Case Study," *Journal of American Culture* 3 (Winter 1980), 619–41.

74. T. J. Jackson Lears, *No Place of Grace: Antimodernism and the Transformation of American Culture 1880–1920* (New York: Pantheon, 1981), 223. Lears notes the "endless dualisms of Victorian culture," such as mastery and submission, free will and determinism; the rationale for the purchase of many new consumer items fits into this analysis.

75. Susan Strasser, *Never Done: A History of American Housework* (New York: Pantheon, 1982), 4–6; for a view of "shopping as a fine art," see *New York Times* (Oct. 4, 1885), 4:1.

76. *Dry Goods Economist* (March 23, 1901), 153; on an earlier occasion the *DGE* wrote, "A man shopping alone and unprotected is simply ludicrous, but

a man with his wife or other female relative is pathetic . . . ," *DGE* (Sept. 10, 1892), 140; see also *Woman's Journal* (April 26, 1873), 135:2. Women's diaries often refer to participation of husbands in shopping for home furnishings and accessories. See Forbes, *Diaries,* May 13, 1872; Richards, *Diaries,* April–May 1885; Pardee, *Diaries,* June 1883, Nov. 1888. See also Seidl, "Consumers' Choices," 183–197. In spite of these examples, men were still very much the exception in the dry-goods stores into the early decades of the 20th century. Clerks at Marshall Field called men who tagged along with their wives "Molly Husbands." Lloyd Wendt and Herman Kogan, *Give the Lady What She Wants! The Story of Marshall Field & Company* (New York: Rand McNally, 1952), 277; see also Wesley Mitchell, "The Backward Art of Spending Money," *The American Economic Review* 2 (June, 1912), 269, 274.

Estimates about the percentage of shoppers who were female varied. The generally recognized figure was about 90%. See *Dry Goods Economist* (June 13, 1896), 16, (Feb. 27, 1897), 65, (Feb. 4, 1899), 4; *Ladies' Home Journal* advertisement in *DGE* (April 3, 1897), 8; *Dry Goods Reporter* (Jan. 21, 1899), 37; *Merchants Trade Journal* (Sept. 1914), 64.

77. Wally Secombe, "The Housewife and Her Labor Under Capitalism," *New Left Review* 83 (Jan.–Feb., 1974), 14. See Forbes diary *re* purchase of gas stove, Aug. 26, 1880; Daniel T. Rodgers, *The Work Ethic in Industrial America, 1850–1920* (Chicago: Univ. of Chicago Press, 1979), 196–98. The *Dry Good Economist* saw a woman's shopping as "a serious and important part of her duties," *Dry Goods Economist* (Nov. 24, 1889), 25. For a contemporary view of women and changing roles, see Kate Gannett Wells, "The Transitional American Woman," *Atlantic Monthly* 46 (Dec. 1880), 817–23.

78. Nina Auerbach, *Woman and The Demon: The Life of Victorian Myth* (Cambridge: Harvard University Press, 1982), 61. For discussion of a new club designed as headquarters for ladies who came to the city for shopping, see *Business Woman's Journal* (Nov.–Dec., 1889), 179. A woman's work was "the shopping tour." See also *Dry Goods Reporter* (Oct. 28, 1905), 49–51.

79. *The Woman's Journal* (April 26, 1873), 135:2.

80. *New York Times* (Sept. 9, 1894), 18:1.

81. Sophie Hall (Mrs. George W. Hall), *Diaries,* NYPL. Feb. 3, 1879; "Shopping in Paris" *New York Daily Graphic* (Aug. 15, 1873), 318:2.

82. Hall, *Diaries,* Feb. 8, 1879.

83. *New York Times* (June 13, 1881), 4:5, editorial; the *Times* editorialist felt that "the amount of money annually spent in shopping by the women of America is so enormous that in comparison with it the amount spent by men for whiskey seems too trifling to deserve notice" *Harper's Weekly* I (Oct. 31, 1857), 689–90.

84. Even sympathetic observers saw shopping in America as a "mania" and a "mild aberration." Katherine G. Busbey, *Home Life in America* (London: Methuen, 1910), 148–9; "Shopping," *The Living Age* 251 (Dec. 22, 1906), 758–60.

85. Lears, *No Place of Grace,* 108–14. Stores reflected and promoted new middle-class interests and social roles; as upper and middle-class women took up active sports, tennis, bicycling, and golf clothes became important com-

modities; the Boston Store in Chicago catered to "every class of society" and was known as "the Gold Mine of State Street." This was unusual enough to cause comment; see also *Dry Goods Reporter* (Dec. 14, 1901), 17.

86. Lawrence Vesey, "Intellectual History and the New Social History," in *New Directions in American Intellectual History,* John Higham and Paul Conkin, eds. (Baltimore: Johns Hopkins University Press, 1979), 6.

87. Wendt and Kogan, *Give the Lady What She Wants!,* 230.

88. Warren Susman, *Culture as History: The Transformation of American Society in the Twentieth Century* (New York: Pantheon, 1984), 214; Lears, *No Place of Grace* 220–23. Shopping was, unequivocally, woman's work, but she was perceived as inadequate even in this area. "The shopper half of the time does not know what she should of the gentle art of buying." *Dry Goods Economist* (Oct. 22, 1892), 11. See also Laura Shapiro, *Perfection Salad: Woman and Cooking at the Turn of the Century* (New York: Farrar, Straus and Giroux, 1986), 85. Shapiro quotes Mrs. Ellen Richards, head of the newly organized Home Economics Association, "The new function of the 20th-century housekeeper was to consume, to spend money wisely." Joan Jacobs Brumberg has pointed out that home economists, through the consumer economics movement, were promoting the idea that there were rational, scientific grounds for all purchases. Telephone conversation with author.

89. Charles Grandison Finney, *Lectures on Revivals of Religion,* William G. McLaughlin, ed. (Cambridge: Belknap Press, 1960), 143, 154; James Fenimore Cooper, *Home as Found* (New York: New York Publ. Co., 1903); Mark Twain, *The Gilded Age: A Tale of Today* (Hartford: American Publ. Co., 1874). For the intellectual history of attitudes toward consumption, see Horowitz, *Morality of Spending,* and Neil Harris, "The Drama of Consumer Desire," in *Yankee Enterprise,* Otto Mayr and Robert C. Post, eds. (Washington, D.C.: Smithsonian Institution, 1981), 189–216. For a discussion of the changes in American thinking about material progress, see Harvey Green, *The Light of the Home: An Intimate View of the Lives of Women in Victorian America* (New York: Pantheon, 1983), 7ff.; also Daniel Bell, *Cultural Contradictions of Capitalism* 55–65.

90. William A. Alcott, *The Young Woman's Guide to Excellence* (New York: Clark, Austin & Smith, 1852), 209; Arthur M. Schlesinger, *Learning How to Behave: A Historical Study of American Etiquette Books* (New York: Macmillan, 1946).

91. *A Peep into Catharine Street, or the Mysteries of Shopping.* By a Late Retailer (New York: John Slater, 1846); for antebellum concern about materialism, production, and consumption see Harris, "The Drama of Consumer Desire," 190–93.

92. Greene, *The Perils of Pearl Street* "The love of sampling is inherent in every American woman," said the *Dry Goods Economist* (April 7, 1894), 21.

93. Rosalind H. Williams, *Dream Worlds: Mass Consumption in Late 19th Century France* (California: University of California Press, 1982), 262; for a discussion of the transformation of sugar from a luxury into a proletarian "goody," see Mintz, *Sweetness and Power, 121, 174.*

94. *Dry Goods Economist* (Aug. 3, 1893), 49 and (Sept. 28, 1901), 53. A woman picked up with a bottle of cologne offered to pay for it when taken into custody. *New York Times* (Jan. 27, 1881), 3:2.

95. Rachael Helena Bowlby, "Commerce, and Culture in Dreiser, Gissing and Zola" (Ph.D. diss., Yale University, December 1983); see also Jules Henry, *Culture Against Man* (New York: Vintage Books, 1965), 9; Susman, *Culture*, introduction.

96. *Dry Goods Reporter* (Feb 6, 1904), 55.

97. Dorothy Davis, *A History of Shopping* (London: Routledge & Kegan Paul, 1966); Roland Marchand notes that the ideology of obsolescence was played out in women's ready-to-wear. Marchand, *Advertising the American Dream*, 156.

98. For a mid-19th-century view of consumption as insignia, see Cooper, *Home as Found;* see also Veblen, *Theory of the Leisure Class* and Busbey, *Home Life*, 102. For modern discussions of consumption see Raymond Williams, *Problems in Materialism and Culture: Selected Essays* (London: Verso Editions and NLB, 1980), 189; Persons, *Decline of American Gentility*, 118ff; Pierre Bourdieu, *Distinction: A Social Critique of the Judgement of Taste*, transl. Richard Nice (Cambridge: Harvard University Press, 1984), 56; also Smith, *Ladies of the Leisure Class*, 69; and Lois W. Banner, *American Beauty* (New York: Knopf, 1983), 28ff. Karen Halttunen deals extensively with this theme and the importance of the ability to "read" others in the new urban world of strangers. Halttunen, *Confidence Men and Painted Women*; see also John Kason, "Civility and Rudeness: Urban Etiquette and the Bourgeois Social Order in Nineteenth-Century America," *Prospects* 9 (1984), 151–52.

99. *Dry Goods Economist* (Dec. 5, 1896), 37; see also George Parsons, "The Growth of Materialism," *Atlantic Monthly* 60 (Aug. 1887), 157–72; Bourdieu, *Distinction*, 2; Hrant Pasdermadjian, *The Department Store: Its Origins, Evolution and Economics* (London: Newman Books, 1954), 129.

100. *Dry Goods Economist* (Feb. 2, 1901), 62. Women often made over old clothes. See Pardee, *Diaries*, April 1, Nov. 19, 1885; Nov. 21, 1887; Jan. 1, 1898; Forbes, *Diaries*, June 15–19, 1880; Margaret Walsh, "The Democratization of Fashion: The Emergence of the Women's Dress Pattern Industry," *Journal of American History* 66 (Sept. 1979): 299–313.

101. Alfred D. Chandler, Jr., *The Visible Hand: The Managerial Revolution in American Business* (Cambridge: Belknap Press, 1977); Alan Trachtenberg, *The Incorporation of America: Culture and Society in the Gilded Age* (New York: Hill and Wang, 1982). A conjunction of well-documented circumstances worked to raise purchasing power among the burgeoning population while major developments in agriculture, technology, transportation, and distribution transformed the material economy. There was a dynamic expansion of output, virtually a "material cornucopia," which in itself furthered the spiral of a rising production-consumption dynamic. See also Fred Hirsch, *Social Limits to Growth* (Cambridge: Harvard University Press, 1976), 123. The growth of national distribution networks furthered the development of stores like Marshall Field & Co. and Macy's. See *Dry Goods Reporter* (July 25, 1903), 19.

102. Hirsch, *Social Limits*, 21; William Leiss, *The Limits to Satisfaction: An Essay on the Problem of Needs and Commodities* (Toronto: University of Toronto Press, 1976), 8. Bourdieu sees an order of succession, a constancy of the gap between groups. Bourdieu, *Distinction*, 163–65; Mintz, *Sweetness and Power*, 93–95.

103. *Dry Goods Economist*—see various issues advertising Trilby items: (March 23, 1895), 58; (May 18, 1895), 38; (June 29, 1895), 48; (July 27, 1895), 53; (Oct. 12, 1895) 69; (Feb. 22, 1896), 79.

104. Stimson *Papers*, Oct. 1894.

105. *Dry Goods Economist* (Feb. 3, 1894), 21; "Events move too quickly now," the Wide-Awake Retailer warned. "A make or weave of dress goods that would be fairly good for years in earlier decades may not live longer than a few weeks now, but be a 'red hot' seller while the rage for it lasted." *DGE* (July 10, 1897), 53.

106. Ibid. (July 27, 1893), 21, editorial.

107. Ibid. (April 6, 1895), 65; Mintz, *Sweetness and Power*, 121.

108. Veblen, *Theory of the Leisure Class*.

109. *Dry Goods Economist* (April 6, 1895), 65.

110. Leiss, *Limits*, 13; also see provocative discussion in Hirsch, *Social Limits*, 85ff.

111. Martin, *Standard of Living*, 191; Victor S. Clark, *The History of Manufactures in the United States*, II, 1860–1893 (New York: McGraw Hill, 1929), 446–47.
Preliminary Report on the Eighth Census, Washington, May 20, 1862, 64, and 175, Table 17, "Clothing Made in the Following States During the Year Ending June 1, 1860"; *Statistics on the Wealth and Industry of the United States*, Washington, 1872; *Ninth Census*, "The General Statistics of Manufactures by Industries," Table VIII B, 394, 426: Clothing.
No women's ready-to-wear appeared in Sears Roebuck Catalog until 1894. Cowan, *More Work*, 74–75.

112. *New York Herald* (Oct. 10, 1875), 1:6. Visitor Katherine Busbey noted that the price, cut, and quality of machine-made items were better in U.S. than in England. Machine-made "stitching is so cleverly done as to resemble hand work." Busbey, *Home Life in America*, 155–56. For a discussion of how industrial capitalism has appropriated the manufacturing functions of the household, see Henry Braverman, *Labor and Monopoly Capitalism: The Degradation of Work in the Twentieth Century* (New York: Monthly Review Press, 1974), 274–78.

113. *New York Herald* (Oct. 17, 1875), 1:6.

114. Not even women on the frontier were immune to the lure of ready-made clothing. Emily Fitzgerald, the wife of an army doctor stationed in Fort Lapwai, Idaho, wrote to a friend in 1876: "There are some people at the Agency who, in some way or other, come across advertisements in New York, the cheap things they get just astonish me [story of a wrapper and cost]. . . . Can you do any better than that? . . . I see in the Altman's Catalogue calico wrappers trimmed with a dark band, pockets and all fixings—for one dollar. *What is the use of sewing any more?*" Quoted in Caludia B. Kidwell and Mar-

garet C. Christman, *Suiting Everyone: The Democratization of Clothing in America* (Washington: Smithsonian Institution Press, 1974), 149.

115. Abba Goold Woolson, *Women in American Society* (Boston: Roberts Brothers, 1873), 235; for a discussion of material, linings, cutting, and mending, see Beecher and Stowe, *The American Woman's Home*, 355–59.

116. Pardee, *Diaries*, Feb. 18, April 25, Jan. 22, 1898. For the time required to prepare a wardrobe, see Woolson, *Women in American Society*, 235.

117. Kidwell and Christman, *Suiting Everyone*, 108. A woman's bust measurement was crucial to early ready-made costumes. The Lord & Taylor catalog of 1881 guaranteed only skirt length and bust size, "the other measurements are in proportion"; for an example of the incredibly complicated dress patterns women followed for home sewing, see *The Delineator* LVII (Butterick Publ. Co., June 1901), 890–913, and Supplement no. 20 to *Harper's Bazar*, 1880.

118. *Dry Goods Reporter* (Sept. 8, 1906), 51; Michael B. Miller, *The Bon Marché: Bourgeois Culture and the Department Store, 1869–1920* (Princeton: Princeton University Press, 1981), 34–35.

119. Christine Stansell, "The Origins of the Sweatshop: Women and Early Industrialization in New York City," in Michael H. Frisch and Daniel J. Walkowitz, eds., *Working-Class America: Essays on Labor, Community and American Society* (Urbana: University of Illinois Press, 1983), 84; Kidwell and Christman, *Suiting Everyone*, 15; Daniel Boorstin, *The Americans: The Democratic Experience* (New York: Vintage Books, 1974), 99–100.

120. Robert Twyman, *A History of Marshall Field & Company, 1852–1906* (Philadelphia: University of Pennsylvania Press, 1954), 45. Dry-goods stores carried few ready-made items before 1865; only cloaks (mantuas), hose, and shawls were generally available. Marshall Field & Co. offered a slightly greater variety after 1871, but the stock was still limited to accessories: gloves, collars, cuffs, and handkerchiefs. Mrs. Caroline Dunstan's diaries suggest the extent to which urban women were engaged in home manufacture. She shopped for shirting muslin, bed sheeting, and for toweling, which she and her daughters fashioned into usable products. Handkerchiefs, stockings, gloves, a shawl, an occasional hat and veil, a damask table cloth, a winter cloak were the types of finished soft goods she was able to purchase in New York City between 1867 and 1870. Caroline A. Dunstan, *Diaries*, 1866–1870 (NYPL). See Lois W. Banner, *American Beauty*, (New York: Alfred A. Knopf, 1983), 28ff; Clark, *History of Manufactures*, II, 446, states that the "value of factory-made women's clothing [was] less than ⅛ that of men's in 1890."

121. *New York Daily Tribune* (Oct. 4, 1875), 5: A. T. Stewart advertisement; (Nov. 1, 1875), 6: Lord & Taylor and Arnold Constable advertisements.

122. *Dry Goods Economist* (July 23, 1898), 13; for a discussion of illusion and reality, see Remy G. Saisselin, *Bourgeois and the Bibelot* (New Brunswick: Rutgers University Press, 1984), 126.

123. *Dry Goods Economist* (July 25, 1891), 66.

124. Ibid. (March 9, 1895), 29 and (Oct. 10, 1903), 77.

125. Ibid. (April 23, 1898), 29.

126. *Dry Goods Reporter* (Aug. 4, 1906), 46.

127. *Dry Goods Economist* (March 3, 1894), 55, and (Jan. 13, 1900), 71.

128. *Dry Goods Reporter* (March 3, 1906), 93; Macy's Fall and Winter Catalogue 1903–04, p. 41, announced "The Macy Manufacturing Method *Makes home sewing obsolete.*" Advertising Catalogues, 1903–1906, RG7, Box 2, R. H. Macy & Co. Archives, New York City (hereafter, Macy Archives).

129. *Dry Goods Economist* (Jan. 29, 1898), 53.

130. *Dry Goods Reporter* (May 30, 1903), 23.

131. *Dry Goods Economist* (Aug. 5, 1899), 95.

132. Smith, *Ladies of the Leisure Class,* 71.

133. Pardee, *Diaries,* May 18, 1898.

134. Williams, *Dream Worlds,* 15; see Saisselin, *Bourgeois and the Bibelot,* 62; *New York Times* (Oct. 4, 1885), 4:1.

135. *Dry Goods Reporter* (Oct. 19, 1901), 39.

136. Pardee, *Diaries,* May 26, 1909.

137. *Dry Goods Economist* (March 9, 1895), 29 and (Jan. 16, 1897), 67; for a traditional view of home-made items, see *The Business Woman's Journal* I (Nov.–Dec. 1889), 176–177.

138. Busbey, *Home Life,* 119.

2. The World of the Store

1. Busbey, *Home Life,* 151. Macy General Manager A. T. LaForge remarked on the "singing birds and moving figures that are so much life like that [*sic*] excite universal wonder." R. H. Macy Archives, extracts from the diary of A. T. LaForge, Oct. 30, 1870. "The important openings are now those made by the great dry-goods houses," *The World* (New York) (March 3, 1872), 2; *New York Times* (Aug. 6, 1905) III, 2.

Neil McKendrick et al. have discussed consumer culture in 18th-century England in much the same terms as the following discussion; however, they were not writing about mass culture, nor were they looking at the great shopping bazaars. Neil McKendrick, John Brewer, and J. H. Plumb, *The Birth of a Consumer Society: The Commercialization of 18th Century England* (Bloomington: Indiana University Press, 1982).

2. *Boston Globe* (Dec. 11, 1897), 4:4, and (Dec. 4, 1897), 6:7.

3. *Dry Goods Reporter* (Jan. 1, 1898), 43; Leach, *True Love and Perfect Union,* Chap. 9; Benson, *Counter Cultures . . . ;* Williams, *Dream Worlds;* Miller, *Bon Marché.* In addition to the stores mentioned in this study, there were department stores in all major American cities by the end of the 19th century. The process of development and change was different in each institution, but the result was often similar. A partial listing of those I have not mentioned would include Rich's (Atlanta), Strawbridge & Clothier (Philadelphia), John Shillito Co. (Cincinnati), The Emporium (San Francisco), The J. L. Hudson Co. (Detroit), Jordan Marsh (Boston), Mandel Bros. (Chicago), and Bamberger's (Newark). There were, of course, many others.

4. Williams, *Dream Worlds,* 265.

5. Émile Zola, *Au bonheur des dames,* trans. John Stirling (Philadelphia: T. B. Peterson & Bros., 1883), 351–52.

6. *Dry Goods Economist* (Feb. 24, 1894), 7; The visual impact of the white fair persisted at the end of the 19th century. Wanamaker's all-white decor elicited this comment: "As one alights from the elevator the eye is greeted with wave after wave of billowy white . . . were we asked for a suggestion which would improve the general effect the only one we could offer would be to dress the saleswomen in white. Then the effect of snowy white would be complete." *Dry Goods Economist* (Jan. 9, 1897), 63. For a late 20th-century view of this phenomenon, see Michael Schudson, *Advertising, the Uneasy Persuasion: Its Dubious Impact on American Society* (New York: Basic Books, 1984), 150.

7. *Dry Goods Economist* (Jan. 13, 1900), 37; Helen Lefkowitz Horowitz, *Culture and the City: Cultural Philanthropy in Chicago from the 1800s to 1917* (Lexington: Univ. Press of Kentucky, 1976).

8. William Leach has elaborated on this theme. See William Leach, "Transformations in a Culture of Consumption," *Journal of American History* 71 (Sept. 1984), 323 and fn 9. *Dry Goods Economist* (Feb. 24, 1894), 7.

9. James Huneker, *New Cosmopolis: A Book of Images* (New York: Scribner's, 1915), 118.

10. *Dry Goods Economist* (June 15, 1893), 22, and (June 29, 1893), 14. The French silk manufacturers, together with the flower and feather manufacturers (Chambre Syndicale des Plumes et des Fleurs), adopted shades and colors for each succeeding season. See *DGE* (Dec. 28, 1889), 5, and (May 2, 1891), 17; *DGE* (June 18, 1892), 8; Pierre Bourdieu, *Distinction,* 311. Fashion included clothing in the correct shade for a particular reason—"a base element in the mode of domination."

11. *Dry Goods Economist* (June 18, 1892), 8, and (Dec. 28, 1889), 30.

12. Ibid. (June 24, 1892), 11, and (May 30, 1896), 14. The importance of improved dyes as well as manufacturing technology contributed to explosion of new colors. *Dry Goods Economist* (Sept. 10, 1892), 66. Louis Hermsdorf, who perfected fast black, was "recognized as being of as great practical importance to the dry-goods trade as was Columbus' find to the monarchs of Europe."

13. Ibid. (Dec. 21, 1895), 16, and (Jan. 12, 1897), 54.

14. Williams, *Dream Worlds,* 69–71. Even the skylights were absorbed into this material economy; we read of the "exquisite effect of translucent banners of lace" attached to the skylights. *Dry Goods Economist* (Jan. 13, 1900), 37.

15. *Dry Goods Economist* (Aug. 3, 1893), 49.

16. *New York Daily Tribune* (Nov. 17, 1896), 2:1; for a description of the theatrical quality of department store interiors, see Miller, *Bon Marché,* 169ff; the lavish settings of the department stores replicated other settings of the Gilded Age: lobster palaces, hotels, restaurants, and vaudeville houses. Banner, *American Beauty,* 184–88.

17. For a 19th-century view of the effects of sentimental literature on girls

and women, see Mary T. Bissell, M.D., "Emotions Versus Health in Women," *Popular Science Monthly* 32 (Feb. 1888), 506; Dee Garrison, "Immoral Fiction in the Late Victorian Library," in Daniel Walker Howe, ed., *Victorian America*, (Philadelphia: University of Pennsylvania Press, 1976), 154–159; *Dry Goods Economist* (March 10, 1900), 21.

18. Bowlby, "Commerce and Culture" 76; Abraham Meyerson, M.D., *The Nervous Housewife* (Boston: Little, Brown, 1920), 125.

19. *Dry Goods Economist* (Sept. 28, 1901), 53; Bissell, "Emotions Versus Health," 506–7.

20. Williams, *Dream Worlds*, 53–59; Leach, *True Love and Perfect Union*, 224. One manufacturer labelled his product "Geisha Waists." *Dry Goods Economist* (Sept. 28, 1901), 53. Banner sees new trend toward open sensual expression in 1890s. Banner, *American Beauty*, 124, 175, 188.

21. Duncan, *Culture and Democracy*, Chaps. X, XI.

22. Dubuisson provides insight into the problems and international dimensions of the new consumer culture. Paul Dubuisson, "Les Voleuses des grands magasins," *Archives d'anthropologie criminelle*, XVI (1901), 1–20, 341–70. Discussions with psychologist Carol F. Reich clarified many aspects of female behavior that appear in this study.

23. Dubuisson, "Les Voleuses des grands magasins," 344. While words did not mean the same thing or have the same connotation that they have for our late–20th-century understanding, the deeper relationship between shoplifting/kleptomania and sex is unmistakable. Dubuisson was not alone in seeing the seduction of the modern department store. Pierre Janet, one of the foremost psychologists of the early 20th century, described the connection between the experience of shoplifting and the relief of depression in terms that left no doubt of the sexual undertones. He cited the case history of "Mme. V," who discussed her shoplifting in frankly sexual terms, saying in her first attempt she experienced a flush of relief and a sense of empowerment that she had not felt before. The memory of that experience and that emotion pushed her to recreate the situation as often as possible, "in spite of the great moral resistance" she felt. "I had too much need to do these things in order to relieve myself and to comfort myself." Janet wrote that the woman recited all this with great calmness and described how the shoplifting made her feel "so good" that she even dreamed about it. Pierre Janet, "La Kleptomanie et la Depression Mentale," *J. de psychologie, normal et pathologique* 8ème Année (1911), 97–103.

See also Henry Putnam Stearns, M.D., *Insanity: Its Causes and Prevention* (New York: G. P. Putnam & Sons, 1883), 14–15, 67–68; *Dry Goods Economist* (Oct. 29, 1900), 57.

A mid-20th-century English study of shoplifting suggested that in some few cases sexual excitement was a contributing factor. T.C.N. Gibbens and Joyce Prince, *Shoplifting* (London: The Institute for the Study and Treatment of Delinquency, 1962), 72–73.

24. Dubuisson, "Les Voleuses," 342, 349; *New York Evening Post* (June 3, 1903), 5:1; Miller, *Bon Marché*, 206; *Dry Goods Economist* (March 15, 1902), 75; *Brooklyn Eagle* (Oct. 27, 1896), 16:2. For a description of the

seductive quality of the ability to "touch with abandon," see Alexandra Artley, ed., *The Golden Age of Shop Design: European Shop Interiors 1880–1939* (New York: Whitney Library of Design, 1976), 7.

Much of the claim of excitability and emotional stimulation emanated from highly conservative views of women in society and the so-called hereditary limitations of woman's nature. See George M. Beard, *American Nervousness: Its Causes and Consequences* (New York: G. P. Putnam, 1881); Bissell, "Emotions Versus Health," 507–8; G.T.W. Patrick, "The Psychology of Women," *Popular Science Monthly* 47 (June 1895), 209, 216–17. Jean Strouse has demonstrated how this understanding of woman's nature colored the life of Alice James and her countemporaries. Jean Strouse, *Alice James: A Biography* (Boston: Houghton Mifflin, 1980), 108.

25. *New York Times* (April 11, 1895); *New York Evening Post* (June 3, 1903), 5:1.

26. *New York Times* (Nov. 3, 1889), 10:1. One of the many articles about "Fair Bargain Seekers," which speaks of the derangement of women as well as the fatigue and anxiety that accompanies their shopping. Gibbens' shoplifting study cited statements about tension and anxiety in accounts of women picked up for shoplifting. Gibbens and Prince, *Shoplifting*, 73.

27. George F. Parsons, "The Growth of Materialism," *The Atlantic Monthly* 60 (Aug. 1887), 164–65; Walt Whitman, *Prose Works* 1892, II, Floyd Stovall, ed. (New York: New York University Press, 1964), 419–25. Noting the brilliant displays, counters piled high with seemingly unwatched goods, and the sheltering crowds, one journalist commented, "The temptation to steal is not to be wondered at." *New York Evening Post* (June 3, 1903), 5:1. Bowlby, "Commerce and Culture," 76.

28. *New York Evening Post* (Feb. 18, 1899), 16.

29. Williams, *Dream Worlds*, 53–59, 265; An article in the *Dry Goods Reporter* echoed Williams: "Who does not remember his first visit to a department store and the feelings of wonder and bewilderment which it inspired?" *DGR* (Jan. 1, 1898), 43. See also Anna Steese Richardson, "The Modern Woman's Paradise," *Woman's Home Companion* 38 (Sept. 1911), 22; Miller, *Bon Marché*, 206.

30. *Dry Goods Reporter* (May 20, 1899), 20.

31. *Dry Goods Economist* (Feb. 3, 1894), 57.

32. *New York Times* (Sept. 27, 1896), 3:2. Newspapers often contributed to the frenzy that accompanied these exhibits. When the Abraham & Straus store in Brooklyn exhibited a statue of Justice—solid silver and 9 feet high—which had been on display at the Chicago Columbian Exposition, the *Brooklyn Eagle* suggested to readers that the crowds that had formed around the railroad car at each stop on its trip to New York would certainly be repeated at Abraham & Straus. *Brooklyn Eagle* (Nov. 5, 1893), 24:6.

33. *Dry Goods Economist* (March 27, 1897), 5.

34. *Dry Goods Economist* (Nov. 17, 1900), 5.

35. Ibid. (April 29, 1899), 42, and (May 3, 1902), 66; Pasdermadjian, *The Department Store*, 125. The pressure to buy was everywhere in evidence. An article, "What Is the Name of Your Sale?" demonstrates, as well, the intense

pressure to sell. See *Dry Goods Economist* (July 30, 1892), 13, and (Feb. 24, 1894), 5. For problems that accompanied this loss of all sense of proportion, see Williams, *Dream Worlds*, 53–54. Patrick Brantlinger discusses stores and "pseudo-events"—staged sales that are a substitution for reality. *Bread and Circuses: Theories of Mass Culture and Social Decay* (Ithaca: Cornell Univ. Press, 1983), 255ff.

36. Saisselin, *The Bourgeois and the Bibelot*, Chap. III, "The Department Store as Cultural Space."

37. *Dry Goods Economist* (June 13, 1896), 15, (May 3, 1902), 26, and (Mar. 27, 1897), 5, 41; *Boston Globe* (Dec. 6, 1897), 2:1. For a discussion of the myriad ways to attract customers and increase sales, see Lucy W. Salmon, "The Economics of Spending," *Outlook* 9 (April 17, 1909), 886–87. When Émile Zola described the bouquet of white violets given to every customer who bought the "smallest article" in the Ladies' Paradise, he was not exaggerating. The *Dry Goods Economist* suggested that a bunch of fresh flowers be given to each woman who made a purchase at the Druggist's Sundries counter. See Zola, *Au bonheur*, 353; and *Dry Goods Economist* (Feb. 22, 1896), 83, and (April 17, 1893), 43.

38. Margarete Bohme, *The Department Store: A Novel of Today* (New York: D. Appleton and Co., 1912), 110–11. For a description of the solid silver statue of Justice, originally displayed at the Chicago World's Fair and subsequently installed in Brooklyn's Abraham & Straus, see *Brooklyn Eagle* (Nov. 5, 1893), 24:6. Duncan, *Culture and Democracy*, 113.

39. *Dry Goods Reporter* (Nov. 18, 1905), 37.

40. *Dry Goods Economist* (Aug. 28, 1897), 73.

41. Ibid. (Nov. 2, 1901), 85; Children's Day at Marshall Field was for the express purpose of "cultivating the good will of children." *Dry Goods Reporter* (Oct. 17, 1903), 72; for children as sales targets in the mid-18th century, see McKendrick et al., *The Birth of a Consumer Society*, chap. VII, "The New World of Children."

42. *Dry Goods Reporter* (April 20, 1901), 31; *Dry Goods Economist* (Aug. 28, 1897), 73, and (Nov. 2, 1901), 85.

43. *Dry Goods Reporter* (Feb. 28, 1903), 38.

44. *Dry Goods Economist* (Oct. 10, 1896), 55, and (May 15, 1897), 39.

45. Ibid. (Nov. 24, 1894), 24. By 1901 Siegel-Cooper had a complete music department, which sold sheet music as well as musical instruments, and "a pianist demonstrated the latest popular tunes throughout the day." Hundreds were reportedly drawn to the department. *Dry Goods Economist* (Dec. 7, 1901), 18. See also Dorothy Davis, *A History of Shopping* (London: Routledge & Kegan Paul, 1966), 289.

46. Hirsch, *Social Limits to Growth*, 65; Paul Goodman and Percival Goodman, *Communitas; Means of Livelihood and Ways of Life* (New York: Vintage Books, 1960), 127.

47. Duncan, *Culture and Democracy*, 140; see also Salmon, "Economics of Spending," 884–85; and Bourdieu, *Distinction*, 55–57.

48. Size and growth of stores will be discussed in chapters III and IV.

49. Wright, *Moralism and the Modern Home:* 19; Bourdieu, *Distinction,* 55–56. Much of the middle class had the economic power to keep necessity "at arm's length . . . life style came increasingly to the fore." See also Smith, *Ladies of the Leisure Class,* 66–67; Veblen, *Theory of the Leisure Class.* Trade journals touted the role of the dry-goods bazaar in formulating middle-class taste. *Dry Goods Reporter* (July 20, 1901), 15; (July 25, 1903), 19; and (Nov. 14, 1903), 57.

50. The *Dry Goods Reporter* advised merchants, "The den has become a very important room" (June 16, 1900), 21. Duncan, *Culture and Democracy,* 117.

51. Richardson, "Modern Woman's Paradise, 22.

52. *Dry Goods Reporter* (July 20, 1901), 15; Colleen McDannell, *The Christian Home in Victorian America, 1840–1900* (Bloomington: Indiana University Press, 1986), 42–43.

53. Ralph M. Hower, *History of Macy's of New York, 1858–1919: Chapters in the Evolution of the Department Store* (Cambridge: Harvard University Press, 1943), 103, 145.

54. Wright, *Moralism and the Modern Home,* 18.

55. *Dry Goods Economist* (April 17, 1897), 45. Even "kitchen furniture" found a place in the new house furnishing departments (May 22, 1897), 61.

56. *New York Daily Tribune* (April 21, 1906), 12:3. The *Dry Goods Reporter* described the House Palatial as "a quarter million dollar mansion with a summer garden" (Oct. 17, 1908), 83.

57. Saisselin, *The Bourgeois and the Bibelot,* 47; Harris, "Museums, Merchandising and Popular Taste" 152.

58. Dubuisson, "Les Voleuses des grands magasins," 342; D.J.K., "Shopping at Stewarts," *Hearth and Home* I (Jan. 9, 1869), 43. Even at this early date the wonders within the store were in stark contrast to "the ugly scenes of the city." For turn of the century views on the modern home environment, see Wright, *Moralism and the Modern Home,* 122–26.

59. Auerbach, *Women and the Demon,* 4–5; Michael Paul Rogin, *Subversive Genealogy: The Politics and Art of Herman Melville* (New York: Knopf, 1983), 28.

60. *Dry Goods Reporter,* Symposium, (Jan. 6, 1906), 33; For a description of the giant new stores see Harris, "Museums, Merchandising and Popular Taste," 150–57. "The manager of the ideal store should be able to say to the customers . . . "Come to see us; this is your house." *Dry Goods Reporter* (Mar. 22, 1902), 55.

61. Lears, *No Place of Grace,* 15–18; Bell, *Cultural Contradictions of Capitalism,* 55, 65.

62. Ade, *Stories of the Streets,* 104–108, "After the Sky-Scrapers, What?" See also Jean Gordon & Jan McArthur, "American Women and Domestic Consumption, 1800–1920: Four Interpretive Themes," *Journal of American Culture* 8 (Fall 1985), 36.

63. Williams, *Problems in Materialism,* 186–89.

64. *Dry Goods Economist* (March 4, 1899), 59; Abraham Cahan picked up on this theme and used almost identical phrasing when describing a woman at a Catskills resort: ". . . she would owe her grocer and butcher rather than go to the country with less than ten big trunks full of duds. . . ." Abraham Cahan, *The Rise of David Levinsky* (New York: Harper & Row, 1960), 421.

65. *Dry Goods Economist* (April 20, 1895), 57, (June 15, 1895), 55, and (Nov. 30, 1895), 57; *Dry Goods Reporter* (Aug. 15, 1903), 41–43. Journalist Anna Richardson described to her readers the "deep easy chairs and new magazines" in the Ladies' Parlor, and added that the quality paper on the mahogany writing desk "is as velvet under her pen, but quite beyond her purse." Richardson, "Modern Woman's Paradise," 22. See also R. H. Macy Co. advertisement touting the new Ladies Waiting Room, described as "the most luxurious and beautiful department devoted to the comfort of ladies to be found in a mercantile establishment in the city. The style of decoration is Louis XV. . . ." *New York Herald* (April 3, 1892), 31, RG 10, Box 2, Doc. # 2101, Macy Archives; see also Benson, *Counter Cultures*, 8.

66. Richards, *Diaries*, (Feb. 8 and 13, 1884). Macy's lunch room opened in 1878; *New York Times* (Oct. 4, 1885), 4:1, and (Dec. 6, 1885), 4:5; *Dry Goods Economist* (March 2, 1895), 74; Richardson, "Modern Women's Paradise," 22; see also Erving Goffman, *Behavior in Public Places: Notes on the Social Organization of Gatherings* (New York: The Free Press, 1963). Lenore Davidoff, *The Best Circles: Women and Society in Victorian England* (New Jersey: Rowman & Littlefield, 1973), 62. Davidoff sees the New York City department stores as "undermining the domination of the home as the only socially correct meeting ground."

67. Twyman, *A History of Marshall Field*, 107. The obituary of merchant Hugh O'Neill cited him as "the first retailer to fit up a reception room for the comfort of women shoppers, ca. 1870s." *Dry Goods Economist* (March 22, 1902), 24; *Dry Goods Reporter* (Aug. 15, 1903), 41.

68. *Dry Goods Reporter* (July 5, 1902), 61; the large department stores in Philadelphia and Boston became settings for discussions about twilight sleep. See *Eliza Taylor Ransom Papers*, "Twilight Sleep Clippings Scrapbook," Schlesinger Library, Radcliffe College, Cambridge, Mass.

69. *Dry Goods Economist* (Jan. 13, 1894), 43; A lengthy article about "Conveniences for Shoppers" at New York's Wanamaker's and Siegel-Cooper was subtitled "The Height of Elaboration and Thoughtfulness Reached by Leading Metropolitan Stores. Rest, Entertainment and Comfort Intermixed with Business." *Dry Goods Economist* (June 3, 1899), 5; *Dry Goods Reporter* (July 5, 1902), 61; Louis E. Kirstein Papers, Notes on Meeting, Oct. 25, 1910, "Modern Stores," Harvard Business School.

70. Leiss, *Limits to Satisfaction*, 67; "things" become expressive of the person in fiction as in life. See Henry James, *The Portrait of a Lady* (New York: New American Library, 1979).

71. *Dry Goods Reporter* (Nov. 14, 1903), 57.

72. Susman, *Culture as History,* introduction.

73. *New York Post* (Feb. 18, 1899), 16.

74. M. Jeune, "The Ethics of Shopping," *Fortnightly Review* 63 (Jan. 1, 1895), 124; Hartly Davis, "The Department Store at Close Range," *Everybody's Magazine* 17 (Sept. 1907), 312.

75. *New York Daily Tribune* (March 16, 1980), 15:6; *Dry Goods Economist* (Feb. 22, 1902), 37 and (Nov. 27, 1909), 28. Some of the problem with merchandise being returned was the result of overselling. *New York Times* (Sept. 9, 1894), 18:1; *Dry Goods Economist* (July 27, 1901), 23. Salespeople not infrequently had quotas, amounts they had to show in their "book." Filene's pushed sales via "The Quota Cup," a store-wide contest for sales above agreed-upon levels. *The Echo* II (March 1904). Such sales contests often resulted in overselling.

76. *Dry Goods Economist* (Sept. 28, 1901), 53; This was a new definition of female responsibility. The husband was saying his wife was an autonomous agent. While we do not know the outcome of this case, in a later case the husband was held responsible for his wife. *DGE* (Nov. 27, 1909), 28. There were many similar court cases. See Chap. IV, note 114. For an earlier view of women and overbuying, see R. Heber Newton, *The Morals of Trade: Two Lectures* (New York: T. Whittaker, 1876), 76. "If women insist upon keeping up appearances, then husbands will very likely fail to pay or fail in paying. Cabinet ministers will not be the only men ruined by their wives."

77. Alice B. Haven, "A Morning at Stewarts," *Godey's* (May, 1863), 431.

78. This discussion has benefited from the interpretation of Jackson Lears in *No Place of Grace,* particularly 41ff. See also Paul A. Carter, *The Spiritual Crisis of the Gilded Age* (De Kalb: Northern Illinois Press, 1971). Boorstin wrote, "The department store was the proper habitat of Santa Claus Americanus." Daniel Boorstin, *The Americans: The Democratic Experience* (New York: Random House, 1973), 160.

79. *Harper's Weekly* (April 26, 1873), 340: "Easter-Sunday. Cracking of the Easter-Egg, and Budding Forth of the Spring Fashions"; *The New York Weekly* (Feb. 10, 1879), 4:2, "Christmas Shopping"; *Dry Goods Economist* (March 15, 1902), 17; James H. Barnett, *The American Christmas: A Study in National Culture* (New York: Macmillan, 1954), 44; In some quarters there was an attempt to promote Easter gift giving. *Dry Goods Reporter* (March 24, 1906), 9; Williams, *Dream Worlds,* 65, 214; see also Arthur A. Ekirch, Jr., *The Idea of Progress in America, 1815–1860* (New York: Columbia University Press, 1944). Duncan, *Culture and Democracy,* 124, sees spending at Christmas "as a kind of secular prayer"; Leach also notes the link between religion and fashion. *True Love and Perfect Union,* 222–23.

80. *Dry Goods Reporter* (April 6, 1901), 25.

81. *Dry Goods Economist* (Sept. 25, 1897), 71, and (Oct. 2, 1897), 37.

82. *San Francisco Chronicle* (Oct. 14, 1896), 1:1; Merchant Fred Lazarus said in an interview that in the long run it was cheaper to take back merchandise "even when the store lost money and the customer was taking advan-

tage." Interview, Jan. 10, 1965, Federated Stores Oral History, Columbia University, New York. There were many stories to this effect. See Annette Austin, "When Woman Buys," *Good Housekeeping* 49 (Dec. 1909), 626.

83. *Boston Globe* (Dec. 5, 1897), 1:6, editorial; Reformers castigated working girls for spending above their income; here middle-class women were doing the same thing. See Kathy Peiss, *Cheap Amusements: Working Women and Leisure in Turn-of-the Century New York* (Philadelphia: Temple Univ. Press, 1986), 52–55, 62–67; Christine Stansell, *City of Women: Sex and Class in New York, 1789–1860* (New York: Knopf, 1986).

84. Richardson, "Modern Woman's Paradise," 22; Jeune, "The Ethics of Shopping," 124–25; Paul Dubuisson recognized this phenomenon as well.

85. C. E. Cake, "Arranging Goods to Make the Shopper Buy," *System* 18 (Dec. 1910), 591.

86. *Dry Goods Economist* (Sept. 11, 1897), 15.

87. Isidore Straus to Mr. Mandel (Mandel's Department Store in Chicago), May 10, 1892, "Leasing," Carton 2, R. H. Macy & Co. (Baker Library, Harvard Business School—hereafter, Macy collection).

88. Interview with William Titon, Sept. 30, 1965, Macy Archives, RG 10, Box 4.

89. Cake, "Arranging Goods," 590–95. Citing the "bewildering variety of styles," the *Economist* sought to impress readers with the importance of stock arrangement and location of goods throughout the store. "Merchandise must be displayed in such a manner as to catch the feminine eye . . . a good share of the success of the department depends on it." *Dry Goods Economist* (July 17, 1897), 45.

90. J. Russell Doubman and John R. Whitaker, *The Organization and Operation of Department Stores* (New York: John Wiley & Sons, 1927), 207; The *Dry Goods Economist* assumed "99% of the people are honest; they won't rob you; if they did you couldn't throw stuff out on your counters so freely, for it would soon be carried off." (Sept. 8, 1900), 57.

91. *Dry Goods Economist* (Aug. 22, 1896), 51.

92. Ibid., (Aug. 3, 1901), 63.

93. Ibid., (Aug. 21, 1897), 78.

94. Elizabeth Beardsley Butler, *Saleswomen in Mercantile Stores* (Baltimore: Survey Associates, 1913), 198; *Dry Goods Reporter* (Nov. 25, 1905), 14.

95. Cake, "Arranging Goods," 590.

96. *Dry Goods Economist* (Feb. 24, 1894), 5.

97. *Dry Goods Reporter* (July 25, 1903), 19. Shoppers were also to be educated to visit the store on a regular basis. "Always have the newest things but don't put them out all at once. A few articles should be added each day. In this way you educate the public to visit this department regularly." *DGR* (Nov. 28, 1908), 37.

98. *Dry Goods Economist* (Feb. 10, 1894), 7.

99. Lears, *No Place of Grace*, 41; See also Twain, *Gilded Age;* Cawelti, *Apostles of the Self-Made Man*, 159ff; *New York Evening Post* (April 23, 1912), 9.

100. *Living Age* 251 (Dec. 22, 1906), 759; Twain, *Gilded Age;* Lewis

Mumford discusses the problem of living with integrity in the Gilded Age. Lewis Mumford, *The Brown Decades: A Study of the Arts in America, 1865–1895* (New York: Dover Publ., 1971), chap. I, "The Brown Decades." Women and men were both vulnerable; men in business and women in the social scene. Both were "disposed to be honest until the pressure of artificial conditions and the tension of artificial effort get too much for them." *New York Evening Post* (April 23, 1912), 9.

101. William N. Gemmill, "Crime and Punishment in Chicago," *Journal of the American Institute of Criminal Law and Criminology* I (July 1910), 31.

102. *Brooklyn Eagle* (Dec. 21, 1897), 2:6; (Oct. 12, 1897), 28:7; and (Oct. 15, 1897), 2:2; *New York Times* (Dec. 8, 1907), II, 5:3.

103. *Boston Globe* (Dec. 21, 1897), 3:7. The title of this article is indicative of the seriousness of the problems: "Saw Others Steal."

104. *New York Times* (Dec. 8, 1907), II, 5:3; Sigmund Freud discusses the contagion of example in *Totem and Taboo*, trans. James Strachey (New York: W. W. Norton, 1950), 34–35.

105. Joan Jacobs Brumberg, *Fasting Girls: The Emergence of Anorexia Nervosa as a Modern Disease* (Cambridge, Mass.: Harvard University Press, 1988), 14. Brumberg discusses the "mimetic or copycat phenomenon" among anorectics.

Numbers of "respectable customers" who pilfered remain murky. Merchants and print journalists reacted as if the numbers were quite alarming. But official statistics were undifferentiated; it is almost impossible to distinguish shoplifting theft from other forms of petty larceny. Stores themselves were rarely the complainants; usually a detective, a salesclerk or a floorwalker was the official complainant. Stores suppressed information out of fear of publicity and effect on sales, and the "vast majority of thefts resulted neither in arrest nor conviction." See Davis, "Department Store at Close Range," 321; *New York Times* (Dec. 11, 1904), III, 1, (April 26, 1908), 8; *Merchants Record and Show Window* (Jan. 1910), 40–42; Patricia O'Brien, "The Kleptomania Diagnosis," *Journal of Social History* 17 (Fall 1983), 65–77.

106. *Dry Goods Economist* (Feb. 6, 1892), 112; Duncan, *Culture and Democracy*, 116–18.

3. The Two-Way Mirror

1. Duncan, *Culture and Democracy*, chaps. X, XI.

2. Williams, *Problems in Materialism*.

3. *Boston Globe* (Dec. 6, 1897), 6:2, editorial.

4. *New York World* (March 3, 1872), 3:5.

5. *New York Times* (Sept. 22, 1912), III, 6:4; *Dry Goods Economist* (Oct. 27, 1900), 57.

6. *Dry Goods Reporter* (April 23, 1904), 19.

7. *New York Times* (March 24, 1893), 7:5 and 9:2. Laura Little, a well-known customer in Stern's in New York City, was arrested after her actions "attracted suspicion of detectives." *New York Times* (Jan. 7, 1897), 7:2.

8. Siegfried Giedion, *Space, Time and Architecture: The Growth of a New Tradition* (Cambridge: Harvard University Press, 1954), 194–95, 206–8, 232–41, 372–73, 388–90.

9. Hower, *History of Macy's of New York 1858–1919*, 305.

10. Ibid. (Feb. 18, 1899), 18, and (March 13, 1897), 58. The latter article made the situation quite clear: "A merchant is necessarily obliged to incur expenses which years ago would have been deemed extravagant. As competition sets a quicker pace in dry goods retailing than in any other business, the man who strives for success must either keep up with that competition or lag behind. . . ."

11. Allan Nevins, ed., *The Diary of Philip Hone, 1828–1851*, II (New York: Dodd, Mead, 1927), 722; see also Harry E. Resseguie, "Alexander Turney Stewart and the Development of the Department Store, 1823–1876," *Business History Review* 39 (Autumn 1965), 310–22.

12. Pittsburg Plate Glass, *Glass: History, Manufacture and its Universal Application* (Pittsburgh, 1923), 31. Neither the machinery for continuous plate glass process nor the skilled workers for grinding, smoothing, and polishing were in the United States in numbers large enough to make manufacturing profitable until 1880.

In *Prose Works*, 1892, Walt Whitman alluded to the limited facilities for plate-glass manufacture in the United States: "St. Louis Missouri, November, '79. What do you think I find manufactur'd out here and of a kind the clearest and largest, best and the most finish'd and luxurious in the world—and with ample demand for it too? Plate Glass!" Walt Whitman, *Prose Works*, II, Floyd Stovall, ed. (New York: New York University Press, 1964), 582.

See also Mary Ann Smith, "John Snook and the Design for A. T. Stewart's Store," *The New-York Historical Society Quarterly* LVIII (Jan. 1974), 25.

13. Nevins, *Diary of Philip Hone*, 772. Defoe wrote of new "shop fitting" techniques in 18th-century London. Part of the new consumer orientation were shop windows measuring 12″ × 16″, "all of looking glass plates." Daniel Defoe, *The Complete English Tradesman* I (London: J. Rivington, 1745), 271.

14. Nevins, *Diary of Philip Hone*, 896–97.

15. Edward Crapsey, "A Monument of Trade," *Galaxy* IX (Jan. 1870), 96.

16. Haven, "A Morning at Stewarts," 430; The *Dry Goods Economist* linked the failure of Hilton Hughes & Co., the successor to the A. T. Stewart store, to the failure to use windows for display (Sept. 12, 1896), 60.

17. While merchants had long recognized the attraction and persuasive quality of goods in shop windows, early attempts at drawing customers into the stores were haphazard and occasionally produced unpredictable results. As the merchant-author of *A Peep into Catharine Street* explained, windows distorted the goods. The merchandise often looked better behind the glass than in the hand, and customers angrily accused merchants of substituting shoddy goods for those displayed so enticingly in the windows. *A Peep into Catharine Street*, 11.

Neil McKendrick writes of "great glass windows" and lights trained on them in early 19th-century London shops. McKendrick et al., *Birth of Consumer Society*, 78–79. For a view of shop windows in early 19th-century Philadelphia, see Ann Royall, *Sketches of History, Life, and Manners, in the United States* (New Haven 1826), 208–9.

18. *New York Herald* (Feb. 7, 1886), 21:3–4, "City Shoplifters." For images of the world through "big polished windows," see Henry Leon Wilson, *The Spenders: A Tale of the Third Generation* (New York: Grosset & Dunlap, 1902), 153; and *Life's Shop Window*, (New York: Darcy & Wolford, 1911).

19. James D. McCabe, Jr., *Lights and Shadows of New York Life; or, the Sights and Sensations of the Great City* (1872) (New York: Farrar, Straus and Giroux, 1970), 131.

20. *Frank Leslie's Illustrated Newspaper* (Jan. 1, 1876), 271; In 1875 a newspaper advertisement for Macy's Christmas windows, "Dolls' Carnival or Skating Party," suggested that the first Macy holiday windows had appeared the preceding year. *New York Herald* (Nov. 28, 1875), 1:6; see also RG10, Box 2, #1997, Macy Archives. See article, "Jumbo—The White Elephant," *Saratoga Eagle* (Dec. 22, 1883), RGI, Box 8, folder 3, Macy Archives. "The wild excitement that prevails among the spectators who block the sidewalks and streets at this corner is laughably reflected in the mirror that forms part of the [scenery], and also in the faces of the doll spectators on the wings of the amphitheatre."

21. *Leslie's*, 271; *Dry Goods Economist* (Dec. 1, 1900), 15.

22. Josiah L. Webster to Mr. Kline (of Macy's), May 22, 1919, "Personnel," Carton 2, Macy Collection. During Christmas of 1879, Macy's 14th Street windows portrayed scenes from the Gilbert and Sullivan operetta *H.M.S. Pinafore*, which was then the rage both in New York and in London. W. A. Darlington, *The World of Gilbert and Sullivan* (New York: Thomas Y. Crowell, 1950), 49.

23. Boorstin, *The Americans*, 104; Duncan, *Culture*, 114. Duncan mentioned window shopping as a "city habit" new in Chicago in the 1890s. Diaries also attest to the pleasure women took in window shopping. Numerous newspaper articles comment about large crowds in front of store windows. See description of crowds in front of early Macy windows. *New York Daily Tribune* (Dec. 16, 1876), 5:2.

24. Jesse Lynch Williams, *New York Sketches* (New York: Scribner, 1902), 46.

25. Busbey, *Home Life,* 158; *Dry Goods Economist* (April 7, 1894), 10; "Our window displays are for the public's benefit, and looked at from that standpoint entirely. They are educational—a panoramic review of the latest and best productions of the whole world." *DGE* (Nov. 2, 1901), 15; see also "The Immorality of Shop-Windows," *Atlantic Monthly*, 106 (December 1910), 853–54; "The shop windows are the poor man's universe." Tudor Jenks, "Before Shop Windows," *Outlook* 51 (April 27, 1895), 689. For a discussion of Parisian shop windows in these decades see Philip G. Nord, *Paris*

Shopkeepers and the Politics of Resentment (Princeton: Princeton University Press, 1986), 72–73.

26. *Dry Goods Economist* (Jan. 18, 1902), 77.

27. Bertha June Richardson, *The Woman Who Spends: A Study of Her Economic Motives* (Boston: Whitcomb & Barrows, 1904), 65.

28. *Dry Goods Economist* (Jan. 10, 1891), 28, said that shop windows were "a city beautifier," which contributed to the public benefit; (Aug. 18, 1896), 135.

29. Goodman and Goodman, *Communitas,* 127.

30. Jenks, "Shop Windows," 688. For a description by Jordan Marsh (Boston) of their elaborate window displays, see Claudia B. Kidwell and Margaret C. Christman, *Suiting Everyone,* 158.

31. *Dry Goods Economist* (Oct. 19, 1889), 25.

32. Ibid. (Nov. 17, 1900), 31, Crowds, of course, presented their own problems. A Boston magistrate declared "window trims illegal if they draw such crowds as to block traffic." (March 9, 1901), 13, editorial.

33. Moses King, *King's Handbook of New York City* (Boston, 1892), 787.

34. Women picked up for shoplifting in New York and Brooklyn department stores gave out-of-town addresses from the earliest reports. Mrs. Catharine King from Trenton, N.J., in December 1880, and Jane Weldon from Boston in 1885 were only two of the more than thirty women in this sample who claimed not to be from New York or the outlying boroughs. *New York Times* (Dec. 19, 1880), 8:1, and (Dec. 12, 1885), 1:6.

35. Richardson, "Modern Woman's Paradise," 90.

36. Twyman, *History of Marshall Field,* 152.

37. *Woman's Wear Daily* (July 8, 1947), 71.

38. Ibid.; see also Duncan, *Culture and Democracy,* 114.

39. *Woman's Wear Daily* (July 8, 1947), 71.

40. Wendt and Kogan, *Give the Lady What She Wants!,* 225.

41. *Dry Goods Economist* (Jan. 9, 1897), 13, editorial.

42. Ibid. (Dec. 25, 1897), 48; May 8, 1897), 54; (June 12, 1897), 51.

43. Ibid. (Dec. 28, 1889), 2. Few windows that year were as elaborate as those of the F. Loesser & Company in Brooklyn, which depicted a scene of the lighthouse in New York harbor, complete with an electric light in the lighthouse and an old ship riding at anchor on real water with undulating waves. Many people were reported "making trips to Fulton Street for the sole purpose of being jammed in the crowd which doth congregate. . . ." *Dry Goods Economist* (Dec. 21, 1889), 15.

44. Ibid. (Sept. 14, 1893), 22; Henry Collins Brown, ed., *Valentine's Manual of Old New York,* no. 5 (New York: Valentines Manual Inc., New Series, 1921), p. 135. Altman's may have been the other store. In 1900 the *Dry Goods Economist* reported that in their windows, "no special display is made or anything to indicate the near approach of Christmas." (Dec. 15, 1900), 16.

45. *Dry Goods Economist* (Oct. 10, 1900), 89. Department store windows were a magnet to the Saturday night crowds on Broadway. In her memoirs of

immigrant life, Mary Antin recalled leaving "imprints of our noses and fingers on plate-glass windows ablaze with electric lights and alluring with display." Mary Antin, *The Promised Land* (Boston: Houghton Mifflin, 1912), 261.

46. *Dry Goods Reporter* (Feb. 1, 1902), 31.

47. *New York Times* (Feb. 18, 1893), 8:6, and (May 24, 1888), 8:2.

48. *Dry Goods Reporter* (July 20, 1901), 33, and (Jan. 9, 1904), 53; An O. Henry short story touched on this theme: The struggling husband, Jim, sells his gold watch that had been his father's and his grandfather's in order to buy his wife combs for her hair that she "had worshipped for long in a Broadway window. . . . They were expensive combs, she knew, and her heart had simply craved and yearned over them without the least hope of possession." O. Henry, "The Gift of the Magi: A Christmas Story" from *The Four Million* (New York: Doubleday, 1919), 13.

49. *Merchants Record and Show Window* (Jan. 1910), 42. For a description of a "continually changing succession of novelties to attract the passer-by," see Lucy M. Salmon, "The Economy of Spending," *Outlook* 91 (April 17, 1909), 886.

50. Susman, *Culture as History,* introduction.

51. "The Immorality of Shop-Windows," 853. Envy and longing were the twin emotions successful windows were supposed to arouse in the passerby. See *The Art of Decorating Show Windows & Interiors,* 4th ed., 1906–1909 (Chicago: The Merchants Record Co.), introduction.

52. Bohme, *The Department Store,* 137–38.

53. *New York Times* (Dec. 27, 1892), 8:7; *Brooklyn Eagle* (Dec. 22, 1896), 4:5, and (Dec. 20, 1901), 2:5.

54. *Dry Goods Economist* (Oct. 13, 1900), 89.

55. *New York Times* (March 27, 1889), 2:5.

56. *Dry Goods Economist* (Oct. 27, 1900), 57.

57. Ellen (Miriam) Gibson Andrews to James Andrews, May 20, 1884. Cited in Seidl, "Consumers' Choices," 183.

58. Crapsey, "Monument of Trade," 96–97. Crapsey's impression of Stewart's is to some extent at odds with the enthusiasm of other observers. See Celia Burleigh's "Letter from New York," *The Woman's Journal* I (April 9, 1870), 1; and D.J.K., "Shopping at Stewarts," 43. Crapsey, however, is usually cited as the authority.

59. Crapsey, "Monument of Trade," 98–99. Disagreeing with Crapsey about Stewart's, Alice Haven described the silk department on the first floor where "we are dazzled by a display of delicate and gorgeous fabrics." See Haven, "A Morning at Stewarts," 431.

60. Godkin, "Stewarts," 332.

61. Twyman, *History of Marshall Field,* 61.

62. Ibid., 60. A. T. Stewart's had a woman's lavatory in the basement of the new store at Astor Place in 1863. Haven, "Morning at Stewarts," 431. For a description of haphazard growth, see Miller, *Bon Marché,* 42.

63. *Dry Goods Economist* (June 4, 1892), 13.

64. Ibid. (Oct. 12, 1889), 17.

65. Ibid. (Feb. 16, 1892), 115.

66. Ibid. (Jan. 11, 1902), 24.

67. Ibid. (Nov. 27, 1900), 57.

68. *New York Times* (Nov. 30, 1904), 1:2.

69. *Dry Goods Economist* (Oct. 24, 1896), 35, and (Aug. 3, 1895), 127.

70. Ibid. (July 22, 1899), 53.

71. *Dry Goods Reporter* (Feb. 16, 1901), 15.

72. Ibid. (Sept. 19, 1908), 30.

73. Walter L. Adamson, *Hegemony and Revolution: A Study of Antonio Gramsci's Political and Cultural Theory* (Berkeley: University of California Press, 1980), 133ff.

74. Bohme, *Department Store,* 72.

75. *Dry Goods Economist* (June 4, 1892), 13.

76. Ibid. (Sept. 19, 1891), 32.

77. Ibid. (June 4, 1892), 13, advertisement.

78. Ibid. (Sept. 10, 1892), 132, advertisement.

79. Ibid. (Jan. 28, 1893), 51, advertisement.

80. Ibid. (April 27, 1901), 57, advertisement.

81. Lew Hahn and Percival White, *The Merchants' Manual* (New York: McGraw Hill, 1924), 52. Almost any issue of the *Dry Goods Economist* in the 1890s carried advertisements for the new glass-enclosed counters and showcases.

82. Interview with George B. Hammond, RG 10, Box 1, Macy Archives. Hammond entered the employ of the Macy store on June 17, 1886, when Charles Webster and Jeremiah Wheeler ran the firm.

83. *Dry Goods Reporter* (April 8, 1905), 39.

84. *Dry Goods Economist* (Sept. 10, 1898), 51.

85. *Dry Goods Reporter* (July 7, 1906), 6.

86. *Dry Goods Economist* (July 30, 1892), 11.

87. Ibid. (March 18, 1893), 32.

88. Ibid. (Aug. 3, 1893), 10.

89. Ibid. (Sept. 28, 1901), 53.

90. Ibid. (March 4, 1893), 48, advertisement.

91. Ibid. (Feb. 6, 1892), 115.

92. Zola, *Au bonheur des dames,* 371.

93. *Dry Goods Economist* (Nov. 26, 1898), 45.

94. Ibid. (May 27, 1899), 51.

95. Ibid. (July 22, 1899), 53.

96. Ibid. (Aug. 26, 1899), 61; Newspapers were full of reports of middle-class women claiming they were overcome by the opportunity. See the *Brooklyn Eagle* (Dec. 21, 1897), 2:6, (Oct. 27, 1896), 16:2, and (Oct. 12, 1897), 28:7.

97. *Dry Goods Economist* (Aug. 12, 1899), 73.

98. Ibid. (April 4, 1891), 4.

99. "Controlling Shortages and Improving Protection," National Re-

tail Dry-Goods Association Store Management Group (New York, Oct. 1953).

100. Pittsburgh Plate Glass, *Glass,* 105.

101. Twyman, *History of Marshall Field,* 5; Wendt and Kogan, *Give the Lady What She Wants!,* 92.

102. Winston Weisman, "Commercial Palaces of New York: 1846–1875," *The Art Bulletin* XXXVI (Dec. 1954), 289. According to the *New York Evening Post* of Sept. 21, 1846, the mirrors were installed in 1846. Cited in Smith, "John Snook," 25.

103. *Dry Goods Economist* (Sept. 24, 1898), 9.

104. *Dry Goods Reporter* (Aug. 16, 1902), 11.

105. *Dry Goods Economist* (Feb. 11, 1893), 57.

106. Ibid. (July 4, 1896), 81.

107. Zola, *Au bonheur des dames,* 4.

108. *Dry Goods Economist* (Feb. 15, 1896), 62.

109. *Dry Goods Reporter* (Feb. 6, 1904), 43.

110. *Dry Goods Economist* (July 4, 1896), 81, and (July 25, 1896), 62.

111. Ibid. (Aug. 22, 1891), 19.

112. Interview with Fred Lazarus, Jr., Feb. 1, 1965, Federated Stores Oral History, Columbia University, New York; In Whiteley's, a large English department store, "there were mirrors on all sides, in which every movement was reflected," of clerks as well as customers. R. S. Lambert, *The Universal Provider: A Study of William Whitely and the Rise of the London Department Store* (London: George G. Harrap & Co., 1939), 142.

113. *Dry Goods Economist* (Sept. 24, 1898), 9.

114. Ibid.

115. Ibid. (April 1, 1899), 17. Queried about how to deal with shoplifting women, the editor suggested the use of mirrors built into shelving: "The salespeople can then watch the customers, even when their backs are turned."

116. *Brooklyn Eagle* (Aug. 10, 1901), 2:6.

117. *Dry Goods Reporter* (Dec. 13, 1902), 17; *Dry Goods Economist* (Feb. 2, 1895), 67. Light was a major concern of the trade journals. Almost any issue in the 1890s had an article about illumination.

118. Zola, *Au bonheur des dames,* 5, 12.

119. Bohme, *Department Store,* 78.

120. D.J.K., "Shopping at Stewarts," 43.

121. Ibid. See discussion of the light and fantasy at Coney Island in the early 20th century in John F. Kasson, *Amusing the Million: Coney Island at the Turn of the Century* (New York: Hill and Wang, 1978), 82–85.

122. Webster to Mr. Kline, May 22, 1919, "Personnel," Carton 2, Macy Collection; *New York Herald* (Dec. 12, 1875), 16:1, RG 10, Box 2, #1998, and (Nov. 30, 1879), 20:3, RG 10, Box 2, #2014, Macy Archives.

123. See correspondence from the United States Electric Lighting Co. to Isidore Straus, June 1, 1888, Box 8, Macy Archives; letter from Isidore Straus to Manhattan Electric Light Co., Sept. 22, "Store," Carton 2, Macy Collection.

124. "Real Estate," Carton 2, Macy Collection, from *New York Times* (Jan. 16, 1902); Macy store biographer Ralph Hower said that the Macy power plant was the largest private one in the city. Hower, *History of Macy's,* 325.

Marshall Field & Co. demonstrated a similarly timed progression. The gaslight of 1868 was amplified by a large glass-domed rotunda and skylight in 1873; electric arc lights supplemented the gas lights in 1882. Illumination in the new Marshall Field store in 1906 was all electric. Twyman, *History of Marshall Field,* 48, 61.

The new Siegel-Cooper store advertised at its opening that it had seven thousand incandescent lamps and eight hundred big arc lights, all of which were powered by nine dynamos in its own engine room. Siegel-Cooper also boasted of having "the largest light ever made," a huge light on its tower that not only promised to annihilate distance within the metropolitan shopping territory but supposedly had a 75-mile range. *New York Times* (Sept. 6, 1896), 10:4.

125. *New York Herald* (Dec. 18, 1881), 1:2, RG 10, Box 2, #2025, Macy Archives.

126. Zola, *Au bonheur des dames,* 24; *Dry Goods Economist* (Dec. 5, 1891), 21.

127. Lambert, *Universal Provider,* 99; Jenks, "Before Shop Windows," 688.

128. Pardee, *Diaries,* Dec. 16, 1885, and Dec. 18, 1893.

129. Jenks, "Before Shop Windows," 688.

130. Davis, *A History of Shopping,* 106–7; Defoe, *The Complete English Tradesman,* 270–71.

131. *Dry Goods Reporter* (Dec. 26, 1903), 42. "Daylight is essential in the cloak department . . . it is well known that artificial light affects colors." *Dry Goods Economist* (March 8, 1902), 89.

132. *Dry Goods Economist* (March 22, 1902), 19. Along with real problems with lights heating up the atmosphere, there were problems with ventilation in all the large stores.

133. *New York Times* (April 11, 1888), 8:2, and (Sept. 6, 1888), 8:4. Describing the grand opening of the new Field, Leiter store in 1868, the *Chicago Tribune* discussed the importance of the daylight the new windows provided: "It is possible to see absolutely the color of any article in any part of the rooms, and no clerk is compelled to take a piece of goods and carry it from his desk to a better lighted portion of the room." *Chicago Tribune* (Oct. 13, 1868), 4:3.

134. *Dry Goods Reporter* (Dec. 26, 1903), 42.

135. *The Detective* XV (Aug. 1899).

136. *Brooklyn Eagle* (Aug. 29, 1899), 2:4.

137. *Dry Goods Economist* (Feb. 15, 1896), 79.

138. Bohme, *Department Store,* 75.

139. *Dry Goods Economist* (Jan. 28, 1893), 57.

4. Invisible Authority

1. Chandler, *Visible Hand*, 48–49.

2. The important new works in the social history of the American department store are Susan Porter Benson, *Counter Cultures: Saleswomen, Managers, and Customers in American Department Stores, 1890–1940* (Urbana: Univ. of Illinois Press, 1986); William Leach, *True Love and Perfect Union: The Feminist Reform of Sex and Society* (New York: Basic Books, 1980), chap. 9, and William Leach, "Transformations in a Culture of Consumption," *Journal of American History* 71 (Sept. 1984); Sarah Smith Malino, "Faces Across the Counter: A Social History of Female Department Store Employees, 1870–1920," (Ph.D. diss., Columbia University, 1982); for stores in France see Philip G. Nord. *Paris Shopkeepers and the Politics of Resentment* (Princeton: Princeton University Press, 1986), chap. II, "Grands Magasins and Small Shops"; Miller, *Bon Marché.*

3. Chandler, *Visible Hand.*

4. Miller, *Bon Marché.*

5. *Echo* IX (May 1911).

6. *Dry Goods Economist* (Dec. 3, 1892), 47.

7. John Wanamaker to Rodman Wanamaker, Dec. 22, 1910, Wanamaker Archives, Philadelphia, Pennsylvania. William Leach uncovered this correspondence and generously shared it with me.

8. Benson, *Counter Cultures,* 128. "The thousands of clerks need espionage as well as the thousands of customers," one journalist wrote in the *New York Post* (Feb. 18, 1899), 16. *Dry Goods Economist* (Oct. 17, 1900), 57. *Memoirs of Miss Abigail Golden,* RG 10, pp. 20, 30, Macy Archives.

9. Lambert, *Universal Provider,* 75.

10. Benson J. Lossing, *History of New York City* (New York: George E. Perine, 1884), 791–93; Like Lossing, Moses King does not use the term "department store"; instead he calls the new institution a "dry-goods store," "large bazaar store," "houses," and distinguishes between the dry-goods store and the modern bazaar store. King, *Handbook of New York City,* 214, 786–88, 796–97. In 1897 Samuel Hopkins Adams said the modern business form was "known generically as the 'department store.'" Samuel Hopkins Adams, "The Department Store," *Scribners* 21 (Jan. 1897), 4. Filene's specifically advertised that it was "NOT a Department Store," ca. 1916. Archives, Wm. Filene & Co.

Not all the so-called merchant princes were equally anxious to expand their operations. Marshall Field considered himself a dry-goods "dealer" and was averse to endlessly increasing the variety of merchandise offered for sale. Field had to be pushed into a more liberal definition of dry-goods. As late as 1890, when almost all the larger stores had restaurants or at least tea rooms for their predominantly female clientele, Field opposed opening one on the grounds that "this is a dry-goods store. We don't feed people here." Wendt and Kogan, *Give the Lady What She Wants!* 213. The *Dry Goods Economist* demonstrated that other merchants sympathized with Field. See a discussion about the House Furnishing departments that had appeared in many of the larger stores (May 22, 1897), 61.

11. Lossing, *History*, 791–93.

12. Chandler, *Visible Hand*, 9, 237–38.

13. Miss Cora Crossman, "Personnel," Carton 2, Macy Collection; Hower, *History of Macy's*, 116. James Woods, a messenger and wagon-boy who was hired in March 1873, also remembered Macy being very much in evidence. Employee Interview #59, RG 10, Box 1, Macy Archives.

14. Mr. H. M. Bowyer, "Personnel," Carton 2, Macy Collection.

15. Miller, *Bon Marché*, 53.

16. Hower, *History of Macy's*, 361. The obituary of Hugh O'Neil, "successful dry-goods retailer of 'Ladies Mile'" described his "personal control of employees on the floor during the greater part of the day." *Dry Goods Economist* (March 22, 1902), 24.

17. Miss Kinnear, "Personnel," Carton 2, Macy Collection.

18. "Straus Letters," Feb. 1, 1889, Carton 2, Macy Collection; H. M. Bowyer remembered that the candy department was an important one in the store. "Employee Interviews," RG 10, Box 1, Macy Archives. Macy advertised "A pound never means 14 ounces, a dozen yards always means 12 times 36 inches," *New York Herald* (April 13, 1890), RG 10, Box 2, Doc. #2073, Macy Archives.

19. "Interview with Mr. Percy," Nov. 22, 1930, Box 4, Folder 7, Macy Collection; Charles Webster retired June 1, 1896; Box 1, Folder 1, Macy Collection.

20. Mr. & Mrs. W. J. Cook, "Personnel," Carton 2, Macy Collection. Miss Golden also noted Jesse Straus coming into the store and "stirring things up." Golden Memoirs, 62.

21. "Interview with Mr. Percy," Nov. 22, 1930, Box 4, Folder 7, Macy Collection.

22. Monte A. Calvert, *The Mechanical Engineer in America, 1830–1910* (Baltimore: Johns Hopkins University Press, 1967), 147; Edward Chase Kirkland, *Dream and Thought in the Business Community: 1860–1890* (Ithaca: Cornell University Press, 1956), 86–87, 107–111. Kirkland discusses businessmen in the 1890s and their views of college education—a useless education to men of practical affairs, which taught wrong attitudes and habits and delayed the start in business.

23. Golden *Memoirs*, 54–55.

24. Jesse I. Straus to Mrs. Elizabeth Friedenberg, Jan. 12, 1910, Box 4, #2895, Macy Collection. The *Dry Goods Reporter* echoed Straus. "The larger business we transact the more necessary is it that every minute detail be correctly and systematically attended to," says Mr. Hughes, superintendent of systems of Marshall Field. "The Modern store now faces the problem of saving seconds, instead of minutes. . . ." *Dry Goods Reporter* (April 9, 1904), 31.

25. Percy Straus, "Personnel," Carton 2, Macy Collection; also in *Dry Goods Economist* (Nov. 25, 1915), 27.

26. Max Weber, *Protestant Ethic and the Spirit of Capitalism* (New York: Scribner, 1958).

27. *Committee of Fourteen*, Miss Habberton's Summary (Oct. 18, 1913).

28. Ibid., Reports of Faith Habberton and Marjorie Sidney (Aug. 7 and Oct. 27, 1913).

29. See discussion in David F. Noble, *American by Design: Science, Technology and the Rise of Corporate Capitalism* (New York: Knopf, 1982), 264–71. See also Chandler, *Invisible Hand;* Braverman, *Labor and Monopoly Capital;* Giedion, *Mechanization Takes Command,* 96–99. Although Winslow Taylor was not writing about production outside an industrial setting, department store executives adopted his theories of efficiency and the organization of work.

30. *Dry Goods Economist* (Sept. 8, 1894), 97.

31. Ibid. (Feb. 15, 1896), 79.

32. Ibid. (Jan. 14, 1899), 65.

33. *Dry Goods Reporter* (April 8, 1905), 39.

34. Ibid. (Jan. 2, 1904), 73. "Leakage" while goods were being wrapped was a serious problem. See *Dry Goods Economist* (March 15, 1898), 13, editorial; Susan Porter Benson, "A Great Theater: Saleswomen, Customers and Managers in American Department Stores, 1890–1940" (Ph.D. diss., Boston University, 1983), 79.

35. *Dry Goods Reporter* (Oct. 14, 1905), 13–14. In the 1890s and the first decade of the 20th century, almost any issue of the major trade journals talks about the problem of clerks. Their potential value was recognized in the hyperbole typical of the period. "A good salesman is as much a necessity to this 19th century civilization of ours as a good hunter was to the Indian tribes who antedated Columbus." *Dry Goods Economist* (June 30, 1894), 93. "Efficient salesmanship is a force as powerful in a progressive wide-awake store as is the force of gravitation in the material world." *Dry Goods Economist* (Nov. 7, 1896), 61.

36. *Dry Goods Economist* (Jan. 22, 1898), 53, and (Jan. 28, 1899), 37.

37. Susan Porter Benson, "The Cinderella of Occupations: Managing the Work of Department Store Saleswomen, 1900–1940, *Business History Review* LV (Spring 1981), 15–16. The work of Susan Benson has been invaluable to my understanding of department store saleswomen and shop floor culture. *Dry Goods Reporter* (April 22, 1905), 27.

38. Adamson, *Hegemony and Revolution,* 34; see also Calvert, *Mechanical Engineer,* 12.

39. *Dry Goods Economist* (Feb. 10, 1894), 48.

40. "The Department Stores of New York City," Final Report and Testimony, U.S. Commission on Industrial Relations, Senate Document 415, III, 1916, 64th Cong., 1st sess., 2217. Daniel Nelson, *Managers and Workers: Origins of the New Factory System in the United States, 1880–1920* (Wisconsin:

University of Wisconsin Press, 1975), 207, note 64. Nelson says department stores were leaders in many forms of welfare work, principally because of their size and the number of women workers.

41. "Mercantile Establishments," State of New York, Fourth Report of the Factory Investigating Commission, II (Albany, 1915), 166. "Department Store Investigation," *Committee of Fourteen* in New York City, Miss Habberton's Summary, (Oct. 18, 1913). The conclusion of this investigator was contrary to factory investigation findings: "The weakness of welfare work lies in the fact that it is considered a kind of philanthropy instead of a part of the business."

42. *Dry Goods Economist* (April 22, 1900), 13.

43. Mr. Schoenfeld, "Employee Interviews," RG 10, Box 1, Macy Archives.

44. *Brooklyn Eagle* (July 11, 1895), 2:3.

45. Pauline Goldmark and George Hall, "Preliminary Report on Employment of Women and Children in Mercantile Establishments," New York State Factory Investigating Commission, vol. II (Jan. 15, 1913), 1213. The expectation that welfare work was a "solid business proposition" was not limited to department stores. Susan Porter Benson, letter to author.

46. *New York Times* (Nov. 12, 1911), V, 3.

47. *Dry Goods Economist* (Sept. 12, 1896), 59.

48. *Dry Goods Reporter* (May 28, 1904), 59; Percy Straus told an interviewer that it was difficult to get the employees to take advantage of what the store offered them. "A job was just a job, and there was no carry-over, no real concern for the institution:" "Welfare," Carton 2, Macy Collection.

49. *Dry Goods Reporter* (June 11, 1904), 8–9; Investigators found that in eleven of the largest New York City department stores, employee turnover was 150% in one year: out of a total average work force of 27,264, 44,308 were added and 41,859 were dropped. Of course the percentages varied by store, and different grades of help flowed through the stores; the greatest turnover was among the lowest-paid employees. "Mercantile Establishments," 92–93.

50. *Thought and Work* (Oct. 1903), 6.

51. Ibid. (Dec. 1903), 11; ". . . It is our patriotic and philanthropic duty to do all we can to promote the sale of Dame Fashion's fancies." *Dry Goods Economist* (Aug. 6, 1892), 21–22, editorial.

52. *Thought and Work* (March 1903), 1; The *Dry Goods Economist* believed that a "store paper's true mission was that of giving instruction, and, if necessary, offer correction and reproof" (March 15, 1902), 19.

53. *Dry Goods Economist* (July 6, 1895), 55, and (Sept. 7, 1895), 27; see also Arlie Russell Hochschild, *The Managed Heart: Commercialization of Human Feeling* (Berkeley: University of California Press, 1983), chap. I.

54. *New York Herald* (Feb. 7, 1886); "Overloaded counters, crowded aisles, and busy clerks all help to make the work of the light-fingered gentry comparatively easy." *Merchants Record & Show Window* (Nov. 1911), 35.

55. Elizabeth Beardsley Butler, *Saleswomen in Mercantile Stores,* Baltimore, 1909 (New York: Survey Associates, 1913), vii.

56. Wm. Filene & Son, *Buyer's Manual,* pt. I:21, ca. 1910.

57. *A Thumb-nail Sketch of the Filene Co-Operative Association* (Boston: Wm. Filene's Son & Co., 1913), 2.

58. *Dry Goods Reporter* (Jan. 2, 1904), 65.

59. Adamson, *Hegemony and Revolution,* 238.

60. Susan Porter Benson, "The Customers Ain't God: The Work Culture of Department Store Saleswomen, 1840–1940," in Michael H. Frisch and Daniel J. Walkowitz, eds., *Working-Class America: Essays on Labor, Community and American Society* (Urbana: University of Illinois Press, 1983), 191, and "Clerking Sisterhood," 46; see also Theresa M. McBride, "A Woman's World: Department Stores and the Evolution of Women's Employment, 1870–1920," *French Historical Studies* X (Fall 1978), 673.

61. *Dry Goods Reporter,* (June 27, 1903), 42; R. H. Macy & Co. (no signature) to Mr. Paul Kyle, Flushing, New York, July 6, 1904, Box 4, Doc. #3375, Macy Collection. "You are perfectly safe in making the assertion that about 150,000 persons visit the establishment of R. H. Macy & Co. daily." Mills, *White Collar,* 68–69.

62. Mills, *White Collar,* 212. The concept of specialization took hold on all levels. The *Echo* rationalized, "even soldiers are specialized . . . they are gunners or guards." *Echo* I (Jan. 1903).

63. Lamson Corp. to Ralph M. Hower, May 21, 1941. The Lamson Cash Carrier Patent was issued in April, 1881. The first installation was probably in Jordan Marsh (Boston) ca. 1880. For pneumatic tubes see "Macy Study," Carton 3, Macy Collection.

64. Diana Hirschler, *The Art of Retail Selling: A Textbook for Salespeople* (New York: The Institute of Mercantile Training, 1909), 3, 33.

65. *Dry Goods Economist* (Sept. 24, 1898), 15.

66. Ibid. (June 11, 1892), 20.

67. "What It Means to Be a Department Store Girl, As Told by the Girl Herself," *Ladies' Home Journal* 30 (June, 1913), 8.

68. "Personnel," and "Work Conditions," Carton 2, Macy Collection. Hower, *History of Macy's,* 203.

69. Wendt and Kogan, *Give the Lady What She Wants!,* 131.

70. *Dry Goods Economist* (Dec. 5, 1891), 19.

71. Ibid. (March 15, 1902), 81.

72. Ibid. (Dec. 23, 1893), 43. A symposium on "Selection and Managing Help" in 1892 took the opposite tack, counseling superintendents to enforce rules to the letter: "Be strict about it, be determined, be exact. No half-way business will do." *Dry Goods Economist* (Sept. 10, 1892), 5.

73. "Mercantile Establishments," 127. Investigators likened the precision and minute gradations of authority and responsibility in large department stores to that found in military organizations. See also *Dry Goods Economist* (April 23, 1898), 13; *Dry Goods Reporter* (Sept. 17, 1898), 13, and (Dec. 3,

1898), 45. Susan Porter Benson suggested to me that rules could also limit the arbitrary exactions of management.

74. *Dry Goods Reporter* (Jan. 2, 1904), 153. An article about employer-employee relations at Filene's declared, "The floor superintendents, buyers and managers maintain a quiet but firm control. . . . There is no store where discipline is better." *Echo* III (Oct. 1905).

75. *Dry Goods Reporter* (Jan. 2, 1904), 153.

76. Twyman, *History of Marshall Field,* 78; *Dry Goods Reporter* (Nov. 20, 1909), 45; *Dry Goods Economist* (April 17, 1897), 83, and (May 4, 1901), 57. One investigator at Macy's reported that "Mr. Straus removed a girl from the flower department because she was made up." Straus is reported to have told the girl "he was not running a theatrical troupe but a department store." *Committee of Fourteen,* Marjorie Sidney Report, (Oct. 30, 1913).

Filene employees were opposed to uniform dress. "Don't dress us all alike," they said. "We should look like an orphan asylum . . . like a crowd of prisoners." *Echo* I (Dec. 1902).

77. *Dry Goods Economist* (Jan. 2, 1904), 160.

78. McBride, "Woman's World," 673.

79. *Dry Goods Economist* (April 23, 1898), 13, and (March 11, 1899), 7; also (May 4, 1901), 57. McBride sees the salespeople becoming part of the presentation, "helping to create an atmosphere of service and contributing to the seductiveness of the merchandise." McBride, "Woman's World," 665.

80. Many of the cases that came before the Arbitration Board of Filene's concerned the attitude of the clerks, most of whom were from the working class. ". . . She tended to be pert and saucy . . . and I did not feel that I could develop her into a courteous, refined girl." "Arbitration Board Meetings," steno notes (March 29, 1905) Filene & Co. Archives, Boston, Massachusetts; Benson, "The Customers Ain't God," 191.

81. "Mercantile Establishments," 137. "Saleswomen are in great measure a class by themselves," Elizabeth Beardsley Butler wrote in her report for the Consumers' League. Even within this occupational category, she found clear social distinctions. Butler, *Saleswomen,* viii, 109. *Dry Goods Economist* (Sept. 10, 1898), 13; Benson, "The Customers Ain't God," 191.

The following are some examples of in-house rules excerpted from the *Dry Goods Reporter* (May 27, 1905), 54:

> DON'T wait on customers with your hands dirty or your fingernails in mourning.
>
> DON'T manicure your nails during business hours.
>
> DON'T address a customer as "lady"—Madame is the proper term.
>
> DON'T disregard instructions from those holding superior positions.

82. *Thought and Work* (June 1903).

83. *Dry Goods Reporter* (May 27, 1905), 54; for a variation on a similar theme, see *Dry Goods Economist* (Nov. 7, 1896), 61.

84. *Dry Goods Economist* (June 24, 1899), 4–5.

85. *Thought and Work* (August 1903).

86. *Dry Goods Economist* (Oct. 27, 1900), 16–17. After interviewing two hundred Chicago "department store girls" during 1909 and 1910, reformer Louise de Koven Bowen acknowledged the ever-present danger of temptation. "She is constantly surrounded by the articles which are so dear to the feminine heart. She sees passing and repassing all day women who are gorgeously arrayed in the very kind of clothes which she naturally covets." Louise de Koven Bowen, *The Department Store Girl* (Chicago: The Juvenile Protection Association, 1911).

87. Miss Golden, "Interviews & Letters from Employees" (n.d.), Carton 2, Macy Collection. Miss Golden, who came to Macy's in the early 1870s, remembered the price wars with Hearn's, particularly the "Challis War." Macy insisted on underselling and had hourly checks made of Hearn's window prices. Mr. & Mrs. W. J. Cook also remembered the fierce price war with Hearn's. Kitty Cook was a comparison shopper for Macy in the 1880s. "Personnel," Carton 2, Macy Collection. See also *Dry Goods Economist* (Jan. 18, 1902), 17: "Battle of Prices: [Macy-Hearn] 41 cent silks went at 1 cent/yd. by end of the day. The next day 2¾ yds. for 1 cent. At 6 o'clock, when the bell rang, the quotation was '11 yds. for 1 cent,' amid scenes of the wildest excitement ever witnessed in a retail store." On Siegel-Cooper see *New York Times* (March 1, 1895), 9:1.

88. *Dry Goods Reporter* (Sept. 17, 1898), 13; for the view of a "shopper," see the revealing article, "The Trials of a Department Store Critic," as told to Gelett Burgess, *Collier's* 44 (Nov. 6, 1909), 20–21.

89. *Dry Goods Economist* (Aug. 24, 1901), 81; Macy Investgator Marjorie Sidney found just the opposite to be the case in some departments: "The girls were quickly on to her . . . [they] claim that it is easy to spot them by the way in which they handle the goods." *Committee of Fourteen,* Report of Majorie Sidney (Oct. 17, 1913).

90. *Dry Goods Reporter* (Sept. 17, 1898), 13; for a report on the "stool pigeon policy" in one department store, see *Dry Goods Economist* (Sept. 29, 1900), 17.

91. *Dry Goods Economist* (Oct. 27, 1900), 16.

92. *New York Times* (May 19, 1869), 5:1. In an article entitled "The Private Detective System and its Abuses," the *Times* reported on "private detectives who spy on the private life of clerks and report to employers."

93. Bohme, *The Department Store,* 353; *Dry Goods Economist* (April 20, 1901), 17. See *Committee of Fourteen,* Miss Habberton's Summary, (July 8, 1913). Habberton quotes advice from a floorwalker to a new saleswoman, which echoes Bohme: The floorwalker warns about shoppers in the employ of the store, who are "paid by the house to tell on us. They'll be after you. . . ." New York State factory investigators found employees' spying on other employees to be a common occurrence. One saleswoman explained the additional $2.00 in her weekly paycheck as encouragement "to keep my eyes open to what goes on in the department." "Mercantile Establishments," 140.

For popular view see the play "Only a Shopgirl, or Eve the Saleslady." Saleswomen were also watched to ensure they obeyed the store rules; they were fined for infractions. "So we are entirely at their mercy. The saleswoman for her starvation wages must be a model of sense, industry and endurance and yet be liable to have even the whole of her meager earnings swept away by the misrepresentations of a contemptible and often a malicious spy." Dorothy S. Pam, "Exploitation, Independence and Solidarity: The Changing Role of American Working Women as Reflected in the Working Girl Melodrama, 1870–1910 (Ph.D. diss., New York University, 1980), 192. For a review of the play, see *New York Dramatic Mirror* (Sept. 11, 1902).

94. "The Department Stores of New York City," Final Report and Testimony, U.S. Commission on Industrial Relations (June 10, 1914). Published as Senate Doc. 415, 64th Congr. 1st Sess., 1916, 2317; *Dry Goods Economist* (Sept. 29, 1900), 16. The New York State Factory Investigating Commission grew out of the federal investigation into conditions in New York department stores. Undertaken with the cooperation of the New York Retail Dry-Goods Association, the state fact-finding commission examined wages, hours, profits, hiring practices, and working conditions in the stores between September 1913 and February 1914. As with the testimony in the Senate investigation, testimony in the state inquiry revealed widespread "internal watchfulness," which tended to pit one employee against the other and discouraged a communality of feeling or of action. "Mercantile Establishments," 140.

95. "The Department Stores of New York City," 2340, 2343; see also Frank Morn, *The Eye That Never Sleeps: A History of the Pinkerton National Detective Agency* (Bloomington: Indiana University Press, 1982), 108.

96. "The Department Stores of New York City," 2340; One "shopper" related how she purposely left her purse on the counter to test employees' honesty. This same woman also placed an open box of candy on the counter to see if the clerk would take a piece. Burgess, "Trials of a Department Store Critic," 21.

97. Goldmark, *Preliminary Report*, 1213.

98. *Dry Goods Economist* (Sept. 8, 1894), 97.

99. *New York Daily Tribune* (Dec. 23, 1883), 6:1.

100. *New York World* (March 14, 1894), 7:4; *New York Daily Tribune* (Dec. 22, 1903), 6:2.

101. R. H. Macy & Co. to Mr. W. E. Sittington of J. L. Hudson Co., May 18, 1915, Box 4, Doc. #3142, Macy Collection.

102. Doubman and Whitaker, *Organization and Operation of Department Stores*, 207. This book was written in the mid-1920s, but the text covers the early decades of the century. Josiah Webster, retired Macy employee, remembered a similar incident with a bolt of black grosgrain silk. *Macy Documentary History*, n.d., Carton I:47, Macy Collection.

103. *New York World* (March 3, 1872), 3:5.

104. *New York Daily Tribune* (Dec. 23, 1883), 6:1.

105. *Woodhull and Claflin's Weekly* (March 18, 1871), 4–5.

106. *New York Daily Tribune* (Dec. 27, 1870), 5:5.

107. See document "From August 7, 1876, to November 4, 1876," Box 4, #2997, Macy Collection; and "Abstract ca. November 1875," Box 4, #2998, Macy Collection.

108. *Dry Goods Economist* (Feb. 25, 1899), 16; see also (Nov. 19, 1892), 51. "We do not believe that one-tenth of the thefts are detected."

109. *New York Daily Tribune* (July 21, 1901), Supplement, 1:4; also (Dec. 22, 1903), 6:2. By the early 1890s comments about the losses suffered at the hands of shoplifters appeared with increasing frequency. *Dry Goods Economist* (April 4, 1891), 4, and (May 30, 1891), 32; *Brooklyn Eagle* (Jan. 21, 1897), 3:7, and (Aug. 2, 1898), 2:6; *Dry Goods Reporter* (Oct. 10, 1903), 19.

110. *Dry Goods Economist* (Sept. 29, 1900), 16. A study conducted in the 1950s revealed that department store estimates of shoplifting loss were still based on guesswork; "wastage" had many causes, of which shoplifting was one. Gibbens and Prince, *Shoplifting,* 148, 152.

111. Siegel-Cooper "Rules and Regulations," 40.

112. *Dry Goods Reporter* (Jan. 2, 1904), 162. Both Marshall Field and Rothchild's (Chicago) had similar warnings. "Employees must be always on the alert and watchful for the protection of the firm's property. Upon detection of any suspicious character, notify floor manager at once in a quiet manner, being careful to avoid attracting attention." (Rothchild's)

113. Marshall Field & Co. *Rule Book,* (Sept. 1911), 38. Filene's floor superintendents were similarly warned against personally interfering against shoplifters. Wm. Filene & Son, *Floor Managers' Manual,* ca. 1910, part 2, 5.

114. *New York Times* (March 16, 1880), 3:3. This was one of the earlier incidents reported. The woman was convicted but merely fined by the judge "in view of her proven good character." The *Times* noted that although the offense was in itself a trivial one, "the result of the trial, by reason of the certainty of a suit for damages in the event of an acquittal, was looked forward to with much interest by proprietors of Broadway establishments, many of whom were in court." See also *New York Times* (Feb. 26, 1886), 8:4, (April 11, 1888), 8:2, (May 30, 1888), 4:7. *Dry Goods Economist* (June 8, 1893), 23, Mrs. Julia Rapp v. Marshall Field & Co. *Brooklyn Eagle* (Dec. 28, 1897), 4:6, Mrs. Thelka Keyes brought suit for damages for false imprisonment and charge of petit larceny. "Stevens v. O'Neill," Appellate Division, 1st Dept. May Term, 1900, v. 51. Defendant Hugh O'Neill fined $3,000 damages for false imprisonment, Dec. 15, 1897. Award affirmed by Appellate Division, 1902, 364–68. "Woodward v. Ragland," Fifth Court of Appeals, District of Columbia, Jan. 20, 1891, 220–40. "People v. Goldberg," Supreme Court, 46 *New York Supplement* and 80 *New York State Reporter,* Aug. 4, 1897, 913–16. See also letter from E. Parmlee Prentice, Esq., to R. H. Macy & Co. regarding false arrest of a Miss Kirkpatrick, Dec. 5, 1904, Box 3, Doc. #2412, 2413. Macy Collection.

William J. Burns discussed the desire of the large stores to avoid notoriety, and their "fear of damage suits in cases of failure of courts to convict." *Protective Department Bulletin,* NRDGA, (1913), 6. The stores did have a quasi-legal form that many shoplifters apparently signed; the form released the store from all damage claims and liabilities. *New York Times* (Dec. 12, 1904), 6:4 and (Jan. 2, 1906), 15:1.

For discussion of mutual dependence and antagonism between clerks and customers, see *New York Times* (Oct. 4, 1885), 4:1 and *New York Herald* (Feb. 7, 1886), 21: 3–4.

115. E. Parmlee Prentice, Esq., to Macy's Dec. 5, 1904, Doc. #2412; Howland, Murray & Prentice to Macy's, Dec. 5, 1904, Doc. #2413, *Macy Documentary History*, Carton II, Macy Collection.

116. *Store Life* VII (April 4, 1910), 10.

117. *Merchants Record and Show Window* (Nov. 1911), 35.

118. Philip Farley, *Criminals of America* (New York: Author's Edition, 1876), 58. Throughout the 1880s and 1890s the *New York Times* frequently carried articles about the inattentiveness and carelessness of dry-goods clerks. Employees have "little direct interest, with their small salaries, in the affairs of the firm." *New York Times* (Dec. 6, 1880), 4:7, editorial.

119. *New York World* (March 3, 1872), 3:5, "New York Shoplifting"; *Dry Goods Economist* (Sept. 27, 1895), 27; "A plan that is used by some stores with good results is to offer a reward to any employee who may detect any person stealing merchandise. The reward serves as an extra inducement. . . ." *Merchants Record and Show Window* (Nov. 1911), 35.

120. "Mercantile Establishments," 133ff.

121. Bohme, *The Department Store*, 234.

122. *New York Times* (June 3, 1894), 1:6.

123. Examples are to be found in the *New York Times, New York Daily Tribune, The Post, New York World, Brooklyn Eagle;* see also *Dry Goods Economist* (May 30, 1891), 32.

124. *New York Times* (Feb. 18, 1895), 7:1. In spite of the high volume of traffic, clerks and detectives seemed to recognize certain individuals. In this sense the department store was not a completely anonymous space. In an article entitled "Shoplifters' Schemes" the *Dry Goods Economist* credited "a suspicious salesgirl" as "the cause of an investigation which showed the working of the apparatus." (May 30, 1891), 32.

125. *Dry Goods Economist* (Sept. 3, 1892), 11. In an article earlier the same year, the "Wide-Awake Retailer" recounted an incident in which a clerk showed two "neatly dressed and very intelligent ladies" a piece of curtain linen, "keeping tight hold on the wound end of the piece, apparently so that the ladies should not snatch it and run." (May 14, 1892), 40.

126. *Store Life* VII (April 4, 1904), 10.

127. Hirschler, *Art of Retail Selling*, 118.

128. *Dry Goods Economist* (Feb. 17, 1894), 53; for a revealing view of this problem, see Hanford Crawford, "Ethics of a Big Store," *Independent* 67 (Aug. 12, 1909), 358–60.

129. *New York Times* (April 26, 1908), V, 8:1.

130. *Protective Department Bulletin* 2, "A Talk to Employees." (July 1, 1913), 3, and (Dec. 1913), n.p.

131. *Dry Goods Economist* (Sept. 29, 1900), 16–17.

132. "Controlling Shortages and Improving Protection," National Retail Dry-Goods Association Store Management Group, 1953; Doubman and Whitaker, *Organization and Operation of Department Stores,* 207; Austin, "When a Woman Buys," 624.

133. Adams, "Department Store," 6.

134. Benson, "A Great Theater," 309.

5. Dilemmas of Detection

1. Mrs. Phelps lived at 49 East 23rd Street; Mrs. Mary Bryant, 117 East 15th Street (husband a dealer/publisher of law books); Miss Sophie Eisner, 324 Second Avenue; Mrs. Elizabeth Claussen, 113 East 13th Street, and Miss Nielson, no address (father a "respectable" leather manufacturer). See the *New York Sun* (Dec. 26, 1870), 2:5; *Phillips Elite Directory, New York City Directory.*

2. *Commerical Advertiser* (Dec. 27, 1870), 2; on Officer Lewis Hall see *New York Tribune* (Dec. 26, 1870), 2:5.

3. *The Sun* (Dec. 26, 1870), 2:5; *New York Daily Tribune* (Dec. 27, 1870), 5:5, "Mr. Macy's Explanation." Macy wrote an open letter to the editors of the various New York daily papers explaining his side of the story.

4. *The Commercial Advertiser,* (Dec. 27, 1870), 2.

5. *The Revolution* (May 6, 1869), 280–81. Although a study of 19th-century prostitution, many of Barbara Hobson's observations about deviant women are suggestive of the way in which middle-class shoplifters were commonly regarded. Barbara Mell Hobson, "Sex in the Marketplace: Prostitution in an American City, Boston, 1820–1880" (Ph.D. diss., Boston University, 1982).

6. *The World* (Dec. 25, 1870), 1:3.

7. Sorosis *Minutes,* Jan. 3, 1871.

8. *Woodhull and Claflin's Weekly* (March 18, 1871), 4–5.

9. Ibid.

10. *The New York World* (Dec. 26, 1870), 5:1; for an account of shoplifting that involved Jane Austen's aunt, see Pierce James, "A Case of Shoplifting in the Eighteenth Century, The Case of Mrs. Jane Leigh-Perrot," *Medicine, Science and the Law* 17 (1977), 201.

11. *The Revolution* (Jan. 5, 1871).

12. Ibid.

13. *Woodhull and Claflin's Weekly* (March 18, 1871), 4–5.

14. Morn, *The Eye That Never Sleeps,* viii.

15. *New York Daily Tribune* (Dec. 28, 1870), 4, editorial.

16. *New York Herald* (Feb. 7, 1886), 21:3.

17. The *New York Sun* (Dec. 27, 1870), 1:5.

18. Richard Wheatley, "The New York Police Department," *Harper's New Monthly Magazine* 74 (March, 1887), 509–10; J.P Shalloo, "Private Police,"

Annals of the American Academy of Political and Social Science, Monograph No. 1 (Philadelphia: 1933), 136.

19. *New York Daily Tribune* (Dec. 27, 1870), 2.

20. *Woodhull and Claflin's Weekly* (March 18, 1871), 5.

21. Morn, *The Eye That Never Sleeps,* 86, viii. There was increasing demand for special policemen that far outstripped the capacity of the municipal police forces. See *New York Daily Tribune* (Dec. 31, 1881), 5:4. Crowd behavior seemed to get worse as the stores increased in size. Describing a sale of bicycles at Siegel-Cooper, the *Times* described a "period of genuine danger" when the doors opened. "One patrolman had two ribs broken . . . and a captain's hand was badly lacerated . . . during the trouble, dresses were torn and a few women fainted." *New York Times* (Sept. 15, 1896), 9:4. Macy's elaborate window displays created such large crowds on 14th Street that "a policeman had to keep free passage." *Dry Goods Economist* (Dec. 1, 1900), 15.

22. *New York Times* (Jan. 27, 1881), 3:2.

23. Ibid. (April 11, 1895), 8:1.

24. Alfred Young, ed., *The American Revolution: Explorations in the History of American Radicalism* (DeKalb: Northern Illinois University Press, 1976); Jesse Lemisch, "Jack Tar in the Streets: Merchant Seamen in the Politics of Revolutionary America," *William & Mary Quarterly* 25 (July, 1968), 371–407; George Rude, *The Crowd in History: 1730–1848* (New York: John Wiley & Sons, 1964); David Montgomery, "The Shuttle and the Cross: Weavers and Artisans in the Kensington Riots of 1844," *Journal of Social History* 5 (Summer 1972), 411–46; Sean Wilentz, *Chants Democratic: New York City and the Rise of the American Working Class: 1788–1850* (New York: Oxford University Press, 1984).

Politically expressive crowds were certainly a continuing part of urban life, but they were short-lived and did not express the sense of the late nineteenth-century city as did the crowds in the commercial center. Paula Hyman, "Immigrant Women and Consumer Protest: The New York City Kosher Meat Boycott of 1902," *American Jewish History* LXX (Sept. 1980), 91–105.

25. *Atlantic Monthly* 100, (Sept. 1, 1907), 289–98. William Dean Howells vividly depicts the street cars in Boston, "where people are brought into the closest contact with one another . . . indecorously huddled and jammed together, without regard to age or sex . . . who otherwise lead lives of at least comfort. . . . These people accept unheard of, unthought of conditions in the horsecars where the courtesies of life are impossible, the inherent dignity of the person is denied." William Dean Howells, *Suburban Sketches* (Boston: James R. Osgood and Company, 1872), 112. See also Busbey, *Home Life in America,* 119.

26 Gerald S. Lee, "The Dominance of the Crowd," *Atlantic Monthly* 86 (Dec. 1900), 755.

27. Ibid. See his broad discussion of department stores in Gerald S. Lee, *Crowds, A Moving Picture of Democracy* (New York: Doubleday, 1914).

28. *Dry Goods Economist* (Sept. 28, 1895), 39. The new Marshall Field store drew two million visitors in the first six days of operation. *Dry Goods Reporter* (Oct. 11, 1902), 35.

29. *Brooklyn Daily Eagle* (Dec. 22, 1901), 1:5. Store entrances were seen as "the bait on the hook," and the small spaces in and around the entrances were intensely utilized. They served "to stop the passerby, and the pocketbook that hesitates is lost." Conversely, some merchants who catered to the "swell trade" felt "artistic beauty," a calm interior, and plenty of room were their major goals. *Dry Goods Economist* (May 14, 1892), 40; see also (May 10, 1902), 59. At the time of the arrest of Mrs. Phelps, Macy cited the crush of people in the store, claiming that at times there were more than 5,000 shoppers. *New York Daily Tribune* (Dec. 27, 1870), 5:5.

30. *Dry Goods Economist* (Aug. 29, 1891), 19; see also Persons, *Decline of American Gentility*, 256.

31. *Boston Herald* (Dec. 5, 1897), 37.

32. *Dry Goods Economist* (Nov. 3, 1900), 16; To highlight the growing importance of bargain counters the *DGE* ran an Essay Contest on "The Bargain Counter." (Aug. 29, 1891), 21; (Sept. 5, 1891), 21; (Sept. 19, 1891), 32. For a description of crowds struggling to get near a silk counter at Macy's see *DGE* (Jan. 18, 1902), 17; see also (April 29, 1899), 18; and *Dry Goods Reporter* (Aug. 30, 1902), 39. Yet another view of the deparment store crowd is offered by James G. Huneker, *New Cosmopolis*, 118–20. The *Boston Globe* printed sketches of crowds of bargain-hunting women with the caption "Cut prices rule in Boston on everything but postage stamps." The only men in the series of six cartoon sketches were at the stamp counter with Uncle Sam. *Boston Globe* (Dec. 1, 1897), 7.

33. *Boston Sunday Herald* (Dec. 12, 1897), 28:4.

34. Bohme, *The Department Store*, 399–401.

35. Zola, *Au bonheur des dames*, 90, 221. The *Dry Goods Economist* carried a description almost identical to Zola's: "At one 6th Avenue dry-goods store the crowd was so great in the silk department that locomotion was simply impossible. . . ." (April 9, 1892), 33.

36. Daniel Defoe, *The Fortunes and Misfortunes of the Famous Moll Flanders* (New York: Penguin Books, 1981).

37. *Brooklyn Eagle* (Dec. 22, 1896), 4:5.

38. *New York Herald* (Feb. 7, 1886), 21:3.

39. *Dry Goods Economist* (Aug. 29, 1891), 19; *New York Evening Post* (June 3, 1903), 5:1; on the concept of "public privacy," see Richard Sennett, *The Fall of Public Man: On the Social Psychology of Capitalism* (New York: Vintage Books, 1977), 217.

40. There are numerous indications of the linkage of the two positions. *New York Daily Tribune* (Dec. 26, 1870), 2:5, and (July 17, 1899), 3:5. Wanamaker's specifically stated that their "aisle men were no longer required to be detectives. We have men for that purpose." *Dry Goods Economist* (Feb. 15, 1902), 36; also Simpson, Crawford & Simpson statement to *New York Daily Tribune* (Dec. 23, 1883), 6:1. *DGE* (Oct. 27, 1900), 16.

41. Roger Lane described many detectives of the mid–nineteenth century as having simply stepped into their jobs over the "blurred line between hunter and hunted." Benjamin P. Eldridge and William B. Watts, *Our Rival the Rascal* (1897) Introduction by Roger Lane (Boston: Pemberton Publishing Co.,

1973), viii; *The National Era* I, no. 3 (Aug. 12, 1847). The author claimed to see little difference between the criminal and the detective: see also T. D. Woolsey, "Nature and Sphere of Police Power," *Journal of Social Science* III (1871), 113–14.

42. *New York Times* (May 19, 22, 23, 28, 1869) "Detectives' Methods"; Woolsey, "Police Power," 114; *New York Daily Tribune* (July 24, 1875), 5:1; Morn, *The Eye That Never Sleeps,* 14; Thomas Beet, "Methods of American Private Detective Agencies," *Appleton's Magazine* VIII (Oct. 1906), 439–445.

Only at the end of the century was the public ready to give grudging acceptance to the private detective. In 1897 the *New York Daily Tribune* could write, "The cry of unreliability is not so loud as it was." As detectives became a "necessity to society," they quickly appeared as "men of good character whose honesty never fails of its daily trial and temptation." No longer, the paper earnestly assured its readers, does it "take a thief to catch a thief." See also *New York Daily Tribune,* (Jan. 30, 1897), II, 16:5. For an opposite view of detectives, see *New York Times* (Aug. 31, 1898), 12:3.

43. *New York World* (Dec. 28, 1870), 4:5, editorial.

44. *New York Tribune* (Dec. 26, 1870), 1.

45. Lloyd Lewis interview with Chief of Special Service, John W. Hughes (n.d.), Marshall Field & Co. Archives, Chicago, Illinois. Hughes went to Marshall Field & Co. in 1881 and spent his entire career of 41 years there.

46. *New York Daily Tribune* (July 17, 1899), 3:5; Shalloo, "Private Police," 135, 168; Morn, *The Eye That Never Sleeps,* 33.

47. *New York Daily Tribune* (Sept. 21, 1897), 1:6; James Kieran, former head of Protection at R. H. Macy & Co., personal interview, Jan. 12, 1982, New York City. In 1911 the licenses of special policemen were again revoked by order of Mayor Rhinelander Waldo. *New York Evening Post* (July 17, 1911), 1:6. The extent of the detectives' authority was unclear. No one actually understood whether or not these special police officers were empowered to make arrests on the premises of the employing store for offenses against the store or its property. See Shalloo, "Private Police," 94.

48. *Dry Goods Economist* (March 14, 1896), 77.

49. *New York Evening Post* (June 3, 1903), 5:1.

50. *A History of Police Training in New York City* (New York: Police Department, City of New York, 1980), 12. "Women became members of the uniform force, May, 1899."

51. *New York Daily Tribune* (Dec. 17, 1905), V, 3:1. Articles in the *Brooklyn Eagle* regularly mention the presence of female detectives all through the 1890s, e.g., (Sept. 11, 1892), 2:7; (Dec. 21, 1897), 2:6; (Nov. 9, 1901), 20:1.

52. *New York Daily Tribune* (Dec. 17, 1905), V, 3:1.

53. Ibid.

54. Ibid (Dec. 23, 1901), 5:1.

55. *New York Evening Post* (June 3, 1903), 5:1.

56. *New York Daily Tribune* (Dec. 17, 1905), V, 3:1.

57. Ibid.
58. *New York Times* (April 11, 1895), 8:1.
59. Ibid.
60. Morn, *The Eye That Never Sleeps*, 68.
61. Eldridge and Watts, *Our Rival the Rascal*, 337.
62. *Chicago Mail* (April 5, 1887), quoted in Morn, *The Eye That Never Sleeps*, 30.
63. Pinkerton National Detective Agency *Timebooks* 1873–1920 Pinkerton National Detective Agency Archives, New York (hereafter, PNDA); Pinkerton *Charge-Off Books*, 1897–1903, PNDA.
64. Pinkerton *Charge-Off Books*; Shalloo, "Private Police." Only Altman's and Lord & Taylor seem not to have used the Pinkerton men in this period. In the interview, James Kerin mentioned that Altman's had a contract with Pinkerton in the 20th century.
65. *The Papers of the Pinkerton National Detective Agency.* The Pinkerton office opened in New York City in November 1865. A "Preventive Police" force appears in 1870.
66. Pinkerton *Timebooks*, PNDA.
67. *New York Times* (April 26, 1908), 8; *New York Evening Post* (Feb. 18, 1899), 16.
68. *Brooklyn Eagle* (Dec. 22, 1896), 4:5. The newspaper noted thirty extra policemen helping out private detectives of the big stores.
69. *Dry Goods Economist* (Nov. 23, 1901), 21.
70. R. H. Macy & Co. to A. J. Manning, Dec. 27, 1906, Box 3, Doc. 2419, Macy Collection.
71. *Dry Goods Economist* (Dec. 3, 1892), 47.
72. Ibid. (Dec. 10, 1892), 20.
73. "Controlling Shortages and Improving Protection," National Retail Dry-Goods Association Store Management Group, (New York, 1953), 17. At one large store in Paris, the code "2-10" meant "keep your 2 eyes on her 10 fingers." *Dry Goods Economist* (May 26, 1900), 27. Susan Benson discusses the various uses of shop-floor vocabulary. See Benson, "The Customers Ain't God," 196.
74. *Dry Goods Economist* (Oct. 27, 1900), 16.
75. Ibid. (Nov. 23, 1901), 21; also *Brooklyn Eagle* (Dec. 20, 1895), 14:5; (Oct. 27, 1896), 16:7; (Dec. 14, 1897), 1:6. This last article described sales-clerk Hilda Almgren, "a young woman who has been useful to the police as a detective."
76. Sennett, *The Fall of Public Man*, 24–25; *Dry Goods Economist* (Oct. 27, 1900), 16.
77. *Dry Goods Economist* (Oct. 27, 1900), 16. See Roger Cooter, "Phrenology and British Alienists, ca. 1825–1845," in Andrew Scull, ed., *Madhouses, Mad-Doctors and Madmen: The Social History of Psychiatry in the Victorian Era* (Philadelphia: University of Pennsylvania Press, 1981). Cooter sees phrenology as a uniquely popular science and a phenomenon of considerable

social significance; for the significance of phrenology in England, see Janet Oppenheim, *The Other World: Spiritualism and Psychical Research in England, 1850–1914* (Cambridge: Cambridge University Press, 1985), 208–10.

78. *Dry Goods Economist* (Sept. 29, 1900), 30.

79. *New York Daily Tribune* (Dec. 23, 1883), 6:1.

80. *Dry Goods Economist* (Nov. 2, 1889), 18.

81. *New York Daily Tribune* (Dec. 23, 1901), 5:1, *Dry Goods Economist* (Sept. 29, 1900), 30. For an exposition of this thesis see Warren I. Susaman, "'Personality' and the Making of Twentieth-Century Culture" in *Culture as History: The Transformation of American Society in the Twentieth Century* (New York: Pantheon Books, 1984), 281–83.

82. *Dry Goods Economist* (Oct. 27, 1900), 16–17.

83. Ibid. (Nov. 23, 1901), 21.

84. Lew Hahn and Percival White, *The Merchants' Manual* (New York: McGraw-Hill, 1924), 518. Initially underwritten by the Women's Educational and Industrial Union, the Prince salesmanship classes began in 1905.

85. Diana Hirschler, *The Art of Retail Selling: A Textbook for Salespeople* (New York: The Institute of Mercantile Training, 1909), 10.

86. Eldridge and Watts, *Our Rival the Rascal*, 27.

87. *Merchants' Trade Journal* (Feb. 1915), 65, 88.

88. Eldridge and Watts, *Our Rival the Rascal*, 344.

89. Ibid., 346, quoting La Fontaine.

90. Capt. Cornelius W. Willemse, *Behind the Green Lights* (New York: Knopf, 1931), 120.

91. After the arrests at Macy's in Dec. 1870, the husband of Mary Bryant and the father of Sophie Eisner threatened to sue for false arrest and imprisonment. Whether or not they followed through is not clear. Suits for false arrest proliferated after 1890, particularly when an arrested woman was discharged by the court. Merchants were understandably fearful of "making a mistake." *Dry Goods Economist* (Dec. 10, 1892), 20, (June 8, 1893), 23, (Oct. 27, 1900), 20; *Brooklyn Eagle* (Dec. 28, 1897), 4:6.

The words to a popular children's clapping and ball-bounding game at the turn of the century are probably not a direct outgrowth of the Phelps incident, but the rhyme obviously served as a reminder that Macy's and policemen remained inextricably linked.

> *I won't go to Macy's any more, more, more,*
> *There's a big fat policeman at the door, door, door,*
> *He'll grab you by the collar,*
> *And make you pay a dollar*
> *So don't go to Macy's any more, more, more.*

Iona and Peter Opie, "Twelve Less Popular Clapping Songs," *The Singing Game* (New York: Oxford University Press, 1985), 478. Margaret Hunt came across these lyrics and, ever–mindful of my project, sent them to me.

92. *Dry Goods Economist* (Sept. 29, 1900), 16. For publicity about new cooperative methods for dealing with shoplifting after 1917, see the following: Pendelton Dudley, Esq., to Jesse I. Straus, Nov. 9, 1917, J. C. Hammond to Jesse I. Straus, May 4, 1918, and R. H. Macy & Co. to "City Editor," May 27, 1919, Stores' Mutual Protective Association Files, Macy Archives.

93. *New York World* (March 3, 1872), 3:5.

94. *New York Daily Tribune* (Dec. 23, 1883), 6:1.

95. *New York Evening Post* (Feb. 18, 1899), 16:1.

96. Zola, *Au bonheur des dames*, 301.

97. *Dry Goods Economist* (Nov. 23, 1901), 21; see also *Merchants Record and Shop Window* (Jan. 1910), 41.

98. *Dry Goods Economist* (Nov. 23, 1901), 21. In an editorial entitled, "Watch the Detective," the *DGE* cautioned that detectives could be dangerous if not kept in check and carefully supervised. (July 21, 1900), 13, editorial.

99. *New York Times* (April 11, 1895), 8:1.

100. *Dry Goods Economist* (Oct. 27, 1900), 20. Barbara Hobson discussed the explicit class bias in handling certain offenses, in this case prostitution. Hobson, "Sex in the Marketplace."

101. *Dry Goods Economist* (April 4, 1891), 4. The *Tribune* quoted one department store chief detective admitting, "If I had an army of detectives at my command, I could not prevent all loss from this source in the store." *New York Daily Tribune* (Dec. 17, 1905), V, 3:1. By 1912 the *New York Evening Post* reported that with increasing losses "insurance rates . . . for jewelry and dry-goods stores have already been advanced." (Feb. 17, 1912), 1:5.

102. *New York Daily Tribune* (Dec. 23, 1883), 6:1.

103. Ibid.

104. Ibid.

105. For Altman's see *New York Times* (Jan. 27, 1888), 3:2; for Bloomingdale's see *New York Daily Tribune* (Feb. 11, 1893), 4:1, The *World* (March 14, 1894), 7:4, and *New York Times* (Dec. 12, 1904), 6:4; for Stern's see *New York Daily Tribune* (Feb. 18, 1893), 12:4, and (Feb. 21, 1893), 3:4, *New York Times* (May 24, 1893), 9:2.

106. *Brooklyn Eagle* (Sept. 13, 1896), 4:7.

107. Ibid. (Sept. 13, 1896), 4:7, (Nov. 12, 1901), 10; *Dry Goods Economist* (May 3, 1902), 26; *New York Tribune* (Sept. 13, 1903), 3.

108. "Harvest Time of the Shoplifter" was the title of a long *New York Times* article that discussed the leniency shown to the good customer who was also a shoplifter. *New York Times* (Dec. 11, 1904), (III) 1. Correspondence between Jesse Isidore Straus of R. H. Macy & Co. and Frederic Kernochan, Chief Justice of the Court of Special Sessions of the City of New York makes it very clear that both men were aware of the lack of severity shown toward shoplifting by amateurs. "The Court," Justice Kernochan wrote, "is not disposed to impose any greater penalties than they have been doing in

shoplifting cases where the defendant appears to be a woman who has simply yielded to temptation." Frederic Kernochan to Jesse Isidore Strauss [*sic*] April 24, 1919, Stores' Mutual Protective Assoc. Files, Macy Archives.

109. By the late 1890s almost any issue of the *Dry Goods Reporter* or the *Dry Goods Economist* carried an article about some aspect of shoplifting.

110. *Dry Goods Economist* (Feb. 28, 1914), 119.

111. The Retail Dry-Goods Association of New York was incorporated Dec. 5, 1895, with virtually all the major New York City stores participating. *Dry Goods Economist* (March 20, 1897), 7. Boston's Retail Merchants Association was incorporated in 1897. *DGE* (Nov. 6, 1897), 14.

112. *Dry Goods Economist* (Nov. 4, 1911), 43; Not until 1918 did New York merchants follow Boston's example with the formation of The Stores' Mutual Protective Association. An experienced former New York City police detective was hired to work in conjunction with the chief detective of each member store, helping him to diagnose the store's particular weakness and work out more effective means for spotting and apprehending suspected thieves. *New York Herald* (Dec. 18, 1918), 3:1, Box 3, Doc. #2420, Macy Collection.

113. *Dry Good Economist* (Nov. 4, 1911), 43.

114. Ibid. (Aug. 2, 1899), 59.

115. *Brooklyn Eagle* (Dec. 22, 1896), 4:5, and (Oct. 27, 1896), 16:2.

116. *Merchants Record and Show Window* (June, 1916), 9.

117. NRDGA Store Management Group, "Controlling Shortages," 2. It is noteworthy that without the benefit of any formal organization, store detectives in Brooklyn discovered a community of interest and would meet "every once in a while and talk about the suspects who came to the shops." They were cooperating with each other even as management was not. *Brooklyn Eagle* (Nov. 9, 1901), 20:1; (Dec. 22, 1896), 4:5. Managers cooperated with each other in respect to inquiries about former employees. *Dry Goods Economist* (Sept. 24, 1898), 15.

118. *Merchants Record and Show Window* (Sept. 1912), 21.

119. *Protective Dept. Bulletin* (Feb. 1915), 3.

120. Ibid.; Bohme, *Department Store*, 353. While it is beyond the scope of this study, it is worth noting that in 1917 the New York City department stores once again formulated plans for a "protective association to prosecute shoplifters." Separate from the Retail Dry-Goods Association, but operating under its direction, the Protective Association seemed to be a serious undertaking; it received funding from the member stores, hired an attorney and a former New York police detective to take charge of all prosecutions, and sent out letters to the New York papers about the problem and its determination to gain control of it (Dec. 1918–1919). It was an experiment in coordination and cooperation that called attention, once again, to the historic leniency toward shoplifters. "We suffer severely through shoplifting," a Macy executive wrote to his counterpart at James McCreery & Co. R. H. Macy & Co. to Louis Stewart, Esq., Oct. 23, 1917, Store's Mutual Protective Assoc. Files, Macy Archives.

121. Marshall Field & Company Archives; Wendt and Kogan, *Give the Lady What She Wants!* 231.

6. Shoplifting Ladies

1. Edwin S. Porter, *The Kleptomaniac,* Edison, 1905. Film.

2. Loren E. Edwards, *Shoplifting and Shrinkage Protection for Stores* (Springfield, Illinois: Charles C. Thomas, 1958), chap. II, 4–15.

3. *New York Times* (April 26, 1908), III, 8.

4. *Dry Goods Economist* (Oct. 27, 1900), 57; *Merchants Record and Show Window* (Jan. 1910), 40.

5. *Boston Globe* (Dec. 6, 1897), 1:1.

6. *New York Times* (Dec. 11, 1897), 1:2; also see *Boston Globe* (Dec. 10, 1897), 1:5.

7. *Dry Goods Economist* (Oct. 27, 1900), 57. The *DGE* wrote that the situation was different in London and Paris. Merchants in those cities were "vengeful," less interested in the good will of friends and relatives. American stores and the general public viewed the middle-class shoplifter very differently from the pickpocket or professional shoplifter; see also Hobson, "Sex in the Marketplace."

8. *New York Herald* (Feb. 7, 1886), 21:3–4; *Dry Goods Economist* (Feb. 1, 1902), 75 and (March 15, 1902), 75.

9. *Boston Globe* (Dec. 6, 1897), 6:2, editorial.

10. *New York Times* (Dec. 11, 1904), III, 1; *New York Daily Tribune* (Dec. 17, 1905), V, 3:1.

11. These trends are evident in the 1880s in the correspondence of John Wanamaker. Wanamaker wrote to one G. Harry Davis that he had reviewed "Mrs. Miller's case, and considering the long period of time that she was stealing from us and the large quantity of goods that you would readily admit, I think the sentence was an extremely light one. . . . I cannot see my way clear to interfere with the sentence of the judge." On the following day he wrote to the judge in the case. "I understand efforts are being made to get you to shorten the sentence of Mrs. Miller who was convicted of stealing at the Grand Depot. But little of her long continued offenses came before you and her sentence was light. I would suggest it stand as it is." See John Wanamaker to G. Harry Davis, May 2, 1883, and John Wanamaker to Judge Allison, May 3, 1883, *Letterbook,* 33–34, Wanamaker Archives, Philadelphia, Pa. Bill Leach was kind enough to share this correspondence with me.

12. *New York Times* (Nov. 30, 1904), 1:2.

13. Ibid.

14. Joan Jacobs Brumberg, *Fasting Girls,* introduction.

15. John Wanamaker to Messrs. Rothermel Brown, *Letterbook,* 493. J.W. Personal from 1881–1883, Wanamaker Archives. Thanks are due, once again, to Bill Leach for uncovering this correspondence and sharing it with me.

16. *New York Times* (Feb. 18, 1893), 12:4.

17. Ibid. (Dec. 11, 1898), 3:5; see also *Brooklyn Eagle* (Dec. 22, 1896), 4:5, and (Oct. 27, 1896), 16:2; note also chap. V, fn 108.

18. *New York Times* (May 23, 1900), 9:2.

19. Ibid. (March 25, 1901), 2:5. The courts became involved early on in the public discussion of shoplifting losses. In an article about shoplifting at McCreery's in 1880, The *Times* quoted Court Recorder Smythe of Special Sessions on the subject: "The large dry-goods establishments in this City suffered great losses by the depredations of shoplifters," Smythe said, and he personally "was determined on administering severe punishment to all offenders brought before him." *New York Times* (April 24, 1880), 3:3. The problem was not simply that of the stores, though they were the most obvious victims: the problem became one of public morality and sensibility. Magistrates and other court personnel could not move beyond public opinion on this highly political issue, much as they might have felt an obligation to uphold what many of them saw as clear distinctions between right and wrong. See Gibbens and Prince, *Shoplifting*, 78.

20. *New York Times* (Dec. 9, 1908), 2:2, and (Dec. 12, 1908), 3:1.

21. *New York Times* (April 27, 1905), 18:5. In her autobiography, the notorious shoplifter Sophie Lyons related how, in the 1880s, she successfully convinced a store detective that she was a kleptomaniac: "Did you pay for that hat?" "No, Sir, I didn't pay a cent for it. You see, I am a Kleptomaniac, and I just cannot help taking any pretty thing I see in the stores. My husband has done everything to stop me, but the habit seems to be incurable." *Autobiography of Sophie Lyons* (Chicago: Star Publishing Co., 1913) typescript, from the files of the Pinkerton National Detective Agency.

22. *New York Times* (Dec. 2, 1904), 7:3. The unequal application of criminal law was a problem at all levels of the legal system. See Gerard C. Brandon, "The Unequal Application of the Criminal Law," *Journal of the American Institute of Criminal Law and Criminology* I, no. 6 (March 1911), 893–95; see also Barbara Hobson's dissertation, "Sex in the Marketplace." The discussion of the varying responses of the courts and the implicit class bias underlying the discretionary practices in the policing and treatment of prostitutes is applicable to the treatment of shoplifters; see personal correspondence of merchant John Wanamaker to attorneys, Messrs. Rothermel Brown, Jan. 8, 1883, *Letterbook*, 493, J. W. Personal from 1881–1883, Wanamaker Archives. Bill Leach passed this correspondence on to me.

23. *New York Times* (Dec. 5, 1904), 12:4. In 1908 the secretary of the RDGA of New York announced, once again, "every case of shoplifting which is henceforth detected will be vigorously prosecuted. The Association has received the assurance of the District Attorney that it shall have his cooperation in obtaining convictions." *New York Times* (Feb. 15, 1908), 3:5.

24. Ibid. (Dec. 23, 1904), 5:2, and (April 26, 1908), V, 8:4. For a view of the unchanging nature of the situation, see a letter from the Stores' Mutual

Protective Association to the city editors of all the morning and evening newspapers in Greater New York, May 27, 1919. "You may have been under the
impression in the past that some of the members of this Association have
shunned publicity in shoplifting cases. Some would prefer not to have their
names mentioned in connection with a report of cases, others are entirely
willing that their names should appear. . . ." Stores' Mutual Protective Assoc.
Files, Macy Archives.

25. *New York Times* (April 26, 1908), V, 8:1.

26. *Merchants Record and Show Window* (June 1916), 9, and (Jan. 1910),
40.

27. Frederic Kernochan, Chief Justice, Court of Special Sessions of the
City of New York, to Jesse Isidore Straus, Oct. 10, 1917. Stores' Mutual Protective Assoc. Files, Macy Archives.

28. Bohme, *The Department Store*, 316–17.

29. Michel Foucault, *Discipline and Punish: The Birth of the Prison*, trans.
Alan Sheridan (New York: Vintage Books, 1979), 104.

30. Gibbens and Prince, *Shoplifting;* T.C.N. Gibbens, Clare Palmer, Joyce
Prince, "Mental Health Aspects of Shoplifting," *British Medical Journal*
(Sept. 11, 1971), 612–15. English psychiatrist T.C.N. Gibbens was the
author of a major study of shoplifting in London stores between July 1959
and August, 1960. Interested in shoplifting trends and the particular character of shoplifting behavior, Gibbens and his associate, Joyce Prince, inves-
tigated 532 cases of female shoplifting. While not applicable in all respects,
the methodology and analytical categories used and the questions asked in
this and in the ten-year follow-up study allowed me to look at my sample of
about 190 shoplifters with a keener eye.

31. I have checked every women mentioned in a shoplifting case in the
New York Times index for the years covered by this study, along with those
so mentioned in the *Brooklyn Eagle* (1891–1903) and the *New York World*
(sporadic index for a few years). I attempted to verify the addresses and occupations of the husbands in one of three New York City directories: *Phillips
Elite Directory, Trows* New York City Directory (some New Jersey towns
included) and the *Brooklyn City Directory*. Only 35 addresses were fully documented. Additional names that appeared in the pages of the store journals
or other New York City newspapers were similarly checked.

The 190 names represent only a tiny fraction of the total number of shoplifting arrests. Other than middle-class female shoplifters, one was the son of
the King of Spain, some were shopgirls, another was a Canadian minister, and
another was a former church sexton. See *New York Times* (July 2, 1911), 3:7,
(Dec. 20, 1907), 1:5, (Dec. 3, 1897), 5:3, and (July 20, 1898), 12:2.

32. Margaret Gibbons Wilson, *The American Woman in Transition: The
Urban Influence, 1870–1920* (Westport: Greenwood Press, 1979), 86; Kath-
erine Kish Sklar, *Catharine Beecher: A Study in American Domesticity* (New
York: W. W. Norton, 1973).

33. *New York Times* (Dec. 9, 1898), 1:3. Mrs. Abbie Long was the Sunday

School Superintendent at The Church of the Puritans, located on 130th Street near Fifth Avenue. About one suspect arrested in 1893 we know nothing more than her name, Mary Arthur, and the intriguing fact that "she spent time in a cell reading a French novel." *New York Times* (Feb. 21, 1893), 3:4.

34. *New York Daily Tribune* (July 21, 1901), supplement, 1:4; Hewitt, *Queen of Home*, 401–43, 458. Hewitt wrote of new avenues of employment opening for women, e.g., bookkeeping, shorthand, and typewriting, but these were careers for single women. She felt married women "should have one profession . . . from choice, let no mother relegate her duties to another, while she preaches science and knowledge away from home."

35. *Dry Goods Economist* (Dec. 4, 1897), 13, editorial, and (March 23, 1901), 153. See also Nathan C. Fowler, Jr. "Reaching the Men Through the Women," *Printers' Ink* 5 (July 22, 1891), 51–53, "The woman buys, or she directs the buying of everything from shoes to shingles."

36. *New York Times* (Nov. 29, 1904), 16:3.

37. Ibid. (Dec. 11, 1898), 3:5.

38. Sheila Rothman, *Woman's Proper Place: A History of Changing Ideals and Practices, 1870 to the Present* (New York: Basic Books, 1978); Karen J. Blair, *The Clubwoman as Feminist: True Womanhood Redefined, 1868–1914* (New York: Holmes & Meier, 1980); see also, Barbara J. Balliet, "What Shall We Do With Our Daughters? Middle-Class Women's Ideas About Work, 1840–1920" (Ph.D. diss., New York University, 1988).

39. Daniel T. Rodgers, *The Work Ethic in Industrial America, 1850–1920* (Chicago: University of Chicago Press, 1979), 183. Among the many articles on the "new woman," see Kate Gannett Wells, "The Transitional American Woman," *Atlantic Monthly* 46 (Dec. 1880), 817–23, and Caroline Ticknor, "The Steel-Engraved Lady and the Gibson Girl," *Atlantic Monthly* 88 (July 1901), 105–8.

40. This scenario appears in a variety of sources. See *New York Times* (April 26, 1908), 8; (Dec. 12, 1904), 6:4; (Jan. 2, 1906), 15:1; *New York Evening Post* (June 3, 1903), 5:1; *New York Tribune* (Dec. 17, 1905), V, 3:1.

41. Many sources deal with the sequence of these events. See *New York Times* (Dec. 11, 1904), III, 1; *New York Evening Post* (Feb. 18, 1899), 16:1. Some stores had women sign a release exonerating the store from any damage claims or suits for false arrest. See *New York Times* (Dec. 12, 1904), 6:4, and (Jan. 2, 1906), 15:1.

42. *Merchants Record and Show Window* (Jan. 1910), 40; *New York Evening Post* (Feb. 18, 1899), 16:1; *New York World* (March 3, 1872).

43. *Dry Goods Economist* (Oct. 27, 1900), 57; *Merchants Record and Show Window* (Jan. 1910), 40–41.

44. *Dry Goods Economist* (Aug. 31, 1901), 75.

45. *New York Times* (Dec. 11, 1904), III, 1.

46. *Dry Goods Economist* (Nov. 23, 1901), 21.

47. *New York Times* (Dec. 11, 1904), III, 1.

48. *Dry Goods Economist* (Nov. 23, 1901), 21.

49. *New York Daily Tribune* (May 24, 1893), 7:5.

50. *New York Times* (Feb. 18, 1895), 7:1.

51. Ibid. (Jan. 7, 1897), 7:2.

52. Ibid. (Jan. 14, 1899), 1:4.

53. Ibid. (Dec. 20, 1900), 1:3.

54. There are numerous citations in the daily press for this practice of giving false names. See for example *New York Times* (Feb. 18, 1893), 12:4; (March 1, 1895), 13:6; (Dec. 19, 1895), 14:2; (Dec. 11, 1904), III:1; *San Francisco Chronicle* (Dec. 1, 1896), 5:2; *Boston Globe* (Dec. 25, 1897), 1:7.

55. *New York Daily Tribune* (Feb. 20, 1893), 12:2, and (Dec. 17, 1905), V, 3:1. One well-dressed woman was reported as crying, "Oh, what will my husband say . . . I shall be disgraced for life."

56. *Boston Globe* (Dec. 21, 1897), 3:7.

57. *New York Times* (Dec. 19, 1880), 8:1 and (Dec. 28, 1880), 8:5.

58. Ibid. (Nov. 8, 1883), 8:2.

59. Ibid. (Dec. 19, 1895), 14:2. The lawyer for many of these cases was Mark Alter. Claiming to have defended over 500 shoplifting cases, Alter gave a dramatic interview to a *Times* reporter. "If I could give the real names of the 500 women whom I have defended on the charge of shoplifting, it would make a sensation that would startle New York. One was the wife of a Supreme Court judge, another a near relative of an ambassador; one, a well-known society woman, had several hundred dollars in her pocketbook when she was arrested for stealing a trinket worth a few dollars. Out of 4000 arrests every year, only about 700 ever get into the courts and of this number not more than 50 are convicted." *New York Times* (Jan. 2, 1906), 15:1.

60. Ibid. (Feb. 2, 1898), 3:4.

61. Twain, *The Gilded Age*, 355; Persons, *The Decline of American Gentility*, 101; Cawelti, *Apostles of the Self-Made Man*, 36, 178–80.

62. *New York Times* (Dec. 20, 1895), 9:6; The *Times* ran a full-page article with illustrations, "Harvest-Time of the Shoplifter," in a Sunday edition in 1904 that discussed the battle of wits between store detectives and women shoppers. "More important than the explanation of the theft . . . is to ascertain the real name and address of the shoplifter." (Dec. 11, 1904), III, 1:1.

63. *Brooklyn Eagle* (Aug. 28, 1899), 2:4; (Aug. 29), 2:4; (Aug. 31), 1:7. It was not an accident that the final court appearance of the richly attired Mrs. Whigham ran on page one.

64. *New York Times* (Jan. 11, 1898), 3:5.

65. Ibid. (Dec. 20, 1895), 9:6.

66. Ibid. (May 16, 1897), 11:2.

67. Ibid. (March 28, 1898), 8:7. Testimony in the Castle shoplifting incident pointed out that "Mr. Castle was very generous with his wife." See *San Francisco Chronicle* (Oct. 14, 1896), 1:1.

68. Psychologists had advanced this very possibility in 1862. Writing in the *Journal of Mental Science* and excerpted in the *American Journal of Insanity*, the prominent English authority on insanity, Dr. John C. Bucknill, analyzed early evidence of "the thieving madness." It is, he wrote, "part of the struggle for existence in the middle and even upper-classes of our complex

social system." Such madness "combined with the prevailing fashion of an emulative and showy expenditure, [to] make the *sense* of want keenly felt . . . where no traces of vulgar poverty are discernible. . . . Women . . . spend no inconsiderable portion of her [*sic*] time in the discharge of that new and peculiar duty of life called 'shopping,' can we be surprised that when the means fail to satisfy the desires thus stimulated . . . that in some few instances the desire of the eye should prove too strong for the moral sense. . . . It would be more true than gallant to consider these fair thieves as an elder kind of children." *AJI* XIX (Oct. 1862), 150–51. See full article "Kleptomania," *Journal of Mental Science* VIII, 42 (London 1863), 262–75.

69. Rogin, *Subversive Genealogy*, 126; for a sardonic view of consumerism, see James Fenimore Cooper, *Autobiography of a Pocket Handkerchief* (Evanston, Illinois: R. R. Donnelley, 1897).

70. *Boston Globe* (Dec. 5, 1897), 2:2.

71. Veblen, *Theory of the Leisure Class;* Woolson, *Women in American Society*, 108–9; Branca, *Silent Sisterhood*, 52–53; McKendrick et al., *The Birth of a Consumer Society*, chap. II, "The Commercialization of Fashion," 34–99. Although he is dealing with Georgian England, McKendrick sees emulative and taste-induced spending among increasingly wide sectors of English society a century before similar developments in the United States. For a new examination of American spending habits and ideology, see Horowitz, *The Morality of Spending.*

For two personal views see Josephine Pitcairn Knowles, *The Upholstered Cage* (New York: Hodder & Stoughton, 1913), 26, and Mrs. Ives, "Pin Money for Married Women," The *Boston Herald* (Sept. 13, 1890), 9:3. For the quintessential statement about the importance of "things" as the expression of the person, see James, *The Portrait of a Lady;* also Theodore Dreiser, *Sister Carrie* (Indianapolis: Bobbs-Merrill, 1970).

72. Richardson, *The Woman Who Spends*, 40.

73. Ibid., 38.

74. Blake, *Fettered for Life;* Abraham Meyerson, M.D., *The Nervous Housewife* (Boston: Little, Brown, 1920), 146; see also Fowler, "Reaching the Men through the Women," 51. For an interpretation of female dependence in a market world in 19th-century France, see Smith, *Ladies of the Leisure Class*, 64–65.

75. Hewitt, *Queen of Home*, 38.

76. Adeline Hibbard Gregory, *A Great Grandmother Remembers* (Chicago: A. Kroch, 1940), 114.

77. William Dean Howells, *A Woman's Reason* (Boston: Osgood & Co., 1883), 185. Describing the fierce concentration of women shopping, Howells asked, "Where does the money all come from? It is a fearful problem, and the imagination must shrink from following these multitudinous shoppers to their homes, in city and suburb, when they arrive frayed and limp and sore, with overspent allowances, and the hard task before them of making the worst appear the better reason." Some historians see women in control of the household budget. See Branca, *Silent Sisterhood*, 22.

78. *Business Woman's Journal* (Feb. 1892), 55–56, and (Nov. 1892), 59,

"Progress." Lucy M. Salamon, "The Economics of Spending," *Outlook* 91 (April 17, 1909), 889; Veblen, *Theory of the Leisure Class*, 193; Blake, *Fettered for Life*, 160.

79. *Boston Herald* (Sept. 13, 1890), 9:3, excerpted from *Forum* magazine, Sept. 1890. For the crippling effects of economic dependence on women, see Charlotte Perkins Gilman, *Women and Economics: A Study of the Economic Relation between Men and Women as a Factor in Social Evolution* (1898) (New York: Harper and Row, 1966).

80. David John Thomas, "The Demographics of Shoplifting" (Ph.D. diss., University of Nebraska–Lincoln, 1979), 222. In 1902 a spokesman for Ehrich Bros. commented, ". . . there is that innate love of shopping which many a woman feels obliged to gratify even with an improverished purse." *Dry Goods Economist* (Feb. 22, 1902), 37.

81. *New York Times* (Dec. 19, 1895), 14:2.

82. David Brion Davis, *Homicide in American Fiction, 1798–1860: A Study in Social Values* (Ithaca: Cornell Univ. Press, 1957), 21. For a discussion about the repression of guilt as an expression of anxiety, see Melvin Zax and George Strickler, *The Study of Abnormal Behavior* (New York: Macmillan Publ. Co., 1974), 28. In an article entitled "City Shoplifters," the *Boston Herald* noted, "conscience stifled by cupidity is dormant, and the lust of possession is all that possesses her." *Boston Herald* (Feb. 7, 1886), 21:3–4. For another statement to this effect, see *Merchants Record and Show Window* (Jan. 1910), 40; see also Freud, *Totem and Taboo*, 29–34, 70–71, 85–87.

83. *Boston Globe* (Dec. 5, 1897), 1:6; *New York Times* (Dec. 8, 1907), 5:3. The former head of protection at Marshall Field suggests that nonprofessional shoplifters maintain conventional attitudes toward theft. Loren E. Edwards, *Shoplifting and Shrinkage Protection for Stores* (Springfield, Ill.: Charles C. Thomas, 1958). It is interesting to note that Lizzie Borden was also a shoplifter. See Edward Rowe Snow, *Piracy, Mutiny and Murder* (New York: Dodd, Mead, 1959), 275–77.

84. *Boston Globe* (Dec. 21, 1897), 3:7; *Brooklyn Eagle* (Nov. 9, 1901), 2:6.

85. *New York Times* (Feb. 4, 1886), 2:6; for a similar, French interpretation, see Maurice Bontemps, *Du vol dans les grands magasins et du vol à l'étalage* (Paris: Étude medico-legale, 1894), 10. American detectives were not unaware of this possibility; see *New York Daily Tribune* (Dec. 17, 1905), V, 3:1.

86. Natalie Zemon Davis, *Fiction in the Archives: Pardon Tales and Their Tellers in Sixteenth-Century France* (Stanford, Calif.: Stanford Univ. Press, 1987), chap. 3, 77–109.

87. *New York Times* (Dec. 10, 1898), 3:2; T.C.N. Gibbens, "Shoplifting," *British Journal of Psychiatry* 138 (April 1981), 347.

88. Leonard I. Sweet, *The Minister's Wife: Her Role in Nineteenth-Century American Evangelism* (Philadelphia: Temple University Press, 1983), 221. Susan Yohn suggested the importance of ministers' wives among the shoplifting suspects.

89. *New York Times* (Feb. 19, 1893), 9:4. The "medical history" of Mrs.

Louisa Schloss, mentioned earlier, was quite similar to this episode, although the two incidents took place fifteen years apart; see Dr. Walker Gill Wylie's obituary in the *New York Times* (March 14, 1923), 19:5.

90. *New York Herald* (Feb. 7, 1886), 21:3–4. Some women "are simply not strong in resisting the temptations to which their sex are most subject." The article continues, "Some really absent-minded have carried some article away from the counter utterly unconscious of it." There are so many comments of this nature that it is difficult to choose only one.

91. *New York Times* (Feb. 18, 1893), 8:6.

92. Ibid. (Dec. 26, 1892), 5:7.

93. Ibid. (May 24, 1893), 9:2. It is interesting that Miss Little was a repeat customer in Stern's. See also *New York Times* (Jan. 18, 1882), 8:6; (Aug. 14, 1887), 1:4; (March 27, 1889), 2:5.

94. Bell, *The Cultural Contradictions of Capitalism*, 224; Williams, *Dream Worlds*, 224.

95. *New York Times* (Jan. 13, 1898), 4:4; see also *Dry Goods Reporter* (Jan. 1, 1898), 45. Issac Ray thought that shame was sufficient punishment for middle-class women. See I. Ray, M.D., *Treatise on the Medical Jurisprudence of Insanity*, 5th ed., (Boston: Little, Brown, 1871), 30–39.

96. *New York Times* (Nov. 8, 1883), 5:4.

97. *New York Times* (March 15, 1894), 5:6. Mrs. Horen was not the only woman to use the excuse of liquor—see *New York Times* (Sept. 9, 1895), 6:5, *Brooklyn Eagle* (June 20, 1897), 32:6, and (Oct. 3, 1899), 18:5; also *Dry Goods Economist* (Feb. 9, 1895), 27.

98. *New York Times* (Jan. 22, 1894), 2:4.

99. Ibid. (Jan. 11, 1896), 9:2.

100. Ibid. (March 16, 1880), 3:3; (Feb. 2, 1893), 7:3; (Feb. 18, 1895), 7:1; (May 16, 1897), 11:2; (Feb. 2, 1898), 3:4; (Jan. 13, 1899), 12:7.

101. Auerbach, *Woman and the Demon*, 186.

102. Gibbens and Prince, *Shoplifting*, 86.

103. Auerbach, *Woman and the Demon*, 189. Gibbens and Prince: "A simple confession does not imply a simple motive." *Shoplifting*, 81. Strout, "The Uses and Abuses of Psychology," 332–39.

7. ". . . Disposition Shady, but a Perfect Lady"

1. Orpheus Everts, M.D., "Are Dipsomania, Kleptomania, Pyromania, Etc., Valid Forms of Mental Disease," *American Journal of Insanity* 44 (July 1887), 57.

2. Ibid., 52.

3. Ibid., 56.

4. Wendy Mitchinson, "Gynecological Operations on Insane Women: London Ontario, 1895–1901," *Journal of Social History* 15 (Spring 1982), 467–84. Bert Hansen very kindly brought this article to my attention.

5. Patricia O'Brien, "The Kleptomania Diagnosis: Bourgeois Women and

Theft in Late Nineteenth-Century France," *Journal of Social History* 17 (Fall 1983), 71.

6. Frances Emily White, "Woman's Place in Nature," *The Popular Science Monthly* 6 (Jan. 1875), 292–301; G.T.W. Patrick, "The Psychology of Woman," *The Popular Science Monthly* 47 (June 1895), 209–25; Alice May Farnham, "Uterine Disease as a Factor in the Production of Insanity," *The Alienist and Neurologist* VIII (October 1887), 532–47: see also John S. Haller, Jr., and Robin M. Haller, *The Physician and Sexuality in Victorian America* (Urbana: Univ. of Illinois Press, 1974), 71; Mary Kelley, *Private Woman, Public Stage: Literary Domesticity in Nineteenth-Century America* (New York: Oxford University Press, 1984), 65; Sandra M. Gilbert and Susan Gubar, *The Mad Woman in the Attic: The Woman Writer and the Nineteenth-Century Literary Imagination* (New Haven: Yale University Press, 1984).

7. Brumberg, *Fasting Girls,* chap. 4, 101–25, "Emergence of the Modern Disease." I have benefited greatly from Joan Brumberg's analysis of the way in which behavior became disease. Hysteria similarly lacked disease characteristics. See Carroll Smith-Rosenberg, "The Hysterical Woman: Sex Roles and Role Conflict in 19th-Century America," *Social Research* 39 (Winter 1972), 654ff. Also Charles Rosenberg, *No Other Gods: On Science and American Social Thought* (Baltimore: Johns Hopkins University Press, 1978), 33.

8. *New York Times* (Oct. 10, 11, 14, 15, 18, 21, 23, and 31. Nov. 3, 4, 7, 8 [three separate articles], 9, 10, 11 [two different articles], 13, 1896).

9. Jean Harris was arrested for the murder of Dr. Herman Tarnower on March 12, 1980, convicted, and sentenced to prison on March 20, 1981. *New York Times* (March 12, 1980), 1:4 and (March 21, 1981), 1:2. Coverage of the trial and the two actors in the case was intense.

10. *San Francisco Chronicle* (Nov. 7, 1896), 1:7; *New York Times* (Oct. 18, 1896), 1:5, (Nov. 11, 1896), 9:5.

11. *New York Times* (Oct. 14, 1896), 9:1.

12. Ibid.

13. "Kleptomania," *Law Times* CII (Nov. 14, 1896), 28; for a full discussion of this case and the issue of moral insanity, see "Kleptomania," *Atlantic Medical Weekly* VI (Dec. 26, 1896), 401–6.

14. *San Francisco Chronicle* (Oct. 13, 1896), 1:4, and (Oct. 14, 1896), 1:1; *New York Times* (Oct. 18, 1896), 1:5.

15. *New York Times* (Oct. 23, 1896), 6:7; S. Weir Mitchell, M.D., "The Relations of Nervous Disorders in Women to Pelvic Disease," *University Medical Magazine* (March 1897), 33, rprnt., remarks by Solomon Solis-Cohen, M.D..

16. *San Francisco Chronicle* (Nov. 18, 1896), 18:1.

17. Ibid. (Nov. 7, 1896), 1:7.

18. *New York Times* (Nov. 7, 1896), 9:5.

19. *San Francisco Chronicle* (Oct. 14, 1896), 1:1; *New York Times* (Oct. 14, 1896), 9:1.

20. *New York Times* (Nov. 7, 1896), 9:5.

21. *San Francisco Chronicle* (Oct. 10, 1896), 1:6. The *Chronicle* published

a partial list of stolen goods found in the Castles' trunks and wardrobes: "18 tortoise shell combs, 7 hand mirrors, 2 sable boas, 2 muffs, 2 neckties, 7 gold watches, 9 clocks, 17 valuable fans, 16 brooches, 7 tortoise shell eye glasses, 2 plated toast ranks [*sic*] marked 'Hotel Cecile,' and a large number of smaller articles of less value. . . ." (Oct. 14, 1896), 1:1–2.

22. Ibid. (Oct. 14, 1896), 1:1.

23. Smith-Rosenberg, *Disorderly Conduct*, 3–52, "Hearing Women's Words."

24. *San Francisco Chronicle* (Nov. 7, 1896), 1:2.

25. Ibid. (Oct. 31, 1896), 1:7.

26. Ibid. (Nov. 11, 1896), 1:4. English law had offered wide latitude in cases of kleptomania earlier in the century, but the defense had been pleaded in "such a depressing multitude of cases," the *New York Times* explained, that the law on a plea of kleptomania had been changed a decade before the Castle case. No longer was it possible for a middle-class woman in England to claim irresistible impulse as a predisposing cause and be assured of acquittal. Prison or the asylum upon a plea of insanity by reason of kleptomania were the choices, and Sir Edward Clarke, the attorney in this case, chose a guilty plea, confident that whatever the sentence, his client would be immediately released. *New York Times* (Nov. 8, 1896), 17:3.

27. Mitchell, "Relations of Nervous Disorders," 35; see also an article by S. Weir Mitchell, "Nervous Disorders (Especially Kleptomania) in Women and Pelvic Disease," *American Journal of Insanity* 53 (April 1897), 605–6.

28. Mitchell, "Relations of Nervous Disorders," 34; *San Francisco Chronicle* (Nov. 7, 1896), 1:7.

29. Mitchell, "Relations of Nervous Disorders," remarks by Solomon Solis-Cohen, M.D., 34.

30. *San Francisco Chronicle* (Oct. 11, 1896), 18:1.

31. Andrew Wynter, M.D., *The Borderlands of Insanity* (London: Robert Hardwicke, 1875), 65; Wynter makes specific mention of the struggle between "the medical advocate and the barrister" over kleptomania. *San Francisco Chronicle* (Oct. 14, 1896), 1:1 and (Nov. 8, 1896), 18:3.

32. *San Francisco Chronicle* (Nov. 10, 1896), 1:4.

33. Helen Merrel Lynd, *On Shame and the Search for Identity* (New York: Harcourt Brace & Co., 1958), 34.

34. Ibid., 183; Mitchell, "Relations of Nervous Disorders," 36.

35. Michel Foucault, *The History of Sexuality*, V. I: An Introduction (New York: Vintage, 1980), 27; Smith-Rosenberg, *Disorderly Conduct*, 11–52; Joan W. Scott, "On Language, Gender, and Working-Class History," *International Labor and Working-Class History* 31 (Spring 1987).

36. For a sample of medical thinking and practice on this subject, see W. B. Goldsmith, M.D., "A Case of Moral Insanity," *American Journal of Insanity* XL (Oct. 1883), 162–77; B. D. Evans, M.D., "Periodic Insanity, in which the Exciting Cause Appears to be the Menstrual Function—Report of a Typical Case," *Medical News* LXII (May 20, 1893), 538–40; Eugene G. Carpenter, M.D., "Pelvic Disease as a Factor of Cause in Insanity of Females and

Surgery as a Factor of Cure," *The Journal of the American Medical Association* XXXV (Sept. 1, 1900), 545–51; John C. Doolittle, "The Relation of Pelvic Disease to Insanity," *Bulletin of Iowa Institutions* III (July 1901), 294–98; L. G. Hanley, M.D., "Mental Aberration Consequent Upon Pelvic Disease," *Buffalo Medical Journal* XL–LVI (March 1901), 672. See also articles by Barbara Ehrenreich and Deirdre English, "Complaints and Disorders: The Sexual Politics of Sickness," and G. J. Barker-Benfield, "Sexual Surgery in Late Nineteenth-Century America," in *Seizing our Bodies: The Politics of Women's Health*, Claudia Driefus, ed. (New York: Vintage Books, 1978).

Medical examination of Mrs. Castle conducted on November 30, 1896, revealed that "the uterus was hypertrophied to one and a half times its normal size; the mucous membrane was irregularly roughened and bled on the slightest touch by the sound [*sic*]. The cervix had a bilateral laceration. . . . The tear was well cicatrized. The rectum was found to be fissured below, ulcerated above. There were evidences of former ulcers that had cicatrized and several large turgescent arterio-venous varicosities (hemorrhoids). . . ."

The operation on Mrs. Castle conducted a few days later consisted of the following procedures: "The sphincter ani dilated, the fissures cauterized . . . the ulcers treated . . . and the hemorrhoids clamped and cauterized. The uterus was curetted and then the trachelorrhaphy performed by denudation of the cicatricial tissue and suturing with silkworm gut." Mitchell, "Relations of Nervous Disorders," remarks by Solomon Solis-Cohen, M.D., 32.

37. Sara Stage, *Female Complaints: Lydia Pinkham and the Business of Women's Medicine* (New York: W. W. Norton, 1979), p. 117; Brumberg, *Fasting Girls*, 162–3.

38. Rosalind Rosenberg, *Beyond Separate Spheres: Intellectual Roots of Modern Feminism* (New Haven: Yale University Press, 1982), 1–12; Charles Darwin, *The Descent of Man, and Selection in Relation to Sex* (Princeton: Princeton University Press, 1981) Part II, Chap. VIII, 271–72ff; Chap. XIX, 316–30; Chap. XX; see also Elizabeth Fee, "The Sexual Politics of Victorian Anthropology," *Clio's Consciousness Raised: New Perspectives on the History of Women*, Mary S. Hartman and Lois Banner, eds. (New York: Harper & Row, 1974), 90–91.

39. Rosenberg, *Beyond Separate Spheres*, chap. I discussion of Dr. Edward Clarke; see also Rosenberg's dissertation, "The Dissent from Darwin, 1898–1930" (Ph.D. diss., Stanford University, 1974), chap. 2; Beecher and Stowe, *The American Woman's Home*, 162. See also a selection of articles from *Popular Science Monthly*: White, "Woman's Place in Nature," 292–301; Mary T. Bissell, M.D., "Emotions Versus Health in Women," *The Popular Science Monthly* 32 (Feb. 1888), 507–8. Bissell quotes Henry Maudsley, the well-known English physician, to support her thesis that in the intimate relation between mind and body, violent emotional disturbances and commotion were a danger to women. Patrick, "Psychology of Woman," 209–25.

40. Edward H. Clarke, M.D., *Sex in Education; or, A Fair Chance for the Girls* (Boston: Osgood and Co., 1873). In an article about Mrs. Castle enti-

tled "Kleptomania," the English legal publication, *Law Times,* still talked in terms of the morally insane. *Law Times* CII (Nov. 14, 1896), 28.

41. Mary Putnam Jacobi, *The Question of Rest for Women during Menstruation* (New York: G. P. Putnam's Sons, 1877); Julia Ward Howe, *Sex and Education: A Reply to Dr. E. H. Clarke's "Sex in Education"* (Boston: Roberts Brothers, 1874). Julia Ward Howe and the other authors in this volume of essays refuted Clarke's conclusions about the deleterious effect of education on women. They saw *Sex in Education* as a polemic that attempted to keep women in dependence and in domestic bondage. See also Louise Michele Newman, ed., *Men's Ideas/Women's Realities: Popular Science, 1870–1915* (New York: Pergamon Press, 1985), chap. I, "The Problem of Biological Determinism (1870–1890)."

42. Mitchinson, "Gynecological Operations," 467; O'Brien, "Kleptomania Diagnosis," 66–67. The work of Carroll Smith-Rosenberg has been fundamental to the understanding of the medicalization of deviant behaviors in the 19th century. In her recent collection of essays, *Disorderly Conduct,* she has underscored the importance of social structure and male medical language in the determination of behavior as disease. Other historians, notably Joan Jacobs Brumberg, Nancy Tomes, and Regina Morantz-Sanchez have moved in another direction and, using clinical case records, have begun to fashion a new social history of medicine.

43. For examples of European use of the concept, see G. E. Berrios, "Obsessional Disorders during the Nineteenth Century: Terminological and Classificatory Issues," in W. F. Bynum, et al., *The Anatomy of Madness: Essays in the History of Psychiatry,* I (London & New York: Tavistock Publications, 1985), 166–87.

44. *American Journal of Mental Sciences* 19 (1836), 99.

45. Rogin, *Subversive Genealogy,* 118–19; Rogin has traced the use of the term "monomania" in the period before the Civil War. See Commonwealth v. Rogers in Leonard W. Levy, *The Laws of the Commonwealth and Chief Justice Shaw* (Cambridge, Massachusetts, 1977), 206–16; for its application to Mrs. Ella Castle see "Kleptomania," *Atlantic Medical Weekly* 26 (Dec. 26, 1896), 403; Vieda Skultans, *Madness and Morals: Ideas on Insanity in the 19th Century* (London: Routledge & Kegan Paul, 1975), 6.

46. Raymond de Saussure, "The Influence of the Concept of Monomania on French Medico-Legal Psychiatry," *Journal of the History of Medicine and Allied Sciences* (July 1946), 365.

47. Charles E. Rosenberg, *The Trial of the Assassin Guiteau: Psychology and Law in the Gilded Age* (Chicago: The University of Chicago Press, 1968), 63–64; see also Skultans, *Madness and Morals,* 22–25; George M. Beard maintained "insanity is a disease of the brain." See *American Nervousness,* 4.

48. Saussure, "Influence of the Concept of Monomania," 366, citing Esquirol, "De la Monomanie"; for a good discussion of Pritchard's definition of moral insanity, see Norman Dain, *Concepts of Insanity in the United States, 1787–1865* (New Brunswick: Rutgers University Press, 1964), 73–74. There was a great deal of confusion in both medical definition and therapeutic practice in the late nineteenth century. See Stage, *Female Complaints.*

49. Saussure, "Influence of the Concept of Monomania," 368. The Concept of monomania became a catch-all. See Neil Harris, *Humbug: The Art of P. T. Barnum* (Boston: Little, Brown, 1973), 53; Rogin, *Subversive Genealogy*, 118.

50. Dain, *Concepts of Insanity*, 78; for a short analysis of John Gray see Gerald Grob, *Mental Illness and American Society 1875–1940* (Princeton: Princeton University Press, 1983), 33–34.

51. James Hendrie Lloyd, "The Claim of Moral Insanity in its Medico-Legal Aspects," *The Medical Record* 31 (May 14, 1887), 542; see also Davis, *Homicide in American Fiction*, 81.

52. Rosenberg, *The Trial of Assassin Guiteau*, 189–95. Guiteau's trial and the medical and legal ideas it dramatized became an expression of American psychiatry in the 1880s and for much of the rest of the century.

53. John P. Gray, *American Journal of Insanity* XIV (April 1858), 319.

54. William A. Hammond, M.D., *Insanity in its Relations to Crime* (New York: D. Appleton & Co., 1873); Dain, *Concepts of Insanity*, 78; Grob, *Mental Illness*, 33–34, 331, fn 6. Both Grob and Dain use the *American Journal of Insanity* (1858–1875) as evidence for Gray's antagonism to the idea of moral insanity. See also Lloyd, "Claim of Moral Insanity," 538–39, 541–42. A supporter of Gray, Lloyd felt that "most kleptomaniacs were thieves with no pathology."

The friction between neurologists and superintendents of American institutions for the insane about classification of insanity appears in a number of sources. Doctors were seriously split over the question of insanity. For many M.D.s, gender issues were completely obscured by scientific questions about the nature of mental illness, its origins, evidences, etc. See for example S.E.D. Shortt, *Victorian Lunacy: Richard M. Bucke and the Practice of Late 19th-Century Psychiatry* (New York: Cambridge Univ. Press, 1986); Grob, *Mental Illness*, 51–2; Personal communication from Steven Stowe, June 2, 1987.

For a description of French attempts to distinguish between insanity and criminality, see Saussure, "The Influence of the Concept of Monomania," 389–93.

55. Ernest Howard Crosby, "The Legal Aspects of Partial Moral Mania," *Physician & Pharmacist and the Bulletin of the Medico-Legal Society* 12 (Dec. 1879), 157–60. For an indication that kleptomania was an item of interest even in the more remote parts of the country, see the *Raton Comet,* (Iowa) March 27, 1885, 4: "An Iowa Female Kleptomaniac" (from a New Orleans dispatch). Susan Yohn found this reference for me.

56. For a sample of this literature, see Henry Maudsley, M.D., "On some of the Causes of Insanity," *British Medical Journal* II (Nov. 24, 1866), 586–90; M. Legrand du Saulle, "The Physical Signs of Reasoning Madness," *Journal of Psychological Medicine and Mental Pathology* II (London, 1876), 317–23; Farnham, "Uterine Disease as a Factor"; Hanley, "Mental Aberration," 672; A. T. Hobbs, M.D., "The Relation of Ovarian Disease to Insanity, and Its Treatment," *American Journal of Obstetrics* XLIII (April 1901), 484–91: Doolittle, "The Relations of Pelvic Disease," 294–98.

57. "Kleptomania," *Law Times* CII (London, Nov. 14, 1896), 28; "Men-

tal Aberration Excited by Uterine Disorder," *The Philadelphia Polyclinic* VI (Feb. 6, 1897), 61.

58. Mitchell, "Relations of Nervous Disorders," 33, remarks by Solomon Solis-Cohen, M.D., quoting English physician; John Young Brown, "Pelvic Disease in its Relationship to Insanity in Women," *American Journal of Obstetrics and Diseases of Women and Children* XXX (Sept. 1894), 360–64; C. C. Hersman, M.D., "Relation of Uterine Disease to Some of the Insanities," *Journal of the American Medical Association* 33 (Sept. 16, 1899), 710; George H. Roche, "Some Causes of Insanity in Women," *American Journal of Obstetrics & Diseases of Women and Children* 34 (Dec. 1896), 801–6.

For a discussion of somatic treatment or behavior disorders in the 20th century, see Nathan G. Hale, Jr., *Freud and the Americans: The Beginnings of Psychoanalysis in the United States, 1876-1917,* I (New York: Oxford University Press, 1971), 94.

59. T. S. Clouston, *Clinical Lectures on Mental Diseases* (Philadelphia: Henry C. Lea's Son & Company, 1884), 171, 339.

60. Mitchell, "Nervous Disorders (Especially Kleptomania), " 605–6. For an earlier but essentially similar view, see V. H. Taliaferro, M.D., "The Corset in its Relations to Uterine Diseases," *Atlanta Medical and Surgical Journal* 10 (March 1873), 683.

61. *New York Times* (Feb. 11, 1893), 4:1; see also Mary E. Greene, "Medical Jurisprudence," Thesis, Women's Medical College of Pennsylvania, 1868.

62. O'Brien, "Kleptomania Diagnosis," 68; Jennie R. M. Eagleson, "Interaction of the Nervous and Reproductive Systems," Thesis, Women's Medical College of Pennsylvania, 1886; Crosby, "Legal Aspects of Partial Moral Mania," 157–60; Roche, "Some Causes of Insanity in Women," 801–6.

63. Wynter, *Borderlands of Insanity,* 49–50. Wynter writes of those who "suffer from a paralysis of the moral sense." H. Tristram Engelhardt, Jr., "The Diseases of Masturbation: Values and the Concept of Disease," in Judith Walzer Leavitt and Ronald Numbers, eds., *Sickness and Health in America: Readings in the History of Medicine and Public Health* (Madison: University of Wisconsin Press, 1985), 18.

64. Carroll Smith-Rosenberg and Charles Rosenberg, "The Female Animal: Medical and Biological Views of Women and Her Role in Nineteenth-Century America," *Journal of American History* 60 (Sept. 1973), 332–56.

65. *American Journal of Insanity* 27 (April 1871), 445; Ely Van de Warker, M.D., "The Relations of Women to Crime," I, *Popular Science Monthly* 8 (Nov. 1895), 2; *New York Times* (Dec. 26, 1905), 4:5.

66. *New York Evening Post* (June 3, 1903), 5:1.

67. *Woodhull and Claflin's Weekly* (March 18, 1871), 4–5; George Ade, "Mr. Benson's Experience with a Maniac," in *Stories of the Streets and of the Town* from the *Chicago Record,* 1893–1900 (Chicago: The Caxton Club, 1941), 124.

68. Dubuisson, "Les Voleuses des grand magasins," 1–20, 341–70; Roger Dupouy, "De La Kleptomanie," *Journal de psychologie normale et pathologique,*

Année 2 (1905), 404–26; Pierre Janet, "La Kleptomanie et la depression mentale," *Journal de psychologie normale et pathologique,* Année 8 (1911), 97–103; for other important French studies see Drs. Francois Boissier and Georges Lachaux, "Contribution a l'étude clinique de la kleptomanie," *Annales medico-psychologiques* 19, *Journal l'aliénation mentale et de la medecine legale des aliénés* (Paris: Librarie de L'Academie de Medecine, 1894); Docteur M. Letulle, "Voleuses honnêtes," *Gazette medicale de Paris,* Tome IV, 7ᵉ Serie 1 Octobre, 1887 (Paris: Librarie Octave Doin), 469–71; "Klepto-manie"—Presentation de malade, *Memoires et bulletins de la societe de medicine et de chirurgie de Bordeaux* 1896 (Séance de 13 Mars, 1896), 160–76. [N.b.: "Voleuse" is the feminine form of "thief."]

69. Dubuisson, "Les Voleuses," 16.

70. Ibid., 343; Thomas Byrnes, *Professional Criminals of America* (New York: Cassell & Co., 1886; reprint, Chelsea House, 1969), 31–32; *New York Times* (Dec. 26, 1905), 6:3, editorial.

71. Dubuisson, "Les Voleuses," 345. Dubuisson conducted clinical studies of 120 women, 100 of whom he labeled "pure cases." His stated goal was to learn about each woman's life, activities, and "the character of her morbid impulsion." In a typical case history a woman arrested for shoplifting related how a trauma changed her life at the age of 48. After her husband lost all his money in the "Panama catastrophe," she began to suffer a series of medical problems—insomnia, amnesia, hallucinations and insanity—all of which were capped by the onset of menopause . . . see 367–70; Dupouy, "De La Kleptomanie," was based on case studies of hospital admissions.

72. This general profile of the kleptomaniac is gathered from a number of sources. Among them see Byrnes, *Professional Criminals,* 31–32; *New York Times* (Jan. 14, 1883), 4, and (April 26, 1908), V. 8:1; *New York Evening Post* (June 3, 1903), 5:1, *Dry Goods Reporter* (Jan. 1, 1898), 45; *Dry Goods Economist* (May 14, 1892), 40, and (Oct. 27, 1900), 57; Dubuisson, "Les Voleuses," 2; Dupouy, "De La Kleptomanie," 404–26; Janet, "La Klepto-manie et la depression mentale," 97–103.

73. Dubuisson, "Les Voleuses," 17; *Dry Goods Economist* (March 15, 1902), 75; Sennett, *The Fall of Public Man,* 141–42. Any history of the American department store mentions the free-entry principle. See Wendt and Kogan, *Give the Lady What She Wants!* 32, 34.

In an article about A. T. Stewart, Henry E. Resseguie attributes the breakdown of the closed door system to Stewart. He also notes that when Harry G. Selfridge, general manager at Marshall Field & Co., established his American-style department store (with its free entry for all) in London in 1902, he was "severely censured by London magistrates for his alleged encouragement of shoplifting in doing so." Henry E. Resseguie, "Alexander Turney Stewart and the Development of the Department Store, 1823–1876." *Business History Review* 39 (Autumn 1965), 310–11. See also *Dry Goods Economist* (Nov. 5, 1892), 30–31. "British dry-goods stores have no goods openly displayed or on counters. . . . The bane of the American stores, the kleptomaniac, is scarcely known here and the force of floorwalkers and inspectors is correspondingly small."

74. *Dry Goods Economist* (March 15, 1902), 75.

75. *New York Herald* (Oct. 10, 1895), 1. Ehrichs invited "ladies who are not prepared to purchase to come in and examine the goods." *Dry Goods Economist* (Jan. 2, 1897), 37, and (Sept. 11, 1897), 61.

76. Hall diaries, week of Feb. 29, 1879.

77. *New York Times* (April 11, 1895), 8:1. Two former police detectives noted "the cloak of kleptomania has been stretched out very thin, sometimes, in the test of compassionate friends and relatives." Eldridge and Watts, *Our Rival the Rascal*, 28–29.

78. *New York Times* (Jan. 14, 1899), 1:4.

79. Ibid. (June 30, 1894), 1:6.

80. *Brooklyn Eagle* (Oct. 5, 1897), 16:4.

81. *New York Times* (Dec. 30, 1904), 1:5.

82. Le Journal *L'Oeuvre*, (June 7, 1925), cited in A. Anthéaume, *Le Roman d'une épidémie Parisienne, la kleptomanie?* (Paris: Librarie Octave Doin, 1925), 90.

83. Dain, *Concepts of Insanity*, 97. Using the records of the Massachusetts General Hospital between 1875 and 1900, Barbara Sicherman demonstrates how neurasthenia and mental disease affected the poor in great numbers by the 1870s. Barbara Sicherman, "The Uses of Diagnosis: Doctors, Patients and Neurasthenia," *Journal of the History of Medicine* (Jan. 1977), 44.

84. Beard, *American Nervousness;* Sicherman, "The Uses of Diagnosis," 44.

85. Skultans, *Madness and Morals*, 24.

86. *Woodhull & Claflin's Weekly* (March 18, 1871), 4–5.

87. Hobson, "Sex in the Marketplace," xx.

88. O'Brien, "The Kleptomania Diagnosis," 70. Building upon the work of Matthey, Pinel, and Esquirol, C. C. Marc was the first doctor to use the term "kleptomania." See also *American Journal of Insanity* (Jan. 1846), 275, ". . . this prompts him to action by a kind of irresistible instinct, while he either retains the most perfect consciousness of its impropriety, and horror at the enormity of the conduct to which it would impel him, and with difficulty, restrains himself or gives way, as in desperation, to the impulse which urges him on. Examples—Cleptomania, or propensity to theft." John C. Bucknill also cites Marc as originator of the term and refers to its usage in the *London Times*, April 1855 n.p. See J. C. Bucknill, M.D., "Kleptomania," *Am. Journal of Insanity*, 19 (Oct. 1862), 148–49. For a popular interpretation of the term, see the *New York World* (March 31, 1872), 6:3, "About Women."

The *Oxford English Dictionary* traces the first public use of the term 'cleptomania' to the *New Monthly Magazine* XXVIII, no. 15, 1830; according to the *Diagnostic and Statistical Manual,* until 1932 there was no standard nomenclature of disease, but a "polyglot of diagnostic labels and systems." See "Kleptomania," *Diagnostic and Statistical Manual of Mental Disorders* III (Washington, D.C.: American Psychiatric Association Task Force on Nomenclature and Statistics, 1980), 293–94 (hereafter, *DSM-III*).

89. *New York Daily Tribune* (Dec. 26, 1870), 2:5.

90. *New York Daily Sun* (Dec. 26, 1870), 2:5.

91. *New York Times* (Jan. 18, 1882), 8:6. The *New York World* (March 31, 1872), 6:3 referred to a "shoplifter's kleptomaneous propensities." By the 1880s middle-class shoplifters were regularly referred to as kleptomaniacs. See *New York Tribune* (Dec. 23, 1883), 6:1.

92. *New York Daily Tribune* (Dec. 23, 1883), 6:1.

93. Smith-Rosenberg and Rosenberg, "The Female Animal," 338.

94. *New York Times* (March 28, 1883), 5:4.

95. Ibid. (Feb. 4, 1886), 2:6.

96. Ibid. (Aug. 14, 1887), 1:4.

97. Byrnes, *Professional Criminals of America*, 31–32. Byrne's language followed French reasoning almost word for word. See Dupouy, "De La Kleptomanie," 410–11. Dupouy describes those women whose ordinary sensibility and will are overcome by the desire for an object. "Reason is subsumed by desire . . . conscious will is diminished."

98. *New York Times* (March 27, 1889), 2:5.

99. Ibid. (Jan. 8, 1892), 10:2. Belief in the persistence of inherited insanity was strong in the second half of the 19th century. See Ray, *Medical Jurisprudence of Insanity*, 173–74; Vieda Skultans discusses the dual and contrasting themes in 19th-century views of insanity: the physical, which depends upon heredity and the moral, which allows individual action and is not as deterministic as the physical. Skultans, *Madness and Morals*, 25.

100. Wynter, *Borderlands of Insanity*, 43–63. On the issue of heredity and insanity, Wynter wrote, "The tendency of the mother to transmit her mental disease is, however, in all cases stronger than the father's; some physicians have, indeed, insisted that it is twice as strong." The *Business Woman's Journal* supported a similar interpretation of heredity. Writing about women's lack of money of their own, and the shoplifting that often accompanied it, the journal added, "It teaches the young girl to purloin pennies from her father's pockets and to bestow an heredity of kleptomania upon her children later in life" (Feb. 1892), 56–7; Skultans, *Madness & Morals*, 24ff.

101. W. A. Newman Dorland, M.D., *The American Illustrated Medical Dictionary* (Philadelphia & London: W. B. Saunders & Co., 1900), 341.

102. *Dry Goods Economist* (Oct. 27, 1900), 57.

103. *Dry Goods Reporter* (Jan. 1, 1898), 45.

104. *New York Times* (Dec. 26, 1905), 4:3.

105. Mitchell, "Relations of Nervous Disorders," 35.

Epilogue

1. Mary Sullivan, *My Double Life: The Story of a New York Policewoman* (New York: Farrar and Rinehart, 1938), 182.

2. See, for example, differences in analysis between Mary Dixon Jones, M.D., "Insanity, Its Causes: Is There in Woman a Correlation of the Sexual Function with Insanity and Crime?" *Medical Record* 58 (Dec. 15, 1900),

925–37, and Doolittle, "Relation of Pelvic Disease to Insanity," 294–98, with Karl Abraham, *Selected Papers*, International Psycho-Analytic Library, no. 13 (London: Hogarth Press, 1965).

3. Jeffrey Weeks, *Sexuality* (New York: Tavistock Publications and Ellis Horwood, 1986), 16.

4. Dr. Wilhelm Stekel, "The Sexual Root of Kleptomania," *Journal of the American Institute of Criminal Law and Criminology* II (July 1911), 239–40ff.

5. While Freudian interpretation achieved a degree of professional recognition in the United States and slowly became part of the *lingua franca* after Sigmund Freud's visit in 1904, there was still no single definition given to the problem of the middle-class shoplifter. Contrasting diagnoses among doctors persisted, as did discontinuities between legal and medical views of the behavior. See *New York Times* (Nov. 30, 1904), 1:2; W. C. Sullivan, M.D., *Crime and Insanity* (New York: Longmans, Green & Co., 1924), 2–3, and chap. 6, 172–78. For the persistence of the popular use of kleptomania, see *Merchants Record and Show Window* (June 1916), 9. For a critical view of kleptomania in France, see Anthéaume, *Le Roman d'une épidémie Parisienne*, 9–13. Anthéaume called the kleptomania diagnosis "an excuse to steal." For an overview, see O'Brien, "Kleptomania Diagnosis," 65–77.

6. Stekel, "Sexual Root of Kleptomania," 240.

7. Abraham, *Selected Papers*, 355, 483–85.

8. For a discussion of the expression of anger in women, see Davis, *Fiction in the Archives*, 82; 187, fn 2, 189, fn 13. See also Gilbert and Gubar, *Mad Woman in the Attic;* Gibbens and Prince, *Shoplifting*, 86. Gibbens and Prince discuss shoplifting by middle-class women as a form of power and control that is also a form of "moral suicide."

9. Fritz Wittels, M.D., "Some Remarks on Kleptomania," *Journal of Nervous and Mental Disease* 69 (March 1929), 245.

10. Ibid., 246. For a discussion of Freud and femininity see Mary Jacobus, *Reading Women: Essays in Feminist Criticism* (New York: Columbia University Press, 1986), 20–21.

11. Fritz Wittels, M.D., "Kleptomania and Other Psychopathic Crimes," *Journal of Criminal Psychopathology* 4 (Oct. 1942), 207–8. This level of interpretation has retained legitimacy, albeit in less crude and decidedly gender-neutral form. *DSM-III* defines kleptomania as an impulse control disorder characterized by, among other things, "an increased sense of tension before committing the act" and the experiencing of "pleasure, gratification or release at the time of committing the act." *DSM-III*, 291–93.

12. Wittels, "Kleptomania and Other Psychopathic Crimes," 208.

13. Weeks, *Sexuality,* 61ff.

14. Ibid., 10.

15. Warren C. Middleton, "Is There a Relation Between Kleptomania and Female Periodicity in Neurotic Individuals?" *The Psychological Clinic* XXII (Dec. 1933–Feb. 1934), 232–47; "To steal is actually the sex life of Kleptomaniacs," Wittels asserted in "Kleptomania and Other Psychopathic Crimes," 208.

16. Middleton, "Is There a Relation?"

17. Mary Sullivan, *My Double Life: The Story of a New York Policewoman* (New York: Farrar and Rhinehart, 1938), 182, 189–90; Popular references to kleptomania appear even toward the end of the twentieth century. "We are impulse eaters, the culinary equivalent of kleptomaniacs," Barbara Raskin wrote in *Hot Flashes* (New York: St. Martin's Press, 1987), 244–45.

18. Middleton, "Is There a Relation?" 246.

19. Dr. Fabian Rouke, "The Psychology of the Retail Criminal," Report of the National Retail Dry-Goods Association, *Controlling Shortages*, ca. 1950, Baker Library, Harvard Business School.

20. Ibid., 21.

21. Ibid., 21–24.

22. "One Out of Sixty Is a Shoplifter," *Life* (Dec. 15, 1967), 66–73. I wish to thank Dick Feldman for recalling this important photo essay.

23. Ibid., 72A.

24. Ibid.

25. Ibid.

26. Kate Ellis, "The Shoplifter," *Village Voice* (Oct. 13, 1987), 15.

27. "One Out of Sixty Is a Shoplifter," 72A.

28. David Finkle, "Sticky Fingers," *New York Woman* (July/August, 1987), 62.

29. "Last year, K-Mart caught people with $13 million worth of stolen merchandise. . . . We're ahead of that this year." *New York Times* (Dec. 20, 1987), III, 7:1–5. With its lead sentence, "There are 39 shoplifting days until Christmas," an article in *Newsday* (Long Island) suggested that shoplifting was rampant. *Newsday* (Nov. 16, 1987), 6, 38. Various sources have estimated losses in the late 1980s. See Louise Bernikow, "Excuse Me, Miss! Did You Pay for This?" *Mademoiselle* (Sept. 1988), 280; Richard Russell, *Dow Theory Letters* (Aug. 10, 1988), 5; and Dody Tsiantar, "Big Brother at the Mall: Retailers Go High Tech in the War on Shoplifters," *Newsweek* (July 3, 1989), 44.

30. Ellis, "The Shoplifter," 16.

31. Finkle, "Sticky Fingers," 62.

32. "Shoplifters," *The Oprah Winfrey Show* (July 14, 1987), Transcript #W217, 3.

33. Ellis, "The Shoplifter," 17.

34. Bernikow, "Excuse Me, Miss!" 281; Jane Pratt, "Women Who Steal," *New Woman* (Oct. 1988), 80.

35. Bernikow, "Excuse Me, Miss!" 281, 312.

36. Pratt, "Women Who Steal," 79.

37. "It's Shoplifting Season Again," *New York Times* (Dec. 15, 1986), D, 1:4; Pratt, "Women Who Steal," 80. The term "kleptomania" appears, surprisingly, in two newspaper articles about shoplifting in the 1980s. In both instances the word is used to describe a compulsive disorder. See *Wall Street Journal* (March 8, 1983), 1:4; and *New York Times* (December 15, 1986), D, 1:4. The analysis of Bess Myerson's shoplifting incorporated many of the ele-

ments of the 19th century definition of kleptomania: class, gender, stage of life, and mental condition. See *New York Times* or *New York Newsday,* almost any issue during October, November, December 1988.

38. Finkle, "Stickly Fingers," 62.

39. Bernikow, "Excuse Me, Miss!" 312.

40. *New York Times* (Dec. 15, 1986), D, 1:4.

41. "If You're Primping in This Store Mirror, Say Hello to Bernard," *Wall Street Journal* (March 8, 1983), 1:4.

42. *New York Times* (Sept. 13, 1987), III:19; *Wall Street Journal* (Sept. 17, 1987), II:33.

43. "To Catch a Thief (and Enroll Him)," *New York Times* (Nov. 24, 1988), D, 1:3.

44. *Oprah Winfrey Show,* "Shoplifters," 12; "Troubled Millions Heed Call of Self-Help Groups," *New York Times* (April 17, 1988), 1:1.

45. Russel, *Dow Theory Letters,* 5. If this is true, it is not a new phenomenon. Kate Simon wrote of her shoplifting exploits in the New York of the 1920s. Kate Simon, *A Wider World: Portraits in Adolescence* (New York: Harper and Row, 1986), 91, 172–74.

46. Statistics about shoplifting losses continue to be unreliable. One retail group, The National Coalition to Prevent Shoplifting, set total losses of $26 billion for 1981. This amount includes losses in all types of retail outlets. Even with such high losses, experts claim dozens of thefts go unreported for every one uncovered. See *Wall Street Journal* (March 8, 1983), 1:4. In 1986 the National Retail Merchants Association, representing 45,000 retailers, estimated shrinkage in individual stores of 1.98 percent of sales in 1986. Included in this figure were shoplifting, employee theft, vendor theft, and bookkeeping error. Peter Berlin, a security expert with Price Waterhouse, said that shoplifting accounts for about 65 percent of all retail shrinkage. Other sources suggest both higher and lower estimates. See *New York Times* (December 15, 1988), D, 1: 4 and (November 24, 1988), D, 1: 3; Russel, *Dow Theory Letters,* (August 10, 1988), 5. Russel estimated that two million Americans would be charged with shoplifting in 1988.

47. *New York Times* (December 15, 1988), D, 1:4.

48. *New York Newsday* (November 16, 1987), 6.

49. *New York Times* (December 15, 1986), D, 1:4.

Index

Abraham & Straus, 89, 100, 138
Abraham, Karl, 199, 205
Ade, George, 15, 53
Administrative hierarchy, 94–97, 99, 103–4, 109–11. *See also* Employee relations
Age, of shoplifters, 157
Altman's. *See* B. Altman & Company
Amenities of department stores, 54–55
Andrews, Ellen, 74–75
Appearances, 24–25, 130–31, 132–33, 138
Arnold & Constable, 72, 133–34, 136, 142, 163
Arrests, 115, 140–41, 143, 144–45, 146, 150, 151, 160–61. *See also* False arrests; *name of specific person*
Athletic women, 24
A. T. Stewart's, 56, 67–68, 71, 74, 75, 83, 86–87, 189–90
Au bonheur des dames. See Zola, Émile
Auerbach, Nina, 171

B. Altman & Company, 142, 163
Bargain counters, 127, 131
Beard, George, 192

Behavior modification, 206
Bell, Daniel, 170
Bellamy, Edward, 27
Benson, Susan Porter, 104
Bernard, George, 153
Biology. *See* Sexuality
Blades, Henry, 11, 134, 135, 136, 140–41, 161, 162
Blake, Lilly Devereux, 165–67
Blame, 12, 147, 171
Bloomingdale Brothers, 110–11, 116–17, 133–34, 142
Blumenthal, Daniel, 154–55
Blumin, Stuart, 15
Bohme, Margarete, 49, 73–74, 78, 89, 110, 116, 127, 156–57
Bolch, Catherine, 138
Boston Globe [newspaper], 64, 150, 151
Boston Herald [newspaper], 127, 167
Boston Store, 31
Bowyer, H. M., 94
Bridal trousseau, 38–39
Brooklyn Eagle [newspaper], 89
Bryant, Mary, 120–25
Burnett, Mrs. W. D., 164
Burns [William J.] Detective Agency, 145–46

Busbey, Katherine, 42, 69
Business Women's Journal, 167
Byrnes, Thomas, 194

Carnival atmosphere, 143
Case studies, 188
Castle, Ella, 58, 175–81, 185–86, 187, 195
Casual shoplifters, 202–3, 206
Chandler, Alfred, 91, 94, 97
Change: obsessive need for, 53–54
Chapin, Robert C., 18
Chicago Record [newspaper], 15
Children, 37–38, 49–50
Christmas, 42–43, 57, 69, 72, 87–88, 89–90, 134–35, 141, 151
Claflin's. *See* H. B. Claflin
Class distinctions: and appearances, 138; and blame, 147; and consumerism/consumption, 6, 26, 27–28, 33–35, 165–66; and courts/judges, 152–55, 157; and department stores as the image of the middle class, 11, 31; and detectives, 131, 138–39, 140–41, 147, 148; and dress codes, 107; and the ease of shoplifting, 172; and the emergence of shoplifting, 4; and justice, 148; and the medicalization of shoplifting, 174, 182, 191–92, 193–94; and middle-class characteristics, 14–15; in the modern culture, 206; paradoxes about, 149; and the Phelps incident, 123–24, 125; and professional shoplifters, 148–49; and prosecutions, 124; and pseudonyms, 164; and salespeople, 107–8, 123–24, 125
Claussen, Elizabeth, 120–25
Clothing, 24–25, 35–39, 50
Clouston, T. S., 186
Color, 44
Commercial Advertiser [newspaper], 121, 122
Competition, 109
Consumerism/consumption: absurdities of, 53; changes in patterns of, 25; and class

distinctions, 6, 27–28, 33–35, 165–67; conspicuous, 165; and display windows, 68–75; emergence of, 4–5, 27–28; encouragement by department stores of, 4–5, 35, 39; and the enticement of shoppers, 6, 11; and identity, 25–26; and the interior of department stores, 43, 47; and the medicalization of shoplifting, 186, 187, 196; and mirrors, 85; and the moral order, 58–62; and nationalism, 102; and the overpowering desires of women, 11; paradoxes of, 149–50, 156–57; pathology of, 169–70; and prosecution for shoplifting, 139; and salespeople, 92–93, 105; and social standing, 165–67; and technology, 27, 33, 37, 39, 40; and the thrift ethic, 95–96; women's role in, 5–6, 13, 26, 28, 165–67. *See also* Materialism; Spending
Control: of employees, 90, 104–9, 118; of money, 166–67
Cooper, W. H., 109
Counters, 75–83, 141
Courts: and class distinctions, 152–55; and the decline of personal morality, 61; and false names/addresses, 163; and first-time shoplifters, 143; and the medicalization of shoplifting, 153–55, 180, 185, 190–91, 193; and the overwhelming desires/temptations of women, 47, 143, 145. *See also* Judges; Prosecutions
Cowan, Ruth, 24
Crapsey, Edward, 75
Crosby, Ernest H., 185
Crowds, 88, 125–29, 143, 172
Customers: and detectives, 137, 138–40, 147; and phrenology, 137; and salespeople, 118, 162; should not see rules/regulations, 106. *See also* Shopping
Cycling, 24

Daggett, J. N., 136
Darwin, Charles, 181–82

Daussé, Augustine, 193
Davis, Dorothy, 33
Defensive salesmanship, 117–18
Definition: of female, 149; of
    kleptomania, 11, 62, 173, 174,
    186–87, 195; of middle class, 14; of
    middle-class women, 13, 159–60,
    204; of the middle-class shoplifter,
    8–9, 207. *See also* Identity
Dengler, Sarah, 190, 191
Department stores: amenities of, 54–
    55; as the arbiters of social mores,
    51; and the authenticating of social
    status, 45–46; and class
    distinctions, 11, 31; desire/
    temptation as focus of, 6;
    emergence of, 4–5, 6–7, 14;
    encouragement of consumption/
    materialism by, 4–5, 6, 35, 39, 56–
    57; extent of shoplifting in, 6–7,
    64–67, 79, 111–14, 143–44, 151,
    156, 197, 207; as a fantasyland, 43–
    48, 64, 68–72, 85, 92–93, 115; as
    the focus of shoplifting, 5; image of
    the, 65, 115, 139, 140, 161;
    influence of the, 5; as ladies' clubs,
    54; and the medicalization of
    shoplifting, 7–8, 188–90, 192; as
    moral communities, 100; and the
    moral order, 47, 51, 53, 56–58,
    61–62; paradoxical situation of, 63–
    67, 118–19; physical expansion of,
    50–51, 65–66, 91–92, 93, 158;
    values/attitudes of, 63–64, 95–96;
    women's relationship with, 28–29,
    40–41. *See also* Enticement of
    shoppers; Interior of department
    stores; Organization of department
    stores
The Department Store. See Bohme,
    Margarete
Detectives: appearances of, 130–31,
    132–33; arrests by, 140–41; and
    class distinctions, 131, 138–39,
    140–41, 147, 148; and crowds,
    125–29; and customers, 138–40,
    147; and employee relations, 129,
    133, 135; fear of, 129; female, 130–
    33, 171; functions of, 130–31;

instincts of, 135–37; and the
    medicalization of shoplifting, 154–
    55, 190–91; overzealousness of,
    140–41, 147; paradoxes for, 147;
    and the Phelps incident, 120–25,
    139, 141; and phrenology, 135–38;
    and professional shoplifters, 134,
    137–38, 142, 144–45, 146;
    professional shoppers as adjuncts to,
    110; role of, 10, 124–26, 129–31;
    salespeople as auxiliaries to, 133,
    135–36; types of, 129–30; as
    working-class people, 138–39
The Detective [journal], 89
Diaz, Abby Morton, 22–23
Discipline of employees, 105–9
Display windows, 67–75, 87–88,
    90
Division of labor, 104
Domesticity, 14, 16, 19–20, 22–23,
    28
Doyle, Arthur Conan, 180
Dress codes, 106–7
Drug use, 204
Dry Goods Economist [trade journal]:
    Blades interview with the, 140–41;
    and consumerism/consumption,
    21, 26, 28, 33–35, 40, 66–67; and
    counters, 77, 78, 80, 81–82, 83;
    and the extent of shoplifting, 113,
    141; and the importance of display,
    90; and the interior of the store, 43,
    45, 52, 53–54, 55, 56, 60; and
    lighting, 87; and the medicalization
    of shoplifting, 189, 195; and
    mirrors, 83, 84; and the need for
    detectives, 134–35, 141; and
    scientific management, 98;
    shoplifting reports in the, 10; and
    window displays, 69, 70, 72, 73, 74
Dry Goods Reporter [trade journal], 10,
    25, 26, 49, 51–52, 60–61, 73, 77,
    98–99
Dubuisson, Paul, 46, 52, 188, 189,
    197
Du Maurier, George, 34
Dunne, Finley Peter, 24–25
Dunstan, Caroline, 17
Dupouy, Roger, 188

Easter season, 57
Economic worries of women, 18
Ehrich Brothers, 36, 48, 111, 133–34, 142, 193
Eisner, Sophie, 120–25
Eldridge, Benjamin, 137–38
Electronic surveillance devices, 205–6
Employee relations: and the administrative hierarchy, 94–97, 99, 103–4, 109–11; and the control of employees, 90, 104–9, 118; and detectives, 129, 133, 135; and the discipline of employees, 105–9; and the indifference of salespeople, 116; and the legitimation of management, 103; and the loyalty of employees, 100–111, 129; and the morale of employees, 110; and professional shoppers, 109–11; and rules and regulations, 104–9, 114–15, 118; and scientific management, 96, 97–98; and social welfare work by stores, 100–102. *See also* Salespeople
Enticement of shoppers: calculation by department stores of the, 28, 48–50, 54–55, 58–62; and consumerism/materialism, 6, 11; and counters, 75–83; and lighting, 86–90; and mirrors, 83–86. *See also* Display windows; Temptations
Esquirol, Jean-Étienne, 183–84
Everts, Orpheus, 173, 174
Evolution, 181–82
Extenuating circumstances, 170–71

Fairness, 154
Fair, The, 54, 106, 114–15
False arrests, 115, 139, 141, 147
False names/addresses, 163–64
Families, 16–17, 19, 172
Fantasyland: department stores as a, 43–48, 64, 68–72, 85, 92–93, 115
Farley, Philip, 116
Fathers. *See* Husbands/fathers
Female detectives, 130–33, 171
Female life cycle. *See* Sexuality
Feminists, 122, 123, 124, 167
Field and Leiter, 76

Filene's. *See* Wm. Filene's Sons Company
F. Loeser & Company, 133–34, 145
Floorwalkers, 129, 146
Forbes, Susan E., 17, 23
Fraser, Arthur, 71–72
Freedom, 189
French contributions to the medicalization of shoplifting, 182–84, 188–89, 195
Freudianism, 197–98, 201–2, 203
Furlong, Julia, 145

Gender: and the Castle case, 175–81; and the emergence of shoplifting, 4; and the medicalization of shoplifting, 8–9, 174, 175–81, 187, 195, 207; and psychiatry, 200, 202, 203–4; and women as shoppers, 30–31
Gimbel Brothers, 109
Gitlow, Benjamin, 110–11, 133
Glamorization of spending, 55–56
Glass: as an enticement to shoppers, 68–86, 90; as counters, 75–83; as display windows, 67–75; as a means of curbing shoplifting, 65, 66, 67–86, 90; mirrors, 83–86
Godey's Lady's Book, 68
Godkin, E. L., 20, 76
Golden, Abigail, 96
Goldmark, Pauline, 101
Gray, John, 184–85
Greene, Asa, 32
Grigg, William Chapman, 176, 178–79
Guilt, 136, 201–2
Guiteau, Charles, 184–85

Hall, Sophie, 30, 158, 189–90
Hammond, George G., 79
H. B. Claflin, 133–34
Hearn & Son. *See* James A. Hearn & Son
Hershey, Julia, 88
Hirschler, Diana, 118, 137
Hobart, Caroline, 76–77, 152–53, 155, 163
Home: importance of, 16, 51–54

Home decor, 51–54
Homicidal mania, 183–84
Hone, Philip, 67
H. O'Neil & Company, 88, 133–34
Horen, Mrs. Peter, 170
Hornig, Mrs. H. A., 170
Household budgets, 17–18
Housework, 23–24
Hudson's. *See* J. L. Hudson Company
Husbands/fathers: and the Castle case, 175–81; and the characteristics of shoplifters, 16; and the medicalization of shoplifting, 175–81, 190–91; occupations of, 159; and power relationships in families, 166–67; shame for, 164–66; and women as shoppers, 30–31
Hysteria, 173–79, 187, 198

Identity of middle-class women, 23–24, 25, 28–29, 37, 180. *See also* Definition
Idleness. *See* Leisure
Image: of department stores, 65, 115, 139, 140, 161; of women, 180
Impulse buying, 55–56, 58, 78, 82–83, 169–70
Income of middle class, 17–18, 25
Interior of department stores: and color, 44; and consumption/materialism, 47, 53; and counters, 75–83; and the enticement of shoppers, 48–50, 54–55; as a fantasyland, 43–48; overpowering desires/temptations of women, 45–47, 59–62
Inventory control, 112

James A. Hearn & Son, 109, 133–34
James McCreery & Company, 126, 139, 194
Janet, Pierre, 188, 197
J. L. Hudson Company, 112
Johnstone, Margaret, 145
John Wanamaker: detectives at, 11, 134, 135, 140; employee relations at, 111; expansion of, 111; home decor department at, 52; and the interior of the store, 44, 45;

scientific management at, 98; shoplifting at, 138; strategies to curb shoplifting at, 66
Judges, 7–8, 121–22, 124, 152–55, 157. *See also* Courts
Justice, 148. *See also* Courts; Judges

Kash, Daniel/David, 155, 161
Kernochan, Frederick, 156
King, Catherine, 163
King, Moses, 70–71
Kinnear, Lillian, 95
Kleptomania: as a class concept, 174, 191–92; decline of the use of the term, 197, 200–201; as a disease, 8; and the excesses of middle-class women, 183; and the inferiority of women, 174; meanings of, 11, 62, 173, 174, 186–87, 195; as a mental disorder, 173; as moral insanity, 183–86; as the recreation of the sex act, 200; as a solution to a problem, 11–12; as a stereotype, 7–8, 62, 148–49, 157; symptoms of, 173–79; and the traditional views of women, 181–82. *See also* Medicalization of shoplifting
Kleptomaniacs Anonymous, 206
The Kleptomaniac [movie], 148, 195
Koch's, 162

Landberg, Dora, 190
Lawyers, 7–8, 155, 163, 169–70, 171, 185, 190–91, 193
Lazarus, Fred and Ralph, 84–85
Lazarus Brothers, 84–85
Lears, T. J. Jackson, 56
Lee, Gerald, 126
Leiss, William, 35
Leisure, 6, 19–23, 40
Lendrum, Fannie, 190
Leslie's Illustrated Newspaper, 69
Liebman's, 145
Life cycle. *See* Sexuality
Life [magazine], 202
Lighting, 65, 66, 86–90, 141
Lingerie, 38, 45
Little, Laura, 162, 169, 170
Lloyd, James Hendrie, 184

Loeser & Company. *See* F. Loeser & Company
Long, Abbie, 168–69
Lord & Taylor, 44, 52, 142, 143
Lossing, Benson J., 93
Loyalty: of employees, 100–111, 129; of shoppers, 161–62
Lynd, Helen, 180
Lynn, Massachusetts, incident, 58, 150, 165, 168, 171–72

McCabe, James, 68
McCauley, Rose, 155
McCreery & Company. *See* James McCreery & Company
McCurdy, W. F., 105
McMahon, Martin T., 47
Macy, Rowland, 9–10, 94, 113, 125, 192
Macy's. *See* R. H. Macy & Company
Management: employees as legitimizing the position of, 103; expansion of, 93–97; and the medicalization of shoplifting, 190–91; and the prosecution of shoplifting, 160–61; and reorganization as a means of curbing shoplifting, 65–67. *See also* Employee relations
Mandel Brothers, 59
Marble Palace. *See* A. T. Stewart's
Marc, C. C., 182–83
Marital status of shoplifters, 157
Markowitz, Janet, 205
Marshall Field & Company: amenities at, 54; and class distinctions, 31; detectives at, 129, 147; display windows at, 70, 71–72; employee relations at, 105–6, 115; home decor department at, 52; as a showcase, 5; strategies to curb shoplifting at, 66
Mass production, 33
Materialism, 6, 27–28, 31–32, 53, 55, 56–57, 81, 165. *See also* Consumerism/consumption; Spending
Medicalization of shoplifting: and the Castle case, 175–81, 185–86, 187,

195; and class distinctions, 174, 182, 191–92, 193–94; and consumerism/consumption, 186, 187, 196; and the courts, 180, 185, 190–91, 193; as a defense for shoplifting, 169–70; and the department stores, 188–90, 192; emergence of the, 5; French contributions to the, 182–84, 188–89, 195; and gender, 8–9, 174, 175–81, 187, 195, 200, 207; and guilt, 195–96; and husbands/ fathers, 175–81, 190–91; and the image of a shoplifter, 207; importance of, 7–8; and the meaning of shoplifting, 11; and modern shoplifting, 207; and moral confusion, 11–12; and moral insanity, 183–86, 193–94; and the overpowering desires/temptations of women, 8, 194; paradoxes of, 174; public attitudes about the, 187–88, 195, 196; and science, 183–86; and sexuality, 7–8, 173–75, 177–79, 181–82, 186–87, 195, 196–201, 204, 205; and the stereotype of middle-class women, 7–8, 169, 174, 175, 187, 188, 192–93, 195–96; and victimization, 205; women's acceptance of the, 8–9, 174, 175, 190–91, 195–96, 198–99. *See also* Kleptomania
Men: as shoplifters, 202. *See also* Husbands/fathers
Menopause, 157
Menstruation, 7, 186–87, 199, 201
Middle class: characteristics of, 14–19; definition of, 14. *See also name of specific person or topic*
Mirrors, 66, 83–86, 90, 118, 141, 205–6
Mitchell, S. Weir, 178, 186, 195
Money: control of, 166–67
Monomania, 183–85
Morale of employees, 110
Moral insanity, 183–86, 193–94
Morality: confusion about, 11–12, 164, 167–68, 192–93; and department stores, 47, 51, 53, 56–

58, 61–62; flexibility toward, 88; paradoxes about, 193; personal, 56–58, 61–62; responsibility for, 195–96, 197–200
Mullenmeister's, 78, 89

Namm's, 145
Nationalism, 102
National Retail Dry-Goods Association [NRDGA], 83, 145–46, 201–2
National Woman's Suffrage Association, 122
Needs and wants, 6, 22, 26, 32–35, 170, 204
Neurotic shoplifters, 202–3
Newspapers: attitudes toward shoplifting by, 65, 155–56, 162; and detectives, 129, 130–31; and the medicalization of shoplifting, 7–8; and the Phelps-Macy's incident, 9–10, 121, 122–23, 192; shoplifting reports in, 10, 162. *See also name of specific paper*
New York Evening Post [newspaper], 17–18, 130, 131, 187
New York Herald [newspaper], 68, 128
New York State Factory Investigation Commission, 116
New York Sun [newspaper], 121, 192
New York Times [newspaper], 134, 141, 149, 150, 151, 162–63, 175, 193–94, 195, 205, 207
New York Tribune [newspaper], 22, 113–14, 122, 125, 131, 132, 136, 139, 142, 170, 192, 193
New York World [newspaper], 112, 122, 123, 129
Nielson, Miss, 120–25
Nymphomania, 183–84

Obsolescence, 33–34, 37–38
Occupations: of husbands/fathers, 159; of shoplifters, 158
O'Neil & Company. *See* H. O'Neil & Company
Organization of department stores: and the administrative hierarchy, 94–97, 99, 103–4, 109; and the

discipline of employees, 105–9; and the division of labor, 104; and owner-managers, 94–97, 98; and the physical expansion of stores, 91–92; and professional shoppers, 109–11; and rules and regulations, 104–9, 114–15, 118; and salespeople as problems, 98–104, 108–9; and scientific management, 96, 97–98; and social welfare, 100–102; and technology, 104–5. *See also* Employee relations
Out-of-town shoppers, 71, 158
Overbuying, 56
Overpowering desires of women, 11, 45–47, 55, 74, 145, 168–72, 194, 198. *See also* Temptations
Overzealousness of detectives, 140–41, 147

Paradoxes: and class distinctions, 149; of consumerism/consumption, 149–50, 156–57; for department stores, 63–67, 118–19; for detectives, 147; of the medicalization of shoplifting, 174; about the morality of Victorian women, 193; for salespeople, 92–93, 105, 119; of wants and needs, 170
Pardee, Clara Burton, 13–14, 16, 17, 18, 19–20, 21, 22, 25, 26–27, 36, 39, 40, 87
Parsons, Helen, 132
Paternalism, 99, 100–101
Paying calls, 20
A Peep into Catharine Street [1846], 32
Personal morality, 56–58, 61–62
Peyser, Eva, 171
Phelps, Elizabeth B., 9–10, 113, 120–25, 129, 139, 141, 147, 170, 171, 192
Philadelphia Polyclinic Hospital, 178
Phillips, C. G., 81–82
Phrenology, 135–38
Phul, Mrs. Henry von, 194–95
Physical expansion of stores, 50–51, 65–66, 91–92, 93, 158

Pinkerton, William, 133–34
Pinkerton Detective Agency, 129–30, 133–34
Plunkett, Mary, 132–33, 141
Porter, Edwin S., 148, 195
Power relationships, 166–67
Prichard, James, 184
Prince, Lucinda, 137
Productivity, 25–26
Professional shoplifters, 134, 137–38, 142, 144–45, 146, 148–49, 161, 202
Professional shoppers, 109–11
Progressive merchandising, 58–62
Prosecutions, 139, 144, 151, 152–56, 160–62
Pseudonyms, 163–64
Psychiatry, 197–207
Psychological explanations for shoplifting, 171–72, 197–207
Public attitudes, 29, 90, 150–51, 187–88, 195, 196
Publicity, 140, 143, 146, 150, 151, 156. *See also name of specific newspaper or person*
Public lives of Victorian women, 16–21, 40
Public voice of women, 8, 204
Punishments, 144, 151, 170, 171–72
Pyromania, 183–84

Raymond, Russell, 159
Raymond, Sarah, 3
Ready-to-wear, 35–40, 45, 50, 84
Religion, 32
Repeat shoppers, 161–63
Reproductive system. *See* Sexuality
Retail associations. *See name of specific association*
Retail Clerks Union, 110
Retail Dry-Goods Association of New York, 144, 151, 152–53, 155, 156
Retailing, 56, 58–62, 96
Retail Merchants Association of Boston, 42–43
Retail Trade Board [Boston], 144
Return of merchandise, 57–58
The Revolution [Woman's Rights Periodical], 123, 124

Rewards, 116
R. H. Macy & Company:
administrative hierarchy at, 94–97; amenities at, 54; Christmas season at, 57, 87; counters at, 79; detectives at, 66, 120–25, 129, 130–31, 132–33, 142; display windows at, 69; employee relations at, 94–97, 100, 105; extent of shoplifting at, 112, 113; history of, 93; home decor department at, 52; and *The Kleptomaniac* [movie], 148; lighting at, 87–88; and the Phelps incident, 9–10, 120–25, 129, 139, 141, 147, 192; physical expansion of, 93–97; rivalries with, 109; salespeople at, 123–24, 125; and the secularization of religious occasions, 57; shoplifting incidents at, 115, 138; as a showcase, 5; strategies to curb shoplifting at, 66. *See also name of specific person*
Richards, Harriet, 13–14, 16, 19–20, 21, 26, 36, 54
Richardson, Anna, 51, 58, 71
Richardson, Bertha June, 70, 166
Ridley & Company, 142
Rouke, Fabian, 201–2
Rubria, Eladia, 169
Rules and regulations, 104–9, 114–15, 118
Russian ladies incident, 193–94
Ryan, Mary, 4, 26

Salespeople: characteristics of, 92–93, 99; and class distinctions, 107–8, 123–24, 125; collusion with shoplifters by, 101; and consumption, 92–93, 105; and customers, 101, 118, 162; as detectives, 133, 135–36; distrust of, 108–11, 118–19; dress codes for, 106–7; and the fantasyland nature of department stores, 92–93; as guardians/watchdogs, 10, 66, 92, 102, 103–4, 108–9, 114–17, 135, 146; importance of, 92, 99; intervention in shoplifting by, 114–15; loyalty of, 100–111, 129;

overlooking of shoplifting by, 116; paradoxes for, 92–93, 105, 119; and the Phelps incident, 123–24, 125; and phrenology, 137; as problems, 98–104, 108–9; and professional shoppers, 109–11; rules and regulations for, 104–9, 114–15, 118; and scientific management, 96, 97–98; showing of merchandise by, 117–18; and technology, 104–5; and temptations, 92–93, 105; working class as, 92–93, 107–8. *See also* Administrative hierarchy; Employee relations
San Francisco Chronicle [newspaper], 175
Sardy, Ellen, 192–93
Savage, George Henry, 176
Schloss, Louisa, 154–55
Science and the medicalization of shoplifting, 181, 183–86
Scientific management, 96, 97–98
Secularization, 32, 56–57
Security, 10, 75–90. *See also* Detectives; Surveillance
Self-denial, 31–32
Servants, 23
Sewing, 26–27, 36
Sexuality, 7–8, 11, 173–75, 177–79, 181–82, 186–87, 195, 196–201, 204, 205
Shame, 164–66, 170, 180, 193
Shoplifters: casual, 202–3, 206; characteristics of, 15–16, 149–51, 157–60, 189; definition of, 8–9, 207; diversity of modern, 206; as epitomizing domestic model, 159–60; men as, 202; neurotic, 202–3; tricks of, 117–18; types of, 202
Shoplifters Anonymous, 206
Shoplifting: in the 1960s, 202–4; as an ancient art, 4; ease of, 172; emergence of, 4, 6–7; extent of the problem of, 6–7, 64–67, 79, 111–14, 143–44, 151, 156, 197, 207; importance of, 6–7, 172; as a major industry, 205–6; reasons for, 168–72. *See also* Medicalization of shoplifting; *name of specific person or department store*
Shopping: frequency of, 21, 39–40; as recreation, 21; satires about, 32; and the stereotype of middle-class women, 29–30; as a woman's responsibility, 5–6, 21, 28–29, 30–31, 39, 40, 158–59. *See also* Consumerism/consumption; Materialism; Spending
Shrinkage. *See* Shoplifting
Siegel-Cooper & Co.: detectives at, 133–34; display windows at, 73; employee relations at, 101–3, 108; and the enticement of shoppers, 48; expansion of, 50, 142–43; and the interior of the store, 48; Macy's rivalry with, 109; prosecution of shoplifting by, 153; salespeople at, 114–15; shoplifting incidents at, 3, 138, 154–55
Simpson, Crawford & Simpson, 112–13, 142, 192
Social status and ambitions, 38, 45–46, 165–67
Solis-Cohen, Solomon, 179, 186
Sorosis, 21, 122
Specialization, 104
Spending, 13, 26, 55–56, 60, 158–59, 165–67. *See also* Consumerism/consumption
Spy system, 109–11
Standard of living, 26, 55
Stekel, Wilhelm, 198, 199
Stereotype: kleptomaniacs as a, 8, 148–49, 157; of working class, 192–93
Stereotype of middle-class women: and the lack of restraint, 16; and the medicalization of shoplifting, 7–8, 157, 174, 175, 187, 188, 192–93, 195–96; and modern shoplifting, 206–7; and moral confusion, 192–93; and shopping, 29–30; and temptations, 8; women's acceptance of the, 164, 174, 175, 195–96
Stern Brothers, 36, 133–34, 142, 153, 162
Stewart, A. T. 136

Stewart's. *See* A. T. Stewart's
Stimson, Alice Bartlett, 19, 21, 34
Straus, Isidor, 59, 87, 94–95, 96
Straus, Jesse, 96–97, 156
Straus, Nathan, 94–95, 96
Straus, Percy, 96, 97
Surveillance, 65–67, 205–6. *See also*
    Detectives; Security
Svenson, Hilda E., 110
Swift, Laura, 3
System [business magazine], 60

Taylor, Frederick Winslow, 97–98
Technology: and consumerism/
    consumption, 10, 25, 27, 33, 37,
    39, 40; and domesticity, 23–24; as a
    means of curbing shoplifting, 10,
    65–67, 143, 205–6; and the
    organization of department stores,
    104–5; and salespeople, 104–5. *See
    also* Glass; Lighting
Temporary insanity, 199
Temptations: and the characteristics of
    shoplifters, 16; and consumption, 6;
    and counters, 75–83; courts' views
    about, 143; and display windows,
    70–71, 72–73, 74; encouragement
    of, 56, 58–62; as the focus of
    department stores, 6; and
    glamorization of spending, 55–56;
    and the interior of department
    stores, 46–47, 59–62; and lighting,
    89–90; and the medicalization of
    shoplifting, 8; and psychiatry, 198–
    200; of salespeople, 92–93, 105;
    and the stereotype of the middle-
    class woman, 8, 151, 168–72. *See
    also* Overwhelming desires of
Theil Detective Service, 129–30
Thrift ethic, 95–96
Titon, William, 59
Trade journals, 10, 26. *See also name
    of specific journal*

Traditional role of women, 9
Trilby mania, 34

Unconscious motivation, 197–200
Underwear/lingerie, 38, 45
Union School for Salesmanship
    [Boston], 137
Urbanization, 4
Uterine disease, 172, 199

Veblen, Thorstein, 165
Victims, 151, 203, 205

Wanamaker, John, 92, 111, 154
Wanamaker, Rodman, 92
Wanamaker's. *See* John Wanamaker
Watts, William B., 137–38
Webster, Charles, 94–95, 96
Welfare capitalism, 100–102
Whitman, Martin, 152–53, 154, 155
Wigham, Mrs. Cornelius, 89, 164
Wilcox, Ella Wheeler, 167
Willemse, Cornelius, 138
Williams, Rosalind, 43
Window shopping, 69–75
Window trimmers, 71
Wittels, Fritz, 199–200, 205
Wm. Filene's Sons Company, 44, 54–
    55, 92, 104, 135
Women's Wear Daily [newspaper], 71
Woodhull and Claflin's Weekly
    [newspaper], 113, 122, 124, 125,
    170
Woolson, Abba Goold, 36
Work ethic, 92–93, 105
Working class, 9, 18, 31, 92–93,
    107–8, 138–39, 192–93
Wylie, W. Gill, 169

Zola, Émile, 81, 84, 86, 87, 88, 117,
    127–28, 140